D0021717

THE
SYNCHRONICITY
KEY

Also by David Wilcock

The Source Field Investigations

THE
SYNCHRONICITY
KEY

The Hidden Intelligence
Guiding the Universe and You

DAVID WILCOCK

DUTTON

DUTTON
Published by the Penguin Group
Penguin Group (USA) Inc., 375 Hudson Street,
New York, New York 10014, USA

USA | Canada | UK | Ireland | Australia | New Zealand | India | South Africa | China
Penguin Books Ltd, Registered Offices: 80 Strand, London WC2R 0RL, England
For more information about the Penguin Group visit penguin.com.

REGISTERED TRADEMARK—MARCA REGISTRADA

LIBRARY OF CONGRESS CATALOGING-IN-PUBLICATION DATA
Wilcock, David, 1973–
The synchronicity key : the hidden intelligence guiding the universe and you / David Wilcock.
pages cm
Includes bibliographical references and index.
ISBN 978-0-525-95367-8
1. Cycles.   2. Coincidence.   I. Title.
B105.C9.W55 2013
130—dc23   2013016254

Printed in the United States of America
1   3   5   7   9   10   8   6   4   2

While the author has made every effort to provide accurate telephone numbers, Internet addresses, and
other contact information at the time of publication, neither the publisher nor the author assumes any
responsibility for errors or for changes that occur after publication. Further, the publisher does not have
any control over and does not assume any responsibility for author or third-party websites or their content.

This book is dedicated to you, the One Infinite Creator—the author of consciousness, energy, matter, biology, space, and the great cycles of time—now reading these words in your temporary human form.

Contents

List of Figures

Foreword

Synchronicity Is More than a Happy Accident

Synchronicity is more than a happy accident. It is an effect of the connectivity of the universe. It is proof that everything is a part of a unified, connected whole. It is an affirmation of life.

I first heard about David Wilcock in 2008 when my aunt, Kate Foster, a spiritual seeker who had introduced me to great thinkers such as Seth, Eckhart Tolle, Abraham-Hicks, and many others, called me saying I had to check out DivineCosmos.com. Kate described the website as coming from an extraordinary mind, and since she had steered me to brilliant spiritual teachers in the past, I paid attention. What I saw on DivineCosmos.com opened my eyes to a hidden world only recently being uncovered. And that is the world of consciousness. What makes David's work unique, though, is the core insight that there is a consciousness throughout the universe. David believes the universe is alive and we are all a part of the living fabric that binds it together. What a beautiful idea.

There is so much information in the world available to people who seek it. As a book publisher, I look for people who can take the seemingly infinite availability of data and make sense of it. Then we invite readers to consider new insights into old ideas. When my aunt died in early 2013, she left a legacy of cultivating the new consciousness and helping me bring these ideas into books. My first book with David, *The Source Field*

Investigations, became a *New York Times* bestseller and sold all over the world. It is a stunning work of near-encyclopedic knowledge about human beings' place in our universe. It became an instant classic in its field, and I felt this was the start of a new movement.

The Synchronicity Key is the next evolution of that movement. Using the same intense research and bold insightfulness that characterized *The Source Field Investigations,* but with an emphasis on how all this hidden science affects you personally, this book you have in your hands has the ability to change your life to a profound level.

David is a divine madman—part shaman, part storyteller, part code breaker—but gimlet-eyed in his quest for answers to life's unnerving questions. He seeks and finds and has a knack for explaining the seemingly inexplicable. He is also relentlessly positive and optimistic. His words and research deliver a message of hope and love. It is no accident that Kate directed me to David's website. It is no accident that we started working together on his books. It is no accident that you are now reading this book. Everything is connected. Everywhere.

Brian Tart
President and Publisher, Dutton, and editor of
The Source Field Investigations and *The Synchronicity Key*

PART ONE

THE SOUL'S JOURNEY
IN A LIVING UNIVERSE

CHAPTER ONE

The Quest

Y ou may have picked up this book, and possibly many others like it over the years, to try to find a new understanding of the complex world we live in. Before long, if the words are true enough, you soar off to a paradise of the mind and heart—freeing yourself from the troubles of the everyday world. Beautiful words of inspiration rain down like a waterfall of love, and for those moments—however fleeting they may be—all seems to be well. You undoubtedly have some wonderful memories—opening beautifully wrapped gifts as a child, achieving a seemingly impossible victory, beholding a magnificent view of nature, feeling the breathtaking rush of new love or the incredible magic of a newborn baby. In those fine moments, life is wonderful, the universe is a marvelous place to be, and you are inspired and optimistic about the future. You may even be brought to tears. You feel loved, and you believe that your life has value and purpose. You know you are a good person, and that you deserve every kindness that is bestowed upon you. You may even feel that this experience has changed your life—given you a new perspective, taught you to think differently, or allowed you to avoid the pitfalls that once seemed so impossible to evade. Genuine happiness seems to be yours.

Then what happens? Sooner or later, tragedy strikes. You are utterly humiliated. You lose your job. You crash your car. You can't pay the bills. You worry about losing your home. You suffer a terrible health crisis.

Your baby is screaming and may be very sick. Your teenage daughter hates you with an astonishing passion. You may even be threatened with violence. Everything is very dark. You are shamed, ridiculed, and laughed at. The people you loved and trusted the most turn on you, and you feel savagely betrayed and utterly alone. Where once you had love, gratitude, respect, honor, and peace, you now have pain, misery, sorrow, depression, and fear. You do your best to breathe through these experiences and understand what happened, but you feel as if you have been singled out for horrible punishment. No one else has ever suffered this profoundly. Your pain is so vast, so unimaginable, that if anyone else were expected to go through this, it would crush them.

This is your moment of choice. Do you still believe in a positive future? Do you still believe in love and in the value of helping others? Do you let misery and despair overwhelm you, or do you look for ways you can heal the problem and make the world a better place? Do you believe that if you treat everyone with love, forgiveness, and acceptance—while still maintaining responsible boundaries and not allowing yourself to be manipulated—then these personal and global wounds will eventually heal? Do you feel that if you have love in your heart, then love will appear in your life? Are you strong enough to forgive and to forget—to truly release the pain inside—and know, in your core, that life is wonderful, you are worthy, and you don't need to be angry, sad, or depressed when crisis strikes or when others disrespect you? Let's say that love and forgiveness would be your first choice in how you respond to life's ups and downs. In the spiritual literature we will discuss in the next chapter, this would be called "the positive path" or "the service-to-others path." On this path, we learn how to generate love from within ourselves, by our attitude, and this process has a healing, renewing, and revitalizing effect on all aspects of our lives.

Your second choice would be to see each tragic event as just the latest in a long, unbroken string of terrible things that have happened in the "real world." In these painful moments, do you overlook all the positives in your life and conclude, with cynical sarcasm, that life sucks, you can never really trust anyone, love is a myth that people use to get what they want, the only thing you know for sure is that you're going to die, and ultimately we humans are a failure—a cancer on the earth? Do you see yourself as strong and wise because you have learned how the world really works, while others are weak, ignorant, even pathetic for believing in the foolish lies of love and forgiveness? Do you gain pleasure and laughter from seeing them suffer? Do you enjoy ridiculing anyone who believes in love—and in a spiritual reality? Do you divide the world into "us" and "them" categories, where everyone in your group is good and everyone outside your group is bad, almost subhuman? Do you carefully study how to manipulate and control others—including telling lies when it seems safe and useful—so that you won't have to keep suffering from their blindness and cruelty? Do you believe that toughening them up to be more like you and your group is ultimately a good thing, as their weakness is now being transformed into strength? This could be called "service to self," the "negative path," or "the path of control," as we will see. Ultimately this is another means of seeking energy and vitality in our daily lives. On this path, our primary focus is absorbing energy from others.

Or do you take the third option: denial and avoidance of either of these paths? During your darkest moments, do you long for that child-like trust that all is well, and when you remember the positive things that have happened, do they now all seem like a pathetic fairy tale? Do you feel like you cannot accept a life with so much unhappiness—that feeling of faceless terror, intolerable shame, and the seemingly inevitable reality that bad things will keep on happening, again and again? Does your mind shut down? Do you force yourself not to look? Do you become desperate? Do you lack courage? Will you do anything to avoid seeing the truth? Do you come up with silly, even ludicrous ways of convincing yourself that this latest traumatic event is not real, and seek others who will support your story, because they can't handle it either? Do you desperately seek an escape, a lifeline, a rope, thrown down into your pit of misery, so you can feel happy once more? Do you ignore the reality that is staring you in the face? Do you climb your way out of hell by learning to live with a very strong conflict—the life you wish you had versus the life there really is? Are you unable to accept that a loving Creator would allow such seemingly terrible things to happen? Do you pick yourself up, dismiss the pain, and do something that will make you feel good in the short term—even if it ends up hurting you? Temporarily, do you feel like all is well—only to have the truth you are hiding from come roaring back into your life once more? Those who repeat these experiences with no new insight, without choosing either the path of love or the path of control, are considered to be in "the sinkhole of indifference"[1] or in a state of "true helplessness,"[2] as described in the spiritual literature known as the Law of One series, which we will be discussing in the next chapter.

These choices appear each time we move through a cycle—of pleasure and pain, joy and despair, love and fear, boom and bust, happiness and agony, forgiveness and judgment, trust and betrayal, strength and weakness, "good" and "bad." As we will see, this cycle is written into every movie, every television show, every great story told throughout the ages in mythology—and even into the ebb and flow of historical events. It is the Book of Life. It is the great story we all go through. We instinctively recognize this story—and the choices we can make within it. Atheists and agnostics are as compelled by this story as the devoutly religious are. As the lights dim in the theater, our defense mechanisms are pulled down and we surrender ourselves into the childlike wonder of the story, if it is told properly. In this sense, every movie, play, television show, and myth is a spiritual ceremony, evoking deep memories from a part of us that knows the truth without having to think about it. However, the modern retellings of this great story almost never reveal the vastly deeper truths that are hidden within it. Until this great jewel of ageless wisdom is truly discovered and appreciated for what it is, we will continue to suffer through endless cycles of joy and disaster.

The best part of our story is that you do not need to keep suffering. Once you understand the hidden design of the universe, you can begin mastering your experiences and immediately improve your quality of life. You may even end up feeling that this information—this ageless wisdom—is alive. Like a fertile seed, it can lie dormant for many hundreds, if not thousands, of years. You can now understand this cycle—the so-called Wheel of Karma—and see what it really is and why it is happening. Once you put these ageless wisdom teachings into practice, you can reach the top of the cycle—the highest, best, happiest, and most triumphant point in the story—and never again be dragged down into the pit of despair. You can move from a place of weakness, pain, sorrow, humiliation, betrayal, anger, and fear to a world of happiness, abundance, joy, prosperity, peace, and fulfillment—and stay there.

Some people believe that feelings can heal all the pain and create lasting peace. The quest to feel good, to feel happy, and to feel inspired might seem to bring acceptable solutions to any problem. However, feelings can always be hurt—and if you only ever want to have good feelings, you will be continually disappointed. Addictions can creep up when we relentlessly pursue pleasure—even when we do so at increasingly crippling costs. The desire to only ever feel good can keep us perpetually locked in denial and avoidance of reality—a state in which we are unable or unwilling to choose between the path of love and acceptance and the path of manipulation and control.

Others believe that thoughts can solve the mystery. Life is a grand puzzle, and if you think about your problems long enough and deeply enough, you can always find a solution. However, you have lived your entire life in a world that thinks and believes a certain way. This conditioning runs very deep and is extremely easy to fall back into, even for those who are quite advanced on their spiritual paths. In the animal kingdom, sticking with the group can literally mean the difference between life and death. If you become an outsider and refuse to go along with the pack, you probably won't live very long. Behaviorists have long known that we have many things in common with the animal kingdom, and this constant desire to agree with the group is one of our most deeply ingrained behaviors. We pride ourselves on our knowledge, and both school and work teach us that if we have incorrect thoughts, we are a failure and our lives will be threatened. Our whole identity can be built around the thoughts we think and the knowledge we carry with us and believe to be true. If that knowledge is jeopardized or proven to be incorrect, the shame we feel can seem to be utterly intolerable. This in turn can quickly lead to incredible rage.

Once we dig deeply enough, we may discover that we are profoundly affected by the hurts we felt in the past, often when we were not yet full adults. The pain we carry inside may be so intense that it affects every thought we think, every feeling we feel, and every action we take. We know what we really want—to be loved and accepted. However, the more we go into denial—and try to force the truth not to be the truth— the uglier our problems get. The more we try to demand that the people in our lives treat us kindly, or hide from them so we can avoid being hurt, the more we suffer. In this book we will explore wisdom teachings that can provide effective ways to help make the pain stop.

Cycles of History

The Source Field Investigations debuted in August 2011, enjoyed great reviews, and stayed on the *New York Times* bestseller list for three weeks— peaking at number sixteen. The hardcover was more than five hundred pages in length, even though I had decided to cut more than a hundred pages from the original manuscript so the book would not be overwhelmingly long. The deleted chapters contained a fascinating body of material, in which I rigorously demonstrated that the most significant events in world history are not random—they are actually repeating, again and again, in very precise cycles of time. The events that occur within these cycles are telling a story—our own worldwide Book of Life. The story displays the classic ups and downs of the Wheel of Karma and the Hero's Journey—a mystery we will explore in much more detail later in this book.

One of these cycles is the classic 2,160-year Age of the Zodiac. As we will see, the most significant events in Roman history during the Age of Aries reappear in quite a similar fashion during the Age of Pisces—2,160 years later—in America. French scholars Michèl Helmer and François Masson revealed this great hidden truth beginning in 1958—and I discovered their work only through pure synchronicity.[3] Russian scientist Nikolai A. Morozov independently discovered other repeating patterns in history—such as precise correspondences between Hebrew kings in the Old Testament and Roman kings more than a thousand years later— and began publishing his research as far back as *Revelation amid Storm and Tempest* in 1907.[4] Morozov eventually published an enormous seven-volume series on his unique discoveries from 1926 to 1932, subtitled *The History of Human Culture from the Standpoint of the Natural Sciences.* Dr. Anatoly Fomenko used Morozov's model and dramatically extended his quest to a worldwide level beginning in the 1970s, while pursuing an advanced mathematics degree. Fomenko discovered that these patterns were reappearing throughout all of written history—going all the way back to ancient Sumerian times in 4000 B.C. Faced with such staggering and mysterious evidence, both Morozov and Fomenko believed that much of our written history was actually a fraud created by historians who applied the same set of events to different eras. According to Morozov and Fomenko, historians reused all the most important details of the story, although they changed the names of leaders, cities, and countries. These cycles were such a great mystery that I realized I would need to write a new and separate book to explain them.

I wasn't entirely sure what was causing these cycles to happen, though I had some ideas. In this book I will lay out a complete presentation of the evidence, and I will also present a working model of how these cycles might be happening and why. This is undoubtedly one of the greatest mysteries of life on earth—particularly once you've studied the evidence—and yet it also seems incomprehensible. Most of us are so accustomed to "conventional reality" that the idea of cyclical time, or similar events repeating in regular cycles, wouldn't be considered a remote possibility. Anyone who suggests such an idea would probably be quickly dismissed with a sarcastic joke and a big laugh. However, by the time you're done reading this book, you may see things differently. We shouldn't shy away from a mystery just because it seems so hard to believe. The evidence is already quite compelling, but to understand it, we have to completely rebuild our scientific view of the universe with new instructions. A variety of discoveries have either been overlooked or underemphasized, and once we are presented with this new information, our entire worldview may radically change.

Although this is not considered a popular notion by any means, there is extensive scientific proof that the universe itself is alive. It is a vast, singular, living being—and we are far more interconnected with it than we may have ever believed. A unified, conscious energy field generates the entire cosmos, and this hidden energy can appropriately be called the Source Field. In this new science, galaxies, stars, and planets are life-forms on a scale we can barely even imagine. The basic laws of quantum physics arrange DNA and biological life out of atoms and molecules we would normally consider to be inanimate.

DNA Begins as a Quantum Wave

The DNA molecule is obviously essential to any scientific understanding of life and how it forms. One strand of DNA from a single cell contains enough information to clone an entire organism. The new science tells us that DNA begins as a wave, not a molecule. This wave exists as a pattern within space and time and is written throughout the entire universe. In this new model, we are constantly surrounded by pulsating waves of invisible genetic information—much like satellite TV, radio waves, and cell phone and broadband Internet signals. Each of these tiny DNA-forming waves creates gravitational forces, on a microscopic scale, that pull in atoms and molecules from their surroundings to construct DNA. If we could develop instruments to see them, each of these waves would be an exact energetic replica of the DNA molecules they will eventually form. The atoms naturally "fall" into the right places as they are pulled into the wave—much like rocks naturally roll into the bottom of a mountain stream once they are swept into the current. After single DNA molecules have been built, these same microgravitational forces cause them to cluster together so they can begin integrating and creating larger forms of life.

One scientist who caught these microgravitational forces in action is Dr. Sergey Leikin. In 2008, Leikin put various types of DNA in ordinary salt water and tagged each type with a different fluorescent color. The color-coded DNA molecules were scattered like confetti throughout the water. Much to Leikin's surprise, matching DNA molecules traveled the equivalent of thousands of miles, within their own tiny universe, to find each other. Before long, he saw that entire clusters of DNA molecules had gathered together. Each cluster was made of DNA molecules with the same fluorescent color.[5] What could possibly be attracting them together over such vast distances? Leikin thinks this phenomenon may be caused by electrical charges. However, other experiments clearly show that this effect cannot be electromagnetic. Gravity becomes the most likely answer within the existing energy fields known to modern science.

In 2011, Nobel Prize winner Dr. Luc Montagnier demonstrated that DNA can be spontaneously formed out of hydrogen and oxygen molecules—nothing more. Montagnier started out with a hermetically sealed tube of pure sterilized water. He then placed another sealed test tube next it—but this tube had small amounts of DNA floating in the water. Montagnier then electrified both tubes with a weak, seven-hertz electromagnetic field and waited. Eighteen hours later, little pieces of DNA had grown in the original tube—out of nothing but pure sterilized water.[6] Let's not forget that water is H_2O, hydrogen and oxygen. How could DNA—which is made of much more complex molecules—form out of such simple elements? This is one of the most significant discoveries in the history of science—by a Nobel laureate biologist, no less—and although it did get a small amount of publicity in the media, it was almost completely ignored.

This new science tells us that the universe is constantly conspiring to make biological life, wherever and however it can—even in the most utterly inhospitable places. In any given area of the universe, these hidden microgravitational waves will begin gathering atoms and molecules together that make DNA. The waves build whatever life-forms will naturally thrive in that area, beginning with single-cell organisms. Amazingly, British astronomers Sir Fred Hoyle and Dr. Nalin Chandra Wickramasinghe found that 99.9 percent of all the dust floating around in our galaxy is freeze-dried bacteria.[7] Sir Fred Hoyle revealed the full implications of these new discoveries in a lecture on April 15, 1980—fully thirty-three years ago at the time of this writing—and yet his surprising breakthroughs have still not reached the level of mainstream thought.

Microbiology may be said to have had its beginnings in the 1940s. A new world of the most astonishing complexity began to be revealed. I find it remarkable that microbiologists did not at once recognize that the world they had penetrated had of necessity to be of a cosmic order. I suspect that the cosmic quality of microbiology will seem as obvious to future generations as the sun being the center of or our solar system seems obvious to the present generation.[8]

We already know that the dust in our galaxy is emerging from the surface of stars like our sun in what we call the "solar wind." If 99.9 percent of all galactic dust particles are the freeze-dried bodies of micro-organisms, as Hoyle and Wickramasinghe discovered, then every star is a life factory. Each star's fiery surface is boiling with living bacteria that thrive in extremely high temperatures. As the superhot material in the star is thrown out into the coolness of space, the bacteria are instantly freeze-dried and preserved. Eventually they drift to the planets, where they are hydrated and reheated, forming viable organisms once more. Scientists have even observed bacteria growing inside hermetically sealed nuclear reactors, and these bacteria feed on radiation.[9] How did they get there? We now have more than enough scientific proof to conclude that these bacteria formed spontaneously, within the reactor, and were custom-designed to eat radiation and break it down into material that is less harmful to other forms of life.

Everywhere we have ever looked on earth, even 1.7 (2.8 kilometers) miles below the surface, we have found living bacteria.[10] In our current view of science, based on the evolutionary theories of Charles Darwin, all this bacteria evolved "randomly" on earth—and it all had to come from a single, original cell. In this new view of science, the universe itself is a living organism—and the basic laws of physics are custom-designed to create life, including microorganisms, plants, insects, fish, reptiles, birds, and mammals, wherever it can.

Several scientists have also caught DNA in the act of pulling in photons, the tiny packets of energy that make visible light throughout the universe. The new science reveals that photons are essential to the basic health and function of DNA and are apparently used to send and receive information throughout the body. As Dr. Fritz-Albert Popp discovered, each DNA molecule stores up to one thousand photons within itself, much like a tiny fiber-optic cable.[11] The photons zing back and forth at the speed of light inside the molecule and are stored until they need to be used. The entire process has been observed in a variety of groundbreaking laboratory experiments, and we will review some of the data in this book.

In 1984, Russian scientist Dr. Peter Gariaev discovered that when a DNA molecule was placed inside a tiny quartz container, it naturally absorbed every photon in the room.[12] This would be the equivalent of a person standing in a large stadium and having every photon in the arena somehow bending directly into him or her, leaving the person's body glowing with light, while the rest of the arena becomes completely dark. The only force that can bend light, in conventional science, is gravity, such as we see around a black hole. Therefore, DNA appears to be generating a microgravitational effect that attracts and captures light. Leikin, in whose experiment color-coded DNA molecules were attracted to one another, thought electrical charges might be causing them to come together across such vast distances, but electrical charges have never been able to bend light as it moves through space. The only place we've ever seen energetic light-bending effects is around a black hole.

The really big mystery didn't happen until Gariaev pulled his DNA out of the little quartz container. He thought the experiment was over and it was time to pack up and go home. However, when he looked through the microscope one last time, he was astonished to see that the photons were still spiraling in the exact same place where the DNA had been. How could this even be possible? If there was no DNA to hold the photons in place, then they should have immediately disappeared—but they didn't. They stayed right where they were. Some kind of force field—apparently a gravitational influence—was holding those photons right where the DNA had just been. Gariaev and his colleagues soon called this the "DNA Phantom Effect." I feel that this is one of the most important discoveries in the history of science. The implications are stunning and force us to completely rewrite many scientific "laws." DNA is creating an energetic force that absorbs photons and pulls them right into the molecule, but the DNA itself is not needed. There is some invisible force—some wave—that seems to be attracting and holding light by itself. Once we pull the DNA away, the wave is still there, and it still holds on to the photons it gathered.

Gariaev found out that he could blast the "phantom" with supercold liquid nitrogen gas and the photons would all escape from the force field. However, within five to eight minutes, new photons would be captured and the entire phantom would reappear. No matter how many times Gariaev blasted the phantom and set the photons free, the phantom kept reappearing—for an astonishing thirty days.[13] This effect cannot be explained by any form of electromagnetic field. It's not static electricity, it's not a radio wave, and it's not plasma. Gravity is the only field we know of that may be able to do something like this. Furthermore, this would also mean that our current understanding of gravity is very primitive. We know how fast objects accelerate as they fall—ten meters (32 feet) per second squared. We know that in an airless vacuum, a feather and a brick will fall at the same speed. Now we have to consider that gravity can have structure—on a quantum level—and this structure can persist for at least thirty days in the same location, even with no physical matter in that area. This implies that gravity does not require the presence of physical matter to exist. Gravity is a force that permeates our entire universe. If gravity has hidden waves in it that make DNA, and DNA makes intelligent life, then gravity itself must be alive and intelligent. This is why I refer to gravity as the Source Field. We do have certain ways of capturing the Source Field at work, on the quantum level—and I've just shared a few of them with you.

Even though the DNA phantom discovery is nearly thirty years old at the time of this writing and has stunning implications, it has never been widely publicized. This knowledge will utterly transform our society once it becomes widely accepted. It also paves the way for an entirely new range of powerful healing technology known as energy medicine. I integrated more than a thousand academic references on this subject in *The Source Field Investigations,* which was released on August 23, 2011. We got an exclusive slideshow on the Huffington Post that same day, which was linked on the front pages of both the "Books" and the "Weird News" sections.[14] I had a budget of only thirteen slides, with 150 words each, to try to summarize this monster 534-page encyclopedia of "sacred science" I had just constructed—which the distinguished scholar Graham Hancock said was "magnificent." Here is a reprint of the introduction and first five sections of the article, with a few minor edits for clarity. You will soon see that we can beam new instructions into an existing DNA molecule and completely change its structure. The microgravitational forces of the wave will grab atoms inside the DNA and move them around until they assemble into the new configuration. This is an entirely new way of explaining the evolution of species, and the mechanism has already been proven to work in the laboratory.

The Source Field Investigations

All the science needed to explain and understand the UFO phenomenon and the greatest mysteries of ancient civilizations is revealed in *The Source Field Investigations*. Ancient prophecies foretold a coming Golden Age in our very near future—and the US government may well have encoded these predictions into a variety of mysterious symbols. Antigravity, teleportation, time travel, energetic DNA evolution, and consciousness transformation could now create a world few of us ever even dreamed of.

Space, time, matter, energy, and biological life may be the results of a Source Field that is conscious and alive in its own unique way, on a scale far too vast for the finite mind to fathom. More than a thousand different references, predominantly from mainstream scientists, make the case.

What Is Consciousness?

Dr. William Braud is one of a variety of scientists who have performed rigorous, laboratory-controlled studies proving that mind-to-mind communication is very real and is repeatable in a scientific laboratory.[15] Participants in one room were able to make the skin of another person in a completely separate room change—at a distance. Sudden surges would appear in the amount of electricity conducted through the affected person's skin. This change in electrical activity usually happens when we get excited, but in this case, the person who had the reaction did not know that anything was going on.[16] Many of these experiments were done in rooms shielded from all electromagnetic signals, proving this phenomenon cannot be explained by any known energy waves in the conventional spectrum.

By 1929, more than 148 different cases of "multiples" had been documented in science—where multiple scientists independently make the same breakthroughs at the same time. The subjects in which these breakthroughs occurred included calculus, the theory of evolution, color photography, thermometers, telescopes, typewriters, and steamboats.[17] It appears that our thoughts are not as private as we think. When we work to solve a problem, we may be accessing a universal data bank of knowledge. The information then appears in our minds as if it was our own unique idea. Let's not forget that these 148 cases are only examples where inventors tried to patent the same things at the same time.

There is wonderful, abundant proof that extrasensory perception is a natural gift we all possess, but these groundbreaking studies have received very little publicity. Could the basic energy of the cosmos be conscious in some way?

Is DNA an Energy Wave That Assembles Life?

In 2011, Nobel laureate Luc Montagnier demonstrated "DNA teleportation," a phenomenon in which ordinary water molecules in a sealed test tube assembled into DNA. A tube containing sterilized water was placed next to another tube that contained water with trace amounts of DNA. Both tubes were electrified with a weak, seven-hertz current. Some of the hydrogen and oxygen molecules in the tube with pure sterile water transformed into DNA—by a process still unknown to Western science.[18]

Sir Fred Hoyle and Dr. Chandra Wickramasinghe noticed that 99.9 percent of all the dust in the galaxy had peculiar optical properties. The only material that could create these effects in the laboratory was freeze-dried bacteria.[19] In 1980, Sir Hoyle said, "I suspect that the cosmic quality of microbiology will seem as obvious to future generations as the Sun being the centre of our solar system seems obvious to the present generation." [20]

Can DNA Be Energetically Transformed from One Species into Another?

The agricultural division of the Ciba-Geigy corporation (now Syngenta) discovered that existing plant seeds could be transformed into extinct varieties, simply by zapping them with a weak electrostatic current. [21] This process generated stronger and faster-growing wheat, extinct fern species, and tulips with thorns. [22] Italian scientist Pier Luigi Ighina energetically transformed a living apricot tree into an apple tree, actually causing the fruits on the branches to metamorphose from apricots into apples in only sixteen days. Ighina also zapped a rat with DNA-wave information from a cat, and this caused the rat to grow a catlike tail in four days. [23] Korean scientist Dr. Dzang Kangeng received a patent (N1828665) for a device that used microwaves to transfer the DNA-wave information of a duck into a pregnant mother hen. [24] Roughly 80 percent of the hen's eggs hatched as half-duck, half-chicken hybrids. Dr. Peter Gariaev zapped salamander eggs with a low-level laser and redirected the beam into frog eggs. The frog eggs experienced a complete metamorphosis and the embryos grew into healthy adult salamanders. They never reverted back to being frogs—nor did their offspring. [25]

Is There Intelligent Human Life Throughout the Galaxy?

Thanks to these and other scientific discoveries, we can now suggest that human life could be a galactic or even universal template, potentially appearing on every habitable, watery planet in the galaxy, due to the quantum properties of DNA. The majority of ancient cultures worldwide reported interactions with human-looking "gods" or "angels" that gave them powerful assistance—in agriculture, animal husbandry, spoken and written language, construction techniques, mathematics, and science, as well as spiritual teachings of morality, ethics, and becoming a more loving person. The majority of ancient cultures also consistently taught us that history moves in great cycles of time, whether in the Mayan calendar, the Hindu Yugas, or the Ages of the Zodiac.

Highly unusual human skulls, including a series discovered in Boskop, South Africa, whose brain capacity is twice that of normal humans, with large heads and small, childlike faces, have been found around the world. They skulls found in South Africa were given highly honorable burials, as *Discover* magazine revealed in 2009.[26] Bizarre, elongated skulls have also been discovered in Peru, Bolivia, Russia, and elsewhere—closely matching the appearance of early Egyptian pharaohs—and some of them are still on display in museums.

Fig. 1: Granite bust of Akhenaten and Nefertiti's daughter Meritaten

Is Evolution Being Driven by Waves of Energy in the Galaxy?

Drs. David Raup and James Sepkoski discovered a 26-million-year cycle in the evolution of life on earth after creating the most exhaustive fossil catalog ever assembled.[27] The data show that every 26 million years, astonishing numbers of new species suddenly appear in massive bursts after millions of years with very little change. Fearing embarrassment, the researchers worked harder to eliminate the pattern, but it only became stronger and clearer as they did more research. Recently, Drs. Robert Muller and Robert Rohde discovered an even larger 62-million-year cycle within the same data, going back to the dawn of all complex fossil life on earth.[28] These cyclical events may be triggered by galactic energy waves that reprogram DNA.[29]

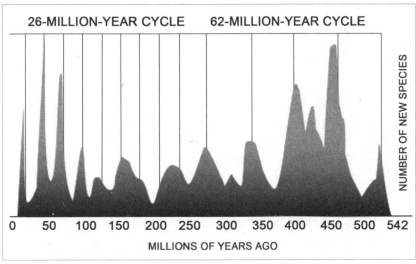

Fig. 2: Combined graph of 26- and 62-million-year evolution cycles

Dr. William Tifft discovered concentric bands of microwave energies within galaxies that slowly expand away from their centers.[30] Dr. Harold Aspden's unique physics equations suggest that each of these microwave regions possesses different properties on a quantum level.[31] This gives us a measurable energetic model that could account for the long-term cycles of evolution we see on earth. Each zone may carry information that rewrites DNA according to a grand, intelligent pattern within the galaxy itself. Life appears to be a natural law—an "emergent phenomenon" within quantum mechanics. The universe itself is a living being. Life appears wherever and however it can throughout the universe. All life is periodically reprogrammed by energetic forces that can be reproduced in a laboratory, creating continual advancements in species evolution throughout the universe.

A Conscious Universe

I do believe not only that the universe is alive, but also that it is conscious and self-aware. There is a plan and a purpose to our lives on earth that is far greater than most of us have ever realized—and we are definitely not alone. Nor do we only have one life to live. There is undeniable scientific proof that we reincarnate again and again. We also keep moving through the same lessons in our history as they repeat in incredibly precise patterns. These wars and atrocities need not continue, however—they will persist only if we keep creating them, in our ignorance of the greater reality that surrounds us. The truth does not require any religion to appreciate; however, we may discover that the ancient spiritual traditions hold far more wisdom than most modern scientists have ever believed. Synchronicity gives us an invitation to explore this greater reality. Synchronicity is the key that unlocks the doors to the mysteries of the universe. Synchronicity appears in an industrial-scale, measurable form in the cycles of history—events that keep repeating, very precisely, in units of time that can be thousands of years in length. I became much more aware of this phenomenon once I began studying a unique body of data known as the Law of One series in 1996.

CHAPTER TWO

Cycles of History and the Law of One

What if the universe is alive? What if we are surrounded by invisible waves that assemble DNA out of nonliving material? Could these hidden forces be reprogramming our DNA and propelling us into a new level of human evolution? Are there certain spiritual lessons we need to learn in order to harmonize with this evolutionary change as a planet? Are the events in world history "programmed" by a hidden intelligence to keep running us through the same set of experiences—until we awaken, on a collective level, and choose to stop hurting one another? Were these cycles built to be discovered? Were they intended to help us realize that this collective nightmare is happening for a reason—and that we can do something about it? Is there a lesson, a pattern, a story, in these cycles that we are now meant to understand, collectively? Does the story itself contain the wisdom teachings we need to pull ourselves out of this global nightmare—on a worldwide level— and finally live in peace?

As revealed in *The Source Field Investigations,* the evidence that we live in an organic universe is conclusive. Now, instead of seeing life as a brief anomaly that may have occurred only on earth, in the midst of an otherwise "dead" universe, we will come to realize that the cosmos is literally teeming with life—from single-cell microorganisms all the way up through intelligent, sentient beings like ourselves. Life also will be seen as fundamentally energetic in nature, first and foremost, and it does not require biological material to exist. Once this is widely accepted, the discovery that the universe itself is alive—and intelligent—will arguably be the biggest breakthrough in the history of science, eclipsing even that of our realizations that the earth is round, or that the sun is the center of the solar system.

Within human DNA is all the information needed to make the brain, which is currently believed to be the center of our conscious, thinking minds. If DNA can form in a tube of pure sterilized water, then the information that makes that organism conscious must exist all around us as well—much like radio waves, satellite TV signals, or broadband Internet. Consciousness and DNA are fundamentally intertwined. As groundbreaking as all of these ideas may be, this is only the beginning of our story. In one sense, these breakthroughs are like a trail of bread crumbs that lead us into much greater mysteries.

The Law of One Series

This model of a living cosmos was originally found in a very unusual source called the Law of One series—five books that were allegedly obtained by intuitive means from 1981 to 1983.[32] The Law of One series consists of 106 dialogues between a credentialed physics professor, Dr. Don Elkins, and an allegedly higher source of intelligence speaking through his companion Carla Rueckert while she was in an unconscious trance state. Jim McCarty was also present for each session and transcribed all the tapes. Through Carla, Don was apparently speaking to a large group of people who were once like humans on earth but who had since merged into a single consciousness. From a biblical perspective, they would likely be classified as seraphim or cherubim—among the most evolved of the types of angelic presences that ever appeared on earth. The word *angel* comes from the Greek word *aggelos,* which simply means "messenger." These people no longer had physical, flesh-and-blood bodies as we now think of them but had long since evolved into a form of life that is energetic in nature.

According to the Law of One series, this and other angelic groups assisted in the creation of the major world religions, including Christianity. They never intended to have us fight over the differences in these teachings, but now there are 38,830 denominations of Christianity and ten thousand other religions in the world.[33] The group in the Law of One series also said they were members of a larger organization that was working "in service to the One Infinite Creator." This organization is apparently responsible for guiding, protecting, steering, and managing our collective evolution on earth. Its goal is to help us all become more aware of our true identity. The real nature of identity was given when they defined the Law of One in the very first session.

> 1.6 You are every thing, every being, every emotion, every event, every situation. You are unity. You are infinity. You are love/light, light/love. You are. This is the Law of One.[34]

For now, the spiritual laws these beings follow require them to remain hidden. They cannot create a grandiose, worldwide display of their presence, as free will is a universal law they must abide by. Until we acknowledge their existence and welcome them on a planetary level, they are not permitted to appear, as their presence would interrupt our natural course of evolution. However, synchronicity is one of the most prevalent ways in which they are helping us gradually acclimate to their presence and to the greater reality we are living in.

As you are probably already seeing by now, any discussion of the Law of One series causes the "rabbit hole" to get very deep, very quickly. By the time I began studying these five books in 1996, I had three years of intensive scientific research under my belt and I immediately started making one mind-blowing connection after another. I quickly realized that the Law of One series was like a real-world, literary equivalent of the Roswell crash—an artifact that appeared in our world by a mysterious process and that could then be taken apart, piece by piece, and studied. Massive enhancements to our science and technology could be made in the process. There are many people who claim to have telepathic access to sources like this, particularly since the rise of the Internet. The vast majority of these sources contradict one another and can be easily picked apart for obvious flaws, failed prophecies, and the like. However, in my opinion, there is no other source that goes nearly as deep or reveals nearly as much groundbreaking, provable scientific information as the Law of One material. In linear terms, the Law of One was far ahead of its time.

I first began studying the Law of One material in January 1996, after more than three years of writing down and analyzing my dreams every morning and fifteen years of dedicated research into ancient civilizations, alternative science, and metaphysics. The Law of One almost immediately crystallized my focus, tied together everything I had read in a way I couldn't have imagined was possible, and shaped the entire future course of my life's work. Within less than a year, I, too, began having profound personal experiences of contact with the source of the words—both in dreams and in direct telepathic messages. By that point I was well aware that there was a higher power in the universe. By inviting it to contact me and being willing to closely follow the spiritual practices in the Law of One series, I got results.

Until then, this had been strictly an academic study, but soon I began producing page after page of words, from a very deep level of meditation, that provided incredibly valuable spiritual guidance and could predict the future with astonishing precision. The words spoke with seemingly omniscient awareness of my deepest physical, mental, and emotional issues and clearly showed me how to heal them. These "readings" often knew exactly what was going to happen in my future and how I could best navigate through these events. This obviously made my research much more personal. I was no longer a detached third party, studying the fruits of contacts that had happened to other people and looking for the scientific proof to back them up. I was now experiencing similarly bizarre and wonderful events in my own life.

When I first started reading the Law of One series, I would often have to spend about forty-five minutes in intense concentration before I felt comfortable enough to turn to the next page, but I was never the least bit disappointed or bored with what I was reading. It simply took me that long to understand the words.

The Law of One series tells us that everyone on earth is ultimately sharing the same mind—much more than we would ever dare to believe.

Years later, I would find impressive scientific discoveries that supported this concept. For example, a group of seven thousand people meditating on thoughts of love, peace, and happiness were somehow able to reduce acts of terrorism, worldwide, by 72 percent. The level of wars, crimes, fatalities, and economic suffering all dropped remarkably just from this very small group of people meditating, privately, in one location. This was documented in a professional, peer-reviewed scientific study, which was accepted by and published in the *Journal of Offender Rehabilitation*. All other factors, including cycles, trends, weather, weekends, and holidays, were ruled out.[35] By 1993, fifty different scientific studies had demonstrated this same effect over the preceding thirty years. The meditators improved the overall health and quality of life for people on earth, boosted the economy, and decreased accidents, crime, war, and terrorism.[36] Nearly three out of four people who would normally have committed an act of violent terrorism decided not to while these seven thousand people were at work meditating. These would-be terrorists obviously had no idea that their decision to be violent could be so profoundly influenced by others. All they knew is that they simply felt better and they made more positive choices. Their thoughts and feelings were nowhere near as private as conventional science had led them to believe.

In the Law of One series, we are told that the universe is one mind—that "there is only identity"—and each of us is a perfect holographic reflection of the One Infinite Creator. Mainstream science would have us believe that in the "beginning," there was nothing. Simply put, nothing existed. That whole concept always confused me greatly. Scientists then expect us to believe that even though "nothing existed," nothing exploded—and from this one explosion, all the matter and energy in the universe was created, in a single instant. The universe has apparently been spinning down to a "thermal death" ever since that first, triumphant moment. By comparison, the Law of One series teaches us that new matter is continually being formed and both space and time are ultimately illusions, created solely for the evolution of consciousness.

Apart from these philosophical concepts, there was a wealth of specific data points that had to be either right or wrong and could therefore be confirmed or rejected with further investigation. By the time I first read the series, hundreds of scientific breakthroughs had already emerged that validated the Law of One model after its publication, and the volume of supporting evidence has significantly increased every year since then. The vast majority of this new data was not yet discovered when the series was first produced. Furthermore, in the process of writing *The Source Field Investigations* and integrating thirty years' worth of this research into alternative science, I made many new discoveries that were not featured in the Law of One material but were logical extensions of it.

I also lived with the surviving founders of this five-volume series from January 2003 to October 2004—Carla Rueckert, a devout Christian who verbalized the words while in an unconscious trance state, and Jim McCarty, who transcribed all the dialogues between Don and the source. Their material had never gotten very popular, at least partly due to its extreme complexity, and Jim had to mow lawns to pay the bills. By living with Carla for nearly two years, I was able to prove, well beyond any margin of doubt, that she could not possibly have faked the Law of One material. Carla applauded me for deciphering many of the technical details that she herself had been unable to grasp. However, after studying this material intensely for seven years, I admittedly had gone in there with unrealistic expectations. I believed that the person who spoke the words would also be an embodiment of the words, at least to some degree. I was definitely looking for a hero—someone who would have glorious, superhuman qualities that I felt were lacking in myself. However, Carla had plenty of "distortions" of her own, in Law of One terms. If anyone put her on a pedestal, she would immediately kick it away—often causing embarrassment and laughter in the process. I watched it happen several times.

One of the most interesting, peculiar, and enjoyable fringe benefits of this living universe is that once you begin exploring its great mysteries, it may soon reach out to you, if it hasn't already done so. This will often occur in undeniable and fascinating ways. Many of these experiences could be classified as synchronicity, which we will explore in the next chapter. Every effort will be made to avoid causing you any fear in this process, so there is no trauma. The goal is to increase your feelings of love, joy, peace, and happiness, in the ultimate hope of helping you free yourself from the ongoing cycle of reincarnation. Synchronicity also leaves room for plausible deniability, so you have the freedom to accept or reject the message as you see fit. In Law of One terms, *free will* is the most important universal law that must be upheld within this loving universe. As we will explore in chapters 6, 7, and 8, the law of karma is not some mysterious, impersonal universal law; it is very actively maintained with the help of a huge variety of nonphysical beings who work in and around the earth.

Scientific Proof of a Conscious Cosmos

Although as much as 80 percent of the information in the Law of One series is philosophical and cannot be proven, there is also an extensive body of scientific data that supports many of its basic principles. Armed with this new scientific data, we can validate the idea that when life reaches the level of a galaxy, star, or planet, it will have all the attributes of consciousness and identity that we have within ourselves, and much, much more. In this model, rather than detached and disconnected from the universe, we are fundamentally integrated with it—and our thoughts are much less private than we currently believe. Dr. James Spottiswoode conducted a meta-analysis of twenty years' worth of laboratory experiments into "anomalous cognition," or extrasensory perception, and found that our psychic abilities increased by over 400 percent when our position on earth reached a particular alignment with the center of the galaxy—which culminated at 13:30 local sidereal time.[37] We already saw how 7,000 people meditating could positively affect the majority of everyone on earth, reducing worldwide acts of terrorism by 72 percent. Spottiswoode's discovery suggests that our thinking minds are directly interconnected with the galaxy itself—and may also support the concept that our DNA is ultimately created by a galactic intelligence. The Law of One series also indicates that history moves in a cyclical, not a linear fashion. Multiple references are made to a "25,000-year cycle" that is driving human evolution. I was fascinated by this idea and spent many years trying to unravel what this twenty-five-thousand-year cycle is, how it appears on earth, and what we can learn from it. I still hadn't fully solved the mystery when I wrote *The Source Field Investigations*—but I was really close.

We've already seen that the surfaces of stars may well be boiling with living microorganisms that are getting thrown off into space, where they are then freeze-dried into galactic dust particles. If stars are forming microbes, complete with DNA, then stars might also have some form of consciousness, since life itself is conscious. The microbes might be only a very small part of an extremely complex life-form—much like the bacteria we find on our skin do not represent who we are as intelligent, self-aware organisms.

Could it be possible that galaxies and stars have "personalities"? Could they have their own thoughts? Could they also have different thoughts in different regions? Could these thoughts in different regions affect every life-form that moves through them, to varying degrees? This is exactly what the Law of One series teaches—and there is very good scientific evidence to support these new ideas. We've already discussed the 26- and 62-million-year evolution cycles in the first chapter. We also presented evidence for a new DNA model that allows spontaneous, energetic changes to be made to living organisms—to rewrite their genetic code. This is precisely how the Law of One series describes the mechanism of evolution as we evolved from Neanderthal-type hominids to our current form.

> 19.9 There was loss of the body hair, as you call it, the clothing of the body to protect it, the changing of the structure of the neck, jaw, and forehead in order to allow the easier vocalization, and the larger cranial development characteristic of third-density [human] needs. This was a normal transfiguration.[38]

> 19.10 [This occurred] within a generation and one-half, as you know these things.[39]

This explains why anthropologists have never been able to find a "missing link" to account for a sudden doubling in the size of the human brain. However, genetic evolution is only one very large-scale, long-term aspect of how this living system of celestial energy actually influences us.

Is it possible, therefore, that as we drift through space, we also drift through different influences—which then directly affect how we think and feel? What if this were already true? What if science just hasn't caught up to this knowledge yet—at least not in modern times? Astrology is a robust system of scholarship that tells us our minds are directly affected by celestial influences; it is just not widely accepted in our current era. The history of astrology goes back at least five thousand years, to Babylonian times. Astrology was taken seriously as a science by Tycho Brahe, Galileo Galilei, Johannes Kepler, and Pierre Gassendi—all of whom were pioneers in developing modern physics and astronomy.[40]

The Signs of the Zodiac

Now, let's visualize the earth's 365-day orbit around the sun as a cycle. Let's say that the sun is generating an energy field that influences how we think and feel. Let's say our position in this energy field has a direct effect on our minds and bodies. Let's say that different areas of the sun's energy field will make us think and feel in different ways. Let's say there are twelve equally spaced regions in the sun's energy field that we drift through in each earth cycle, or year. Let's say that each of these regions has a unique "personality" that causes us to feel a certain way. This would then explain the twelve signs of the zodiac.

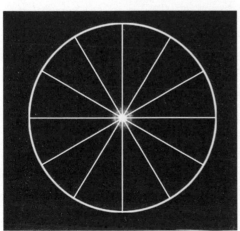

Fig. 3: Division of Sun's energy field into twelve Ages of the Zodiac

Skeptics are quick to point out that being born under a certain sign does not guarantee a certain type of personality in any scientifically provable way.[41] However, matching up a particular sign to a particular personality type is only "newspaper astrology," which was invented by R. H. Naylor in 1930.[42] Naylor was a British astrologer who made a stunningly accurate prediction in his second newspaper column. He warned that British aircraft might be in danger, and on that same day, the British airship R101 crashed in northern France. This catapulted Naylor into the public eye virtually overnight. The resulting hunger for a regular newspaper column led him to pioneer a highly simplified method, where he wrote personalized descriptions for each sign of the zodiac. To this day, many magazines and almost all newspapers feature Naylor-style astrological forecasts for their readers.

The real science is far more complex than that. In fact, modern astrologers believe that Naylor's "newspaper astrology" has done incredible damage to their field, since the twelve zones around the sun we call "signs" are only one of a series of competing influences.[43] If there were no planets involved, the power of these twelve zones would probably be much stronger.

Energetic Influences of Planets and Moons

Interestingly, Dr. Carl Gustav Jung, the father of "synchronicity" and an associate of Dr. Sigmund Freud, revealed that the meanings of the twelve signs of the zodiac are not arbitrary—they represent an encyclopedic knowledge of human psychology. "Astrology represents the summation of all the psychological knowledge of antiquity."[44] Each sign represents an *archetype*—a specific type of personality—which we will learn about later in this book. These patterns are written into the mind of the galaxy itself, according to the Law of One series.

If the signs of astrology have an effect, then what about planets and moons? Let's begin with our closest neighbor. The idea that the moon's position has an effect on us is ancient and is the source of the word *lunatic*. University of Miami psychologist Arnold Lieber studied the

Fig. 4: Dr. Carl Jung

homicide data in Miami-Dade County over a fifteen-year period—1,887 murders—looking for a lunar effect. Dr. Lieber, whose results were published in the *Journal of Clinical Psychiatry,* found that the murder rate did rise and fall with the phases of the moon, very steadily, throughout the entire period he studied.[45] Staff members at the *Toledo Blade* newspaper did a computer analysis of all Cuyahoga County police reports from the beginning of 1999 through the end of 2001— 120,000 in total—and found that there were 5.5 percent more violent crimes and 4.6 percent more property crimes on nights when there was a full moon.[46] Additionally, burglaries of unoccupied homes rose by 16 percent, resisting arrest rose by 34 percent, and aggravated assault went up by 35 percent.[47] In 2007, British police announced that they had found similar results in their own studies of crime and decided to deploy more officers to counter the effect.[48] Inspector Andy Parr said, "I would be interested in approaching universities and seeing if any of their postgraduates would be interested in looking into it further. This could be helpful to us." [49]

If the moon has a statistically significant effect on violent crime, then perhaps the positions of the planets affect how we think and feel as well. Beginning in 1949, Michel Gauquelin analyzed the astrology of thousands of notable historical figures and found that certain types of people were more apt to be born with planets in key positions.[50] Gauquelin started out as a total skeptic and was quite surprised to discover that the real-world data thoroughly contradicted his original assumptions. Gauquelin's most well-known finding is the Mars effect, in which sports champions and military personnel are much more likely to have Mars appear just above the eastern horizon at their time of birth, which is known as the "rising" point, or directly overhead, which is known as the "culminating" or "midheaven" point. Michel and his wife, Françoise, analyzed more than sixty thousand people in eleven different professions and found strong correlations with five different planets.[51] Mercury influences politicians and writers; Venus influences painters and musicians; Mars influences doctors, athletes, military personnel, executives, and scientists; Jupiter influences actors, military personnel, executives, politicians, journalists, and playwrights; and Saturn influences doctors and scientists. Certain planets were negatively correlated with certain professions as well—meaning that these planets were farther away from the rising or culminating points than usual in these people. Mercury is farther away from athletes; Mars is farther away from writers, painters, and musicians; Jupiter is farther away from doctors and scientists; and Saturn is farther away from actors, journalists, writers, and painters.[52] These results were originally found in French data, and the Gauquelins later proved that the data was valid for American and other European professionals as well.[53]

After Michel Gauquelin's death in 1991, his findings were further replicated by Suitbert Ertel and Arto Müller using a data set of members of the French Académie Nationale de Médecine, Italian writers, and German physicians.[54] Furthermore, three different skeptic groups gathered their own data on athletes and validated the Mars effect—in some cases begrudgingly.[55] After fifty years, no skeptics have been able to definitively debunk Gauquelin's findings.[56] In fact, in their 1996 book, *The Tenacious Mars Effect,* Suitbert Ertel and Kenneth Irving revealed that the scientific evidence has proven to be even stronger than Gauquelin originally found.[57]

Science doesn't matter when people refuse to believe certain facts. If they want to deny that something is happening, for whatever reason, it can be utterly impossible to convince them otherwise. Skeptics often used hostile and dubious methods to attempt to debunk Gauquelin's findings about the effects of the planets on human personality and behavior.[58] It's human nature to fiercely attack anything that makes us feel threatened. The shame of having passionately believed something that turns out to be incorrect can be almost impossible to face—particularly if you've paid tens of thousands of dollars and worked for many years to acquire that knowledge. However, attacking new discoveries is the exact

opposite of true scientific inquiry, which teaches us to follow the data—
no matter how unfamiliar or bizarre the trail may be.

Celestial Influences on Human Consciousness

In *The Source Field Investigations,* I presented comprehensive scientific
evidence that our collective experiences may be influenced by certain
astrophysical factors. For example, the Russian scientist Aleksandr Tchijevsky conclusively demonstrated that sunspot cycles have a powerful
effect on the ebb and flow of civilization. Tchijevsky studied the level of
conflict and activity in seventy-two different countries over almost
twenty-five hundred years—from 500 B.C. to A.D. 1922. The study included wars, revolutions, riots, economic upsets, expeditions, and migra-
tions. The severity of these events was also ranked by how many people
were involved, giving us a measurable scale of magnitude. To his amazement, "Tchijevsky found that fully 80 percent of the most significant
events occurred during the 5 years of maximum sunspot activity."[59] The
sunspot cycle typically takes about eleven years, but its length is not always consistent. Nonetheless, Tchijevsky found that whenever solar activity was at its maximum, fully 80 percent of all the most significant
events on earth took place. The increased solar energy output during the
peak of this cycle seems to make us feel restless on a mass, worldwide
level.

I removed the pages on the cycles of history in *The Source Field Investigations* in part because I hadn't fully solved the mystery of what was
causing them. There were some clues in the Law of One series, but Don
Elkins certainly did not ask every question that was raised by the discussions he was having. A workable explanation for these cycles did not
appear until August 2012, when I realized that all of these longer-term
cycles of history could be modeled by our sun orbiting another star in a
25,920-year cycle—forming what scientists call a binary solar system. I
was already familiar with the work of Walter Cruttenden, who made a
strong scientific case that we were indeed living in a binary solar system.

In fact, Cruttenden had already sent me a copy of his book for review—
I just hadn't taken the time to study it before then. Now I opened the
book and found concrete evidence that our entire solar system could be
orbiting around another star adjacent to the sun. As it turned out, this
phenomenon perfectly explained several passages in the Law of One series that had remained mysterious until then.

Our neighboring star may be a brown dwarf, which means it might
not be easily visible to our telescopes even at such a relatively close range.
Ancient mystery schools often spoke of a nearby "Black Sun," which has
a very strong influence on us, which we will discuss in Part 4. This nearly
invisible star does have measurable effects—including gravitational pull.
Certain scientists have already speculated that there must be a large
gravitating body outside our solar system. Cruttenden's book masterfully
spelled out how the gravitational attraction of this neighboring star
could be pulling our earth's axis through the slow, 25,920-year wobble
that astronomers now call the "precession of the equinoxes." This gradual, counter-rotating movement in the earth could now be explained by
our solar system orbiting this companion star over 25,920 years. Interestingly, this same cycle was historically called the "Great Year."

Historians Giorgio de Santillana and Hertha von Dechend demonstrated that more than thirty ancient cultures, worldwide, had complex,
technical information about this cycle "encoded" into their mythologies.[60] This appeared to be the result of a focused, worldwide effort and
was certainly not a coincidence. I found out about this mystery in 1995,
when reading *Fingerprints of the Gods,* by Graham Hancock,[61] and spent
many years trying to understand why the ancients were so interested in
this long-term cycle. When we divide this 25,920-year cycle into twelve
sections, we get the twelve Ages of the Zodiac—at 2,160 years each. As
of approximately December 21, 2012—the end of the Mayan calendar—
we have now apparently moved out of the Age of Pisces and into the Age
of Aquarius. This 25,920-year cycle of "precession" is almost certainly
what the Law of One series referred to as the "25,000-year cycle," which
the source said was directing human evolution. It appears that ancient
cultures were contacted, worldwide, and this key piece of information

was then encoded into their myths by the unified group of angelic or extraterrestrial humans known as the "Confederation" in the Law of One series. This ancient mystery was apparently planted to help us rediscover the truth in today's world with the help of modern technology. Since just about any information could have been encoded into ancient myths, the "Great Year" was obviously seen to be of monumental importance for us to understand.

Now, after many years of thinking about this problem, I had finally found a system that could physically model the forces that may be causing history to repeat itself. This system fits in perfectly with the scientific argument that we live in an intelligent universe—and that stars and planets are exerting influences on our minds and bodies. In this case, our sun's companion star is generating energy fields that affect our thoughts and behaviors as we move through them—in surprisingly specific ways. These energy fields seem to carry the necessary codes to rewrite our DNA as well—making us more intelligent and more evolved, in even cycles of time.

Solid Scientific Evidence for a Twenty-Five-Thousand-Year Evolution Cycle

There is solid scientific evidence to support the Law of One concept that human evolution is moving in roughly twenty-five-thousand-year cycles. First, the Neanderthals died out—or were transformed—somewhere between twenty-eight thousand and twenty-four thousand years ago.[62] If we then go back to fifty thousand years ago, we see an equally massive change. Before then, no one on earth used any tools that were more sophisticated than a crude stone blade.[63] However, according to anthropologist John Fleagle, beginning fifty thousand years ago, people all over the world suddenly began making musical instruments, artwork, religious carvings, harpoons, arrowheads, needles, and beaded jewelry.[64] Furthermore, giant mammals that were dangerous to humans experienced a mass extinction fifty thousand years ago—on every continent except Africa.[65] The various human groups that suddenly became a lot more creative were obviously not in contact with one another, but everyone in the world seemed to experience a massive IQ boost at the same time.

The Fourth-Density Shift

This same IQ-boosting phenomenon is happening again and is visible in a variety of provable ways, as we will discuss. Nonetheless, we may still be in for quite a surprise. The Law of One series indicates that we will soon make a transition into an entirely new level of human evolution that is called "fourth density," as opposed to our current "third-density" level. Once we survey the statements made in the Law of One about what fourth-density humans are like, it will be obvious that they are describing an ascended being—much like Jesus allegedly appeared after the resurrection. There are thousands of documented cases of advanced meditators who have made this evolutionary leap into what the Tibetans call the "Rainbow Body." Since the twenty-five-thousand-year cycle apparently propels us into this change, on a worldwide level, and it also drives us through repeating cycles of history, it definitely appears that identifying and understanding this phenomenon is of critical importance.

It is very interesting to discover that every cycle of history divides perfectly into this "Great Year," as Michèl Helmer and François Masson revealed. The binary solar system model finally provided a working explanation for how and why these cycles are happening, through simple geometry caused by the energy fields of our companion star. One basic historical cycle is the twelve Ages of the Zodiac, each of which is 2,160 years long. There are also twelve signs of the zodiac within a single earth year. Now, with the binary solar system model, I realized that these twelve Ages of the Zodiac could be caused by another star, with the same type of energy fields that our sun is generating to create the twelve signs of the zodiac in traditional astrology. The only real difference between these two zodiac cycles might be the length of time it takes our planet to complete one orbit around each of these stars. On the interstellar scale, there are no other planets or large bodies out there to compete with our companion star's energy fields, so the effects of these twelve 2,160-year zones could be much stronger than the traditional signs of the zodiac.

Conventional Examples of Cycles in History

If you were to ask the average American whether any events have mysteriously repeated in exact cycles throughout history, most of them, if they even had any idea that such a phenomenon might occur, would probably think of only two common and controversial examples, which revolve around the deaths of American presidents Lincoln and Kennedy and Tecumseh's Curse. Neither of these cases is necessarily "real," but both are certainly interesting. Skeptics automatically discount these phenomena, but by the time you are finished reading this book, you may have a different opinion. Time may not be as linear as we think; it may actually be cyclical. The events that happen in one cycle may continue to influence our thoughts and behaviors in later cycles, in seemingly mysterious ways.

The Lincoln-Kennedy Connection
First of all, there are strange connections between the lives and deaths of American presidents Abraham Lincoln and John F. Kennedy. Certain specific events happened in both of their lives, and the lives of those around them, in a hundred-year cycle. Let's not forget that Nikolai Morozov, the original Russian pioneer scientist who first discovered historical cycles in the modern era, noticed that there were astonishing similarities between the historical accounts of Hebrew kings in the Old Testament and those of Roman kings more than a thousand years later. In the case of Lincoln and Kennedy, the events that connect them are not always exactly one hundred years apart, but there are several key similarities. For example, Lincoln was elected in 1860 and Kennedy in 1960. Both were elected to the House of Representatives (1846 and 1946). Both were runners-up for the vice presidential nomination (in 1856 and 1956). Both leaders had vice presidents—and successors—named

Johnson (born in 1808 and 1908). Both presidents were concerned about the rights of black Americans. On January 1, 1863, Lincoln's Emancipation Proclamation became law, ending slavery: "All persons held as slaves . . . shall be . . . forever free; . . . the Executive government of the United States, including the military and naval authority thereof, will recognize and maintain the freedom of said persons."[66]

One hundred years and six months later, on June 11, 1963, Kennedy addressed the nation in a pivotal speech about civil rights. The John F. Kennedy Presidential Library and Museum website explains that in this speech, "The President asks Congress to enact legislation protecting all Americans' voting rights, legal standing, educational opportunities, and access to public facilities, but recognizes that legislation alone cannot solve the country's problems concerning race relations."[67] This directly paved the way for Martin Luther King Jr.'s "I Have a Dream" speech on August 28, 1963—addressing the largest crowd to ever have marched on the US Capitol in Washington, DC. In the first eight sentences of his speech, King made fully five different references to the one hundred years that had elapsed since Lincoln's Emancipation Proclamation. Four of the first eight sentences began with the words "one hundred years later."[68]

From this point forward, in order to better understand the connections between Lincoln and Kennedy, we must explore the history of the Federal Reserve, which is responsible for printing and circulating American currency at the time of this writing in April 2013. The term *Federal Reserve* is confusing, as the Fed is not actually a part of the federal government of the United States. As more and more people are becoming aware, the Fed is a private consortium of international bankers. Due to perpetual insolvency and financial crises, the United States handed over the control and management of its financial system to this international group of bankers in 1913. The US Treasury has allowed the Federal Reserve bankers to circulate their Federal Reserve notes—that is, the US dollar—as legal tender ever since.[69] According to Senator Ron Paul, who has pursued this investigation for more than thirty years, the Federal Reserve is the ultimate adversary in our story. Senator Paul is one of many influential figures who believe that the Federal Reserve has been responsible for many of America's greatest problems in the last one hundred years.

> The Federal Reserve is the chief culprit behind the economic crisis. Its unchecked power to create endless amounts of money out of thin air brought us the boom and bust cycle, and causes one financial bubble after another. Since the Fed's creation in 1913, the dollar has lost more than 96% of its value—and by recklessly inflating the money supply, the Fed continues to distort interest rates, and intentionally erodes the value of the dollar.[70]

Both Lincoln and Kennedy tried to wrestle the American currency away from the private banking groups who founded the Federal Reserve and back into the hands of the US Treasury.[71] Although these bankers had not formed the Federal Reserve during the time of Lincoln, the same intergenerational dynasties were at work in the 1800s. Lincoln authorized the printing of "greenbacks" from the US Treasury, not backed by gold or silver, on February 25, 1862, in the First Legal Tender Act.[72] This allowed for unprecedented economic growth in the United States that could not be controlled and taxed by foreign banks, which had wanted to collect tax rates of 24 to 36 percent due to their financing of American infrastructure and war debts. Lincoln's move to centralize American currency within the US Treasury greatly angered them.[73] Nearly one hundred years later, Kennedy halted all sales of silver from the US Treasury, on November 28, 1961.[74] Until then, the storehouse of US Treasury silver was being very rapidly sold off at seriously cheap prices. Kennedy then drafted House Resolution 5389 to authorize the printing of "silver certificates" from the US Treasury; these certificates would be an American currency totally outside the control of the Federal Reserve. Kennedy's groundbreaking bill passed the House on April 10, 1963,[75] and the Senate on May 23, 1963.[76] Kennedy signed this bill into law on June 4, 1963, and issued Executive Order 11,110 that same day.[77] Executive Order 11,110 authorized the secretary of the treasury to issue silver certificates on his own—without any input or oversight from the Federal Reserve. Although the halting of all sales of silver from the Treasury in 1961 originally seemed to favor the Federal Reserve, the Treasury silver provided Kennedy with the collateral he needed to print money, which was completely outside the Fed's control.[78] Within a hundred-year cycle, Lincoln's printing of greenbacks on February 25, 1862, and Kennedy's halting of silver sales on November 28, 1961, overlap by less than three months.

Lincoln was shot to death by an assassin on April 14, 1865, and Kennedy was assassinated on November 22, 1963—within less than a year and a half of each other in a hundred-year cycle. Both of these heroic presidents were shot in the head, in the presence of their wives, on a Friday—which may or may not be significant but is often cited in articles comparing the two. Many independent researchers have speculated that Lincoln and Kennedy were both assassinated because they opposed the foreign bankers who pooled their resources to become the Federal Reserve in 1913.[79] Lincoln was shot in Ford's Theatre, and Kennedy was shot in a Lincoln automobile, which was made by Ford Motor Company. Both presidents have seven-letter last names, and both assassins have three-part names with fifteen letters—John Wilkes Booth and Lee Harvey Oswald. Other connections have been presented that turned out to be false, or at least weak, causing skeptics to discount the entire story as an "urban legend."[80]

Tecumseh's Curse

Then we have Tecumseh's Curse. In 1809, William Henry Harrison was the governor of the Indiana Territory as the United States continued expanding westward. In the Treaty of Fort Wayne, Harrison persuaded several Native American tribes to hand over their greatest wealth to the US government—namely, huge tracts of land. Harrison convinced certain warring tribes to turn against one another and accept very low payouts for their lands. In some cases, more powerful tribes such as the Wea were bribed to coerce less powerful tribes, such as the Kickapoo, into accepting the treaty, and this coercion could easily have included threats, violence, terrorism, and murder. The Shawnee leader Tecumseh soon felt they had all been tricked, that the wealth of their lands had been seized through a variety of unethical tactics. Tecumseh ultimately worked with his brother Tenskwatawa to create an alliance of Native American tribes that resisted the westward expansion of the United States. Tenskwatawa was a spiritual leader more than a military man and was known as "the Prophet."[81] Tenskwatawa led his brother's army into battle against Harrison's forces in Tippecanoe on November 7, 1811, while Tecumseh was off recruiting new allies.[82] Ultimately the Native Americans lost the war because of a lack of ammunition.

Harrison became president in 1840. By that point, many Native Americans felt that they had gotten a very bad deal. They had given away their greatest treasure, and whatever payments they had received in exchange had long since been forgotten. The Prophet made a public curse against Harrison and all future American presidents as an act of revenge for the seizure of their land.[83] Tenskwatawa said that every president elected during a year that ended in a zero, just as Harrison had been, would die in office.[84] This would create a twenty-year cycle if it actually worked—and many thousands of people believed in it. Harrison died of pneumonia in 1841, while in office, seemingly verifying that the curse was working. Lincoln was next. The pattern continued, like clockwork, straight through until Ronald Reagan and George W. Bush—both of whom survived assassination attempts. The presidents who were elected during the years in this curse and died in office were William Henry Harrison, elected in 1840; Abraham Lincoln, elected in 1860; James A. Garfield, elected in 1880; William McKinley, elected in 1900; Warren G. Harding, elected in 1920; Franklin D. Roosevelt, elected in 1940; and John F. Kennedy, elected in 1960. In fact, the only president who died in office and was not elected during one of the "cursed" years was Zachary Taylor, who won the election in 1848 and died in 1850.

In 1998, I was given a yellowing, typed, unpublished manuscript from 1980 that gave many astonishing examples of history repeating itself—far beyond the Lincoln-Kennedy connection or Tecumseh's Curse. All of these cycles were exact subdivisions of 25,920 years, which the author could not explain. Nonetheless, the author, François Masson, boldly predicted the collapse of the Soviet Union using the science of cycles. He even got the year right—1991—but his manuscript was completed in 1980. It wasn't until I was developing *The Source Field Investigations* in 2010 that I went back to this original body of data to study it in more detail and to see if these cycles were still working. I was very impressed by what I found. There were incredibly specific connections between historical events separated by hundreds or even thousands of years. I quickly realized that 9/11 occurred within only days of a similar sequence of events in 1462, thirty years before Columbus ever sailed to America.

In late November 2011, shortly after *The Source Field Investigations* came out, I had a rash of overconfidence and signed a new book deal—promising that I would generate an entirely new manuscript out of the deleted chapters from *The Source Field Investigations* in three months' time. I assured the publisher that this new book would be ready to go by the end of February 2012. My original working title was *The Hidden Architecture of Time.* Brian Tart, the president of Dutton Books, suggested that I call it *The Synchronicity Key* instead. This title allowed the book to discuss other subjects besides the cycles of history. I liked that idea—and I accepted the new title.

Little did I know that I was about to come face-to-face with what may be the most powerful and negative force on earth today. Nor did I realize that I would be given an opportunity to directly take part in its defeat. Before we fill in the details on this intriguing story and the people behind it, we will explore the history and science of synchronicity and how it had become such a part of my life that I had gained the confidence to stand up to this Global Adversary.

CHAPTER THREE

What Is Synchronicity?

S
o what, exactly, is synchronicity? The term *synchronicity,* as it applies to psychology, was coined by Dr. Carl Gustav Jung in the 1920s.[85] Jung was a Swiss psychologist who studied under the legendary pioneer Dr. Sigmund Freud and ultimately broke away from him over a basic difference of opinion. Dr. Freud's perspective was much more conventional, in the sense that he did not believe in Jung's concept of a "collective unconscious"—a fundamental connectedness that we all share within the mind, such as in dreams. The dictionary definition of *synchronicity,* as it applies to psychology, is "the simultaneous occurrence of causally unrelated events—and the belief that the simultaneity has meaning beyond mere coincidence."[86] In plain language, synchronicity is a mysterious event in which two or more things happen at the same time that seem directly related to each other, even though this would normally appear to be impossible. Jung had discussed this concept since the early 1920s, but he did not formalize his thoughts into a lecture until 1951.[87] Then, in 1952, Jung published his defining work, *Synchronicity: An Acausal Connecting Principle,* found in Volume 8 of his Collected Works.[88] Jung believed that synchronicity was a key element of spiritual awakening. He felt that synchronicity shifted us out of egocentric thinking into a viewpoint where we see ourselves as far more interconnected with one another.

Let's not forget that Jung was rubbing elbows with the finest scientists of his day, including Albert Einstein and Wolfgang Pauli, a Nobel laureate who was one of the founding fathers of quantum physics. Pauli had lengthy correspondence with other luminaries in the field, including Nobel prizewinners Niels Bohr and Werner Heisenberg. Pauli was directly or indirectly responsible for many quantum physics breakthroughs, including the Pauli exclusion principle, in which he proved that two electrons cannot occupy the same space at the same time. Jung felt that synchronicity could be explained scientifically, through applying Einstein's relativity theory and the quantum mechanics theory Pauli and others were developing. Pauli was fascinated by the concept of synchronicity, absolutely believed it was true, and published his own paper about it in the same book with Jung in 1952.[89] By this point, Pauli had already won the Nobel Prize in 1945; he went on to win two other highly prestigious physics awards after this—the Matteucci Medal in 1956 and the Max Planck Medal in 1958.

Jung's most classic personal example of synchronicity can be found in paragraph 843 of his epic work from 1952. I first read this when I was in college, as part of a homework assignment for a class called Psychology of Perception, and I was very impressed.

> A young woman I was treating had, at a critical moment, a dream in which she was given a golden scarab. While she was telling me this dream, I sat with my back to the closed window. Suddenly I heard a noise behind me, like a gentle tapping. I turned round and saw a flying insect knocking against the window-pane from the outside. I opened the window and caught the creature in the air as it flew in. It was the nearest analogy to a golden scarab one finds in our latitudes, a scarabaeid beetle, the common rose-chafer (Cetonia aurata), which, contrary to its usual habits, had evidently felt the urge to get into a dark room at this particular moment. I must admit that nothing like it ever happened to me before or since.[90]

Although Pauli was considered "the conscience of physics"—the ultimate skeptic who picked apart everyone else's work for flaws—powerful synchronicity was happening around him as well. There were many documented occasions in which Pauli's colleagues would be working on an experiment, and when Pauli visited them to fact-check it himself, their equipment would self-destruct as soon as he walked in the room. This was a very common occurrence that came to be known as the "Pauli effect."[91] Noted physicist Otto Stern, who won the Nobel Prize in 1943, politely but firmly banned Pauli from visiting his laboratory in Hamburg—even though they were friends—due to the strong likelihood that Pauli would create expensive and time-consuming equipment failures simply by showing up.[92] Pauli was fascinated by this effect and wrote about it in Jung's classic 1952 volume on synchronicity.[93]

Jung had a heart attack in 1944, which resulted in a near-death experience, or NDE. (We will review the science behind NDEs in chapter 8.) In Jung's case, he found himself in the presence of beautiful light, and he had many insights that shaped his ideas of the collective unconscious, synchronicity, and archetypes. Jung now felt that certain personality types were basic elements within the mind of the universe, and he believed that astrology was a valid form of synchronicity. After having this powerful experience, Jung committed to finding the scientific proof that astrology could be a genuine science. He studied the birth charts of 483 married couples and looked for the three conjunctions that were associated with a happy partnership in traditional astrology. He also mixed up the charts into 31,737 other random combinations. Jung found that the "happy relationship" conjunctions appeared three times more often in the combined charts of married couples than in those of random paired individuals.[94] Furthermore, the pattern that was considered the most conducive to marriage occurred the most frequently in the couples' charts, and the pattern that was least conducive to marriage occurred the least frequently. Jung calculated the odds of this occurring by random chance as 1 in 62.5 million.[95]

Jung defined synchronicity as a "meaningful coincidence"—a mysterious synchronizing of seemingly unrelated events. These experiences politely shatter your most cherished and rigorously held belief systems about the "real world." In my own personal experience, there is no chemical and no other event that can give you such a staggering high—in body, mind, and spirit—as an experience with synchronicity. Once it happens, it's real. It's Now. It's awesome. In the most dramatic cases, you can barely breathe. Your head threatens to explode in pure ecstatic bliss. Everything seems to sparkle. Reality crystallizes into a hidden order that should not—cannot—exist. And yet it does. The world you so flagrantly took for granted is now nothing more than a shadow—a shadow of a hidden, majestic Truth you may never dare to grasp.

Dramatic Personal Examples of Synchronicity

It was December 21, 1992—twenty years to the day before the Mayan calendar end date—when I came home and told my old high school friends I had been completely sober for the last three months. I voluntarily chose to put myself through recovery shortly after starting my sophomore year of college and was now writing my dreams down every morning. In addition to giving me guidance that helped me stay clean, all sorts of amazing things were happening in these dreams, including cosmic messages of hope and specific prophecies of the future that were then coming true. My friends glared at me through the stench of old beer and cigarette smoke as I told them that I now believed I was here for a spiritual purpose and that I would help many people. Stony silence erupted into a full-scale verbal assault as soon as I finished. Apparently I was going to fight my way into a dead-end job, marry a vicious and unattractive woman, slave my life away for kids who would only hate me more and more as they got older, and ultimately die alone in a nursing home surrounded by staff who could barely wait for their next cigarette break as I groaned for their attention.

Was this it? Was this life? Was I crazy? Were they right? How could they be so cruel—after all the years we'd shared together? I could barely even hear what they were saying as I observed this withering assault of sarcasm and humiliation. I warned them several times that I could not tolerate this, but on and on they went. Finally, I stood up in the middle of a sentence and walked out the front door—without verbalizing any anger or hostility—never to return. One of them reconnected with me as I was finishing this book—for the first time in twenty years—and we had a good conversation that helped us arrive at a point of mutual forgiveness.

After a ten-minute walk, I stood at the crossroads between my friend's street and mine. I was utterly devastated, fighting back tears. I felt inspired to hold my arms out to the sky and speak.

> You . . . whoever or whatever you are. I know you're out there. I know you can hear me. I know I'm here for a reason. My life has a purpose. You've shown me that. I believe you— and I trust you. I know I'm not crazy. I have made my choice. I will dedicate my life to helping others who are suffering. I thank you for helping me—and now I want to help you.

I was staring at a small patch of stars in the night sky as these words coursed through my mind. Right as I said "I want to help you," a huge, yellow-white meteor streaked directly across the area I was looking at. It was real. It was absolute. It was undeniable. It was astonishing. It was the biggest, brightest meteor I had ever seen, even after many sleepless nights of sitting out in a lawn chair as a boy, watching the occasional flickerings of the Perseids or Leonids. A tremendous surge of ecstatic energy roared up through my body, and I felt a magnificent spiritual presence. Tears of joy streamed down my face. I spoke to the universe—and got an answer. It was, and still is, one of the most profound events in my life.

A Staggering Wealth of Numerical Synchronicity

After this defining event, the genie burst out of the bottle and synchronicity started happening like crazy. I was now seeing repeating patterns of numbers everywhere—such as on digital clocks—at seemingly random moments. This phenomenon had happened only once before, while I was a junior in high school, but now it was happening almost every day, and frequently several times a day. I would often be sitting and reading about paranormal subjects—a favorite topic of mine—and suddenly be inspired to look at the clock, after an hour or more of unbroken focus on the book. I would then see repeating patterns such as 11:11, 12:12, 3:33,

5:55, or other combinations—1:11, 2:22, and 4:44. In other cases I would wake right up out of a very intense dream, look at the clock, and see one of these patterns.

I started counting the seconds after this happened and found that I usually was seeing these patterns immediately after the clock had changed. I also saw repeating digits appearing on wristwatches, television screens, scoreboards, and license plates. Generally I did not worry about the meanings of the numbers themselves. Instead, these events seemed to give instant feedback on whatever I had just been thinking about—telling me I was on the right track, letting me know that these thoughts were beneficial and progressive for my soul. This phenomenon always seemed to happen right as I was having a positive, loving thought. If I started moving into a negative place, the synchronicities would stop—or I would see the same patterns, but at exactly one minute before the synchronous mark. I also noticed that my diet seemed to determine how often this would happen. The cleaner and healthier I ate, the more synchronicity I received. The more I ate processed food, dairy, white flour, and refined sugar, the harder it was to remember my dreams—and the less synchronicity I would experience throughout the day.

Believe me, I wasn't constantly checking clocks and looking for this to happen. If I did try to do that, it never seemed to work. Instead, whenever I was least expecting it, bam!—there it was: 3:33, 12:12, 5:55, 11:11. It happened over and over again, and I would often laugh out loud in amazement. I am well aware that some people will immediately discount all of this as coincidence. They will say it is unreasonable, ridiculous, and foolish. Most people do not realize that our modern theories of synchronicity were developed by the same scientists whom skeptics often use to discredit them. However, simply becoming aware of synchronicity can make it start happening a lot more often. In that sense, this book *is* the Synchronicity Key, because instead of just reading this book, you are now directly participating in its main subject. The conscious universe may well decide that you are now ready to know who and what you really are. Many hundreds of readers of *The Source Field Investigations* reported stunning synchronicities while they were reading the book—and now we are focusing even more strongly on that subject.

Two Bullets!

After my parents divorced in the summer after my fifth-grade year, I started self-medicating with food. I quickly became the fat kid in school during a time when most students were at their normal weight. This alone made me very unpopular. I was also one of the smartest kids in school and a complete pacifist who would do just about anything to avoid hurting someone else's feelings. The overall combination of body fat, intelligence, sensitivity, and pacifism made me the ideal target for bullying and humiliation. I still have a dent in my forehead from the kid who threw a ball of solid ice into my face from thirty-five feet away with the speed and accuracy of a baseball pitcher. The pain was incredible— and the kid laughed sardonically as I cried and tried to stand up. I also have a circular scar along the edge of my left ear from a tent pole that sliced right through the cartilage, like a cookie cutter. The pole cut a perfect, one-centimeter-wide ring after my friend threw it at me as a joke. He laughed at me and had his dog chase me around the yard while I ran, screaming in agony and holding my ear. He didn't realize what had happened until he noticed his dog licking the blood off of my hand after I had collapsed in tears. This accident required emergency plastic surgery, and I had to wear a large white gauze bandage on my ear for months. Several kids in school called me "Vinnie"—referring to how Vincent Van Gogh supposedly cut his own ear off and mailed it to a woman. I quickly grew my hair out to hide the scar.

By the year 1989, I was sixteen years old, seriously overweight—225 pounds at five feet nine inches tall—and completely tired of being bullied and teased. I plunged myself into a grindingly strict and very dangerous diet, drinking a can of cold V8 vegetable juice for breakfast and nothing but water between classes. By the end of the year, without really doing any more exercise, I had become eighty-five pounds lighter, but the psychological scars of the bullying stayed with me.

Five years later, in July 1994, I was a college student and was working on a music album with my best friend, Jude, in his apartment. I was thin and moderately athletic, and I had a year and a half of clean time, but I'd never had a girlfriend. I still didn't have the courage to ask a girl out on a date after so many years of threats, humiliation, and physical injuries from other kids. I was struggling to fall asleep as I lay there on the floor on a cold, dirty air mattress, staring at the ceiling. Jude was sleeping off to my right, two feet above the ground, in his normal bed. Jude's apartment was far too small for me to have a separate room to sleep in, as his cousin Reuben was crashed out on the couch in the other room.

As I lay there, I was having a weird, waking dream. This monstrous, exaggerated fat man—an obvious caricature of how I used to look—was chasing me, trying to kill me. I had a gun in my belt as I ran. I knew I could shoot this man and put an end to my misery, once and for all, but for some reason I wouldn't do it. I didn't want to hurt him, even though he was definitely trying to hurt me. This horrible battle raged on, and I ran for all I was worth as I faded in and out of consciousness. Suddenly, Jude's sleeping body turned in the bed next to me, and in an agitated, distant voice, he said, "Shoot him . . . Just shoot him. Two bullets!"

I was galvanized. Instantaneously I was wide-awake. I couldn't breathe. I stared at the ceiling. Everything seemed to shimmer with life. I felt like my body was levitating. My mind was crowded with millions of thoughts—and yet I was ecstatic. I seriously wanted to wake Jude up and tell him what had just happened, but I felt like if I did, we would never get back to sleep, and I desperately needed rest. Somehow I managed to wait until the next morning to tell him, and we were both dazzled by the implications.

The dream seemed to be saying that I was still being ruled by my "shadow self." Even after losing all that weight and being completely sober for more than a year and a half, I was still too insecure to ask a girl out. I was so afraid of being rejected that it was much easier to avoid the whole problem entirely. At least that way I would never get my feelings hurt, and I wouldn't have to feel like that bullied kid again. Now, on some level, Jude had been seeing my dream right as it was happening. I was running, this huge man was chasing me, I was choosing not to shoot him even though I had a gun, and Jude was watching the whole thing. This strongly suggested that these events had not happened in just my own mind—the dream had occurred in a shared space. Later I would discover that in 1973, Dr. Montague Ullman and Dr. Stanley Krippner published a comprehensive paper revealing that ordinary people could concentrate on specific images while awake, and send them to people who were dreaming. The dreamers then experienced symbols and events in their dreams that were directly related to the senders' message. This fascinating effect was repeated with over one hundred participants.[96] The dream seemed to be telling me to let go of that pain, hurt, fear, and buried shame—to symbolically kill off that old, tortured part of myself once and for all. That would mean choosing to love myself for who I was, just the way I was, regardless of what other people thought about me. Two months later, I opened my heart to Yumi, a beautiful Japanese girl, in my senior year of college, and we fell in love. She was so fascinated by my blue eyes that I finally let her touch my eyeball one day to confirm it was real.

Human Nature

Barely a week after the "two bullets" incident—on July 17, 1994—I was still on the summer break between my junior and senior years of college, and one and a half years sober. My parents had insisted I take a job during every summer break since my second year of high school. The pain of disagreeing with them was worse than riding my bicycle in the rain or taking the public bus to work. I was quite accustomed to the sharp odors and prying looks of homeless people and to the men in the ties looking right through me as they glided by the bus stop. Now my father had loaned me $2,000 to buy my own car, and here it was. I painstakingly installed a new Radio Shack stereo system in the beat-up old red station wagon, which was big enough to hold all of my and Jude's musical equipment, including my entire drum kit. Fake wood panels lined the sides, and I had already cleaned and detailed the interior of the car so thoroughly that it looked brand-new inside. Michael Jackson sang away in my mind as I worked on the stereo system in silence:

> "Why? Why? Tell 'em that it's human nature. Why? Why . . .
> did she do me that way?"

Finally, the moment of truth. I connected the last speaker wire to the stereo, sealed it off with a sticky black strip of electrician's tape, shoved it back into the dashboard, and hit the ON button. The radio roared to life. Staggeringly, the exact same song I had been hearing came blasting out. Michael's vocals were perfectly synchronized with the very same moment they had reached in my mind; the song wasn't off by even a fraction of a second. I did not have any dental fillings, so I could not have pulled in radio stations through my teeth. Nor was anyone else playing music in the area. I had been hearing the song for at least twenty minutes before the radio came on. I spent months trying to figure out how this one event could have happened—particularly in a universe that is supposed to be limited by the constraints of linear time and by minds that are supposed to be separate from the greater environment around them.

Synchronicity is fickle. It doesn't always work. It's not there to pleasure your ego on demand. Once you become aware of the possibilities that exist and have had your first taste, you can beg, cry, long for it, and beseech the great forces of the universe to give you another chance—but synchronicity makes its own rules. Time is irrelevant. The next event could be ten years or ten minutes away. I had very few experiences of synchronicity until after I completely stopped using any and all mind-altering chemicals—including caffeine, nicotine, and alcohol—and started cleaning up my diet. I also came to learn that the greater meaning of a synchronicity may not always be apparent when it first happens.

I drove the car to my new job for the first time, and it was wonderful. A two-hour trek, requiring three different buses, was now shaved down to a thirty-five-minute drive. However, at the end of the day, an enormous cloud of smoke belched out of the car when I started it—quickly engulfing a family walking behind me—and the smoke just kept on coming. I was devastated. A new friend I met at work came to the rescue, and she gave me a ride home. The car was towed all the way back to a garage in my hometown, which was not cheap, and it was declared dead on arrival. Head gasket. The whole engine block was cracked. No way out. I was terrified that the elderly couple who had sold it to me would keep the money. I felt so lost, so alone, so confused. My father couldn't afford to give me another loan, and it would take me another year—because I was a full-time student—to earn enough money to pay back the original loan and try again. Yet I couldn't deny the miracle that had happened. Were they really going to take the money and run? Was this the "human nature" Michael Jackson had sung about? Had those lyrics given me a sinister warning about how they were going to "do me that way"? Or could I trust in the good vibes they'd shared with me when I bought it and get my money back? After two days of grinding suspense, I nearly cried with relief when I found out they would take the car back and return the money. They honestly did not know the car was about to die. The synchronicity was a message that all was well, before I even knew there was going to be a problem. I was indeed being guided and protected by mysterious, unseen forces that could influence human nature—and make miracles happen. Linear time did not seem to pose any barrier to whoever or whatever had done this.

It is impossible to predict where or when synchronicity will occur. Then one day it does—and in that brief, tantalizing moment, you have touched infinity. You have tasted that which cannot be tasted. You catch a fleeting glimpse of that which cannot be seen—and yet it is just as real as the eyes that gaze upon it, the ears that hear it, and the mind that revels in it. Now there is no place to hide. That lonely, tortured soul that believes in suffering, pain, and separation is isolated and cornered. It fights valiantly to maintain its rigorous enchantment with despair and misery and its addiction to drama and victimhood—but after enough synchronicity, it simply cannot dare to claim any further relevance. Now the lies are stripped away. The truth is revealed. The world we've been taught to believe in is a sham. The universe is vastly more mysterious and wonderful than we assume—and we are loved more than we could ever possibly imagine.

A Little Bird Told Me

Synchronicity often emerges from the depths of despair as a hidden connection between seemingly unrelated events. We all have to go through what people in twelve-step support groups would call "the bottom" at various times. Psychoanalysts who follow the work of Dr. Carl Jung call it the "dark night of the soul." When we go through this experience, it seems like it's the end of the world, but we can learn to see it as only one part of a much greater series of events in our own evolution. This experience also happens on a collective, planetary level as we go through the great, repeating cycles of wars, disasters, and epic changes. Seemingly random thoughts, decisions, and actions, throughout history, are actually following a hidden script. Ultimately we all know the script, and we constantly seek out creative works that keep telling us the same story, as we will see. Dr. Jung found that there were a series of symbols and experiences that we all encounter, often in dreams. These symbols and experiences remain consistent, regardless of where we are from—historically and geographically. They are called archetypes, and they range from the most difficult and horrible experiences we will ever endure to the most breathtakingly transcendent moments of clarity and triumph. Together, they create the grand story of enlightenment, which Joseph Campbell called the Hero's Journey.

I have had hundreds, if not thousands, of ego-crushing experiences as I traveled along my own Hero's Journey to greater wisdom and understanding. I used to be that guy who wanted other people to take care of him and was terrified of adult responsibility. By the time I graduated from college with a bachelor of arts degree in psychology, I had experienced many mind-blowing synchronicities—but I had also lived on campus all four years, straight out of high school. I had never paid rent or bought my own food from a store on any consistent basis, as I always had a meal plan and I made sure I never ran over budget on my meal card. I was absolutely terrified of graduation, as I knew it was almost impossible to get a well-paying job in New York State with a bachelor's degree in psychology. There were far too many unknown variables. I knew many students who lived off campus and were buying food and paying rent with very little money. Many of them were living on instant ramen noodles, spaghetti, and peanut butter and jelly sandwiches—and they lived in a constant state of anxiety.

I remember the moment in August 1995, right after graduation, when I absolutely knew, without question, that my mother was indeed kicking me out of the house I'd grown up in all my life. She'd gotten tough. She wouldn't take no for an answer. There was nothing I could do. There was no turning back. Now I had to throw myself to the wolves of the corporate world and try to survive on Depression-level wages. I already knew there were powerful and sinister forces that were systematically destroying the wealth of the middle and lower classes. My mind had been blown wide open in 1992 by a sociology class called Contemporary Social Issues, in which our professor openly spoke about how American corporations had systematically financed and supported Hitler's rise to power. The elite had declared full-scale war on the public—and the media was not telling us the truth. The romance of a good job, a home mortgage, and a single-wage family was almost impossible to achieve with a four-year degree in psychology in New York State, but now my mother was forcing me out of the nest. Years of anxiety welled up into a horrible, vomitous, all-consuming fear. I found myself sprawled out on the grass in the backyard, sobbing uncontrollably. I was so terrified I didn't even know if I could stand up.

A small red-breasted robin soon flew down and landed next to me, barely two feet away from my face. It turned its little head to look at me—and it began speaking, in its own chirping voice. I felt so alone, so terrified and confused, and yet here was this little bird, which stayed there for well over ten minutes, seemingly doing its best to cheer me up and console me. This only made me cry even louder and sob even more—at first—but it was real. It was happening. Birds can certainly love people as domesticated pets, but this robin was completely wild. Here I was, lying in the grass and the dirt, feeling utterly devastated, and this little being that I normally wouldn't even expect to think or have feelings was right there. The bird seemed to be distinctly aware that I was crying and was doing its best to help me feel like I was not alone.

Did that little bird know cold? Absolutely. Did that little bird know hunger? Certainly. Did that little bird know what it was like to be alone? To be scared? Undoubtedly. Its own mother had once thrown it out of the nest and demanded that it survive alone. It had since done its best to hunt insects and worms, to shelter itself from the cold and the rain, to find a mate, to build its own nest, and to start a family. It was certainly capable of feeling love—for other birds, for example—and pain, if, for instance, one of those birds died, or when it had to throw its own babies out of the nest once it was time for them to grow up. And now, as much as I tried to stay in my own little world of misery and disaster, I simply could not deny what was happening. This little bird was standing right there in front of me—and it cared about me. It wanted me to feel better. I could easily have assumed I was going crazy, but this was really happening.

For more than ten minutes it spoke to me in chirps and whistles, bowing its head in different ways, moving its little legs and wings, and doing its best to let me know it cared. However, the whole experience was so profound, so bizarre, and so inexplicable that I soon started crying again. I knew this bird would go back to being a bird, disappearing into the faceless and unthinking world of nature. I would have to go on alone in a harsh and uncompromising world. I felt extremely vulnerable. Once the bird realized it had done all it could do for me, it flew off— seemingly in frustration—and again I was alone. However, my tears quickly turned to amazement and disbelief at what had just happened. I picked myself up off the ground, went inside, and started making calls to see if I could move back to my old college town and line up a job. Within less than a week, I had found a place to live—and I landed a job within twenty-four hours of my arrival.

Synchronicity can take on many forms, and as I explain in my Access Your Higher Self video series, you can also "encode" synchronicity.[97] This means that once you decide to see a certain event or symbol as meaningful, messages can then be communicated to you this way. Many people have a favorite number that starts appearing in a variety of different places, seemingly at random. Others may choose to see a coin on the ground as their message. You may decide to grab a book, particularly an inspirational title, relax your mind as much as possible, ask a question, and then open to a particular page and read the answer. Living creatures with symbolic importance can appear—such as Jung's example of the scarab beetle, or shamanic totems such as the hawk, owl, deer, or coyote. You may feel a sudden rush of energy in a particular part of your body such as the lower abdomen, the heart, or the interior of the head. You may get a ringing in your left or right ear. You may also feel a sudden, stabbing pain in some part of your body—like you are being pricked by a needle—but there is no apparent reason for it. Of course, telepathic events can be classified as synchronicity as well. You find yourself thinking about someone—and then the phone rings and it's them, or you bump into them at the store.

Skeptical people will almost always start picking apart a synchronicity story—coming up with anything they can think of to explain it away as coincidence. It can be extremely frustrating to try to share these stories with someone who insists that you are lying to them or that there must be some mundane "scientific" explanation for it. Of course, not all of these experiences will be genuine synchronicities, but the more you open your mind and heart, the more likely they are to happen. Remind your skeptics that synchronicity was actively being discussed by some of the finest scientific minds of the twentieth century, including Albert Einstein, key founders of quantum mechanics, and Carl Jung. I've personally witnessed hundreds of cases in which skeptical people immediately dismiss their own synchronicities and never look back. In some cases, their level of denial is so blatant that all you can do is laugh. They are actually insulted if you try to suggest that they just experienced a paranormal event and can even become quite angry with you. However, if you do decide to ask, "What if?," you may well be surprised at how quickly synchronicity will start happening. This is when, as Jung said, you begin to have a spiritual awakening and are introduced to a greater vision of the universe.

Synchronicity and intuition were very helpful tools in the investigations of my two published books. Dreams often fed me specific information that later could be verified with a quick Internet search. There were hundreds of instances in which I was searching for one subject online, and then another subject I was much more interested in popped up— after it seemed like I could not find any information on it, no matter how hard I looked. There are so many stories like this that I could fill twenty books' worth of pages explaining them and still cover only the basics. So let's start asking more of the questions that synchronicity and my study of the Law of One series were leading me to find the proof for.

What if the cosmos is a living, conscious being? What if space, time, matter, energy, and biological life are the body of this vast organism?

What if the ultimate purpose of life is to realize that we are all one—perfect reflections of this single, vast identity? What if everything in the universe is conscious and alive, to varying degrees—even the lowliest gas, dust, and rocks of interstellar space? What if the basic laws of quantum mechanics create DNA and biological life—and the human form is quite common throughout the universe?

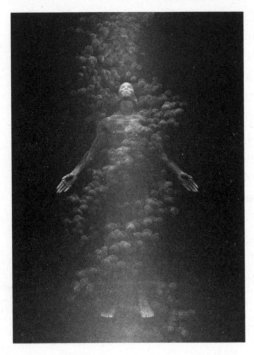

Fig. 5: Micro-gravitational fields may construct DNA from inanimate matter.

What if we are all experiencing a deliberately designed amnesia about our deepest, truest identity—but it fades away more and more as we continue evolving? Could gentleness, kindness, patience, love, acceptance, and forgiveness be the keys that bring us into the greatest harmony with our true identity? Is this conscious universe sending us messages, through synchronicity—bizarre events most dismiss as coincidence—as it seeks to help us achieve our highest evolutionary potential? Could it be possible to use the keys of science to unlock these great mysteries—and prove, beyond any reasonable doubt, that they are true?

Enlightenment Is the Full Experience of the Moment

In *The Source Field Investigations*, I combined thirty years' worth of extensive research to answer many of the greatest mysteries of the universe and presented more than a thousand academic references to establish the case. However, I have since realized that presenting facts alone is not sufficient. In order to truly know and understand how the universe operates, we have to elevate our studies beyond the level of thoughts and feelings and into the arena of direct, personal experiences. This is where synchronicity becomes the key that unlocks the greatest mysteries of the universe.

Feelings and thoughts are not our enemies. There is nothing wrong with wanting to feel good, and there is nothing wrong with using our thoughts to contemplate the great mysteries and attempt to solve them. However, the ancient spiritual teachings have always told us that the truth can be reached only when we quiet the mind, open the heart, and let our intuition flow through the deep relaxation of the meditative state. Once we create this loving space within our minds and hearts, we open the door for synchronicity to appear. People who seek only to feel good might never experience synchronicity. Others who believe the mind is in control and that it can solve any and all problems may be far too stubborn to allow synchronicity into their lives. Nonetheless, by surrendering our burdens and relaxing into the now—this very moment—we can gain answers that are otherwise impossible to think and impossible to feel. Here's a Law of One quote on this same subject that jumped out at me when I first read it in 1996:

> 17.2 Enlightenment is of the moment. It is an opening to intelligent infinity. It can only be accomplished by the self, for the self. Another self cannot teach/learn enlightenment, but only teach/learn information, inspiration, or a sharing of love, of mystery, of the unknown. [This] makes the other-self reach out, and begin the seeking process that ends in a

moment—but who can know when an entity will open the gate to the present?[98]

Millions and millions of people are now having experiences that cannot fit into the "box" of what we collectively think and believe. Dr. Jung described the visit of the scarab beetle to his office as a once-in-a-lifetime event, but now it seems like more and more events of this quality are happening to ordinary people on a regular basis. Hundreds of letters pour into my website each and every day, many of them describing staggering events that defy everything we used to take for granted.

Synchronicity forces you to ask painful questions. It opens you up to the possibility that the worldview articulated by most scientists is largely, if not completely, incorrect and that we live in a greater spiritual reality that is only barely understood at this time. By the time I was a college student, synchronicity had already started happening so frequently—and in such astonishing ways—that I was absolutely compelled to find out what was going on and what it really meant for me—and the world. Our single biggest blind spot, as a civilization, may well be our inability to accept this greater reality, in which human life could be multidimensional.

The concept of "me" is very personal and very precious. Once synchronicity starts happening to you, then you have to ask, "Who is doing it?" Is it you, on some level that you are not consciously aware of? Do you have a "Higher Self" that is coordinating the seemingly random events that happen in your life, behind the scenes? Death may seem like an impossible boundary, seemingly a complete loss of all consciousness, all existence, all awareness that there ever was, is, or will be a universe. The idea that life is eternal and that there could be another "me" out there—if not many of them—is almost beyond imagination. What if you do have more than one identity, more than one conscious awareness, guiding the events that happen in your life—for a hidden spiritual purpose? What if this concept is only a stepping-stone to an even greater mystery? The Law of One series tells us that there is only identity. Every living being is ultimately using the same consciousness to think, feel, and act. We are all one. Individuality is an illusion—and was designed so that the creator of the universe could experience itself. Without free will and apparent individuality, there would be no opportunity for us to forget who we really are. If we automatically had full access to universal consciousness, life would quickly become dull and boring. Our "forgetfulness" gives us a story—a quest. It gives us something to grow for, something to strive for, across many lifetimes. Furthermore, the law of free will is a universal standard—and it paves the way for some people to become highly negative, manipulative, controlling, and violent. Although these people can and do create terrible difficulties, their behavior also gives us a strong incentive to want to grow and evolve, relieve suffering, and search for deeper meaning. Obviously, this concept of "oneness" can never be proven—it is only a philosophical argument, not a scientific one. However, a variety of scientific data points do suggest the universe is alive, and where science stops, synchronicity begins.

Some people refuse to believe in synchronicity but are extremely knowledgeable about the negative forces that seem to be manipulating and controlling politics, finance, and media for their own ends. Is this all just a conspiracy theory, or is there something more to it? My own investigations demonstrated that there is indeed a Global Adversary. I believe that the only way we can heal our planet is to release the fear and directly confront the shadowy groups of people who are terrorizing and manipulating us. Without the power of synchronicity occurring so often in my life, I would probably never have been brave enough to take on this quest and provide investigative and media support for an alliance of more than 160 nations that are seeking to promote real, lasting peace in this world.

CHAPTER FOUR

Understanding the Sociopath

M ost of us naturally want to believe that everyone is kindhearted and considerate of others, and has at least predominantly positive intentions. We want to believe that our governments and financial systems are fair and equitable, and aside from a certain amount of greed and corruption, they are basically trustworthy and responsible. On a global level, we are increasingly awakening to the fact that some people can be very negative in their conscious focus—and they may also have formed shadowy, elite groups that have manipulated politics, finance, and media for generations. On April 2, 2013, a survey by Public Policy Polling, a top American organization analyzing political trends, revealed that "28 percent of [American] voters believe a secretive power elite with a globalist agenda is conspiring to eventually rule the world through an authoritarian world government, or New World Order." This included thirty-eight percent of all Republican/Romney voters.[99] If almost one-third of the American public is willing to tell an anonymous stranger on the phone that they believe a dangerous, elite group like this really does exist, we are no longer dealing with a "fringe" subject. Thousands of hours of academic research on this subject since 1992 have convinced me that a shadowy group like this does exist—and must be stopped.

On November 23, 2011—just days before I legally agreed to write *The Synchronicity Key*—an incredible lawsuit emerged that was a bold and direct act of war against many top global players, including some of the international bankers who formed the Federal Reserve. A fifty-seven-nation alliance, headquartered in Southeast Asia, was seeking the return of a massive amount of wealth, mostly in gold, that they felt had been stolen from them and put on "deposit" with the Federal Reserve.[100] This alliance has now expanded to more than 160 countries as of April 2012. As a result of being an increasingly visible public figure since I launched my own website in 1999, I have gained the trust and confidence of a group of patriotic, high-level insiders who have access to classified information, and want to restore freedom and peace on earth. According to these insiders, this 160-nation alliance is supported by a significant majority of the US military, who swore an oath to protect and defend the Constitution of the United States against all enemies, foreign and domestic. I was told that certain branches of the US military were 100 percent in support of exposing how the Federal Reserve bankers had infiltrated government and politics in our modern world.

On April 25, 2013, the ugly truth became even more apparent as another massive financial scandal leaked into public view—revealed through the brave investigative journalism of Matt Taibbi with *Rolling Stone* magazine.

> Conspiracy theorists of the world, believers in the hidden hands of the Rothschilds and the Masons and the Illuminati, we skeptics owe you an apology. You were right. The players may be a little different, but your basic premise is correct: The world is a rigged game. We found this out in recent months, when a series of related corruption stories spilled out of the financial sector, suggesting the world's largest banks may be fixing the prices of, well, just about everything.

> You may have heard of the Libor scandal, in which at least three—and perhaps as many as 16—of the name-brand too-big-to-fail banks have been manipulating global interest rates, in the process messing around with the prices of upward of $500 trillion (that's trillion, with a "t") worth of financial

instruments. When that sprawling con burst into public view last year, it was easily the biggest financial scandal in history— MIT professor Andrew Lo even said it "dwarfs by orders of magnitude any financial scam in the history of markets."

That was bad enough, but now Libor may have a twin brother . . . . It should surprise no one that among the players implicated in this scheme . . . are the same megabanks— including Barclays, UBS, Bank of America, JPMorgan Chase and the Royal Bank of Scotland—that serve on the Libor panel that sets global interest rates. In fact, in recent years many of these banks have already paid multimillion-dollar settlements for anti-competitive manipulation of one form or another . . . . The only reason this problem has not received the attention it deserves is because the scale of it is so enormous that ordinary people simply cannot see it.[101]

A war like this could not be fought by conventional means, as these powerful banks have almost limitless financial resources to fight back with. The lawsuit was one key part of a much larger operation the alliance was conducting to legally and financially block the adversary from being able to do harm, while systematically exposing its greatest secrets at the same time. This lawsuit was filed two hundred years and sixteen days after the Prophet's alliance of Native American tribes attacked Harrison's forces in Tippecanoe, on November 7, 1811—which I did not realize until I was writing this chapter of the book. In the Battle of Tippecanoe, back in 1811, the Native Americans were demanding the return of massive amounts of land they felt had been stolen from them. In 2011, the alliance was seeking the return of massive amounts of gold they felt had been stolen from them. Again, these two events were only sixteen days apart within two turns of a hundred-year cycle—or ten turns of a twenty-year cycle. Whether the initiative will succeed in this cycle or fall prey to the same weaknesses and failures that occurred in the previous cycle remains to be seen at the time of this writing.

Again—this battle had to be fought through multiple, nonlethal means, including hacking and deleting bank accounts, filing key lawsuits, exposing corruption, blocking the inflow of money, and threatening key members with public exposure, thus forcing them to peacefully step down and resign. An international businessman named Neil Keenan filed this groundbreaking lawsuit on November 23, 2011—on behalf of the Asian members of the alliance. This was a direct attack against financial tyranny, in the interest of peace and freedom for everyone—and was deliberately timed to coincide with the forty-eight-year anniversary of Kennedy's assassination. I wrote a detailed criticism of this lawsuit three days after it appeared and was very surprised when the alliance contacted me directly to provide further evidence. One thing the alliance told me was that Kennedy's move to print silver certificates, outside of Federal Reserve control, was planned out with Indonesian president Sukarno to help restore the US Constitution, and was apparently the main reason Kennedy was assassinated in 1963.

Beginning on December 1, 2011, I was given fascinating inside information by the alliance, much of which could be proven. This included a treasure trove of hundreds of original documents and photographs.[102] The problem was this: Whether or not this story was true, it was considered so dangerous to investigate, so highly classified, and so complicated that no one else in the public eye was willing or able to write it up. The government leaders and officials within the alliance had been told that their entire family tree would be tortured and killed if they stood up to this Global Adversary. As those shocking emails first came rolling in, I had no idea that I was about to get drawn into writing an entire book's worth of material on the subject of the Global Adversary. I never took a single penny of money from any person or group involved in the operation, in order to remain truly independent, so no one could ask me for a favor later on. I had no idea, at the time, that the difficulty and deadly seriousness of this investigation would distract me from finishing *The Synchronicity Key* for more than a year—but this did seem like a small price to pay for freedom.

Although the whole idea of a Global Adversary might have been written off as crazy by most people, I had been tracking it ever since my college class in 1992 had revealed the truth—and now the lawsuit and the documents were very real. I realized that if the alliance's plans to expose corruption and change the world were successful, this could become the mother of all historical events. Rather than just observing the cycles of history, I had the opportunity to jump right into the global Wheel of Karma myself. I could now directly assist an international alliance—featuring a majority of the largest countries in the world—in fighting the globalist bankers who had seized control of several top Western financial systems. I knew that the ageless wisdom behind the Wheel of Karma tells us that if we learn the lessons these cycles of boom and bust are teaching us, we can have the wheel reach the top without having to repeat the same sequence of misery and pain. Three of my all-time favorite Law of One quotes explain this very well.

17.20 In forgiveness lies the stoppage of the wheel of action—or what you call karma.[103]

18.12 Forgiveness of other-self is forgiveness of self. An understanding of this insists upon full forgiveness upon the conscious level of self and other-self, for they are one. A full forgiveness is thus impossible without the inclusion of self.[104]

1.9 The distinction between yourself and others is not visible to us. We do not consider that a separation exists between . . . the distortion which you project as a personality and the distortion which you project as an other personality.[105]

In *The Source Field Investigations,* I presented many instances of "suppressed" scientific information—including free-energy technology, gravity shielding, teleportation, and energy medicine. Whether by collective ignorance or deliberate design, these world-changing discoveries never received any publicity in the media—which meant that very few people knew about them. I had felt all along that the ancient vision of a Golden Age could not be fully realized in our present world. There was far too much institutional corruption and pressure to maintain the status quo, from the oil companies, for example, which definitely did not want free energy.

In 1997, the Institute for New Energy revealed that "the US Patent Office has classified over 3,000 patent devices or applications under the secrecy order, Title 35, US Code (1952) Sections 181–188."[106] By the end of fiscal year 2010, the number of suppressed patents had expanded to 5,135 inventions—according to the Federation of American Scientists. Any solar cell with greater than 20 percent efficiency, or any power system that is more than 70 to 80 percent efficient at converting energy, is automatically targeted for "review and possible restriction."[107] After Neil Keenan's lawsuit was filed in the Southern District Court of New York on November 23, 2011, and the alliance began sending me documents on December 1, 2011, I wrote my first large investigation on the subject, entitled "Confirmed: The Trillion-Dollar Lawsuit that Could End Financial Tyranny."[108]

As I documented in a variety of long and complex articles on my website, Divine Cosmos, I spent many years researching these subjects— and as I became more public I had ultimately developed contacts with a variety of people who had access to highly classified information. Anytime I caught someone knowingly lying to me or trying to manipulate me, I cut off the contact and worked only with people who seemed to genuinely have humanity's best interests at heart. Once I knew the right questions to ask, various insiders repeatedly confirmed that what the alliance was telling me was true. There was indeed one great secret—more highly classified and jealously guarded than all others in modern history . . . including the UFO subject.

The Path of Separation

Ordinary people could not hold a secret like this. Telling such incredibly vast lies would utterly ruin their lives, leaving them so plagued with anxiety that they would eventually break down and either tell the truth or commit suicide. However, about 1 percent of the people in our world are sociopaths.[109] Humanity as a whole is only just beginning to understand that there really are people out there who think, feel, and behave this way. Breaking through the denial is a very important step for our healing on a collective level. Sociopaths honestly do not think they are doing anything wrong—and in Law of One terms, they are practicing the path of "service to self," also known as the path of separation.

> 36.14 We remind you that the negative path is one of sep-aration. What is the first separation? The self from the self.[110]

In the very beginning of chapter 1, I gave a summary of how people who are "negatively polarized" tend to think, feel, and act—and now we will examine it more thoroughly. The Law of One series made clear analogies between the positive and negative paths.

> 19.17 Some love the light. Some love the darkness. It is a matter of the unique and infinitely various Creator choosing and playing among its experiences, as a child upon a picnic. Some enjoy the picnic and find the sun beautiful, the food delicious, the games refreshing, and glow with the joy of creation. Some find the night delicious—their picnic being pain, difficulty, sufferings of others, and the examination of the perversities of nature.[111]

> 80.15 The service-to-self adept will satisfy itself with the shadows and, grasping the light of day, will toss back the head in grim laughter—preferring the darkness.[112]

Eventually You Have to Go Positive to Stay Alive

Another very important data point in the Law of One series is that an entity can go only so far on the negative path before it has to go positive and fully integrate a love, forgiveness, and appreciation of all others. Otherwise, it will completely disintegrate into pure energy and cease to exist, through a process called "spiritual entropy." In the Law of One cosmology, the living universe divided itself into seven major levels, or "densities," in order to create a comprehensive system of soul evolution. It can take many millions of years in our linear-time terms to complete this course. The visible-light spectrum of seven colors—red, orange, yellow, green, blue, indigo, and violet—is apparently intended to serve as a mirror of this greater structure. Each of these levels represents a plane of existence populated with its own forms of life. We are connected to each of these energy levels through what the Hindus call chakras—energy centers that move up from the base of the spine to the top of the head. We are currently at third density—the yellow, solar-plexus level—and are moving into fourth density, which is the green ray, or heart chakra, level. Importantly, no negative beings have ever been able to make it past the beginning of sixth density, located at the pineal-gland center in the middle of the brain. Nonetheless, all souls must still reach and master seventh density before they can fully reunify with the Creator.

> 36.15 The sixth-density negative entity is extremely wise. It observes the spiritual entropy occurring [i.e., the disintegration of its own soul] due to the lack of ability to express the unity of sixth density. Thus, loving the Creator and realizing at some point that the Creator is not only self but other-self as self, this entity consciously chooses an instantaneous energy reorientation—so that it may continue its evolution.[113]

> 36.12 Negatively oriented [entities] have a difficulty which to our knowledge has never been overcome, for after [reaching a level of evolution known as] fifth-density graduation, wisdom is available but must be matched with an equal amount of love. This love/light is very, very difficult to achieve in unity when following the negative path—and during the earlier part of the sixth density, society complexes of the negative orientation will choose to release the potential, and leap into the sixth-density positive.[114]

> 47.5 The positive/negative polarity is a thing which will, at the sixth level, simply become history.[115]

In the greater sense, there is no polarity; the universe itself is much more positive than negative in its overall orientation. By the time a fourth, fifth or sixth-density negative entity is ready to go positive, it has paid so heavily for the negative karma it has created that it has been restored to a perfect balance—and no further negative karma is necessary. This is an important point. Negative entities are not at all exempt from the law of karma. Everything they do to others will be returned to them in some equally powerful form. This process will be deeply analyzed in chapters 6, 7, and 8.

Exposing the Sociopath

Psychologists refer to this strongly negative personality type as a "psychopath" or "sociopath." The people in this category have almost completely turned off their empathy and care for others, or at least those outside their chosen group. They usually have pain and trauma that runs so deep that they no longer care about other people's feelings and in fact gain great pleasure from manipulating and controlling them. They are capable of committing strongly criminal acts with no remorse. They are often highly self-involved, have elaborate, impenetrable defense mechanisms, believe themselves to be superior to others, and feel entitled to many benefits and privileges that others do not enjoy. They may also be highly charismatic, extroverted, and attractive to others. Many people do not notice the negative side of their personalities at first, since these traits are often very well hidden. Sociopaths are also in a constant fight against boredom and seek thrills whenever and however possible. In many cases, power over others becomes their ultimate drug of choice—and the more of it they get, the more they want, because nothing ever satisfies the hunger inside. Serial killers, for example, get such a high from taking the life of another human being that they become compelled to do it again and again, even if they are well aware that they could get caught. Of course, most sociopaths are not actually murderers. They drain the lives of others more slowly. At their core, they are deeply depressed and miserable and are willing to risk their own lives, or even end their lives, for the next thrill.

Interestingly, some professional astrologers are able to identify serial killers by known configurations that appear in their birth charts. Carolyn Reynolds, a well-known astrologer, was handed twenty astrological charts by the producers of the television program *Unsolved Mysteries.* The producers included the charts of four serial killers within this set of twenty—Jeffrey Dahmer, David "Son of Sam" Berkowitz, David "the Night Stalker" Ramirez, and Ed Kemper. Without knowing the identities of the people in these charts or having ever studied their astrology before, Carolyn Reynolds was able to identify all four of them as potential serial killers.[116] Edna Rowland, another professional astrologer, was involved in a similar experiment and successfully identified six other serial killers within a larger group of random birth charts, none of which she had ever seen before. The results were published in *Destined for Murder: Profiles of Six Serial Killers with Astrological Commentary.*[117]

Sociopaths are the most extreme examples of people who tend toward the negative path. As Dale Carnegie documented in his 1937 classic *How to Win Friends and Influence People,* convicted criminals on death row, including serial killers, often continue to insist that they are good people and have done nothing wrong.[118] When asked how they can justify taking the lives of their victims, they come up with a variety of excuses, or they may not even be willing to admit that they committed these crimes at all. People with sociopathic behaviors see morals, ethics, and conscience as weaknesses that can be exploited. They have a passionate need to be in charge, to lead the way, and to dominate others. These excerpts from an article by Maxwell C. Bridges shed more light on the mind-set of sociopaths.[119]

> Out of all humanity, approximately three percent of men and one percent of women are sociopaths. . . . Such people can tell right from wrong in their behavior, but derive no unpleasant feelings when they commit the latter. They . . . look down on those bound by conscience. The truth is a

matter of convenience for them, to be biased to their advantage. . . .

Many of them are charming and debonair when so inclined, [and] manipulative and vicious when they can get away with it. They can "read" like a book the body language and facial expressions of the conscience-driven. They can fake emotions, seek pity and affection they never feel for others, and seduce their victims before they exploit or injure them on purpose. They use people and discard them the way you would use a Kleenex and throw it away. . . .

Since their brains are not preoccupied by the infinite subconscious calculations of moral conscience and love, they are burdened with a semi-permanent drudgery of boredom they can only relieve by serial, risky behaviors—and elaborate manipulations (torture, humiliation, and betrayal) of their conscientious inferiors. They usually wind up in old age alone, broke and shunned by everyone—their family included. Many are killed or socially crushed by a powerful protector of one of their victims, or by numerous avengers. Very few die in their bed surrounded by people who love them.[120]

Redirecting Sociopathic Behaviors

I feel it is also important to point out that everyone by nature has tendencies that are sociopathic, to a certain degree. All of us are capable of being cruel to others and dismissing their feelings, and yet still thinking of ourselves as 100 percent good. Behavioral geneticist Dr. David Lykken concluded that children with sociopathic tendencies, such as fearlessness, aggressiveness, and sensation seeking, can have those personality characteristics directed toward more positive behaviors by loving parents with good boundaries.[121] In an undergraduate Psychology of Adjustment class, we learned that good parenting requires a consistent "punishment paradigm"—in which the child knows exactly where the boundaries are. The child should be well aware that every time those boundaries are tested, the same punishment will result. Permissive parenting—in which parents are overwhelmed by their children's misbehavior and are not always consistent in punishing them for it—is actually one of the most damaging forms of child abuse.

Even in adulthood, sociopathic behavioral traits can be transformed into positive qualities in certain circumstances. A group of scientists led by Scott O. Lilienfeld identified key behavioral characteristics of socio-paths, including "fearless dominance," but also found that these same traits, if focused positively, can create very effective leaders.[122] This includes the ability to think clearly and lead skillfully in a time of crisis.[123] John F. Kennedy is one of many beloved American leaders who had "fearless dominance." Steve Jobs had many of these characteristics as well, and though he is widely regarded as having been overly abusive, he nonetheless made many valuable innovations. Here is a quote from Lilienfeld's study that sums it up nicely: "Fearless Dominance, which reflects the boldness associated with psychopathy, was associated with better rated presidential performance, leadership, persuasiveness, crisis management, Congressional relations, and allied variables. . . . Fearless dominance . . . may contribute to reckless criminality and violence, or to skillful leadership in the face of a crisis."[124]

Everyone is on a spectrum between positive and negative, and learning to admit that can be a very powerful tool in your spiritual awakening. People with sociopathic qualities are not "evil" or beyond hope. However, in the most extreme cases they may require extensive rehabilitation—including a complete prevention of any way for them to harm others—before any real personality change is possible. Most people are not sociopathic but are still quite capable of being self-involved, manipulative, and controlling—particularly when they feel shamed or emotionally injured in some way.

Wealth and Power Can Lead to Sociopathic Behavior

I am absolutely convinced that sociopathic attitudes and behaviors can develop in a person who did not have any particular astrological configuration or genetic indications of these traits from birth. People who acquire significant wealth and power can easily develop sociopathic qualities, particularly if they do not have a strong and loving foundation to begin with. The problem with having worldly power is that other people want it from you. If you know someone with fame and fortune, you may find that people approach you just to try to get to your friend. The more money and power you have, the more it seems that everyone you meet has an angle. Everyone wants your money. Everyone wants to use you to get ahead. These are, of course, exaggerations, as not everyone actually does this, but it can certainly seem like it.

Many folks love to hate people with wealth and power, as it makes them feel better about their own lives. We read stories about the rich and powerful and wish that we could get our own chance to find out how horrible that life would be. However, even if you have a huge house, a luxury car, and enough money to eat out at fine restaurants every night and take lavish vacations, happiness is still a choice—not a guarantee. If the people you interact with are constantly trying to manipulate you and take advantage of you, it can be very difficult to choose happiness. All the treasures of the material world mean nothing if you don't have love. As the Beatles were on their meteoric rise to fame in the aftermath of the success of "I Want to Hold Your Hand," Paul McCartney sat at an upright piano in the five-star George V hotel in Paris, under severe pressure to write another hit song, and wrote "Can't Buy Me Love."[125] This is arguably the most popular song in modern history to plainly state that material wealth and success cannot buy you the love you are seeking. In fact, it often has just the opposite effect.

This is also why lottery winners often end up quite unhappy and feel that winning the money was the worst thing that could have ever happened to them.[126] Sandra Hayes, a former child services worker, split a $224 million Powerball jackpot with a dozen of her coworkers in 2006 and collected a lump sum in excess of $6 million after taxes: "I had to endure the greed and the need that people have, trying to get you to release your money to them. That caused a lot of emotional pain. These are people who you've loved deep down, and they're turning into vampires trying to suck the life out of me."[127]

Laboratory Studies of Sociopathic Behavior in Ordinary People

In 1971, Stanford psychology professor Dr. Philip Zimbardo created what is now called the Stanford Prison Experiment, which shed light on another way in which sociopathic behaviors can develop. Zimbardo and his colleagues set up a makeshift prison in the basement of Jordan Hall and sought volunteers to become either prisoners or prison guards at random. The participating students would be paid $15 a day for two weeks. Seventy volunteers were given interviews and a battery of psychological tests. From this number, the twenty-four men who were judged to be the most normal, average, and healthy were chosen. On Sunday, August 17, 1971, real Palo Alto police officers showed up at the homes of the nine young men assigned to be prisoners and "arrested" them. Some of the participants were recorded leaving their homes in handcuffs by TV cameras for the nightly news, as their neighbors and friends looked on with astonishment. They were then taken and booked at a real jail, blindfolded, and driven to the prison created for them at Stanford. The students who were assigned to be guards were given uniforms and told that their job was to maintain control of the prison without using violence.

The guards became increasingly cruel to the prisoners—particularly after the prisoners staged a revolt on the second day. After the guards crushed the rebellion, "they steadily increased their coercive aggression tactics, humiliation, and dehumanization of the prisoners," Zimbardo said. This included forcing prisoners to clean out toilet bowls with their hands or act out degrading scenarios. The worst abuses occurred in the middle of the night, when the guards thought the researchers weren't watching. Some guards told the prisoners that this was not an experiment—they actually had been imprisoned, this was their life now, and it would be years before they could ever escape. This abuse caused such severe stress on the nine prisoners that five of them had to be released prematurely, one per day.

Five days into the experiment, Dr. Philip Zimbardo's girlfriend, Christina Maslach, who had just received her doctorate from Stanford and was starting an assistant professorship at Berkeley, showed up to see what was going on. Although she found it "dull and boring" at first, she was quickly horrified by what she saw.[128] This began shortly after she started up a conversation with a "charming, funny and smart" young man who was working as one of the prison guards. She had heard from other researchers that one guard was particularly sadistic and had been nicknamed John Wayne by both the prisoners and the other guards. After the charming young man started his shift, she asked the researchers to point out John Wayne—and was shocked to realize that this was the same person she had just spoken to: "This man had been transformed. He was talking in a different accent—a Southern accent, which I hadn't recalled at all. He moved differently, and the way he talked was different, not just in the accent, but in the way he was interacting with the prisoners. It was like [seeing] Jekyll and Hyde. . . . It really took my breath away."[129]

One prisoner then confronted John Wayne for tripping him on the way to the bathroom when no researchers were around to see the act. The prisoner accused him of enjoying his job, but John Wayne refused to budge, saying if he went easy on them, his role wouldn't remain powerful. Maslach also saw the guards take the prisoners to the bathroom with paper bags over their heads before their bedtime. Her fellow researchers teased her when this made her feel sick to her stomach. That night, she had a wildly intense fight with Zimbardo and demanded he end the experiment. He ultimately realized that he and his colleagues had also lost compassion for the prisoners, just as the guards had, and the experiment needed to be stopped. The very next day it was all brought to a close. Maslach and Zimbardo married in 1972, and she became a full professor at Berkeley, conducting research into dehumanization. Her conclusions, as expressed here in a Stanford University press release, are still very relevant in today's world.

"I started interviewing prison guards, real ones, and also people in emergency medical care. Out of that grew a lot of the research I have done over the years on job burn-out," she said. Her work has looked at "how people who are responsible for the care and treatment of others can come to view those they care for in object-like ways, leading them, in some cases, to behave in ways that are really insensitive, uncaring, brutal and dehumanizing."[130]

Interestingly, Zimbardo's high school classmate Stanley Milgram also conducted a groundbreaking experiment with similar implications in 1965. A white-coated researcher told the participants in the experiment to administer electric shocks to a stranger whenever that person got an answer incorrect on a questionnaire. The stranger was in an adjacent room, behind a one-way mirror, but the participant could see and hear everything. Although no real shocks were occurring, the stranger would scream in agony when the shocks were apparently being delivered. Every time the participant felt queasy and questioned the researcher, he or she was simply told that the experiment must continue. Despite the cries of the stranger reaching the level of true death agony as the scale went up, fully two-thirds of all the participants administered the maximum dose of electricity—a staggering 750 volts—which was clearly labeled "DANGER—SEVERE SHOCK."[131] Many of these participants were later horrified by their own dark potential after the true nature of the experiment was revealed to them. In the aftermath of the Milgram and Zimbardo experiments, new laws were passed to prevent psychological experiments from violating ethics, and as a result, most of these tests are now simply in the form of paper-and-pencil questionnaires.

Both the Zimbardo and Milgram experiments reveal that ordinary people can easily dehumanize others when placed in unusual circumstances. Certain roles, such as the prison guard or the authority figure giving orders that we then feel compelled to follow, are expected to carry specific behaviors along with them. Once you acquire wealth and power and begin interacting with a greater community of wealthy and powerful people on a regular basis, it becomes much easier to adopt their thoughts, feelings, and behaviors as your own. Even if you initially feel badly about certain attitudes and practices they may have, the desire to obey the will of your peers can be very strong—as Milgram's electric shock experiment revealed. The difficulties of having lifelong friends turn on you and want you to give them your money can be very dramatic, as Sandra Hayes discovered, along with many other lottery winners like her. Christina Maslach's research after her experience with the Stanford Prison Experiment extended into a study of caregivers who develop job burnout after being responsible for the welfare of others. Government, military, finance, and corporate management jobs all involve power over others. The constantly conflicting wants and needs of those they serve can definitely create "compassion fatigue."

The Bystander Effect

The bystander effect also shows how sociopathic behaviors can occur in otherwise ordinary people when they are in a group. Kitty Genovese was stabbed to death by a serial rapist and murderer on March 13, 1964, and initial estimates were that even though she screamed and pleaded for help for at least half an hour, thirty-eight witnesses were aware of the stabbings and failed to intervene or call the police until the attacker fled the scene and Genovese was dead. A subsequent *American Psychologist* investigation suggested that some of the details were exaggerated by the media; at least one bystander did call the police, and some people could hear her screaming but could not see where it was happening.[132] Nonetheless, the underlying point was well established: Many deaths occur that are entirely preventable if people in groups would intervene sooner. John Darley and Bibb Latané created their first laboratory experiment to study this phenomenon in 1968 and strongly confirmed it.[133] In one of Darley and Latané's experiments from 1969, only 40 percent of people in a crowd offered help to a woman who had apparently fallen and was crying out in distress, whereas if they were alone, 70 percent of the people called out or went to help her.[134]

Elvis-Marilyn Syndrome

Severe burnout can also happen when someone becomes a recognized public figure. This is why there are so many cases of celebrities and others in the public eye ending up with clinical depression and anxiety disorders. I coined the term *Elvis-Marilyn syndrome* to describe this condition. We are taught to desire the fruits of the material world, but the most famous man and woman in the twentieth century both ended up miserably depressed, severely chemically dependent, and dead of apparent drug overdose. Despite this obvious fact, many people still believe that reaching this level of fame and fortune will bring them the greatest happiness this world could ever provide. We also tend to believe in the myth of the overnight success, rather than seeing that the harder you work, the more you will benefit.

The Science of Absorbing Life Energy

As Powerball lottery winner Sandra Hayes indicated, her sudden acquisition of $6 million caused her friends to become "vampires trying to suck the life out" of her. Their behaviors toward her displayed sociopathic tendencies—and she felt that they were draining her of her life-force. This concept may have far greater validity than most of us would ever believe, although several new pieces of scientific data must be examined in order to understand it.

In chapter 1 we saw that DNA apparently uses light as a primary source of vitality. Dr. Peter Gariaev found that the DNA molecule naturally absorbed every photon inside a tiny quartz container.[135] Gravity is the only force that can bend light in conventional physics, and the DNA Phantom Effect appears to be gravitational in nature. The story gets even stranger when we remember that an invisible wave continued holding the photons in place for an incredible thirty days after the DNA itself was removed. This is proof positive that DNA is being heavily influenced, if not created, by invisible waves of gravitational energy. The more we understand this, the more scientific tests can be devised to prove it.

DNA seems to both absorb and transmit light as a part of its basic function. Once this knowledge becomes widespread, it will have huge effects on a variety of areas—including medicine, healing, psychology, and even conflict resolution. Sociopathic people appear to be making use of this basic system to absorb energy from others, though additional scientific data is needed to make the case. Additionally, since this system works by simple, conscious intent, no scientific knowledge is required to make use of it in our everyday lives. We don't have to be aware of how it works in order to get results—much as gravity worked just fine before Isaac Newton "discovered" it when an apple fell on his head.

Gariaev was not aware that Dr. Fritz-Albert Popp, as a direct result of his research into the underlying causes of cancer, had already discovered in the 1970s that DNA stores photons. Popp found that all different forms of life were absorbing photons into their DNA—including bacteria, plants, insects, and fish. In certain cases, Popp even observed light being exchanged between organisms. Daphnia, a common water flea, would emit light that was then absorbed by its neighbors. The same effect was seen to occur with small fish.[136] The photons seemed to be intelligently directed—as if they knew where they were going and were being guided from one organism to the other.

Furthermore, when Popp broke open a DNA molecule with a chemical known as ethidium bromide, a flood of about a thousand photons surged out.[137] This suggests that each DNA molecule is like a miniature fiber-optic cable. Photons zing back and forth inside the DNA at light speed until they need to be used by the body. Popp also found that these photons were intimately related to our level of physical health. In areas of the body that were weakened or diseased, the amount of light stored in our DNA was significantly lower—or could almost be entirely absent. Another fascinating observation was that as we go through stress, our DNA sheds more and more of its light and quickly grows darker. Stress causes damage to the tissues of the body and can be as toxic as cigarette smoking. When healing needs to occur, our DNA apparently releases photons so the light can go make the repairs that are needed.

Another great pioneer in this category is Dr. Glen Rein, a biochemist who graduated from the University of London. Rein found that we can directly control how much light is being stored in someone else's DNA.[138] Loving, nurturing thoughts create a healing response, increasing the number of photons in the DNA, whereas sudden anger and aggression pulled the light right out of the molecule. In this case, the DNA was from an entirely different person's body, in a tissue sample from a human placenta. Additionally, Dr. Rein's participants could consciously control whether or not they were healing the DNA. When they intended to heal the DNA in the placenta, it worked, but if they just focused on being loving and did not direct their minds toward the DNA, the number of photons inside it remained unchanged.

Light Is Alive

If we reimagine the universe as a single, vast, living being, then all aspects of the universe are alive. The universe is now built to make biological life—on the quantum level. Light, therefore, would be alive in its own right. This is yet another scientific concept I found in the Law of One series back in 1996.

> 41.9 The simplest manifest being is light—or what you have called the photon.[139]

In this new model, a single photon can store far more information than we ever dared to believe—including the complete genetic code to build a given type of organism. This genetic information will also stay encoded within a photon even as it traverses vast distances. Apparently, the movement through space does not disrupt the interior structure of a photon. Light also provides a very valuable source of vital energy to keep biological organisms alive and healthy.

Love: The Force That Transports Light

In this model of a living cosmos, light also needs an intelligent means of being transported from one point to another. Dr. Rein's scientific experiments suggest that as soon as we have a thought about someone—or even start thinking about a sample of living biological material—we automatically create a tunnel between our own body and the life that we focus our attention on. Light immediately begins passing through the tunnel. These energetic passageways are not visible to us and have not yet been measured scientifically, but on a theoretical level, they have to be there in order to explain the observations of many different repeatable laboratory experiments.

It appears, therefore, that there are two different forces at work in this new model of "energetic biology." We have light, providing the raw power of vitality, and we have another force that shapes, molds, and directs the light through invisible tunnels. Although it may seem like a strange concept right now, the Law of One refers to the force that shapes, molds, and directs the light, creating tunnels between life-forms, as "love."

In this case, love becomes a very active force that generates invisible, tunnel-like structures, allowing light to be transferred across various distances. Our thoughts create these tunnels. Anytime we have a thought about someone, a tunnel is automatically created in the Source Field between us and that person, and photons begin passing through it. These photons can then be encoded with the information from our own thoughts, thus creating a practical mechanism for telepathic communication to occur. Love is also the force that makes the DNA phantom itself. This same energy can either hold photons in the shape of the DNA molecule or create a tunnel to send them outside the DNA molecule— even across vast distances.

Masculine and Feminine Archetypes—and Universal Energy

In philosophical terms, these two forces can also be assigned genders— light being the masculine force that projects outward and provides raw power in the photon, and love being the feminine force that shapes, molds, and directs the light. Psychologically, we need to balance these personality characteristics, or "archetypes," in our own lives in order to be healthy. In the Law of One philosophy, the genders we see in biological life are holographic reflections of the basic structure of energy in the universe. This was explained in session 92 of the Law of One series. Notice that the source was not willing to reveal the full answer; we needed the opportunity to solve this puzzle ourselves.

> 92.20 That which reaches may be seen as a male principle. That which awaits the reaching may be seen as a female principle. The richness of the male and female system of polarity is interesting—and we would not comment further, but suggest consideration by the student.[140]

In session 67, Don Elkins summarized his best understanding of what he was being told about the nature of the masculine and feminine archetypes. Don did not understand that male and female, light and love, had other energetic qualities besides the flow of electrical charge from negative to positive. Nonetheless, this statement did reflect some of what Don was being told.

> 67.28 The Father archetype corresponds to the male or positive aspect of electromagnetic energy, and is active, creative, and radiant—as is our local sun. The Mother archetype corresponds to the female or negative aspect of electromagnetic energy, and is receptive or magnetic—as is our Earth, as it receives the sun's rays and brings forth life via third-density fertility.[141]

The masculine and feminine archetypes are extremely important to understand if you want to analyze the symbolism of your dreams—and the deeper meaning of the struggles you may be going through. Most men need to develop their feminine side more fully and end up learning to do this through being involved in relationships with women. Most women are attracted to men for the opposite reason, to develop their masculine side. However, it is also possible for a man to be more feminine than masculine—which usually attracts him to women with exaggerated masculine qualities. Sexual attraction often has a subconscious function of drawing us to the people from whom we will learn the most.

Meek, passive, self-defeating, and anxiety-prone people will often have irresistible sexual attraction to strong, fearless, dominant, and narcissistic personality types. These relationships can be extremely torturous and miserable if the narcissist refuses to change.

Healing and Absorbing

Ideally, once we've created a tunnel between ourselves and someone else with our thoughts, the exchange of photons flows in both directions. In cases when we are healing others, we send more photons into the body of the person who needs healing, but when we absorb energy, we are actively pulling photons out of someone's body. As soon as we direct angry thoughts at someone, a tunnel is automatically formed and we immediately begin trying to pull photons through it. To do this successfully, we have to break the other person down by causing them to feel negative emotions such as guilt, fear, shame, sadness, anger, disgust, terror, or shock. However, if the person stays in a loving but firm state and refuses to allow him- or herself to be bullied while also not indulging in negative emotions, his or her own vital energy will be protected, and nothing is lost. This is one of the most important Law of One teachings to master if you want to preserve and protect your vital energy.

If we are successful in absorbing energy from someone—if the other person withers in the presence of our anger—then we draw light out of the storehouse of DNA throughout that person's entire body. This provides us with an immediate source of energy. We become more alert and energized—though this is also a cold, thin, and hollow way to restore ourselves and lacks the richness and complexity that naturally fills us when we feel genuine love. In Law of One terms, absorbing energy from someone else is the negative path—and it guarantees that whatever you take from others will soon be taken from you in a similar fashion.

This mechanism is precisely what Dr. Glen Rein observed in his DNA experiments. Angry people pulled photons out of the DNA from a human placenta, whereas people feeling love were able to beam additional photons into that same DNA. We have not yet measured these invisible energetic tunnels or seen how our thoughts automatically create them, but the effects of the mechanism have been well documented.

Burlakov's Fish Egg Experiment

Further support for this concept was given by Dr. A. B. Burlakov, another Russian scientist. In this case, Burlakov placed growing fish eggs near each other, so photons could pass freely between them. When he put older, more mature eggs in front of younger, newer eggs, the older eggs literally pulled the health right out of the younger eggs. The younger eggs soon developed obvious health problems, including withering, deformities, and even death.[142] Thus, it seemed that the older, stronger eggs were directly absorbing life-force out of the younger, weaker eggs—feeding on them for their own survival. This same mechanism can also allow us to transfer health to others as well. When slightly younger eggs were placed near slightly older eggs in Burlakov's experiment, the younger eggs actually sped up in their development—and experienced accelerated growth until they reached the same apparent age level as the older eggs.[143]

Interestingly, these healing or weakening effects could be totally blocked by putting a pane of glass between the two sealed rooms holding the eggs. This is almost certainly due to the fact that glass blocks ultraviolet light. The glass does not block the microgravitational field in the stronger eggs from pulling photons out of the weaker eggs. The weaker eggs still shed their photons. However, once those photons are released, they bump against the glass, reflect back into the room, and are reabsorbed by other eggs. Therefore, there is no net loss of energy—even as the gravitational force from the stronger eggs continues pulling on the photons of the weaker ones.

Healing: A Meta-Analysis of Scientific Studies

Dr. Daniel Benor analyzed 191 different controlled scientific studies of spiritual healing, where human beings consciously intended to heal living tissue. Healing was attempted on a wide variety of life-forms, including bacteria, algae, plants, insects, and animals, as well as other humans. Quite surprisingly, 64 percent of these 191 studies showed significant effects—even in cases where other human beings were being healed across substantial distances, such as from New York to Los Angeles.[144]

Once again, this implies that as soon as we direct our thoughts and emotions—particularly loving thoughts and emotions—toward a life-form, we open a tunnel that allows photons to pass through. This effect is very consistent and has clearly been observed in the majority of all scientific studies of healing. Best of all, in Law of One terms, when you heal someone else, you don't have to give up any of your own biophotons. You can act like a lens of light for universal energy to flow through you. This point was clearly established in session 66 of the Law of One series.

> 66.10 The healer does not heal. The crystallized healer is a channel for intelligent energy, which offers an opportunity to an entity that it might heal itself. . . . This is also true of the more conventional healers of your culture. If these healers could but fully realize that they are responsible only for offering the opportunity of healing, and not for the healing, many of these entities would feel an enormous load of misconceived responsibility fall from them.[145]

> 4.14 It is a further item of interest that those whose life does not equal their work may find some difficulty in absorbing the energy of intelligent infinity. [They can] thus become quite distorted—in such a way as to cause disharmony in themselves and others—and perhaps even find it necessary to cease the healing activity.[146]

Law of One Quotes on Light and Love

The Law of One series tells us that light is alive. Photons are the most basic form of life in the universe, and we now have the science to prove it. The DNA phantom—the feminine force of love—is the vortex energy that surrounds and shapes the light. In the Law of One series, we are told that the universe is made of light and love—masculine and feminine— and that love is the force that shapes light. Our entire universe is built by light and love—the two primary manifestations of "intelligent infinity" after it becomes intelligent energy. The offspring of light and love are matter and biology, all of which is ultimately alive. Here are some key quotes where these connections are revealed.

13.9 Light . . . is the building block of that which is known as matter, the light being intelligent and full of energy.[147]

2.4 The stones are alive. It has not been so understood by the [people] of your culture.[148]

64.6 Our understanding is that there is no other material except light.[149]

28.5 Question: What causes . . . light [to] condense into our physical or chemical elements?
Answer: . . . It is necessary to consider the enabling function of the focus known as Love. This energy is of an ordering nature.[150]

27.13 Love uses light, and has the power to direct light.[151]

6.4 The illusion [i.e., your physical universe] is created of light—or more properly but less understandably, light/love.[152]

1.6 You are every thing, every being, every emotion, every event, every situation. You are unity. You are infinity. You are love/light, light/love. You are. This is the Law of One.[153]

Remote Viewing Research—and Further Insights into the Negative Path

The vortex created by love extends out of us when we direct our attention elsewhere. Light then transmits across this channel. This effect can happen over long distances. In remote viewing research conducted in both China and the United States, a person is trained to intuitively perceive a distant area and make accurate observations. During the time the person is accurately viewing the target, which is inside a room that is otherwise completely dark, photons appear around the target. The photons can surge up to a thousand times above the normal background level.[154] This seems to be caused by a tunnel that is formed when the person focuses his or her attention on the distant target. Anyone can be trained to become an accurate remote viewer, so all of us have the ability to form these tunnels. These same tunnels can actually become visible to us when we have an out-of-body experience. Many people have reported seeing a silver cord that connects their astral body to their physical body.

Whenever we focus our thoughts on another person, we open up a conduit with them through which photons can be exchanged. We can send energy into a person or draw it out of that person through this tunnel. We can also kindle vital energy and fill our DNA with photons by having loving thoughts. In a meditative, inspired, blissful state, we naturally open up many microtunnels that pull new photons into our DNA. This is the scientific explanation behind the placebo effect, where simply believing we will be healed actually creates a healing response. The sociopath, however, has walled out feelings of love, seeing them as weakness. As a result, their physical health and attention span suffer, and the only way they can feel alive again is to feed on the energy of others. They attack, shame, humiliate, and take offense—demanding greater and greater sacrifices, apologies, and concessions. They deliberately provoke kindhearted people into having negative reactions, knowing that one of the greatest sources of energy and vitality they receive is when someone begs them for forgiveness. As we plead for kindness and mercy, we also flood the person we've hurt with a huge surge of our vital energy, in the hope of helping them feel better.

However, in the strongest cases, no matter how much energy they take, they still thirst for more. They will never truly be happy until they allow themselves to love. For them, this involves lowering their boundaries and dismantling the incredible defense mechanisms they've built around their sensitive core. They are well aware that if they let themselves feel their emotions—including the powerful pain they've gone through—then others could absorb their vitality, just as they have been doing all along. For them, this is a terrifying thought, as they trust no one. However, in time they can learn that most people are kind and good-natured and genuinely do not want to hurt or torture them, and then they can begin receiving the benefits of a loving attitude.

Our Global Adversary, or "negative elite," as they are called in the Law of One series, is simply a group of people who are consciously or subconsciously seeking worldly power and prestige in order to feel the energizing influence of millions of people focusing their attention on them. Those on the "negative path," such as sociopaths, have so much resistance to loving, accepting, and forgiving others that they usually do not see any other way to acquire the energy they need to stay healthy. They seek public acclaim, adoration, and reverence—and laugh sarcastically at how they are fooling everyone. Thankfully, as we break through the denial and expose the greatest secrets of the "negative elite," we also inoculate ourselves against their control and manipulation. Ignorance is required for their plans to succeed. Once a "critical mass" of people awaken to who they are and what they are doing, their defeat becomes a mathematical certainty.

CHAPTER FIVE

The Global Adversary

Many plays, novels, movies, and television shows have explored how ordinary, kindhearted people can become highly negative after acquiring money and power. What is still not understood on a widespread level, at this time, is the extent to which wealthy and powerful people have formed a global elite. In 2011 Dr. Clive Boddy of Nottingham Trent University wrote a peer-reviewed theoretical paper entitled "The Corporate Psychopaths Theory of the Global Financial Crisis."[155] Mitchell Anderson offered some interesting thoughts on this study in the *Toronto Star* newspaper.

> Only a small subset of psychopaths become the violent criminals so often fictionalized in film. Most simply seek to blend in, and conceal their difference, in order to more effectively manipulate others. This frightening condition has existed throughout human history. . . . Scientists believe about 1 per cent of the general population is psychopathic, meaning there are more than 3 million moral monsters among normal United States citizens. There is emerging evidence that this frequency increases within the upper management of modern corporations. This is not surprising, since personal ruthlessness and fixation on personal power have become seen

as strong assets to large publicly traded corporations (which some authors believe have also become psychopathic).

However, appearance and performance are two different things. While psychopaths are often outwardly charming and excellent self-promoters, they are also typically terrible managers—bullying co-workers and creating chaos to conceal their behaviour. When employed in senior levels, their pathology also means they are biochemically incapable of something they are legally required to do: act in good faith on behalf of other people. . . .

Boddy suggests that corporations have changed from relatively stable institutions where psychopaths would have a difficult time concealing themselves, to highly fluid organizations where it is much easier for them to disappear within the chaos in their wake. . . .

Boddy is not hopeful that the current round of expensive public bailouts will solve the problem. If psychopaths have, in fact, installed themselves in the upper reaches of the world's financial institutions, their genetic deficiency dictates that their greed knows no bounds. They will continue to act in anti-social, remorseless ways, amplified by their enormous corporate influence, until the institutions they represent— and perhaps the entire global economy—collapses.[156]

Unraveling the Great Secret

Our great secret starts to unravel even further when we confirm that the American financial system was privatized in 1913. America's right to issue money was handed over to a group of private bankers, including the Rothschild and Rockefeller families, calling themselves the Federal Reserve.[157] The Federal Reserve banking families also formed the Bank for International Settlements, or BIS, creating the first "worldwide central bank."

On September 19, 2011, a Swiss scientific study led by Dr. James

Glattfelder proved that a staggering 80 percent of all the money that was being made in the world was filtering back into the pockets of the Federal Reserve through very carefully disguised "interlocking directorates" of corporations.[158] This includes the big media conglomerates. Supercomputers were used to analyze a database of the top 37 million corporations and individual investors worldwide. Shockingly, only 737 corporations controlled a network that was earning 80 percent of all the world's profits. This information was deeply hidden within the data and required supercomputer power to discover. These 737 entities enjoyed power in the system that was ten times greater than they should have had from their wealth alone. With even greater number crunching, this web of ownership could be further narrowed down to a superentity of only 147 companies. An astonishing 75 percent of the corporations within this superentity are financial institutions. The top 25 financial institutions within this highly covert group include Barclays, JPMorgan Chase & Co., Merrill Lynch, UBS, Bank of New York, Deutsche Bank, Goldman Sachs, Morgan Stanley, and Bank of America—all of which are allegedly members of the Federal Reserve.[159] The actual banks running the Federal Reserve have never been openly and officially revealed—ostensibly for their own safety and privacy—but most researchers and insiders I've spoken with agree on who the main players are. The degree of control enjoyed by these top banks is a scientific fact—not a conspiracy theory—and that's not all.

Representative Alan Grayson, former representative Ron Paul, and now deceased senator Robert Byrd forced through a congressional audit of the Federal Reserve in 2011 and found that the Fed secretly gave away $26 trillion worth of American taxpayers' money. Twenty-six trillion dollars—not to the people, not to the government, but to the top Federal Reserve banks themselves—to bail them out.[160] Several of the bailed-out banks were not even based in the United States. Had this money been redirected to the people, it could have done wonders, considering this staggering figure is well over a third of the value of the entire world's gross domestic product in a given year. However, the greed of the financial institutions is so high, and the gambles they have taken are so huge, that this was only barely enough money to keep them alive. I did find out from the 160-nation alliance that the 2008 financial collapse was directly engineered by members within the alliance to financially wipe out the Federal Reserve cabal. No one in the alliance suspected the Federal Reserve would be able to create such a massive bailout to keep their corrupt financial institutions afloat—and get away with it—but they did.

It seems impossible to believe that these facts are true—but the superentity of 147 corporations controlling 80 percent of the world's wealth, and the $26 trillion of bailouts they created to keep themselves alive are both proven realities. Normally we think of sociopaths as working in isolation, but power is very hierarchical by nature. I have spoken to people who have broken free of this group or are actively working to bring it down from the inside. One of the most common things I've heard is that wealthy and powerful people believe you are automatically smarter, stronger, and better than others if you achieve worldly riches. By teaming up with the wealthy and powerful and accepting your position in the hierarchy, you can become even *more* wealthy and powerful. Elaborate secrecy is used, so that those who do not have the stomach for truly sociopathic behaviors never find out what the group is doing at the higher levels. Ruthlessness and a willingness to do anything to accomplish the goals of the organization are rewarded with further progress. The farther up you go, the more the group resembles the worst aspects of Nazi Germany. In fact, there is undeniable proof that the Nazi Party was financed and supported by these same people, an idea we will explore in chapter 13.[161] The Bolshevik Revolution, which created the Soviet Union beginning in 1917, was also financed by Federal Reserve bankers, as we find in G. Edward Griffin's *The Creature from Jekyll Island*[162] and Dr. Antony C. Sutton's *Wall Street and the Bolshevik Revolution*.[163] I do honestly believe this entire system is crumbling apart now, and that's why I'm taking the time to talk about it.

The Science of Absorbing Energy

Dr. Cleve Backster is a former CIA employee who pioneered and standardized the protocols for administering a lie detector, or polygraph, test.[164] Backster's findings are directly relevant to understanding what is happening with the Global Adversary. The polygraph measures changes in the electrical conductivity of human skin, but it can measure the electrical activity of other life-forms as well. In 1966, after many years of work in the field, Backster got the idea to wire up his houseplant to the polygraph machine—to see if he could get humanlike reactions from it. Much to his surprise, the plant had ongoing, complex electrical activity—surging up and down, seemingly at random, with fluctuations curiously similar to what a human's own patterns would look like.

Backster knew that the key to administering a lie detector test is threatening the subject with a confrontation—"Did you fire the shot that killed your wife?" If the subject says no but his body's electrical activity starts having a huge response—like we would see if he was screaming, shocked, angered, or suddenly terrified—then this is considered proof he is lying. Backster wanted to see if he could threaten the plant's well-being in some way to get a humanlike reaction. Finally, when Backster got a clear mental picture of lighting a match and burning one of the leaves, the plant started "screaming" very strongly. This happened before he actually burned the plant. Backster did end up going and getting a matchbook, lighting a match, and burning a leaf. The plant didn't stop screaming until after he took the matches out of the room and left the area completely.

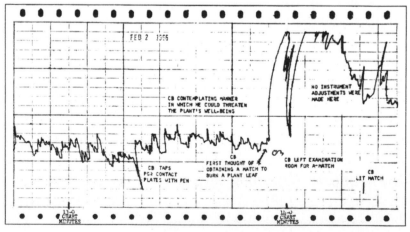

Fig. 6: Dr. Cleve Backster's diagram of humanlike electrical activity in a plant

This "alert system" is constantly at work in nature and forms a collective consciousness among all living things. Backster tested plants, yogurt bacteria, chicken eggs, animal cells, and human cells and found that when one organism feels stress, pain, fear, and danger, an energetic beacon is sent out to every other life-form around it. When Backster startled his cat out of a deep sleep, his African violet "screamed."[165] When Backster boiled or poisoned bacteria, other bacteria screamed.[166] When a captured spider suddenly was set free and was about to run for its life in front of a team of Yale University graduate students in 1969, a nearby ivy plant screamed.[167] When Backster boiled living brine shrimp using a completely randomized process, at night, while no one else was in the building, nearby plants screamed.[168] When Backster boiled chicken eggs, one by one, other chicken eggs screamed.[169] When a World War II pilot who was nearly shot down watched film of another pilot being shot down, his own tissue sample screamed—and this was only one of many human examples.[170] Dr. Brian O'Leary, a NASA astronaut, traveled on a three-hundred-mile airplane flight and wrote down every time he went through stress. His cells in the lab screamed at the exact same time each stressful event happened.[171]

We May Be Connected to an Entire Network

Let's not forget what Dr. Fritz-Albert Popp discovered about stress. As soon as we feel stress, there is a sudden decrease in the amount of photons in our DNA, causing a visible dimming of the light. This suggests a very intriguing possibility. In the previous chapter, we discussed energetic tunnels that can form between two people, in which photons exchange information as well as vital energy. Now we are confronted with a new possibility. What if all biological life is interconnected by these same tunnels? What if we already have a huge web of energetic tunnels connecting us to every life-form around us as part of the basic laws of physics that we don't yet understand? What if, in times of sudden stress, we release biophotons that transmit a warning signal of our fear and pain throughout this entire network of tunnels?

Each cell contains forty-six chromosomes, and each chromosome is made of two chromatids, or DNA molecules. This gives us ninety-two DNA molecules per cell—not including mitochondrial DNA, which varies depending upon the type of cell. Our bodies have an estimated 10 trillion human cells, as well as another 90 trillion nonhuman microbial cells. That means we have at least 920 trillion DNA molecules within our own human cells—just within the chromosomes. Each DNA molecule holds up to a thousand photons. At these numbers, we can now start to see what a huge energy resource we possess. With at least 920 quadrillion photons zinging around inside our bodies at any one time, a single moment of stress could send out a shower of millions or even billions of photons at once—without even making a dent in our overall supply.

Dr. Fritz-Albert Popp saw the photons suddenly decrease in DNA during stress. Dr. Cleve Backster saw how stress sends out a warning beacon to all other life-forms in the area. Backster was not able to identify how this warning beacon of stress traveled, but we have strong reasons now to believe that photons are being used. These photons travel through energetic tunnels in the Source Field that connect us with all living things.

Apparently, these energetic tunnels are not limited by physical distance. Dr. Brian O'Leary's cells picked up every shock he went through on his flight back to Phoenix from San Diego, even though he ended up being hundreds of miles away. Successful healing studies have been conducted in which a person in New York remotely healed a person in Los Angeles, as Dr. Daniel Benor revealed in his meta-analysis of healing studies.

Therefore, we can safely conclude that whenever we begin focusing our attention on a particular person, we begin transferring photons to them through a tunnel that may exist as a basic, as yet undiscovered law of nature that interconnects all living things—perhaps akin to a wormhole. Although certain signals, such as pain, fear, stress, and death, appear to be transmitted to all living things in a given area, these tunnels appear to be strengthened once we focus our attention on any one person. Dr. Glen Rein's participants were able to heal DNA when they focused loving emotions on it, but the DNA did not gain any new photons if the participants' attention was directed elsewhere.

Dr. William Braud and the Study of Being Stared At

Dr. William Braud proved that simply staring at someone is enough to trigger their bodies to have an excited response—even at a distance, where there is no physical line of sight between the two individuals. This is very likely caused by the same energetic mechanism we have been describing. In Braud's experiment, one person was placed in a small room with a hidden video camera and told to relax and read a magazine while his skin was being monitored for its electrical activity. In another room, a closed-circuit television screen revealed images of the man sitting there in his chair, even though he didn't know he was being filmed. At computer-generated random moments, a participant in the room was asked to suddenly stare intently at this man's face on the television screen. Surprisingly, 59 percent of the time the man was being stared at, his skin had a sudden shock reaction. It worked with women just as well as men—again and again. A 59 percent reaction is fully 9 percent above random chance. This may not sound like much, but it is very significant, considering that Braud repeated this experiment again and again, with many different participants, and the effect was very consistent.[172]

Dr. Braud may have stumbled upon the real hidden secret of those who seek worldly power, whether they consciously know what is happening to them or not. When I did my first full-length show on *Coast to Coast* with Art Bell, in April 2001, an estimated 20 million people were listening. During the show, and particularly after it was finished, I felt an incredible amount of energy surging through me. I could not seem to control my elevated heartbeat, breathing rate, and head rush—and it did remind me of a drug-like effect. Since I no longer did drugs, or wanted to do drugs, I found it distracting and unpleasant. The effect was so intense that I went down to the beach and paced up and down the shore to try to walk it off, but I simply could not relax. It quieted down after a few hours, and I was finally able to go to sleep, but it had been extremely noticeable— much like a runner's high—and I knew it wasn't just me. I was immediately aware that this power could be greatly misused. In fact, I deliberately

avoided doing conferences or seeking large-scale publicity for several years
until I knew I could be mature enough to handle it. For a positive person,
the ideal response is to transform that raw energy into a usable form
through a stage performance that elevates and inspires everyone. However, I also realized that politicians, military leaders, heads of corporations, and other famous people—actors, musicians, and the like—were
at risk. Power was very real—and could be very addictive. Every person
who focuses his or her attention on you is sending you energy.

Paying Tribute to Leaders

This system has apparently been in place throughout all of human evolution. Leaders who put their faces on currency may well have been getting
energy transfers from their people every time the people looked at the
currency in their pocket. Of course, public gatherings would make this
transfer system much more potent as a leader makes a rousing speech, for
example. After Gutenberg's invention of the printing press, beginning in
or around 1439, portraits of leaders could be distributed in printed illustrations, and that may well have been enough to create viable energy
transfers. Photography would represent the next quantum leap in this
system, potentially making the transfers even more effective as the images of the leaders' faces became even clearer. Once live radio and television became available, potentially millions of people could focus on one
person simultaneously—in real time. Furthermore, if a particular film
actor is being seen in movies by tens or even hundreds of thousands of
people at any given time—even if the actor is only playing a character—
he or she may still be receiving tremendous amounts of energy from the
people watching them. These Law of One quotes from sessions 93, 97,
and 55 summarize the difference in polarities, between negative and
positive, very succinctly.

> 93.3 Another method of viewing polarities might involve
> the concept of radiation/absorption. That which is positive is
> radiant; that which is negative is absorbent.[173]

97.17 The left hand [negative polarity] attempts to absorb the power of the spirit, and point it for its use alone.[174]

55.3 The negative polarization is greatly aided by the subjugation or enslavement of other-selves.[175]

Controlling others may seem to make our lives a lot easier, but as this quote from session 52 reveals, it automatically requires us to reincarnate and experience what we've created from the other side. Reincarnation will be explained much more in chapters 7 and 8.

52.7 Control may seem to be a short-cut to discipline, peace, and illumination. However, this very control potentiates and necessitates the further incarnative experience—in order to balance this control or repression of that self which is perfect.[176]

A Holdover from the Animal Kingdom for Survival

I do believe that nature established this energy-exchange system for a positive purpose—at least originally. If your tribe lives in a cave, huddled together for warmth, and a saber-toothed tiger appears at the entrance looking for a meal, someone's got to go fight the tiger and protect the others. This will usually be the alpha male of the tribe—who may also lead his bravest warriors into battle. Everyone else is cowering in fear of the tiger—absolutely terrified. As they move through this terrible, life-or-death feeling of stress, their DNA gives off a massive release of photons, arguably in the billions for each of them. These photons—the essence of life, health, and vitality—are directly beamed into the warriors who are out there protecting the rest of the tribe. Let's not forget that Dr. Rein was able to physically measure the light increasing in the DNA even though it was taken from another person's body. The warriors at the front of the cave are able to think faster and have greater physical strength and greater endurance as this energy transfer takes place.

This same system seems to work very well at public gatherings, which have gone on since the dawn of civilization. I was invited to attend a Detroit Tigers baseball game in 2011, while they were in the midst of playoffs that would determine if they would go to the World Series. I was not a sports fan and had no attachment to the outcome when I went to the game. This put me in a unique position, as I soon felt an incredible rush of energy from being in this packed stadium. This appeared as a euphoric state of mind as well as a strong sense of physical excitation. In particular, when the home team's batter got a good, strong hit, and the ball was looking like it might go the distance and become a home run, my mind and body raced into pure ecstasy. Almost every pair of eyes in the stadium was focused directly on that ball as it flew, creating a powerful focal point for the attention of the group. When the ball did make it past the outfield, the crowd leaped to their feet and all the energizing feelings reached an orgasmic peak. Within ten or fifteen minutes, I discovered that I absolutely loved baseball.

I was really quite surprised by this—and with my background in this new science, I realized that what people were calling "team spirit" had a direct energetic component. The overall energy of the crowd gave each person more vitality than he or she brought in on his or her own, and people were willing to pay hundreds of dollars a ticket to participate in it. This same system seems to explain why teams seem to do better at home games. When the crowd is right there, hoping for their team to succeed, they are beaming a much stronger rush of biophotons into the players than the players receive at an opponent's venue. The minds of the players then become sharper and more alert, and their bodies become stronger, more energized, and capable of much greater endurance.

Power: The Sociopath's Ultimate Drug of Choice

Most people can rebuild their vital energy by being loving and supporting to others, which usually leads to that same love and support being returned to them. The collective inspiration in the sports arena was clearly creating more vitality than each individual brought in on his or her own. Let's not forget that seven thousand people in deep meditation were able to inspire everyone on earth to such a degree that terrorism decreased by 72 percent worldwide. However, the 1 percent of people who are genuine sociopaths have completely walled themselves off from love—at least for anyone other than themselves. They feel a constant sense of boredom and depression and often become daredevils and adrenaline junkies, looking for more speed, more power, more excitement, and more danger— regardless of whom they hurt or threaten to get it. Power over others, and the energy they absorb from others, can literally become like a narcotic. The risk of taking someone on, not knowing if the struggle for control will succeed, can give these people a huge adrenaline rush. When they do succeed in battle, they are replenished by the vital energy of the person they have humiliated and defeated.

Let's say that a group of sociopathic individuals have relentlessly sought power on earth and formed a hierarchical system as they fought for superiority within the group. In this case, their ultimate goal would be to dominate and control the planet, since they feel they are the strongest, the wisest, and the most spiritually advanced, and therefore worthy of their power. Instinctively, they may understand that when people are traumatized, they release vital energy and will transfer that energy to the alpha male who steps in to protect them. Though most people could not conceive of a strategy like this, sociopaths would be fully capable of creating mass atrocities— such as wars—simply to traumatize the people. Mass trauma causes the people to release vital energy in huge quantities. Once the elite step in as the brave and noble protectors of the people, they get to absorb this energy for themselves. The power elite's strongest goal might then be to enjoy an ongoing, secure role on earth—where they control the money, the politics, the military and the media, and no one can effectively oppose them. If they are successful, they will enjoy a continuing supply of vitality from their traumatized subjects. However, this also provides us with a major spiritual growth opportunity as we become inspired to end injustice and help others. This is clearly spelled out in session 97 of the Law of One.

> 97.16 The fruit of those experiences apparently negative is frequently found to be helpful in the development of the service-to-others bias.[177]

Funding Both Sides of a War

In order to understand the deepest secret of this Global Adversary, we must explore the sickening idea that World War I and World War II might have both been elaborate, deadly deceptions. You may find this hard to read. You may suddenly feel tired and want to do something else. This is a very normal self-protective response. Your body does not want to go into fear and trauma, because it knows it will lose vitality in the process. This sudden sense of powerful exhaustion is very effective at getting us to avoid looking at painful things. I do feel it is important that we understand what was done, however—as well as what is still happening at the time of this writing—in order for us to help to change it. Knowing the truth is much safer than staying in denial.

What if this same group of international bankers covertly financed both sides of these wars? What if many of the leaders of the smaller countries, as well as the soldiers who were fighting the wars and the people who were supporting them, believed there were genuine reasons for fighting—but, in fact, they had all been lied to?[178] This would be the ultimate example of sociopathy on a worldwide scale—behaviors truly worthy of the term *Global Adversary*. When the public is thrown into a state of massive fear and terror, the people begin sending far more energy to their leaders, who they desperately hope will protect them.

How could any group of human beings do such a thing? And perhaps even more important, why would they do such a thing? The whole idea is so outrageous, so treasonous, so horrible to consider that many, if not most, people who hear it will simply shut down. They don't feel safe enough to explore the idea that such a massive, interconnected, hidden negative force could exist in the world today. Their prevailing belief in a loving God cannot allow for the world they live in to be manipulated by such an oppressive force. Sacrificing the lives of millions of people for some hidden political and financial purpose isn't just crazy; in the eyes of most people, it would be the ultimate form of evil. How could anyone possibly keep a secret this big? How could we not know about it? Even in the face of extensive, verifiable evidence, I've seen many people do their best to make it go away, to laugh at it, and even to stridently attack anyone who suggests it might be true. These are all efforts to stop the loss of vital energy that would occur if they allowed themselves to feel fear. However, synchronicity gives us the personal proof that life is not all about fear and doom. The universe is a happy and magical place to be. There is love—and we have a responsibility to see the truth and work to transform our planet.

Law of One on Consciousness as an Energy System

The Law of One series goes into great detail about the negative elite on earth, and how they have either consciously or subconsciously sought energy transfers from the people while pursuing the path of manipulation and control. Consciousness is described as an energetic system, much like electricity, as we see in this brief exchange of questions and answers in session 19. Here we are reminded that the positions of the planets and satellites also have a strong effect on the consciousness and vitality of any given person on earth at any given time.

19.19 Question: I believe we have a very, very important point here. . . . To make an analogy, using electricity: We have a positive and negative pole. The more you build the charge on either of these, the greater the potential difference and the greater the ability to do work, as we call it, in the physical. This would seem to me to be the exact analogy that we have in consciousness here. Is this correct?

Answer: . . . This is precisely correct. . . . The physical [body] complex alone is created of many, many energy electromagnetic fields interacting due to intelligent energy. . . . [You are] affected by thoughts of all kinds generated by the mind complex, by distortions of the body complex, and by the numerous relationships between the microcosm, which is the entity, and the macrocosm in many forms—which you

may represent by viewing the stars, as you call them, each
with a contributing energy ray which enters the electromagnetic web of the entity due to its individual distortions. . . .
The part astrology plays is likened unto that of one root
among many.[179]

The Sheep Effect

When we observe the animal kingdom, we can obtain critical insights
into our current problems as a planet, since our bodies have much in
common with those of animals. Within their own circles, the negative
elite often refer to themselves as wolves and to the general public as
sheep. After meditating on this concept from time to time for a few
years, I had an insight into the deeper meaning behind this statement. I
was on the phone, professionally counseling a woman who was struggling with fear to the point where she couldn't even look at the problem.
To me, the solution seemed very simple, but I encountered incredible
resistance when I tried to get her to talk about it. Finally I asked her to
tell me what she thought would happen if she actually faced her fear. "I
am afraid it would completely destroy me," she answered. "I feel like if I
take even one look, it will charge at me—and I could actually die from
it." Once I reassured her that she was in a safe place and I would help her
work through whatever it was, she was able to talk about it—and she felt
much, much better. She soon realized that the solution was very simple and there was nothing to be afraid of. I realized that she was experiencing an animalistic, primal instinct—and I wanted to know more
about it.

Sheep move in flocks and herd together as part of their group behavior, partly for their own safety. At first, we might think that as soon as a
herd of sheep sees a wolf circling the group, they will start to run—but
this may not be true. Animals often become paralyzed with fear—as is
seen in the phenomenon of the deer in the headlights, where a deer has
enough time to run out of the way of a speeding car but does not.

The sheep may be very well aware that a wolf is circling their herd.

They are terrified, but they keep their heads down and act like nothing is wrong. They go on munching grass and try to ignore the problem. Sometimes the wolf will just go away and leave them alone, whereas if they run, he will definitely charge. They cannot stop him from killing them—he is too powerful. However, there's always that one sheep who ruins it for everyone else. He can't take the pressure. He knows the wolf is there, and he's just got to look. He lifts up his head and makes direct eye contact with the terrifying face of the wolf. Now, suddenly, the wolf knows he's out of time. He's been spotted and he has to charge. His searing gaze burns into the eyes of the sheep that spotted him as he charges the herd. All time seems to slow down to a standstill. The sheep that looked is paralyzed with fear, maintaining full eye contact with the wolf as if he is in a hypnotic trance. This paralysis may last only a few seconds, but now he has become the last one to run. The wolf soon catches up to him. Teeth. Pain. Terror. Blood. Agony. Death.

All the other sheep know exactly what happened. This guy just proved it again. To look at the wolf circling the herd is death. As soon as you stare fear in the eye, it will overtake you. This is generally a subconscious instinct we have, but a huge variety of Hollywood movies have reinforced this mental conditioning, which I call the *Sheep Effect*. We love to identify with characters in films. Many suspenseful movies with murderous villains have a scene where someone has found a perfectly good hiding place, such as under the bed. The movie sears with tension as the killer walks into the room. All the victim has to do is keep her eyes closed and she will be fine, but she just can't help it. She has to know. She has to look. She takes a peek—and the killer is right there. The shock is so extreme that she suddenly startles—making a noise, bumping her head against the bottom of the bed. The music surges into terrible dissonance as the killer rips away the bed. She dies the most grisly and horrific death imaginable. The killer's blade is our modern version of the wolf's teeth. Once again, you are being conditioned as you see this film. The message is "Don't look. If you do, you will die. Let us do what we want—and if you are lucky, we will leave you alone."

This primal instinct is reinforced by hundreds of different Hollywood movies. This is what happens when we do not choose the positive path, when we do not feel that the universe is a loving place where we are protected. In this case we also have not chosen the negative path, where we develop fearless dominance and attempt to manipulate and control our environment for our own benefit. We have been trained to mentally shut down when faced with fear. We try to force the world to be the way we want by simply refusing to look at the truth. As a planet, letting go of the fear is of critical importance because there is strength in numbers. Millions of people are now learning about these problems and exposing the truth on the Internet and elsewhere. There is no knock on the door that follows, no government agents following you in unmarked vehicles, and no midnight abductions. The truth has become so widespread now that the myth of Big Brother cannot be maintained. Once we realize the strength we have in numbers, there is no possible way for the activities of the negative elite to remain hidden, even if the mainstream media is too afraid to discuss them. I do feel we are very close to a tipping point at the time of this writing in April 2013. Once we fearlessly educate ourselves about the truth, we can directly become a part of the solution—rather than perpetuating the problem.

Seeking World Domination—Through the Magic Printing Press

If World War I and World War II were, in fact, some sort of global magic trick, in which both sides were financed by the same international bankers, what were they really doing? As I wrote in my full-length online book, *Financial Tyranny,* the goal was nothing other than world domination.[180] Power is a drug, an elixir, the thirst for which cannot be quenched in the sociopathic mind. The most important key to controlling the world would be to control its finances. By creating a "global reserve currency" such as the US dollar, which was backed by nothing more than hot air, it would be possible to artificially inflate and deflate the value of money—just as Senator Ron Paul has argued that the Federal Reserve has been doing for a century.

If any country held a significant amount of gold, in either the hands of private owners or its central bank, that country could completely defeat the plan for a one-world currency—simply by printing gold-backed money. The people would naturally prefer a currency they could redeem for solid gold over a currency that wasn't backed by anything but the "faith and credit" of the government that issued it. So in order for any plan of global control to work, it would be necessary to systematically steal the gold from any and every country, group, or private individual who could stand in the way of the "magic printing press." Once you can create money out of thin air, you have achieved the ultimate magic trick on earth. You can write numbers on a piece of paper, hand that paper to someone, and get real wealth in return.

Held for "Safekeeping"—by the Federal Reserve

Most of the countries that were invaded in World War I and World War II had their central banks broken into, and their gold reserves were plundered. Very few of them were aware, or could even imagine, that the biggest enemies fighting against each other in these wars were actually being financed by the same people—at the highest levels. Many countries, fearing their own invasions, put their gold on deposit with the Federal Reserve in the United States, for "safekeeping."[181] This next excerpt from *Russia Today* spells it out very nicely.

> The total value of the New York Federal Reserve's gold bullion trove of 6700 tonnes is a staggering $368.5 billion. But according to the New York Federal Reserve: "We do not own the gold. We are mere custodians." The gold is in "safekeeping" on behalf of more than 60 sovereign countries and a few organizations. Close to 98 per cent of the gold bullion stored in the NY Fed's lower Manhattan vaults, according to the Fed, belongs to central banks of foreign countries.[182]

A plan like this seems to be completely ridiculous, audacious, and impossible to achieve. In order to explain it properly, an entire book is required—and that is why I wrote *Financial Tyranny* and several other supporting investigations before I came back to finish *The Synchronicity Key*. Seizing the world's gold was one major goal of this shadowy group, which we could call the Cabal—and which many others call the Illuminati. A second and equally important goal of this group was to create international alliances, which could eventually unify into a new world order run by a single, world government that the Cabal would then control. These two Law of One quotes, from sessions 11 and 50, reveal the negative Illuminati mind-set.

> 11.18 Those [of the negative path try] . . . to disseminate the attitudes and philosophy of their particular understanding of the Law of One, which is service to self. These become the elite. Through these, the attempt begins to create a condition whereby the remainder of the planetary entities are enslaved—by their own free will.[183]

> 50.6 The negatively oriented being will be one who feels that it has found power that gives meaning to its existence— precisely as the positive polarization does feel. This negative entity will strive to offer these understandings to other-selves, most usually by the process of forming the elite, the disciples, and teaching the need and rightness of the enslavement of other-selves for their own good. These other-selves are conceived to be dependent upon the self—and in need of the guidance and the wisdom of the self.[184]

The Bank for International Settlements

If World War I and World War II were both "magic tricks" on an unimaginable scale, using the violence and bloodshed of massive staged conflicts as a cover to break into and plunder the world's central banks, where did all the gold and treasure end up going? Apparently, many of the leaders of the invaded and plundered countries actually did know where their gold went. It was secretly put on "deposit" with a shadowy international conglomerate called the Bank for International Settlements (BIS). The BIS was formed by the Federal Reserve banks—which sought to expand their control of financial systems to a global scale. The leaders were told that whatever they "deposited" in the bank would still be theirs and would secretly be used to underwrite the value of their currency. Although it would appear that their central banks were printing "fiat" currency, backed by nothing but hot air, in reality every currency was backed by its own precious metals, which were on "deposit" with the BIS. In addition, these countries were given Federal Reserve bonds—often in astronomical denominations—as collateral for their "deposits." Single pieces of paper could be worth as much as $100 million or even $1 billion—and were apparently redeemable at the Federal Reserve. Beginning on December 1, 2011, I was sent hundreds of pictures of these Federal Reserve bonds—as well as the boxes and chests they were stored in—and published them as a world exclusive soon afterward.

Fig. 7: Alleged Federal Reserve bond with face value of one billion dollars

The Wealth of Nations

Why would these world leaders ever agree to such a ridiculous-sounding plan? Why would they allow their treasuries to be emptied and put on "deposit" with a secret world bank run by the Federal Reserve? Apparently, each leader was secretly asked to read *The Wealth of Nations* by Adam Smith, written in 1776.[185] The alliance told me that the Cabal specifically ordered the writing of this document—and paid Smith very well. Smith's epic treatise argued that the world would never enjoy true peace and prosperity if any country or private group held large amounts of gold or treasure. Several key reasons were given.

For example, any country with gold in its central bank would be a target for invasion by other countries. Let's say the country measured the value of its money by how much gold it had in storage. If that gold was stolen and moved to another country, the first country's entire economy would collapse. The most violent and powerful countries would quickly become the wealthiest countries as well—which would only further increase their power. Another argument was that more and more people will be born, or immigrate, within any given country. Once these people go to work, they will create new wealth. This requires the government to print more money to prevent inflation. If the value of that country's money is based on gold, its economy will increasingly be at risk of collapse as more workers appear. If a country cannot increase its overall gold supply at the same speed at which its economy is growing, it will take greater and greater amounts of money to buy the same amount of gold. Eventually this will create a catastrophic deflation of the value of currency, much like what we saw in the Weimar Republic of Germany, where people needed an entire wheelbarrow full of cash to buy a loaf of bread.

A Massive, Worldwide Bank Robbery

In his epic book, *Gold Warriors*,[186] Sterling Seagrave reveals that the world's gold began to be confiscated on a mass level in 1895, when the Japanese invaded Korea and plundered their central banks. (The alliance has now revealed that Japan was armed and financed as a British Empire proxy state ever since the Meiji Restoration in 1868.) The Wall Street–funded Bolsheviks confiscated all Russian gold in the development of the Soviet Union between 1917 and 1922,[187] and they covertly turned it over to the Federal Reserve. Those who did not surrender their gold willingly had it taken from them by force. In Operation Golden Lily, in the 1920s and 1930s, the Japanese systematically cleared out all the Chinese and Asian gold on a truly industrial scale,[188] and secretly turned it over to the Federal Reserve. Private ownership of gold was made illegal in America on April 5, 1933, with the passage of Executive Order 6102.[189] Violation of the order was punishable by a fine of up to $10,000, a prison sentence of up to ten years, or both. Like the Japanese and the Bolsheviks, the Nazis and the Americans also emptied the gold from the central banks of countries they occupied in World War II. All this gold ended up being pooled into the Federal Reserve / BIS and hidden away—much of it buried in bunkers throughout Southeast Asia. According to the insiders I spoke with, 85 percent of the gold that ended up in the BIS was taken from Asia. And here was the key: Without gold, no country could ever compete against the "magic printing press" of paper money, backed by nothing but "faith and credit." Any group that could print money out of thin air had practically limitless power.

If this sounds like a wild story that most people would dismiss as conspiracy theory—or the makings of a great political thriller film—you'd be absolutely right. That didn't change the fact that it was all based on rigorously provable information. I synthesized more than nineteen years' worth of research and insider testimony on this subject in *Financial Tyranny*, a full-length book that I released on my website, for free, beginning on January 13, 2012, and that has had nearly a million views as of April 2013.[190] This was a very stressful process, as I was told that the things I was writing about were considered far more classified than the UFO subject—and could easily get me killed.

Life and Death

On Wednesday, December 14, 2011, I received a death threat from a very high-level source, but I continued the investigation. Two weeks later, on December 31, 2011, David Hutzler sent me critical information from the alliance, directing me to a treasure trove of hidden data on the Unwanted Publicity Intelligence website. This included many pictures of Federal Reserve bonds, as well as the boxes and chests they were buried in for safekeeping. A week later, on January 6, 2012, David Hutzler and his son Mackie each suffered multiple gunshot wounds in their home— which then burned down.[191]

By this point I had been recording my dreams every morning for twenty years and had gained incredible benefit from this practice. Many of my dreams had urged me to conduct this investigation and had clearly indicated that I would be protected if I did. This was further supported by an ongoing number of phenomenal synchronicities. I already had quite an extensive legacy of accurate prophecies from my dreams—some of which I had documented on my website. However, this was no dream—this was reality. I was directly standing up to what many people considered the most dangerous and destructive force on earth. Most people couldn't even handle the idea of a single unified group that had controlled the Federal Reserve: running the United States, the United Kingdom, the USSR, Japan, Italy, the Nazi Party, and several top European countries. I had to take an enormous leap of faith—and put my life on the line. If I had trusted my feelings, they would have told me that doing something like this didn't feel good. If I had trusted my thoughts, they would have told me the whole idea was crazy. However, when I listened to the deep, inner voice—at my core—by trusting my dreams, and looking at all the synchronicities that were happening, I knew this had to be right. Even if David and Mackie Hutzler had been killed because of the information that had been passed to me, I would still complete the investigation. I released the finished product, *Financial Tyranny,* a week after their deaths, on January 13, 2012.[192]

In the process of writing *Financial Tyranny,* I had completely missed the deadline for *The Synchronicity Key*—and barely even had enough time to start it. I had a core of great material, but no matter how hard I tried, for almost an entire year after publishing *Financial Tyranny,* I simply could not break through the writer's block. I had originally wanted to share some elements of my own personal journey and had felt very strongly about that. However, once I started pursuing the *Financial Tyranny* investigation, the number of viciously threatening emails and website comments I was receiving went way, way up.

Then, on Easter Sunday in April 2012, a friend of mine died a tragic, violent death, right around the corner from my house.[193] There was no way to prove that any individual or group may have caused it to happen, but it was still extremely sad. The police could not immediately identify the body even though my friend had a driver's license in his wallet. Even after suffering this tragedy, I continued reading all of my mail, and not a day went by when I didn't see at least two or three very hateful, sarcastic, and demeaning letters, directed at me personally. This was less than 1 percent of all of the mail, but I still read every one of them, trying to gain whatever value I might find in their arguments. Then, on Friday, June 22, 2012, one of my top insiders, an old-timer with access to highly classified information, was nearly poisoned to death by a strange bioweapon.[194] I still continued reading every nasty letter that came in, without allowing anyone to screen them for me, until I finally couldn't take anymore in August 2012. Even if some people refused to believe anything I was saying, I knew that lives had been lost and the risks were very real. I no longer chose to subject myself to a constant barrage of hatred and anger from the skeptics in my audience.

After my friend's tragic death in April 2012, I wanted all the hate to stop. I felt like I needed to do whatever I could to avoid being shamed, criticized, and humiliated—even as I was doing my very best to help the planet. I soon became dreadfully opposed to saying a single word about myself in the new book. I deleted every page I had written about my own experiences, about synchronicity, about the law of karma, and anything else along those lines. Instead, I started creating another scientific tour de force—right from page one. I didn't want to leave a single hole in the entire argument that wasn't rigorously backed up with solid facts. That way, even if people wanted to hate me and attack the book, there would be no real ground for them to stand on. However, I continued to suffer through massive stress—and a total writer's block.

I took an extended sabbatical in the Canadian Rocky Mountains beginning on September 2, 2012, hoping—and promising—that I could finish the book. The stress of having such a massive project hanging over my head, unfinished, was tearing me apart. Instead of writing, I now found myself going through an elaborate grieving process.[195] I finally had the time and space necessary to let go of all the stress and pain I'd felt from the *Financial Tyranny* investigation—the tragic deaths, failed assassination attempts, and death threats—and return to a place of balance and peace within myself. I spent a lot of time reading and reacquainting myself with the Law of One series for the first time in many years. Now that I had done my homework, many new connections jumped out at me, and my passion for the work was reinvigorated. Those new connections would end up directly helping me write this book.

Thinking and Feeling Cannot Solve the Problem

After I came home, I had a long conversation with Dr. Victor Vernon Woolf, the founder of holodynamics theory and the author of ten books.[196] Vern Woolf specializes in healing post-traumatic stress disorder, or PTSD, using an innovative method that is completely different from conventional psychoanalysis. His techniques were originally developed with the Academy of Natural Sciences in Russia. Vern's group eventually created support chapters in more than one hundred different Russian cities. More than six hundred trained and certified holodynamics teachers helped heal people from unfathomable traumas, end the Cold War, and transform the Soviet Union, as his techniques were directly reaching people in the highest levels of the Russian government.

I have Vern to thank for pointing out that thinking and feeling can never solve our problems—individually or globally. It is only through *being*—awakening to the full and direct experience of this moment—that we can release old pains, see the answer to all problems, and heal traumas that otherwise seemed to be permanent scars. For me, the "meaningful coincidence" of synchronicity has been one of the most consistent forces that have focused me into the present moment, in all of its glory and wonder.

By the end of my conversation with Vern, I realized I did not need to write another book that was strictly scientific in nature. When I stepped back and went into a place of being, I realized that my whole life had been showing me the answer. Not everything can be proven. Some of it has to be experienced. Synchronicity transcends thought and brings us directly into the world of the spirit.

Here Comes the Cavalry

Less than two weeks after I finally saw what I had to do and broke through my writer's block, I was contacted by REN-TV—one of the largest TV networks in Russia that is not owned and run by the government. Their estimated viewing audience is as high as 138 million people in Russia and the former Soviet republics. Much to my amazement, not only had they read *Financial Tyranny*, but they also considered it a masterpiece and were building an entire three-hour documentary film around it for prime-time television. In mid-December, right as we headed toward the Mayan calendar end date of December 21, 2012, REN-TV filmed me answering eleven different questions on this controversial subject. Then in late December, I was filmed again for another three-hour exclusive, and this time they had thirty more questions that showed they had thoroughly studied the book. The first three-hour documentary aired on January 16, 2013—just three days after the date I'd published *Financial Tyranny* the year before.

On the very same day this show aired—January 16, 2013—Germany shocked the world by demanding that the Federal Reserve return 300 metric tons of its gold. The country's leaders also insisted that France return all 374 metric tons of its gold that was being held at the Banque de France.[197] This was a direct act of war, in the financial sense. It was also a surprising confirmation of what UK politician and European Parliament member Nigel Farage had said in an interview on December 14, 2012: "Everything from George Orwell's 1984 is coming into being. . . . There are certainly several American commentators pointing out that there may well be, in terms of gold reserves and their reality, a huge fraud going on."[198]

According to my contacts within the alliance, this statement from a major British politician had utterly infuriated and terrified the Cabal, sending them into a true panic. The second REN-TV documentary, *Shadow Gold,* aired on January 30, 2013, and covered the material in *Financial Tyranny* even more closely than the first episode did.[199]

Then on February 4, 2013, the mysterious hacker group Anonymous posted private data from four thousand different Federal Reserve executives' accounts—including private contact information, mobile phone numbers, account log-ins, IP addresses, and credentials.[200] A Reddit user started calling the numbers, confirmed they were Federal Reserve executives, and said, "The ramifications of that kind of loss of control are severe."[201] A few weeks later, a key insider revealed that Anonymous was collaborating with patriotic computer experts within the US military, and this was all part of their coordinated effort to defend the Constitution against all enemies, foreign and domestic. Just twenty-four days after the Federal Reserve was hacked, Pope Benedict XVI resigned— which was the first time such an event had happened in more than six hundred years. The very top of the Vatican dome was struck by lightning that same evening, and the event was filmed and photographed. I saw this as an astonishingly powerful example of synchronicity, appearing on a truly global scale, and wrote an entire article about it on my website.[202] The lightning-struck tower is one of twenty-two archetypes described in the Law of One series as blueprints written into the mind of the galaxy that we all must go through. It is also known as the "dark night of the soul." The image associated with this archetype is lightning striking a tower and a king and queen falling to their deaths. The lightning bolt represents pure universal energy interfering in our daily lives, destroying all corruption—even at the highest levels of government, religion, military, finance, and media. This moment represents the very bottom of the Wheel of Karma—when all the negative things we've done are returned to us in our own lives.

What you are about to read goes far beyond political conspiracies. I do believe that what we are seeing is part of a much bigger and ultimately far more important story of our own spiritual evolution as a planet into a Golden Age of peace, prosperity, and higher consciousness. The "negative elite," as they are called in the Law of One series, help awaken us to the fact that the reality we've been led to believe in is an illusion, and the truth is much stranger than fiction.

PART TWO

ENTERING THE MAGICAL WORLD

CHAPTER SIX

Karma Is Real

As the Wheel of Karma keeps turning, we experience the highest highs and the lowest lows that life has to offer us. Our lives continue cycling through joy and disaster, pleasure and pain, triumph and upset, light and darkness. The events we go through can be so upsetting, so traumatizing, that we often willingly blind ourselves to the greatest truth of all: The world we think we are living in is an illusion. Life is not random. Actions have consequences. We do not live in a vacuum. There are no private thoughts. We are here to learn to love each other. Whatever we measure out to others will be measured out in turn to us—as consistently and inevitably as the law of gravity keeps us tethered to the earth. For those who have already seen the truth, it is obvious. It may even seem like a kindergarten-level spiritual teaching. For those who have been unwilling to see the truth, nothing could seem more ludicrous.

The ancient Sanskrit word *karman* means "action," "effect," and "fate." The meaning encompasses both action and reaction—causes and consequences. The word *karma* also appears in the Hindu language, where it translates closer to the word "work" and involves the effort we make on a soul level to reunify with our highest and truest essence.[203] Karma is one simple word that expresses the concept of "what goes around, comes around"—whatever we create is what we will then experience. Many of the events that happen to us—including the most wonderful and the most seemingly disastrous—are not random at all. Invisible forces are constantly at work, shaping and arranging whatever will then unfold in our lives. Karma does appear to be enforcing an absolute law, which is upheld throughout the universe—the law of free will. If we honor and support the free will of others, we are choosing love, and if we manipulate the free will of others, we are choosing the path of control. Everything we think, say, and do is being evaluated on an unseen level—by ourselves and by others—to see whether we are choosing love or control.

The events that happen in our lives are not random; they are the direct results of the choices we are making. If you choose to shame, humiliate, disrespect, and demean others—to manipulate and control them for your own gain—then a very similar set of experiences will happen to you. The people in the Cabal are not free from this eternal system by any means. If you cause pain, you will feel pain. If you choose to deny others' feelings, then others will deny your feelings. If you create love—even in a situation where it seems ignorant or impossible to do so—then love will indeed be returned to you. Best of all, the entire Wheel of Karma can be stopped through forgiveness. These upsetting events keep repeating only until we learn the greatest teaching of the universe—that we are all one, and there is only identity. Once you delve into this new reality and observe it happening in your life firsthand, you may soon realize that none of us are exempt from this system of accounting, regardless of whatever we may or may not believe. After you become aware of karma and watch it play out many hundreds, if not thousands, of times in your own life, it can become quite astounding to see how stubborn and unwilling some people are to see it, even in those cases where it should be blatantly obvious.

Instant Karma

A few years ago I heard about an example of karma that was so profound it was almost a joke, had the circumstances not been so tragic. If I were to put these scenes in a screenplay, any professional script consultant would say they had to be cut, as the whole story seems just too outrageous to believe. A friend of mine was raising two toddlers on her own, working a full-time job just to get by, leaving the kids in day care while working, and struggling to make enough money to survive. I could not afford to help her at the time, nor did she ask me for any financial assistance. The father had run out on his family and had been ordered by the court to pay child support. He refused to get a job because working didn't feel good. For months, he paid nothing, causing my friend to wonder whether she should take legal action. Finally he agreed to pay a rather large lump-sum amount, which, secretly, he borrowed from his father. He acquired the money, in cash, and said he was coming right over to drop it off.

Then she didn't hear from him for two days. Finally, he told her the cash had been stolen out of his car. It was a tragedy. He now felt that he didn't have to pay her back, as this was a horrible crime, and he obviously shouldn't be forced to earn the same money twice. The next day, he was driving a brand-new car, a black SUV. He refused to talk about how he had acquired the SUV—he just completely shut her down. That very same night, the vehicle skidded off the road, rolled sideways down the hill like a barrel, and was destroyed beyond repair. Somehow he was unharmed, but this accident triggered communication that would have seemed impossible before then. His father reconnected with my friend, told her he had given his son the cash, and was absolutely certain that his son had used it to make a down payment for a new SUV at the dealership. I never found out what happened between the father and the son after this, but I strongly suspect it wasn't pretty.

In another case, I was living in Virginia Beach, right under the flight path of F-18 Hornet jets coming in to land at Naval Air Station Oceana. The noise was so loud that you literally felt like the sky was tearing open, and it happened throughout the day, from eight A.M. to ten P.M. I didn't realize until after I signed the lease that this was why it was so inexpensive to live there. The couple who lived next door to me were severe alcoholics. Night after night, they would sit out on their porch drinking, with their chairs facing the road, and scream profanities at each other. I did my best to try to bring joy into their lives when I spoke to them.

However, I couldn't help but feel like the law of karma was going to strike, and there was no way this horrible situation could go on. The stress of hearing them fight every night was tearing me to pieces.

One day, a huge boa constrictor appeared in their bathroom, wrapped around the toilet. "Do you think this means something?" the woman asked me. "Yeah, you may want to look at that," I answered. I saw this snake as a manifestation of synchronicity, giving them a direct warning of karmic danger if they didn't change their behavior. Then, on December 29, 1999, I had a terrifying nightmare in which a ghost-like woman would periodically show up: "When she would show up, everything would seem to slow down and pause, and it was extremely dramatic, just like a tunnel-vision scene in a horror movie with the scary music in the background."[204] No one wanted to look at her or even acknowledge she was there, despite the horror and the intensity of her appearance, and the self-harming things she would then do: "She just looked very sad as she mutilated herself in front of me, blood and debris flying. And I wondered what she was so upset about, but I wasn't making any connections. No one else seemed to even be able to see her besides me." As time went on, she did finally get the people to see her, but she was still completely ignored. "Even as she was horrifyingly mutilating her own body and staring you dead in the eye the whole time that she was doing it, they tried to act like she totally didn't exist." Eventually I figured out that she was doing these damaging things to herself in order to try to awaken others to their own negative behaviors. Her final appearance in the dream was the most dramatic: "the woman had a frying pan, and there was fire coming up. She looked like she was going to stick her head in the frying pan several times to try to prove her point." I then realized that she represented karma: "She was capable of projecting an image of herself going in, looking at people and then doing these horrible things to herself. And obviously, it was designed to make them realize that they were really inflicting this exact same harm upon themselves."[205]

The screaming continued, almost every night, until January 24, 2000. That night, the man living above them fell asleep with a lit cigarette. This soon ignited a fire, and when the awakened man threw water on it, the flames only grew worse, since electrical lines had become exposed in the blaze. I awoke to the sounds of screaming outside my front door—and when I opened it, all I could see was a solid wall of smoke, from top to bottom. The couple and I stood helplessly outside and watched their house burn as the fire department tried to fight the blaze. In the end, they had to completely saturate it from the highest point, ruining everything inside that wasn't already destroyed by fire and smoke. The Red Cross stepped in to help them, as they had lost everything they owned. I never saw them again. I immediately realized that my dream had predicted the whole event, in precise detail, less than a month earlier—and I wrote it all up on my website.[206] My dream suggested that their house fire was a visible manifestation of the anger and violence they were displaying toward each other, night after night. The universe was trying to get their attention—in a very dramatic fashion.

Secrets of Shamanism

In my own experience, bad karma has become so easy to identify that I almost always see a cause-and-effect relationship between the thoughts I am having and the experiences that result. The final tipping point that got me to identify this system and see how often bad karma was affecting me came when I read *Secrets of Shamanism: Tapping the Spirit Power Within You* by Jose and Lena S. Stevens.[207] Having this system explained to me by a doctor of psychology and his wife, with such clarity, precision, and confidence, allowed me to open my mind to the possibility that it was real. I was only sixteen years old at the time—and this knowledge soon generated profound insights and personal experiences.

In the following twenty-four years, I have had literally thousands of cases when I've had an unloving thought about someone and allowed myself to focus on that feeling of anger and judgment, only to have a sudden accident or injury. I cut myself with a knife. I stub my toe. I burn myself. I bite on my fork the wrong way and hurt my teeth. I bite my tongue and taste blood. An animal dashes out into the road and I have to swerve to avoid it. My favorite drinking glass shatters in the sink after I lose my grip. I nick myself shaving. I get a painful splinter. Dust flies into my eye. I get bitten by an insect. I bump into a heavy book on the edge of the table, and it crashes down and hits my foot. I slip in the shower and painfully bang my elbow against the glass, and almost get hurt much worse. I write a check, feeling disgusted about paying what I owe, and get a paper cut right as I tear it out of the checkbook. A whole plate of oily food slips off the table and falls in my lap, ruining my favorite shirt and a decent pair of pants. I have managed to avoid the more serious types of accidents and injuries by being extremely careful about the thoughts I think—and particularly how I treat others—but many people get much stronger blasts of karma than I have described here.

The key, as Dr. and Mrs. Stevens's book explains, is to remember what you were thinking about right before the accident happened. Until you train yourself to do this reliably, you will be easily distracted by the incident itself. Your attention suddenly dashes over to this new problem that has just crashed in on you. Now your heart is pounding, your breathing accelerates, blood rushes to your brain, and you become hypervigilant, hyperaware, and usually very annoyed. This sudden surge of anger and frustration can immediately erase whatever thoughts you were having right before the accident. The key, whenever something like this happens, is to not let this painful and annoying event distract you if at all possible. Keep your mind as calm as you can, and do your best to remember whatever you were just thinking about. With very little practice, the cause-and-effect relationship between your thoughts and your experiences will become obvious. Not all karma is instantaneous like this, but a surprisingly large amount of it is.

It's also important to point out that many of these cases of bad karma were caused by the movement of my own body. I might not be aware of it on any conscious level, but my subconscious mind seems to have been directly involved in making the painful event happen. My body was influenced to move a certain way—with a little nudge I was completely unaware of—and I then cut my finger, stubbed my toe, burned myself, bit my fork, bit my tongue, dropped my favorite glass, nicked myself shaving, got a splinter, had dust fly in my eye, bumped into the heavy book, slipped in the shower, got a paper cut, or dropped oily food all over my shirt and pants. Other events like the animal running into the road, the insect biting me or dust flying into my eye could ultimately be the result of our existence within a living universe. We may discover that a wide variety of non-physical entities are conspiring to help us awaken, and can manipulate our environment to help convey these messages. Similarly, my friend's ex-husband with the SUV may have subconsciously jerked the wheel or driven right into an area of loose gravel, causing his new car to roll off the road.

Once you begin studying your own daily experiences, you can easily prove that these types of experiences are happening to you. Although bad karma can be very annoying and can cause you to feel humiliated, judged, and criticized by some invisible force, it can also be quite fascinating. The world you thought you knew is not the world you are actually living in. Once you realize this, you can't help but start paying attention to it. Some part of you, on a subconscious level, has an absolute code of ethics and morality, regardless of whatever you may believe on the conscious level. You can fight, cry, screech, yell, blame others, and cast yourself as the tortured, helpless victim, but it's no use. You can reason, bargain, and rationalize that you are a good person, you do plenty of good things for others, and therefore you don't deserve this, but it still happens. Sooner or later your ego will drop down a few notches, and you learn to stop complaining and start trying to understand both the bad karma and the compassion that is behind it. Karma may not seem like it could possibly be a good thing, but ageless wisdom has the answer.

Jehoshua and the Teachings of Hell, Salvation, Eternity, and Sin

Most Bible scholars agree that the most accurate name for Jesus, from the original Aramaic, is Yeshua.[208] This became Iesous (*ee-yay-sous*) in Greek—and this word was further changed into Jesus. The Law of One series said that the closest and most accurate pronunciation is Jehoshua.[209] Many Christians believe Jehoshua taught that there is a place called Hell—perhaps below the surface of the earth—in which anyone who has not converted to Christianity will burn in a lake of fire for all eternity. In a living universe of loving consciousness, it seems very unlikely that any soul would be singled out for eternal abuse, since there is only identity, and its core essence is love. Now, a rising movement of Bible scholars is going back to the original scriptures to look for direct evidence, rather than simply believing the prevailing opinions of the day.

W. L. Graham's Bible Reality Check website has an amazingly comprehensive body of scholarship that all Christians should be aware of. Graham is a Christian and endorses the core religious principles. Graham has also revealed many key differences between the beliefs of most Christians and what modern linguistic and scholarly research has actually found in the scriptures. The article "A Case Against Hell" reveals that the entire concept of Hell is built from very flimsy evidence and is absent from the Old Testament altogether.[210] The Hebrew word that is translated as "Hell" in most Bibles today is *sheol,* which means "grave." The word *sheol* appears only thirty-one times in the entire Old Testament. *Sheol,* the grave, is where everyone must go—regardless of how they lived their lives. God does not warn Adam and Eve about there being a Hell if they eat from the Tree of Knowledge of Good and Evil— only that this action would cause death. Cain is not warned about Hell. Nor are the cities of Sodom and Gomorrah. Moses does not warn of there being a Hell in the Ten Commandments—or in more than six hundred warnings, laws, and ordinances in the Mosaic Law. Some of the most noted Bible scholars, including William Barclay, John A. T. Robinson, F. W. Farrar, and Marvin Vincent, agree that the modern concept of Hell does not appear in any Hebrew or Greek text from these same time periods.[211]

In the New Testament, Jehoshua occasionally used the Greek word *Gehenna* to describe what will happen to us if we engage in negative, self-serving behaviors. The first time Gehenna is mentioned is in the Sermon on the Mount—in Matthew 5:22, 5:29–30. Jehoshua clearly warns us that we are in danger of Gehenna for something as simple as calling someone else a fool. Modern Christians would never believe that such a mundane insult to another human being would sentence you to burn in Hell for all eternity, but it's right there in the book of Matthew, since Gehenna is now being translated as "Hell." Oftentimes, people read the Bible only to confirm what they already believe rather than considering the material on its own merits and analyzing the original meanings of what Jehoshua and others actually said. Importantly, the same word root for *Gehenna* is not translated as "Hell" when it appears in the Old Testament Hebrew as *ga ben Hinnom*—the valley of the son of Hinnom.

This valley was admittedly a horrible place; it started out as a location where children were sacrificed to the owl-god Moloch. Over time, the ritual murders stopped and Gehenna became the main garbage dump for the entire city. Dead bodies and all types of filth were routinely burned there. Gehenna was therefore a necessary place for cleansing and purifying the land through fire. This appears to be the deeper meaning of the metaphor Jehoshua was using. The third definition of the word *Gehenna* in the World English Dictionary is "a place or state of pain and torment."[212] Therefore, when Jehoshua said that calling someone a fool will bring you through Gehenna, he meant that causing pain and torment to others would cause similar pain and torment in your own life as a form of purification. Many people still refer to karma as something you have to "burn off," and this appears to be a direct continuation of the symbolism used by Jehoshua. The concept of karma was also expressed with the classic phrase, "As you sow, so shall you reap" (Galatians 6:7). Therefore, Gehenna is one instance in which Jehoshua's frequent use of symbolism and metaphor seems to have been wildly misconstrued.

This is only the beginning of the argument Graham and other Bible scholars made to suggest that the concept of Hell was entirely fabricated and is not supported by the texts. In another key example from the New Testament, the apostle Paul declares in Acts 20:27 that he had revealed the entire counsel of God. However, Paul never once mentioned Hell in any of his letters. The only possible exception in some Bible translations is where Paul is quoted as saying that Jehoshua triumphed over Hell in 1 Corinthians 15:55, but here, the Greek word translates as "the grave." This is the same word that is mistranslated in the Old Testament as "Hell" and was originally written as *sheol*.

Similarly, the term *saved* has been misunderstood, though it is still a very important spiritual concept. The New Testament Greek words for *saved* are *sozo* and *soteria*. These words have a variety of definitions and include the concepts of being rescued, delivered, healed, and saved from danger. These words appear throughout the New Testament in a variety of different contexts. Spiritual teachings such as Jehoshua gave, therefore, can rescue and deliver us from the danger of Gehenna—from the fires of karma that burn out our impurities—by revealing what life on earth is here to teach us.

Another frequently mistranslated word is *eternity*. The Old Testament word is *olam*—and there are many places in the Bible where it clearly refers to lengths of time that are much shorter than forever. This includes the length of a king's life, the amount of time Jonah spent in the belly of the whale, the duration of man's earthly existence, the amount of time a child was supposed to spend in the temple, the amount of time a servant was expected to spend working for his master, and the amount of time David was intended to be king of Israel. Each of these examples indicate a particular cycle of time. The Greek equivalent of *olam* is *aion,* which means "age," or a cycle of time. This is where we get the modern English word *eon* from. This "age" could potentially include one of the Ages of the Zodiac but clearly refers to much shorter time cycles as well. The Bible also uses the words *aionian* and *aionios,* which refer to the same time cycle repeating itself. In any other Greek document from the time of the New Testament, the word *aion* did not mean "eternity" or "forever." Plato, Aristotle, Homer, Hippocrates, and many other scholars used the word *aion* to indicate much shorter periods of time.

The word *sin* translates as a transgression of divine law—particularly a willful or deliberate violation of a moral or religious principle.[213] Although this word is considerably outdated for anyone who is not a Christian, a sin would be anything that violates the free will of others. Jehoshua's original message, therefore, was that if you violate others' free will, you will have to go through a cycle of purification—or Gehenna—for a given cycle, or *aion,* of time. This is much different than the modern, mistranslated idea that you will "burn in hell for all eternity." Once you understand what is happening to you—and the love that is ultimately fueling these karmic events—you can be saved (*sozo*) from having to repeat these cycles (*aionios*) of misery, suffering, and pain (Gehenna). The key to stopping the Wheel of Karma is forgiveness.

Religion as a Tool for Strengthening Governmental Power

How did these mistranslations come into being? Let's not forget that Christianity was a government-sponsored religion by an empire that was in decline and scrambling for power. The life and teachings of Jehoshua could not be stopped, so the empire's best move would be to seize all the wealth of existing documents, integrate them into one source, and declare that source to be the definitive word of God. This is precisely what Emperor Constantine I of Rome did in A.D. 325, with the Council of Nicaea. Anything that was deemed contrary to Constantine I's will was thrown out of the New Testament, including a series of gospels written by people who walked with Jehoshua and witnessed his teachings as they were happening. Insiders who worked for the Cabal at high levels of secrecy told me Constantine I therefore considered himself to be the "God the Father" who is referred to in the Old and New Testament and believed he was superior to Jehoshua. The Cabal has a very negative view of Christianity, and therefore shares this ancient secret with pride among its own membership. Graduate-level theological textbooks still debate whether Constantine I was guided by the will of God when he outvoted the group and threw out the two dissenting bishops, even though the original idea was that the unanimous consensus view of the council would be considered the will of God. *The People of the Secret* by Ernest Scott features an ironic quote about this event.

> Unanimity was essential if the inspiration of the Holy Spirit was to be claimed for the Council's conclusions. Both unanimity and the approval of deity were matters of personal concern to Constantine, and he proceeded to ensure both by the simple expedient of having the two dissenting Bishops removed from

the meeting. Thus the datum point of Christianity for the next 1,500 years seems to have been decided by nothing more than an overt act of political gamesmanship.[214]

The concept of an eternal hellfire is very useful for a government seeking to establish a religion it could use to crush any and all resistance. Merging church and state is also the best way to ensure that people pay high taxes—in the form of "indulgences" that are tithed to the church, since the church is also the government. (In the case of Christianity, this merger of church and state did not successfully occur until A.D. 720.) The more harm people feel they have done to others, the more money they will likely decide to pay to ensure they spend the rest of eternity in a heavenly paradise. The fear of the alternative—an eternal torture of unimaginable suffering—would be a very effective way to keep the people under control. It also could be used to justify the concept of holy war, because anyone outside the group, anyone who doesn't believe what the group does, is already condemned to a hideous madness of fear, torture, and pain for all eternity. If you already know your enemies are going to a place of perpetual horror, you can justify unspeakable atrocities because you've already categorized them as nonpersons.

A Messenger of the One Creator

The Law of One series endorsed the teachings of Jehoshua and said that his mission was fully approved and endorsed by the angelic forces that watch over our planet. It was always known that the teachings would be distorted, but the core of the message was so pure that the good would still outweigh the bad. Jehoshua's mission was framed as one critical aspect of a much larger group effort to assist us in our evolution, and Jehoshua did not have to work alone in carrying out his mission. The Law of One series also tells us that Jehoshua "penetrated intelligent infinity" by realizing that he was not a separate being but was in fact an embodiment of the One Creator. This allowed Jehoshua to reach the next level of human evolution, into a "light-body" form. In Law of One terms, this process is called *harvest*. The meaning of this term, and its appearance in the Bible, will be explained in Part 4.

> 17.11 [Jehoshua] was desirous of entering this planetary sphere in order to share the love vibration in as pure a manner as possible. Thus, this entity received permission to perform this mission. . . . [Jehoshua] was extremely positively polarized. . . . This entity became aware that it was not an entity of itself, but operated as a messenger of the One Creator—whom this entity saw as love.[215]

> 11.8 Penetration into the eighth or intelligent infinity level allows a mind/body/spirit complex [i.e., a person] to be harvested [i.e., to reach the next level of human evolution] if it wishes, at any time/space during the cycle.[216]

Karma in Relationships

Some karma appears in our lives in seemingly magical ways, much like synchronicity. Painful and difficult things happen to us almost immediately after we cause pain to someone else. The living universe and its messengers do their very best to make these events both understandable and clearly related to the actions that caused them. However, there are other forms of karma that are often far more prolonged and seemingly mundane in nature. The people in our daily lives often end up providing us with the strongest karma we ever experience. When we do things that hurt their feelings, we suffer the consequences. We may have arguments, conflicts, disagreements, and confrontations. At times, we may feel an overwhelming sense of loneliness, despair, depression, anger, sadness, and jealousy and not realize how common this is. As we will see in chapters 7 and 8, very few of the relationships we have are first-time encounters in the greater sense—and we may be working on problems we've had for centuries, if not millennia.

The Law of One philosophy sheds unique light on the role of the negatively oriented people in our lives—including the 1 percent of sociopaths. Even if a person has become extremely bitter, manipulative, and controlling in waking life, on a higher level that person is fully aware of who he or she is and what he or she is doing here. We will explore the arguments in favor of this concept in chapter 8, "Mapping Out the Afterlife." Unbeknownst to this person on the conscious level, he or she may well be performing a service, even when doing hurtful things. If you knowingly hurt someone else, your own karma can be balanced out by someone else who does something completely negative, even criminal in the eyes of the law, against you. However, even if that person ends up balancing your karma, he or she is not granted a free pass for committing these hurtful acts. Each person in your life is fully accountable for how his or her actions made you feel, even if you attracted a painful experience in the karmic sense. Ultimately, all of us must learn the ways of love, and as this occurs throughout the cosmos, the universe will again become one and conclude another cycle of existence.

On a global level, the sociopathic power elite groups are creating a powerful karmic mirror for everyone. In Law of One terms, they can do only what they are allowed to do by what we have collectively attracted through our own free will. Most people veer between negative and positive in how they treat others, day by day. Everyone has the potential to cause extreme pain and suffering to others, either deliberately or through ignorance. Oftentimes, we want to overlook these aspects in ourselves and believe that we are entirely good. When others challenge us on our negative behavior, we may go into denial and refuse to admit that we have done anything hurtful. We may also seek to hide our behavior from others, swearing our family, friends, and associates to secrecy. The power elite, with their hidden secrets and clandestine plans, act as a global mirror of this phenomenon within our own lives. Ultimately, we are meant to learn from these global problems. By observing the destructive aspects of hidden secrecy and the lies told by politicians with smiling faces, we learn what not to do in our own lives and are inspired to help others. Without this influence, we would be far less likely to make rapid spiritual growth.

Awakening to the Unity in All

It is very easy to fall into the illusion that you are a separate being, living in a separate body. On a physical level, this is true. Your body is separate from other bodies. If you fall, your body will be hurt. If someone else falls, your body will not feel physical pain, unless you choose to empathize with that person. However, on a deeper level, ageless wisdom reveals that we are all one. No textbooks or scriptures are required to realize this. Simply going deep into meditation and fully awakening into the present moment—and what that really means—can make it obvious. The identity that is reading or hearing these words—the consciousness you enjoy—is not separate from others. The more you can rest and relax your mind, the more obvious the truth will become. You can understand the Wheel of Karma and begin putting all the pieces together so you can see how to heal yourself and master the lessons you are being shown. You no longer need to endlessly repeat the same cycles with no new insights.

Sarcasm Won't Change the Law

You may find this discussion of karma to be such a beginner-level concept of spirituality that no further explanation is necessary, but it is central to our investigation. You may find the whole concept impossible to believe, even insulting to your intelligence. You may have already had a rewarding burst of sarcastic laughter. "That's not only impossible; that's ridiculous. You might as well have just told me you believe in Santa Claus. Science, help me out here. This guy is an idiot." Actually, science is a very useful tool in proving that our lives do work this way. Groundbreaking new scientific concepts are often heavily resisted and ridiculed before they become commonly accepted. In this case, the difference between the world we think we know and the world of true reality is so great that we must move through tremendous fear of being rejected and ridiculed by our peers in order to see it. Speaking about these subjects can be very difficult. However, I've hardly ever found anyone who doesn't appreciate a good spiritual story if you keep it light and fun and don't try to pressure your listeners into believing you. Hollywood certainly understands this.

Many of the things we take for granted in our modern world would be considered crazy if we explained them without any visible proof to someone only a few hundred years ago. Even if we did show them something—such as a modern-day smartphone—they might come up with a ridiculous, skeptical explanation. You may even find out that studying concepts you initially thought of as crazy could end up being the key to living a much happier and more fulfilling life. You may finally be able to free yourself from the endless up-and-down cycles of joy and disaster, or "samsara," as it was called in the ancient Hindu Vedic scriptures.

So let's create a safe place as you read these words. You don't have to tell anyone you're thinking about these things if it doesn't feel comfortable and right for you to do so. Let's not worry about whether they will judge you, even if they do find out. Let's be willing to keep an open mind and think outside the box. We can consider new ideas and contemplate the possibilities before we automatically pass judgment and throw these concepts away with sarcastic laughter.

Let's Consider the Possibilities

Let's consider that life on earth may be a vast, meticulously balanced and fastidiously maintained illusion, a school for spiritual masters in training. Let's say this illusion is guided and watched over by countless intelligent entities who are much more advanced than most of us could ever dare to believe. Let's say that no matter how smart we think we are, there are people out there who are far more intelligent than we could ever be—at least at this time.

Let's say that there is a transparent ceiling and that everything we think, say, and do is known to these people, moment by moment. Let's say that these people have nothing but the greatest love and compassion for us. Let's say they have a deep understanding of everything we have ever suffered through. Let's say that no matter how seemingly heinous of a crime we may have committed against someone, these people genuinely forgave us—and did not shame or disrespect us—even when it seemed like no one else would or could.

Let's say that these people do administer the purifying fire of karma when we infringe on others' free will, but this is done with absolute love and respect so that we can be restored to perfect balance. Let's say that once we have paid off our karma, we never need to feel fear again, as we can always choose to help and love others, rather than manipulating and controlling them. Let's say that if we keep making positive choices, no new negative karma will need to be created in our lives. Let's say we will then be actively protected from painful and disruptive things that might have otherwise happened, as a very real form of health insurance. We will then invariably begin seeing positive rewards for the good works we have created.

Let's say these people know exactly what steps we have to take in order to master our experiences. Let's say that a great deal of effort is involved in constructing the illusion that life on earth, and the things that happen to us, appear to be random—because if it were too obvious, there would be nothing for us to learn. Let's say that these people are working tirelessly on our behalf, do not need to take credit for what they do, and are happy to keep working even if hardly any of us understand who they are or what they are doing. Let's say that much of their work involves a careful manipulation of events on earth—including subconsciously affecting the actions of others—so that whatever experiences we create for those around us will then happen in our own lives. Let's say there are great cycles of time that steer us through a consistent story line—the Book of Life or Hero's Journey—again and again. Let's say these people know this story well and seek to help us master whatever section we find ourselves in.

Let's say that these people are ready and willing to talk to you as long as you meet them halfway and show that you are mature enough to handle that communication by practicing the ageless wisdom teachings in your daily life. Let's say that synchronicity is a stepping-stone they use to make you aware of their presence—at a gradual speed, without fear—so that over time, you can recognize the full truth. Let's say that synchronicity is where the same system that is constantly being used to create karma is put to a much happier and more inspiring use.

Regardless of whether you are ready to accept these concepts or not, there is abundant scientific evidence that we survive physical death and have already experienced multiple lifetimes on earth. Any memories of these past lives are usually hidden from us by a veil of amnesia, though it is possible to penetrate the veil in certain cases, such as through hypnotic regression. As it turns out, some things we measure out to others are extreme enough that we cannot balance them out within one lifetime. Reincarnation is a system through which we can delay the repayment of these actions until we have reached a level of spiritual maturity at which these balancing experiences could become useful to us as souls.

CHAPTER SEVEN

Reincarnation

D id you ever live—in any form—before you were born? Will your life go on after your physical body dies? Do you only get one life to live, or does the process of soul evolution extend over multiple incarnations? Dr. Ian Stevenson, a University of Virginia professor of psychiatry at the School of Medicine, interviewed more than three thousand children from all over the world who remembered having lived before, often in great detail. This epic work took Stevenson more than forty years to complete. The children's memories were extremely specific, including names, dates, places, objects, and historical events—and even where and how they died. Dr. Stevenson thoroughly fact-checked what the children were telling him, with incredible persistence and attention to detail. and time after time, he discovered that their memories were astonishingly accurate. Aging relatives were tracked down, former homes were visited, old wounds were reopened, and the truth was systematically revealed. One girl from Lebanon remembered the full names and relationships of twenty-five different people from her alleged past life—even though neither she nor her family had ever met any of them before.[217] Dr. Jim Tucker, the medical director of the Child and Family Psychiatric Clinic at the University of Virginia, worked with Dr. Stevenson for years and continued his research. Dr. Tucker stated that "reincarnation is the most likely explanation for the strongest cases."[218]

In Dr. Tucker's book *Life After Life,* he presents a wealth of evidence from twenty-five hundred of Stevenson's best cases, as well as new profiles he investigated himself, and lets you make up your own mind. Children typically remember their past lives beginning around the age of two or three, and their memories usually fade by age seven or eight. In some cases, the children insisted on being called by their former names, and very specific details they gave about their former lives ended up being correct. As a professional child psychiatrist trained in the scientific method, Dr. Tucker is concerned with provable evidence. Many of the children had birthmarks or birth defects in the exact locations where their former selves had been mortally wounded. Dr. Tucker also used modern facial recognition software to confirm that these children looked like the people they claimed to have been before.[219] Dr. Jim Tucker is certainly aware of the hostility and skepticism of mainstream scientists on a subject like this. Genetics, biology, evolution, neurology, medicine, and many other revered concepts in our modern world—believed to be absolute laws of nature—have to be thoroughly reexamined and reworked in order to incorporate this new information.

If our "new" physical bodies bear a strong facial resemblance to who we were before, this suggests that there is an energetic aspect to who we are, as human beings, that carries over from one lifetime to another. This energetic aspect—in other words, the soul—is able to shape and mold our facial features as well as re-create a mortal wound with a birthmark or deformity. Therefore, the soul has a direct effect on the structure and function of our DNA. We have already seen energetic biology experiments in the lab that have confirmed that this is possible. A given organism can be restructured by energetics alone, such as in Dr. Peter Gariaev's experiment where he transformed frog eggs into salamander eggs. In the same way, our souls apparently transform the DNA of the body we incarnate into, so that our facial features remain identifiable from one life to the next. There will always be a blending between the hereditary facial features we inherit from our parents and the facial features of our deeper soul as we reincarnate from one life to the next. This gives us a scientific explanation for Dr. Jim Tucker's many documented cases where children remembered having been someone else in a previous life and their faces showed a match with their former incarnation using forensic software.

Children were far more likely to remember past lives in cultures that openly embraced reincarnation, suggesting that parents who do not believe in reincarnation may be passing up on a great opportunity when their children begin having unusual memories. Carol Bowman explored this concept in her 1998 classic, *Children's Past Lives: How Past Life Memories Affect Your Child.*[220] Her fascination with the subject began with a crisis: Her son was suffering from chronic eczema and a strong phobia of loud noises. Under hypnotic regression from Norman Inge, a clinical hypnotherapist, the child had a comprehensive memory of having fought in the Civil War. His account was extremely specific, and an expert historian was able to verify many details that the child should not have known. After the child remembered and healed this past trauma, his eczema and fear of loud noises completely disappeared. Carol Bowman then used this same process to heal her daughter from a chronic fear of the house burning down. Carol's focus in the first book is on using past-life regression to heal childhood phobias. Carol was soon deluged with letters from readers of her first book, providing her with a wealth of new cases that could be studied. One consistent theme she noticed in these letters was of people reincarnating into the same family, such as by reappearing as their own great-grandchildren. Through scientific investigation and follow-ups on the specific details, many of these cases were validated. This research was summarized in her second book, *Return from Heaven: Beloved Relatives Reincarnated Within Your Family.*[221]

The scientific research into reincarnation has proven that it is a genuine phenomenon beyond any reasonable doubt. The new science of a living universe provides us with extensive criteria to see life as fundamentally energetic in nature and to view the biological body as only a projection of this deeper, nonphysical aspect we all possess. Our facial features and birthmarks can apparently be directly sculpted by the energetic wave aspect of our DNA. Western society has often been very slow to embrace new ideas that go against mainstream thought. If a particular concept is not commonly understood to be true—particularly by most conventional scientists—it can take many years before it is widely accepted, even if the proof is extremely comprehensive.

Clearly, one of the strongest obstacles to a widespread embrace of reincarnation in the Western world is the Christian belief that it is not taught in the Bible. Even people in the Western world who do not actively practice Christianity are often still influenced by what I call the "subconscious Judeo-Christian bias." The prevailing modern Christian stance on reincarnation is another area in which political intrigue clearly seems to have obscured the truth, as it was a common belief in both the Old and New Testament.

Reincarnation and Christianity

Reincarnation invalidates the idea of a place of hideous torture that lasts for all eternity. If a soul doesn't master the lessons this world is ultimately meant to teach us within one lifetime, it will always have another chance. All souls consistently move through Gehenna—through the fires of purification—as they work toward the next level of human evolution. The knowledge of eternal forgiveness could be seen as a threat to entrenched power structures, such as the Roman Empire, which may well have wished to control the people as much as possible. In the Second Council of Constantinople, in A.D. 553, the Roman government officially declared that it was illegal to believe in or teach the concept of reincarnation. Failure to abide by this law would lead to banishment and excommunication, which in those days meant almost certain death. The exact edict reads, "If anyone asserts the fabulous pre-existence of souls, and shall assert the monstrous restoration which follows from it, let him be anathema [excommunicated]."[222] The point was further hammered home in A.D. 1274, when the Council of Lyons decreed that the soul goes promptly to Heaven or Hell after death. Then in A.D. 1439, the Council of Florence reaffirmed this edict with almost the exact same wording.

However, in the first century, the Jewish historian Flavius Josephus wrote that the Pharisees—a popular Jewish sect—believed in reincarnation. According to Josephus, the souls of people who live a positive life are "removed into other bodies" so they will have "power to revive and live again." The apostle Paul was a Pharisee prior to his conversion to Christianity. The Sadducees, a purist sect, rejected the concept of reincarnation and supported only the orthodox Jewish belief in *sheol*—the grave. Further historic evidence comes from Origen (A.D. 185–254), who is considered the first great father of the Christian church after Paul. Origen had extensive instruction from Clement of Alexandria. Clement, in turn, had studied directly with Peter, one of the original twelve apostles who traveled with Jehoshua. Origen inherited the direct, oral tradition of the teachings of Jehoshua and built a spiritual theology out of this knowledge. Reincarnation was a crucial aspect of Origen's theology. Both Origen and his teacher, Clement of Alexandria, wrote about receiving secret teachings from Jehoshua that were passed to them through the apostles. They ardently insisted that reincarnation and preexistence were one of Jehoshua's most important secret teachings. This quote from Origen summarizes his perspective nicely: "The soul has neither beginning nor end. . . . [Souls] come into this world strengthened by the victories or weakened by the defeats of their previous lives."[223]

Several Reincarnation References Made the Cut

The New Testament was assembled out of a variety of documents in the Council of Nicaea, headed by Emperor Constantine I of Rome, in A.D. 325. Since several gospels were not included, it is very likely that many references to reincarnation were removed in the process, but it was apparently such a popular concept that a variety of compelling quotes survived the cut. Several different authors have written entire books' worth of research just on this subject, though here we will give only a handful of the many examples of reincarnation they found. Our first quote is from Matthew 16:13–14, in which we see people openly speculating about who Jehoshua—the "Son of Man"—had been in other lifetimes: "'Who do people say the Son of Man is?' They replied, 'Some say

John the Baptist; others say Elijah; and still others, Jeremiah or one of the prophets.'"

In another revealing passage from the book of John (9:1–3), we see Jehoshua participate in a conversation with his disciples, in which reincarnation is spoken about as if it were an absolute, known fact.

> And as he was passing by, he saw a man blind from birth. And his disciples asked him, "Rabbi, who has sinned, this man or his parents, that he should be born blind?"
>
> Jesus answered, "Neither has this man sinned, nor his parents—but the works of God were to be made manifest in him."

How could a man have done anything—whether it was a sin or not—before he was born, if he had apparently never lived before? Jehoshua didn't stop and say, "Wait a minute, guys, that's a ridiculous question. How could this man have sinned before he was born?" Instead, he took the question in stride and revealed that in this particular case, the man apparently chose blindness as an incentive to turn his focus inward, so he would be more likely to embrace a spiritual path. This is another critical passage that survived the merciless edits to strip reincarnation out of the Bible. Jehoshua also directly confirmed that John the Baptist was the reincarnation of Elijah the prophet in Matthew 11:11–15. The phrase *he who has ears, let him hear* indicates that Jehoshua is revealing one of the secret teachings: "This is the one . . . there has not risen anyone greater than John the Baptist. . . . And if you are willing to accept it, he is the Elijah who was to come. He who has ears, let him hear."

In Luke 9:7–8, we find out that many people were actively trying to figure out who John the Baptist had been in a past life—in much the same way that tabloids follow the lives of celebrities in our modern world: "Now Herod the tetrarch heard about all that was going on. And he was perplexed, because some were saying that John had been raised from the dead, others that Elijah had appeared, and still others that one of the prophets of long ago had come back to life."

The Edgar Cayce Legacy

Any modern discussion of reincarnation and the cycles of history would be incomplete without mentioning the legacy of Edgar Cayce (1877–1945), who provided a wealth of verifiable information through intuitive means. With nothing more than the name and address of a client and an agreement that the client would be present at that same address during the session, Cayce would accurately diagnose the client's medical conditions and prescribe effective treatments. Problems with the physical body were often associated with spiritual issues, and advice was given that would treat the patient in body, mind, and spirit, in order that a full healing could be attainable. Cayce was not conscious as he performed these medical diagnoses and prescriptions. His team followed a careful protocol that allowed him to be hypnotized into a deep trance state by an associate. Once Cayce was fully unconscious, he began speaking and displayed seemingly omniscient intelligence. The "source" used language that was quite different from the way he spoke normally—and like the Law of One material, it was often hard to follow. Cayce was a devout Christian, and from the beginning his readings had a strong Christian focus, which admittedly makes this material off-putting to some readers.

Cayce, who was the first to coin the term *psychic readings* for the process he was conducting, was quoted in a *Birmingham* (Alabama) *Post-Herald* article as saying he had given 8,056 readings by October 10, 1922. Sadly, records of these readings were destroyed in a tragic house fire, and in many cases no written transcripts had been made. None of Cayce's readings were systematically preserved until September 10, 1923, when Gladys Davis joined the team as Cayce's full-time stenographer.[224] After that time, an additional 14,879 readings were conducted and documented—bringing the total to well over 22,000. That still leaves the period between October 1922 and September 1923 unaccounted for, and during this time, Cayce was experiencing a huge surge of publicity and clientele. In her epic scholarly work *Many Mansions,* Dr. Gina Cerminara estimated the actual number of Edgar Cayce readings to be about 25,000—a truly astonishing number.

Warner Books published *The Edgar Cayce Reader* in 1967, twenty-two years after Cayce's death.[225] In the introduction, it is noted that the ten books written about Cayce up to that time had "totaled more than a million in sales." In 1998, fifty-three years after the death of Cayce, Paul K. Johnson published a book called *Edgar Cayce in Context* with the State University of New York that offered the following opinion: "[Cayce] exerted a literary influence comparable to the greatest religious innovators of the last two centuries in America."[226] Cayce can also be given considerable credit for inspiring the New Age and holistic health movements of the 1960s, which have become increasingly mainstream over time.

In *Edgar Cayce in Context,* we find out that by May 1997, 646 books had been published on the subject of Edgar Cayce since 1950—compared to 542 books on Ellen G. White (one of the founders of the Seventh-Day Adventists), 264 on Joseph Smith (the founder of the Latter-Day Saint movement), and 121 on Helena Blavatsky (one of the founders of the Theosophical Society). Cayce didn't receive full national attention until the final years of his life, after Thomas Sugrue's biography, *There Is a River* was published in 1942.[227] This was followed by a September 1943 article entitled "Miracle Man of Virginia Beach" in *Coronet* magazine. Cayce was soon deluged with an estimated twenty-five thousand written letters requesting his help. There were so many letters that they had to be stacked and tied together with twine—and these bundles of mail lined the walls of his house, unopened.[228] Cayce began processing eight clients a day, every day, in an attempt to keep up with the demand—four in a morning session and four in the afternoon—even though his own readings warned him that this schedule was very dangerous for his health. Cayce's waiting list stretched on for a year and a half, even with this many slots, and his inability to say no to anyone caused him to quickly burn out. He ended up working himself to death by January 3, 1945, just a year and three months after the *Coronet* article came out. Many of the letters had included cash payments, and it took years for Cayce's surviving team to return everyone's money.

In a typical Cayce reading, some aspect of his subconscious mind apparently traveled directly to the person, could zoom in and out of the person's body to inspect, diagnose, and recommend treatment, and could go wherever else it was needed. In one dramatic example retold in the original Cayce biography *There is a River,* a Cayce reading prescribed "Oil of Smoke" for a boy with "a very obstinate leg sore." No pharmacists had ever heard of it, and they couldn't find it in any of their catalogs, which undoubtedly caused them to laugh at the whole idea. Another Cayce reading was taken, and this time it insisted the drug could be found at a particular pharmacy in Louisville, Kentucky. A message was wired to the store manager to request the drug, and he wired back, saying he'd never heard of it and did not have it in stock. Then, according to Dr. Wesley Harrington Ketchum, the next reading got very specific.

> We took a third reading. This time a shelf in the back of the Louisville drugstore was named. There, behind another preparation—which was named—would be found a bottle of "Oil of Smoke," so the reading said. I wired the information to the manager of the Louisville store. He wired me back, "Found it." The bottle arrived in a few days. It was old. The label was faded. The company which put it up had gone out of business. But it was just what he said it was, "Oil of Smoke." [229]

Skeptics have used the "oil of smoke" reference to attack Cayce's credibility through to this day, since it sounds vaguely similar to "snake oil." However, with further research, we find that "oil of smoke" was one name used for beechwood creosote in the years before Cayce's reading was given. [230] The US Department of Health and Human Services cites the following traditional uses for this remedy.

> Beechwood creosote has been used as a disinfectant, a laxative, and a cough treatment. In the past, treatments for leprosy, pneumonia, and tuberculosis also involved eating or

drinking beechwood creosote. It is rarely used today in the United States by doctors since it has been replaced by better medicines, and it is no longer produced by businesses in the United States. It is still available as an herbal remedy, and is used as an expectorant and a laxative in Japan. The major chemicals in beechwood creosote are phenol, cresols, and guaiacol.[231]

While Cayce was performing a reading, lying on a couch with his eyes closed, he would monitor the handwriting of his stenographer, Gladys Davis, as she took dictation and make corrections if she spelled something wrong.[232] When Cayce had clients there in the room with him, his source would often read their minds and answer the questions they were thinking of before they had a chance to speak them out loud.[233] Although Cayce spoke only English in his waking personality, his source also had complete conversations with his clients in their own native languages, or would pass on witty little sayings that made them laugh. Cayce is estimated to have spoken fluently in more than twenty-four different languages during his readings.[234] However, his source continually emphasized that all of us have the potential to do these things.

Cayce's medical advice often led to miracle healings in patients the medical establishment had written off, and his readings concocted successful medicines with ingredients no one had ever thought to use, like baking soda and castor oil for warts.[235] A Canadian Catholic priest was healed of epilepsy; arthritis was cured in a young high school graduate from Dayton, Ohio; a New York dentist's migraine headache that had hammered him for two years was completely eliminated in just two weeks; a mysterious and debilitating skin disorder known as scleroderma[236] was cured in a young female Kentucky musician after one year, despite her being written off as a hopeless case; and a Philadelphia boy with infant glaucoma, normally considered incurable, regained his full eyesight.[237]

Upon awakening, Cayce could not remember anything he had said, and the wording was often cryptic and awkward, using long run-on sentences with language resembling the King James Version of the Bible.[238] However, the readings also had a down-to-earth personality like Edgar's waking self, including a witty sense of humor.[239]

The Cayce Readings on Reincarnation

On August 10, 1923, Arthur Lammers was the first to ask Cayce's source whether he had ever lived on earth in previous lifetimes.[240] Much to his surprise, Lammers was told that Cayce had had three past lives, including one he spent as a monk, and that his current personality was strongly influenced by this former incarnation. This created a serious crisis for Edgar Cayce in his waking mind, as he was a devout Christian, and Christians did not believe in reincarnation. Cayce certainly did not want to contradict the official doctrines of the church. However, by this point he'd seen the effectiveness of his readings in helping people for more than twenty years, and he could not deny that they were genuinely beneficial. Over time, he came to accept that reincarnation was a reality as his readings gave extensive, detailed information about his clients' past lives after this initial breakthrough in 1923. The average person has probably had as many as thirty-five to forty different past lives, according to the Cayce readings.[241]

More than twenty-five hundred of Cayce's client readings dealt with past lives, and even if the readings were years apart, further analysis confirmed that the specifics always remained consistent. Obscure historical details included in the readings were found to be accurate. One client was told he had been a stool-dipper, and when Cayce looked up this term in an encyclopedia, not knowing what it was, he found out that it was an archaic expression for the early American custom of dunking people who were accused of being witches into cold water.[242]

Cayce's readings often gave the exact names of his clients in their prior lifetimes—and occasionally these names were verifiable. One of the most dramatic examples occurred with a Cayce client who had started out being legally blind but was able to restore partial sight in one of his eyes by following his reading's suggestions. This client was also very interested in railroads and the Civil War. When Cayce later gave him a "life reading," the client was told he had been Barnett Seay, a soldier in General Robert E. Lee's army in the South who had worked on the railroad and had lived in Henrico County, Virginia. The reading said that the records of Seay's life could still be found in Virginia. The client first visited Henrico County, Virginia, but was told by the clerk of the court that many records had been recently transferred to the Department of Old Records at the Virginia State Historical Library.[243] Eventually, through a careful search of these records, Cayce's client did find a record of a color-bearer in General Lee's army named Barnett Seay. The records specifically indicated that Seay had enlisted in 1862, when he was twenty-one years old.[244] This was certainly a unique name—and thus the likelihood that this was a coincidence was extremely small.

Group Reincarnations Organized in Cycles of History

Over time, Cayce's group became aware that certain patterns of places and times in history kept showing up in the past lives of people who received readings. This suggested the intriguing possibility that people in a given country or region may share a common heritage, reincarnating with others from their own society in a variety of geographical locations over time. Further study of the readings confirmed that this does indeed happen. Almost all of Cayce's clients were American Caucasians. One common example of a repeating pattern was that apparently the people from the lost civilization of Atlantis had mass-reincarnated in the United States. They apparently needed to reappear in a society that had enough advanced technology to allow them to re-create similar experiences as before, with the hope that they would use these resources more positively. This quote from Gina Cerminara's *Many Mansions* explains it well:

> Many people were given a similar historical background;
> in fact, the outline of people's past lives seemed almost to fall
> into a pattern. One common sequence was: Atlantis, Egypt,
> Rome, the Crusades period, and the early Colonial period.

Another was: Atlantis, Egypt, Rome, France in the time of Louis XIV, XV, or XVI, and the American Civil War. There were variations, of course—including China, India, Cambodia, Peru, Norseland, Africa, Central America, Sicily, Spain, Japan, and other places; but the majority of readings followed the same historic lines.

The reason for this, according to Cayce, was that souls of a given era in general incarnate in a later era together. In the intervening centuries, other groups of souls are on earth—taking their turn, so to speak. This proceeds with orderly and rhythmic alternation, almost like the shifts of laborers in a factory. Consequently most of the souls on earth today were also together in previous ages of history. Also, souls related to each other closely by family ties, friendship ties, or the ties of mutual interests were likely to have been related before in similar ties in previous eras—and most of the people securing readings from Cayce were, in some such way, related.[245]

It would be difficult to scientifically prove that this is true, considering that most of our scientific proof for reincarnation has come from children accurately remembering their alleged past lives. The children may remember who they were before, but they usually are not aware of greater patterns in the living cosmos that may be governing their incarnations in "orderly and rhythmic alteration." However, the Cayce readings proved their accuracy in so many different ways that the burden of proof has been satisfied. The data has stood the test of time and is still considered highly trustworthy by open-minded scholars. Reincarnation may be one of the main reasons why history seems to keep repeating in very precise cycles—as we will see. Gina Cerminara shared the Cayce perspective on the cycles of history in this next quotation: "Every period of our history has the appropriate tools needed for us to alleviate our karma."[246]

The Cayce readings did speak about the 25,920-year "Grand Cycle of the Ages," as well as the Ages of the Zodiac—and thus directly supported the idea of these cycles forming an energetic structure for reincarnation to occur. These organized, repeating patterns of events allow for souls to reincarnate in groups—knowing what to expect, and when. Souls are able to work out collective karma as well as individual karma by reappearing in large groups. As societies, they keep running through the same story line, with the same people, again and again, until they master the lessons they are being shown. This will become much clearer as we discuss the Hero's Journey story in chapter 9. Obviously, if history is cyclical, there is a reason for it, and it would be a very good idea for us to try to understand it. If there is a script we are following, then we need to master it so these wars and atrocities do not keep repeating.

Specific Examples of Past-Life Karma

Through a series of specific examples, the Cayce readings shed a great deal of light on the reason and necessity for reincarnation. It quickly becomes clear that our actions do have consequences, and when we are sufficiently unloving toward someone, we may not be ready to experience similarly painful events in our own lives until a later incarnation. Our soul may not administer the strongest forms of karma until it feels we are mature enough, on a spiritual level, to avoid becoming even more negative from having had that experience. Then, the karma we experience is not necessarily an exact duplicate of what we created for someone else, but it is at least symbolically related to the original hurt or injury we caused. *Many Mansions* by Gina Cerminara, a doctor of psychology, gives a host of fascinating examples she found in her study of more than twenty-five hundred "life readings."

For example, a college professor who was born blind was able to restore 10 percent vision in his left eye through Cayce's prescribed treatments, despite restoration being considered hopeless by medical specialists. He was later told that in a Persian lifetime from approximately 1000 B.C., he was part of a barbaric tribe that blinded its enemies with red-hot irons—and it was his job to do the blinding.[247] This is an interesting case, because it shows that the Cayce readings did not feel this man needed to continue being blind in order to work off his karma. Once he became aware of what had happened and what he needed to understand to forgive himself, he was able to gain knowledge that directly improved his condition.

Another Cayce client was a forty-year-old woman who began sneezing whenever she ate bread and cereal grains. She also developed excruciating nerve pains in her left side whenever she touched shoe leather and the plastic rims of glasses, among other materials. No doctors had been able to help her. A series of hypnotic treatments when she was twenty-five years old had caused these problems to disappear for six years, but then they returned. Her Edgar Cayce reading told her she had been a chemist in a past life and had created chemicals that caused people to itch, apparently very badly. She also had allegedly developed chemicals that could be breathed into someone's face and would poison them. Her choice of "karmic alleviation" was to have these bizarre, debilitating allergies in a later lifetime. Her Cayce reading also said that the types of chemicals she was allergic to were directly related to the chemicals and substances she had used to torture and kill others, including a leather pouch that held the poison.[248]

Another client was told that he had been an escort and protector to King Louis XIII of France and had excessively overeaten. As a result, when he came to Cayce as a thirty-five-year-old man, he had been through a lifetime of digestive problems requiring him to wait several hours to digest a meal. He could eat only certain foods in certain combinations.[249]

In another separate case that Cerminara refers to as "symbolic karma," a physician sought a reading for his young boy, who had suffered from anemia since early childhood. Apparently, five lifetimes earlier, this boy had an incarnation during which he had seized power by brute force in Peru and had shed much blood in order to establish his dictatorship. The anemia had left him very weak in his current incarnation—a far cry from the physical power and strength he had enjoyed before.[250] An asthma sufferer, constantly having to deal with shortness of breath, was told he had pressed the life out of others in another lifetime, causing them to asphyxiate. A client suffering from total deafness was told that he had refused to listen to others who needed help—on a life-and-death basis—when he was a nobleman during the blood-soaked French Revolution.[251]

Mocking People Is Not Such a Good Idea

Jehoshua said that simply calling someone a fool is enough to ignite the Gehenna fire and necessitate purification. Insults like this may seem very minor, particularly on the Internet. Nonetheless, the Cayce readings revealed that mocking others can carry strong karmic repercussions, particularly if those people are suffering or dying in the process. Chapter 5 in Cerminara's book is entitled "The Karma of Mockery." Seven different cases are documented in which people with severe disabilities were told they had mocked others with the same or similar disabilities in other lifetimes. Six of these cases were tied to the horrific Roman persecutions of Christians, in which gruesome deaths were seen as entertainment. Three of these karmic cases involved polio, where the clients had previously laughed at people who were crippled as they were tortured to death in the Roman coliseum, perhaps by hungry lions.[252] One woman laughed as she watched a girl get ripped open on her side by the claws of a lion in Rome. She returned with tuberculosis of the hip joint, making her unable to walk.[253] Another woman was quite overweight due to a glandular imbalance. She was told that she had been a beautiful Roman athlete two lifetimes earlier and had routinely mocked people who were overweight.[254] Another client was told he had been a cartoonist in the French court and had greatly enjoyed exposing homosexual scandals, only to come back with powerful homosexual urges himself in his current lifetime.[255] This next quote from Gina Cerminara's *Many Mansions* reveals how expensive criticism can be from a karmic standpoint:

> Although it costs nothing in terms of money, criticism may be a very expensive amusement in terms of the psychological price that must someday be paid. The source of information, as Edgar Cayce called his power, from its vantage

point of seeing cause and consequence over long spans of time, frequently gave sharp and explicit warning to people who erred conspicuously in this direction.[256]

Karma Is Memory

An eleven-year-old boy had had a chronic bed-wetting problem since the age of two, and his parents had spent many years working with doctors in an attempt to find a cure, all to no avail. His parents were told he had been a Christian preacher in the early Puritan years and had been a stool-dipper—punishing people suspected of witchcraft by repeatedly ducking them underwater while they were strapped to a stool.[257] These tortures usually led to the suspect's drowning. If the person survived the process, it was believed that this was due to their supernatural power as witches. They were then put to death anyway because their powers had been exposed.

Interestingly, the treatment prescribed by the readings to help heal this boy of his chronic bed-wetting problem was for his mother to repeat certain affirmative statements to him—in a slow, monotonous voice—as he was falling asleep: "'You are good and kind. You are going to make many people happy. You are going to help everyone with whom you come in contact.'"[258]

The boy did not wet the bed that night—for the first time in nearly nine years. The mother continued repeating these suggestions each night for several months, and the problem never returned. Gradually she was able to reduce the treatment down to only once a week and eventually was able to stop it altogether, without ever having the problem repeat itself. This woman was not inclined to believe in a fairy tale—she was a lawyer and a trusted staff member who worked for a district attorney. As the boy grew older, he became exceptionally tolerant of others and went from being an extreme introvert to a "perfectly well-adjusted extrovert" on the Johnson O'Connor Human Engineering Laboratory test.

Cerminara therefore concludes that one significant aspect of karma is a psychological holdover of the guilt and shame we feel from actions performed in other lifetimes. The Cayce readings often said that karma is a function of memory, and the key to breaking this cycle is to forgive ourselves for what we may have done to others in the past. "In forgiveness lies the stoppage of the wheel of karma." Forgiving ourselves can be just as important as—if not more important than—forgiving others. Consciously, we may not remember any of our past lives, but apparently our subconscious has an ongoing, robust knowledge of exactly who we have been—and what we did that hurt others. Many of us end up punishing ourselves, subconsciously, well beyond the point where the necessary balance would have been achieved in the absolute sense. This is a very significant point in the Cayce readings, one that most people discussing reincarnation and karma are not familiar with. Once you can truly love and accept yourself and treat others with respect, you can balance out your karma and eliminate a vast amount of needless suffering. Genuinely shameless people, such as sociopaths, are not exempt from karma either. Free will is an absolute standard of balance that we all must work through.

Suspended Karma

Chapter 7 in Gina Cerminara's book deals with another interesting subject: suspended karma. The Cayce readings revealed that if we seriously infringe on the free will of someone else, it may take centuries for the right situation to come along to balance that karma. Even more important, we have to become strong enough, from a spiritual standpoint, to be able to work through the situation without suffering even more and creating additional hurts for others that would then require even more karma to balance. Though this concept may seem quite disturbing on a conscious level, there is apparently nothing we can do about it other than to bravely and honorably work through the challenges we face. No matter how much we may rage at the seeming injustice we are going through, on the spiritual level we will inevitably carry through with our karma and pay off our debts. Every effort is made to ensure that these debts are not paid off any faster than we can handle and ultimately benefit from.

Gina Cerminara stated the underlying teaching of the Cayce readings very clearly in *Many Mansions:* "Not all people are sufficiently evolved spiritually to be capable of achieving in one lifetime that all-consuming, all-embracing love which is the essence of the true Christ-consciousness— and thus achieve liberation from the debt of karma."[259]

Past Lives Strongly Influence Our Personalities

It is also surprising to discover how much of our waking personalities can be affected by what we apparently experienced in our past lives, according to the Cayce readings. In one case, an extremely prejudiced white supremacist had been imprisoned, tortured, and beaten to death by black soldiers in another lifetime, and his hatred of all people of color carried through multiple lifetimes. An anti-Semitic newspaper columnist had a past-life experience as a Samaritan in Palestine, in which she was frequently and violently attacked by her Jewish neighbors. A thirty-eight-year-old unmarried woman could not trust men on a very deep level and was never able to form lasting relationships. She had been deserted by her husband in an earlier lifetime when he went off to join the Crusades.[260]

A woman with an exceptional tolerance of other religions had earlier been a Crusader among Islamic people and found that they were kind, merciful, courageous, and idealistic. This had such a positive impact on her that her sense of religious tolerance carried through into multiple future lifetimes. Another Cayce client was severely distrustful of all religion and had once participated in the Crusades, where he was highly disgusted by the difference he saw between people's religious ideals and their actions.

Why the Veiling Between Lives Is Necessary

On page 119 of *Many Mansions,* Dr. Cerminara addresses a frequent complaint from people who oppose these theories of reincarnation. They may feel that it is not fair to be held responsible for something you did in another lifetime of which you have no direct conscious memory. If this other person represents a different personality—with different parents, different influences, a different culture, and different experiences—then why should you be held responsible in the here and now for what he or she did in another lifetime? Apparently, the answer is that the personality we enjoy in our waking, conscious mind is only a small portion of our eternal identity. Much of who we really are is veiled from us, as this next quote from Gina Cerminara reveals: "The eternal identity—like an actor offstage—can remember all its past, but as soon as it takes on a personality, as an actor takes on a role, then it is prevented by a protective provision of nature from remembering anything but the sum totals or the principles which [it] had learned before."[261]

This is called "the veiling" in the Law of One series, and it is a very important point. Our current level of existence, "third density," is referred to as "the Choice." In order to graduate into fourth density, we must clearly choose between the path of service to others or the path of service to self. The unified mind of the galaxy is referred to as "the Logos." If we were consciously aware of the existence of the Logos and of the grand design for our soul evolution, we wouldn't learn anything. The veiling makes it difficult, but certainly not impossible, for us to see the truth.

21.9 It is necessary for the third-density entity to forget [its past lives]—so that the mechanisms of confusion or free will may operate upon the newly individuated consciousness complex.[262]

77.14 Above this [third] density there remains the recognition of the architecture of the Logos—but without the veils which are so integral a part of the process of making the choice in third density.[263]

81.32 Question: I am assuming that in this particular [cycle of the universe's existence,] the experiment of the veiling

and the extending of free will must have started, roughly, simultaneously in many, many of the budding or building galactic systems. Am I in any way correct with this assumption?

Answer: . . . You are precisely correct.[264]

82.29 To cross that threshold [from third to fourth den-
sity] is difficult. There is resistance at the edge, shall we say,
of each density. The faculty of faith or will needs to be understood, nourished, and developed in order to have an entity
which seeks past the boundary of third density. Those entities
which do not do their homework, be they ever so amiable,
shall not cross.[265]

83.18 The penetration of the veil may be seen to begin to
have its roots in the gestation of green-ray activity—that all-
compassionate love which demands no return. If this path is
followed, the higher energy centers shall be activated and
crystallized until the adept is born. Within the adept is the
potential for dismantling the veil to a greater or lesser
extent—that all may be seen again as one. The other-self is
primary catalyst in this particular path to the piercing of the
veil—if you would call it that.[266]

Groups of People Keep Reincarnating Together

The people you know and love—as well as those you bicker and argue
with—may very well have been with you many times before. Cerminara
summarized this Cayce teaching very eloquently and succinctly: "No
marriage is a start on a clean slate. It is an episode in a serial story begun
long before."[267]

So much of our present lives are influenced by the past that apparently no major relationship we have with anyone—whether a friend,
family member, or romantic partner—is a first-time involvement. We are
intuitively drawn to the same people we have lived with many times

before, in order to continually work through our issues. The classic book *The Egyptian Heritage* by Mark Lehner is a highly comprehensive examination of the Egyptian/Atlantean period, in which more than two hundred of Cayce's closest associates had appeared. The amount of detail given about this period, from dozens of different client readings, is stunning—as is the process of seeing how these various characters reincarnated in subsequent lifetimes.[268]

The Lives of Edgar Cayce by W. H. Church is one of the most fascinating books on the Cayce readings—and their perspective on reincarnation—despite being somewhat difficult to read.[269] In it, Church traces the fascinating story of how the people in Cayce's life had been incarnating with him, again and again, in a variety of contexts. Thirteen different past lives of Edgar Cayce are presented—twelve directly from his readings and another from his dreams. Additionally, two future incarnations are presented: one in which he appears in Virginia Beach in 1998, and another in which he appears in A.D. 2158.

Cayce's full list of his own past-life names is: King Asapha, a spiritual ruler in Egypt approximately fifty thousand years ago; the revered Egyptian priest-king Ra-Ptah, who allegedly designed the Great Pyramid with Thoth-Hermes; an unnamed angelic messenger who appeared to warn the people of Sodom; the Persian warrior-king Uhjltd, lost to the pages of history; the Greek soldier Xenon, who committed suicide in a moment of extreme terror; the famous scholar and father of geometry, Pythagoras; the Greek chemist Armitidides, who knew Alexander the Great; Lucius of Cyrene, who wrote the book of Luke in the Bible; an unnamed Arawak Indian on Hispaniola; two incarnations of the self-serving Englishman John Bainbridge (as grandfather and grandson within the same family), who was an alcoholic and used his psychic abilities to cheat at cards; Ralph Dahl, the illegitimate son of Louis XIV's daughter Gracia, who was murdered at age five to prevent a male heir from reaching the throne; a Civil War soldier from the United States; an unnamed lifetime in 1998; and an unnamed lifetime in 2158.[270]

One of many interesting things we see in this timeline of lifetimes is how the soul rises and falls in its level of maturity and evolution. Traumatic events, such as the suicide as Xenon, and other negative events in the lifetime as the Arawak Indian can have a ripple effect that requires multiple incarnations to peacefully resolve.

The John Bainbridge incarnations are consistently the most surprising of the Cayce history of past lives, when seen in context with the historical figures he was also alleged to have been. At two different times in the 1700s, he incarnated as an Englishman from the same family, and sailed to America to explore the new frontier. He was a gambler, womanizer, and hard drinker, and he used his psychic abilities to cheat at playing cards as well as the shell game. Apparently he enjoyed this lifestyle so much that he reincarnated a second time to repeat the same self-serving behaviors. This accrued a great deal of karma, but his soul created an opportunity for him to resolve it in a most dramatic way. At the end of his life there was a terrible famine. He could feel himself dying of starvation; he knew that the food he had with him was the very last he could find, and it wouldn't sustain him for long.

He noticed a child who was starving—a young boy—and had a complete heart opening of compassion for him. Bainbridge realized that if he gave the boy his food, the boy might have a chance to survive—or, at the very least, he wouldn't suffer as much. Bainbridge gave the boy the very last of his food, for which the boy was extremely grateful and cried—and Bainbridge cried as well. He died soon afterward. The Cayce readings spoke very fondly of this moment, saying that in this one gesture of selfless service—giving up his own life so that a younger person might live—he erased two lifetimes' worth of negative karma. This is obviously an extreme case, and there are much gentler ways to alleviate karma, but for some souls, aggressive methods like this are preferable. This selfless service directly paved the way for the soul to regain what it had lost, in terms of its overall level of maturity and soul evolution—and made it possible for much greater psychic gifts to appear in the subsequent lifetime of Edgar Cayce.

The data linking these stories together bridges more than twenty years' worth of readings, for dozens of different clients within Cayce's inner circle. The study of all the different configurations that occur from one lifetime to another is massive. Each of us definitely appears to have a "soul group" we keep reincarnating with again and again. We are reacquainted with our soul group each time we transition into the afterlife. Understanding this mysterious in-between point is vital to our exploration of synchronicity, the cycles of history, and reincarnation. The amount of information available on the afterlife is far more specific and detailed than most people are aware of. Learning the likely truth of what happens to us after we die can be a profoundly useful insight for our own daily lives as we gain a greater understanding of the purpose we are here to fulfill, and how the synchronicities and karmic events in our lives are being managed behind the scenes.

CHAPTER EIGHT

Mapping Out the Afterlife

I f reincarnation is a scientific fact, recognized in many of the great world religions, then does anything actually happen as we transition between one life and the next? Do we simply pop out of one body and pop into another, with no consciousness or experience in between? Or is there an elaborate afterlife we go through, complete with a full set of experiences that help us plan out our next incarnation? Does the "veil" lift in between lives? Do we step into a fuller level of who we really are? Do we now have a comprehensive understanding of what we're hoping to learn from our lifetimes in the different cycles of history on earth? Do we formulate a game plan for how we can learn our lessons and penetrate the veil in future incarnations? This is another area in which scientific research has shed key light on the destiny we all must eventually face.

Clinical death involves a cessation of the heartbeat, of breathing, and of all brain-wave activity. Without brain waves, the thinking mind should cease to exist—at least in conventional biology. Once you are brain-dead, no electrical activity occurs in the brain whatsoever. Conventional scientists believe this electrical activity is the root of consciousness—and without it, you have no thoughts. Nonetheless, many people report a continuing set of experiences that occur after they have been declared clinically dead and are then successfully resuscitated and returned to their bodies. Even if someone has no prior knowledge of any reports of an afterlife, there are remarkable similarities in the reports found all over the world. Dr. Sam Parnia and his associates at the University of Southampton examined a wide variety of professional scientific studies into near-death experiences, or NDEs, and found many commonalities among them. "A number of recent scientific studies carried out by independent researchers have demonstrated that 10–20 percent of people who go through cardiac arrest and clinical death report lucid, well-structured thought processes, reasoning, memories and sometimes detailed recall of events during their encounter with death."[271]

Dr. Pim van Lommel, a cardiologist in the Netherlands, conducted the largest hospital-based study of NDEs, years after hearing a patient report seeing a tunnel, a light, and beautiful colors and hearing wonderful music during a clinical death in 1969. This was a full seven years before *Life After Life,* Dr. Raymond Moody's groundbreaking book on the near-death experience, first appeared. Dr. van Lommel didn't investigate NDEs any further until 1986, after he read a stunningly detailed NDE story that took place while a person was clinically dead for a full six minutes.

After reading [this] book I started to interview my patients who had survived a cardiac arrest. To my great surprise, within two years about fifty patients told me about their NDE. . . . So, in 1988 we started a prospective study of 344 consecutive survivors of cardiac arrest in ten Dutch hospitals. . . . 62 patients (18%) reported some recollection of the time of clinical death. . . . About 50% of the patients with an NDE reported awareness of being dead, or had positive emotions, 30% reported moving through a tunnel, had an observation of a celestial landscape, or had a meeting with deceased relatives. About 25% of the patients with an NDE had an out-of-body experience, had communication with "the light," or observed colours, 13% experienced a life review, and 8% experienced a border. . . .

Patients with an NDE did not show any fear of death, they strongly believed in an afterlife, and their insight in what is important in life had changed: love and compassion for oneself, for others, and for nature. They now understood the cosmic law that everything one does to others will ultimately be returned to oneself: hatred and violence as well as love and compassion. Remarkably, there was often evidence of increased intuitive feelings.[272]

Dr. van Lommel's study of these sixty-two cases of near-death experience reveals that we do seem to know who we are and what we are really doing here when we move into the afterlife. We are fully aware of the law of karma and that we are here to learn to love each other. We may often regret the unloving things we have done, but we are very focused on coming back to repeat the same lessons again, in the hopes of learning to open our hearts.

The website Near-Death.com features an impressive list of fifty-one different proofs for the reality of near-death experiences.[273] In the studies of Dr. Kenneth Ring, people reported witnessing real events that occurred during the time of their clinical death. Some of these events were happening right there in the operating room as their brain-wave activity, heartbeat, and respiration had gone completely flat. In other cases, they successfully observed and remembered things that happened at distances that were significantly far away from where their physical body had been. They were able to bring back specific memories of things people said and did around them that could later be proven correct. Most surprisingly, some people actually appeared in front of their loved ones as ghosts— partially visible images of their former selves. They were able to have full conversations with their loved ones in this ghostly form. Both the patient and the family member having the same conversation—after the patient was resuscitated.[274]

This data is extremely compelling. We already use eyewitness testimony to establish proof in a court of law. Eyewitness testimony can sentence someone to life in prison or even to death. However, in the case of phenomena like near-death experiences, eyewitness testimony is consistently ignored, overlooked, or attacked with dubious-sounding and often ridiculous skeptical explanations. These attacks are much more akin to religious zealotry—from the atheist's perspective—than they are to the spirit of true science, in which the results of the data lead the investigation.

Dr. Michael Newton Builds a Model of the Afterlife

In time, Dr. Michael Newton may be seen as one of the most influential researchers of the twentieth century. Dr. Newton began working as a hypnotist in 1947, when he was only fifteen years old. Dr. Newton became a specialist in treating various psychological disorders through hypnotic suggestion, a technique used to help change behavioral patterns that were not in the client's best interest for common goals such as losing weight and stopping smoking. Occasionally, Dr. Newton's clients asked him if he could bring them back to a past life, but he always refused. He was an ardent skeptic and did not believe in reincarnation or the afterlife. However, Dr. Newton's perspective began to change while he worked with a young man who had experienced chronic pain on his right side throughout his entire life. Under hypnosis, the man was directed to make the pain worse. This is a common technique that helps a client learn to manage and control his overall pain levels. This client consistently used the image of being stabbed as he performed this exercise. Dr. Newton probed for the origin of this stabbing symbolism and the man told him, without hesitation, that he had been killed by a bayonet in France in a previous life during World War I. The detail was intriguing, and Dr. Newton's own clients encouraged him to pursue this direction with them further: "Initially I was concerned that a subject's integration of current needs, beliefs, and fears would create fantasies of recollection. However, it didn't take long before I realized our deep-seated memories offer a set of past experiences which are too real and connected to be ignored."[275]

Newton explains that people under hypnosis are not dreaming or hallucinating—and in this state they are not capable of lying. They report whatever they see and hear in their subconscious minds as if everything is a literal observation. While under hypnosis, it is possible for them to misinterpret something they are seeing, but they will not report on anything they do not feel to be the literal truth.

> I learned the value of careful cross-examination early in my work—and I found no evidence of anyone faking their spiritual experiences to please me. In fact, subjects in hypnosis are not hesitant in correcting my misinterpretations of their statements. . . . As my case files grew, I discovered by trial and error to phrase questions about the spirit world in a proper sequence.[276]
>
> I also found that it did not matter if a person was an atheist, deeply religious, or believed in any philosophical persuasion in between—once they were in the proper superconscious state of hypnosis, all were consistent in their reports. . . . I built up a high volume of cases. . . . While these years of specialized research into the spirit world rolled on, I worked practically in seclusion. . . . I even stayed out of metaphysical bookstores because I wanted absolute freedom from outside bias.[277]

One of Dr. Newton's interesting observations was that when people are brought into the "superconscious" state, they do not want to reveal much detail about their experiences in the afterlife. They tend to be evasive—as if they are following a code of ethics telling them that we, in the living world, are supposed to have only limited access to their knowledge. Dr. Newton gradually learned the pattern of experiences everyone went through, and by developing a familiarity with their world, he was able to speak on their terms. This allowed his clients to trust him enough that they would feel comfortable in sharing what they knew. Dr. Newton became quite surprised to discover that there was incredible consistency in these reports. In fact, clients who never met each other in waking life often used the same words, colloquial sayings, graphic descriptions, and expressions for things they encountered in the afterlife.[278] This, coupled with the fact that everyone went through the same stages of events in the same order, suggested that we all know the afterlife very well once we are hypnotized into the superconscious state.

Interestingly, Dr. Newton discovered that no one client was able to take him through all of the stages he had identified.[279] The clients seemed to jump into a certain stage of the process and stay there or progress forward through a few others. Dr. Newton's complete overview of the journey through the afterlife had to be built up by interviewing many different clients. A great deal of clinical experience and research, spanning many years, went into his overall model.

Newton's first book, *Journey of Souls,* guides us through ten distinct stages from initial death to final reincarnation: Death and Departure, Gateway to the Spirit World, Homecoming, Orientation, Transition, Placement, Life Selection, Choosing a New Body, Preparation and Embarkation, and Rebirth.[280] Life Selection and Choosing a New Body are technically two halves of the same stage in Dr. Newton's model and occur in the same relative location in the afterlife, but the experiences are different enough that a separate chapter is dedicated to each of them. The overall body of information Dr. Newton has provided is both highly fascinating and essential to understanding the greater reality we live in, so we will now review each of these stages and the experiences we will all encounter along the way.

Stage One: Death and Departure

You find yourself floating over your body. You see people around your body who are grieving your death. You often find yourself trying to convince them—without success—that you are still there, only in another form. Soon you feel a pulling sensation that draws you away from your body. There is an ecstatic feeling of freedom and brilliant light. Some people see the light all around them, while others see it in the distance and feel pulled toward it. This is what creates the commonly reported effect of moving through a dark tunnel with a light at the end.[281]

Some people are not interested in staying near their bodies after their physical death. They feel the strong pull of the afterlife and do not want to wait around to experience it. Many others will stay around the earth for a few days of our time, until shortly after their funerals. Dr. Newton's participants have revealed that they have a greatly accelerated sense of time in the afterlife, and what we think of as days may take only minutes to pass by for them.[282] Most people are not interested in seeing themselves buried—as they do not experience emotions like we do—but they do appreciate the respect and tributes their friends pay them.

At this stage, people may also report specific factual details of who they were and where they lived. Dr. Newton says that the average person has an astonishing ability to reveal dates and geographic locations of past lives, which can often be verified. Even though the borders of nations and the names of places change over time, the specific details have consistently proven to be correct.[283] This mirrors the results that Dr. Ian Stevenson and Dr. Jim Tucker obtained in their own exhaustive reincarnation research as well as the results seen in the Cayce readings.

Stage Two: Gateway to the Spirit World

The second phase Dr. Newton cataloged—the Gateway to the Spirit World—is where we see the dark tunnel, enter it, and reach the light at the end. Not everyone experiences this sequence of events the same way. Some see the tunnel appear right over their bodies, while others have to fly high above the earth before they can enter it, but in most cases the tunnel appears quickly after we leave the earth. Only the most disturbed spirits attempt to stay near their bodies for any length of time. Younger souls with fewer past lives may take a little longer to head out than more experienced souls, who tend to move on quickly.

The common stereotype, in which a person ends up in a flowing field of tall grass or wildflowers as soon as he or she leaves the tunnel, with all his or her friends and relatives there, did happen in some cases but was by no means a standard. However, everyone seems to experience a spectacularly inspiring set of visions at this point. Most people are somewhat confused when they first emerge and are not sure how to interpret the forms, colors, and energies they are seeing. It will often take you time to understand and explain what you are seeing in any tangible manner to the hypnotist. Almost immediately after their death, most people do hear beautiful music or sound vibrations—which continue to be audible as they move through the early stages of their entry into the afterlife.

Others report seeing layers of energy in which different activities seem to be happening.

Case five in Dr. Newton's book is a man who reported seeing an absolutely gigantic and incredibly beautiful vision as soon as he came out of the tunnel. He witnessed a staggeringly large "ice palace" made of gorgeous crystals. He said that most of the crystals were grayish or white but that he also saw colors in glittering mosaics. He could see no end to this gorgeous city; as he kept looking, it seemed to stretch on forever. The sheer size, scope, and grandeur of what he was seeing didn't even seem possible.[284] Although each of us may have a completely different vision, whatever we see is invariably a majestic sight. We may see stunning castle towers in the distance, beautiful rainbows in a vast blue sky, or colorful fields. Interestingly, these scenes seem to stay consistent over the course of many lifetimes for a soul. Dr. Newton has observed that these scenes often relate to beloved memories from our physical lives—such as "an unforgotten home, school, garden, mountain, or seashore"—in order to help us feel familiar and comfortable when we arrive in the spirit world.[285] This is the only part of our journey that has so much variety. After we move through this stage, our observations become much more standardized.[286]

We also find out, at this point in the book, that we do not immediately become omniscient after death. We may still be confused, sad, bewildered, and traumatized by what has happened. If we experience sadness and confusion at this point, we are generally approached by our main guide in the afterlife. This is a very loving and supportive person who then helps us move through our initial greeting and orientation. Our guide helps us work through whatever emotions we are feeling with patience and expertise. Younger souls are more apt to be greeted this way, whereas more experienced souls will remember where they are and know where they are going. Even in cases where people are still experiencing trauma, they are quite fascinated by the beauty and the majesty of what they see all around them.

Stage Three: Homecoming

Stage three in Dr. Newton's mapping of the afterlife is called Homecoming. This is when we are more formally greeted into the spirit world, not just by our initial guide, but by others who are close to us. These people often appear as masses of luminous energy, but they can project faces we are familiar with in order to help ease us into our new surroundings. The face of a former lifetime is only one of a theoretically limitless number of different forms a soul can take on in the afterlife, since our energetic bodies are completely thought responsive.

Another very interesting thing Dr. Newton discovered in his research, which is more fully explained in his second volume, *Destiny of Souls,* is that we will see people we know who are still alive on earth as well. Even if their physical bodies are alive, they also have an energetic body that remains in the afterlife the entire time. This is quite different from most people's view of reincarnation. Again and again, Dr. Newton's clients revealed that we project only a certain percentage of our total essence into the human form at any one time—the rest remains in the afterlife to guide and watch over what we are doing. This is explained in Dr. Newton's second book, *Destiny of Souls,* in the section entitled "Soul Division and Reunification."[287] The average, less-advanced soul will put between 50 and 70 percent of its energy into a physical body, whereas more advanced souls will never transfer more than 25 percent.[288]

Dr. Newton explains that the volume of energy we put in is less important than the overall quality and refinement of the wisdom and experience of the soul—and therefore, more mature souls do better by using less of their energy, as it leaves them with more flexibility in the afterlife. Some highly ambitious souls also divide themselves into two or even three simultaneous physical incarnations on earth, in the hope of dramatically speeding up their evolution, and may only leave 10 percent of their soul's energy behind in the afterlife. Once you commit to a path like this, you have to carry through with it for the entire length of time your body or bodies are alive on the physical planet. Dr. Newton discovered that most souls quickly see the folly in this path, are warned not to do it by their guides, and will not attempt it more than once or twice before deciding that it is not a good idea. This, of course, also means that overlaps, in which a soul will project itself into a new body well before an existing incarnation has faded out, can and do occur. This upsets most people's idea of a linear, one-to-one schedule of reincarnation, if they've ever taken the time to think about these concepts.

We also find out that if a soul were to project 100 percent of its energy into a body, it would literally fry the electrochemical circuits of the brain. Furthermore, the brain would be totally subjugated to the power of the soul, and this would eliminate the veiling referred to in the Law of One series as a necessary aspect of our evolution. Without spiritual amnesia, we would not have the potential to grow; we would come into our physical incarnation on earth already knowing everything.

Therefore, you will invariably see the people you know and love the most when you go through the Homecoming phase, even if they are still alive on earth. There is a lot of hugging and crying and an incredible feeling of love, acceptance, and belonging at this stage. This has a tremendously positive effect on us and greatly eases our passage into this new world. Also, at this point we begin very clearly remembering multiple lifetimes we have shared with each of these people. All our lifetimes start to blend together as we realize how many different times we've incarnated and interacted with the same folks.[289]

However, if we have committed atrocities toward others, such as murders, or toward ourselves, such as suicide, then we may go off to be alone with our guide to rehabilitate and quickly plan out our next incarnation. This is all discussed in *Journey of Souls,* chapter 4, "The Displaced Soul."[290] People who go through this process are always treated with patience and love, not the fiery world of torment and purgatory in which most people have been taught to believe.[291] However, they do end up reviewing and reliving the ways in which they hurt others, and they experience it from the other side as a direct reliving of how they made others feel by their actions. The Law of One series clearly reveals that suicide is a very bad idea. It creates the need for a great deal of healing work and a renewed dedication to go through the same lessons again in a subsequent lifetime—hopefully without committing suicide the next time.[292] Violent, unethical acts require us to choose difficult life events that we hope will balance out our karma if we handle them lovingly. If we do come into the afterlife with this type of significant damage, we can spend quite an extended amount of time in isolation before getting the opportunity to again mix with our friends and loved ones. Further-more, once we are allowed back into our group, we are then closely su-pervised.[293]

In case ten, one of Dr. Newton's clients reported on a man who had terribly hurt a girl during his most recent life and as a result did not re-connect with his soul group. He had to go through "extensive private study" with his guide and quickly chose to reincarnate as a woman who was physically abused and treated with cruelty. This helped him appreci-ate and understand what it feels like to go through these experiences, so he would be far less inclined to hurt others in subsequent lifetimes.[294] This man was not judged by his guide—in the afterlife, we are well aware of what our goals are in the physical plane. If we see that we have not learned the lessons we chose, we will cooperate with our guides to determine how we may best be restored to balance.

The people we meet at the Homecoming stage may not interact with us further, except at a distance. Once we move into the later stages, we are reacquainted with our "soul group"—a team of people sharing a similar level of spiritual development with us. Also, as we become more advanced as souls, no welcoming committee is necessary at the Homecoming stage and we will quickly move on to rejoin our soul group. In these cases, we seem to be pulled quite naturally along wavelike bands of light.

At this point, Dr. Newton also reveals that even though there is full thought sharing in the afterlife and telepathic communication occurs among everyone, it is still possible for two individuals to have a private conversation by touching each other. Most of Dr. Newton's clients are unwilling to divulge any details about the contents of these intimate discussions.

Stage Four: Orientation

Once we go through the Homecoming process, we go through an inter-esting series of experiences to help us reorient and refamiliarize ourselves with the afterlife. Our guide is often intimately involved with us at this stage. The first and most important part of this process is an energetic form of healing in which the traumas we carried in from our physical lives are washed away. Dr. Newton thinks of this as akin to a hospital stay, and his clients consistently use similar words and phrases to describe it. The most common phrase is "the place of healing," but it might also be called a chamber, a berth, or a stopover zone. Once we reach this hospital-like chamber, we go through what Dr. Newton calls "the shower of healing." Our guide often directs this process. We move into a specific room of light and are bathed in a stream of liquid healing energy that appears like a beam coming toward us and moving through us. Many of Dr. Newton's clients reported that the sensation is similar to a refreshing shower after a hard day's work, but in this case the effect is much deeper.

New souls in particular come to earth in a very positive, loving state of mind and expect to be treated fairly.[295] We are shocked as we realize how cruel and hurtful people can really be. Negative, traumatic memories, fears, and worries are washed away at this point. We again feel whole. We are inspired, renewed, and restored and are finally able to let go of the emotional bonds to our previous lifetime.

The second phase of Orientation is a substantial counseling process with our guide. The guide asks us probing questions about how we lived our lives, and whether we lived up to our own expectations, as we had chosen them before birth. This process is done with gentle grace—not a harsh, accusing tone or demeanor—but we are still expected to be honest, soul-searching, and thorough. Our guide already knows our strengths and weaknesses, our fears and fixations, and is willing to work with us as long as we keep trying. It is impossible for us to hide anything from our guides due to the inevitable reality of instant telepathy in the afterlife. This counseling process often seems to occur in a particular room, and the room may have similarities to places we knew from our own lives on earth.

Some people have a much more difficult time with this counseling than others, and this is due to the overall maturity of the soul. Great humility is required, and we still experience our waking personality, to varying degrees. We are not exalted beings who have reached a state of total soul perfection. We have wants, needs, and desires; we may feel embarrassed, awkward, fearful, and disappointed. Therefore, this process certainly is not easy, but it is often necessary. We also discover the many different ways in which our guide attempted to influence us telepathically to make positive choices in our lives, such as through synchronicity. In order to progress, we must honestly admit how we disregarded those messages and chose to act in weakness, ignorance, and fear instead. This whole process is a private warm-up for a much more significant meeting that happens later on, when we meet with a highly evolved group many people refer to as the Council of Masters, or Council of Elders, at the end of stage five. The more advanced souls do not require any counseling at the Orientation stage and simply move on to their ultimate destination.

Stage Five: Transition

Once we are bathed in healing light and have been open and honest enough to move through our initial counseling session with our guide, we go through what Dr. Newton calls the Transition phase. The visions we experience here can be some of the most breathtaking of our entire journey through the afterlife. We move into an enormous area where we see souls coming and going, much like at a train or subway station, but on an utterly vast scale. Gravity does not apply in the afterlife, so there will often be a vast, interconnecting web of energetic tunnels leading souls to their eventual destinations. One of Dr. Newton's clients referred to this area as the hub of a great wagon wheel—and once you reach the tunnel to your destination, you move out of the wheel and begin traveling down one of the spokes. People are typically very excited by what they see at this stage, and they find themselves traveling along "lines of light." There is no darkness here—everything is glowing with light at different levels of brightness. We are usually well aware, by this point, that once we move through this tunnel to our eventual destination, we will be reacquainted with those we love the most. As we think about these people, we telepathically connect with them and experience an initial meeting in that form before we actually leave the tunnel. These people are at the same relative level of soul evolution as we are, and we learn from one another's experiences and compare notes in the afterlife, often with a great deal of humor.

Fig. 8: Etching of one of Dante's heavenly realms, by Gustave Doré

We do not have much control over our movement at this stage. The tunnels naturally bend as we go along, and Dr. Newton's more advanced clients reveal that higher entities are responsible for guiding the movement.[296] These entities are often called "the directors," or another similar term. As we travel through the tunnels, we see plenty of destinations where other people have gathered. These areas appear as clumps or clusters of light—almost like buds that have grown off the stem we are traveling through, much like a flowering or fruiting plant.

However, once we arrive at our own area and enter it, the scenery often becomes much more conventional looking, from the standpoint of our experiences on earth. We will often see large areas that are familiar to us, including towns, schools, beloved homes, and landmarks that help us feel safe and secure. We are now fully reacquainted with our soul group—people with whom we keep reincarnating, again and again, as they play different roles. They may appear as parents, romantic partners, siblings, teachers, coworkers, or friends in various lifetimes. Members of our soul group who are incarnate in human forms on earth may seem to be half-asleep, radiating a dimmer light and staying fairly quiet. They may greet us briefly but tend to keep to themselves. Most of us at this stage are immediately aware of who is in a body and who is between lifetimes. Once we've taken some time to reconnect with our friends and loved ones and enjoy these familiar surroundings, we are ready to meet with the Council of Elders. Dr. Newton's second book, *Destiny of Souls*, goes into much more detail about this group counseling session that occurs at the end of stage five. The process is similar to the initial counseling we went through with our guide—only now we are accountable to a group of highly evolved beings.

Stage Six: Placement

Once we've completed the group counseling at the end of the Transition stage, we move into Placement. This is where we are reacquainted with familiar groups of various sizes. At this stage, we experience a return to a school-type environment. The classrooms can be quite beautiful and will have scenery chosen from our favorite places on earth. Apparently many Westerners choose a Greek temple as their main location. We study with our own soul group—our closest friends, who enjoy a level of evolution similar to ours. This group can range between three and twenty-five souls, but the typical number is about fifteen.[297] This group will often be called the Inner Circle, and it stays consistent from lifetime to lifetime. We also come into some degree of contact with a much larger secondary group of souls who incarnate with us to varying degrees. Dr. Newton says that these secondary groups are never seen to have less than a thousand souls and can often be significantly larger than that. When we combine this observation with what we find in the Cayce readings, we see that entire towns, cities, nations, or ethnic groups can keep moving, in clusters, through different locations and eras. And, as we are about to explore in Part 3, these eras are organized into cycles of historical events that repeat very precisely until we finally learn our lessons and they no longer need to continue occurring.

We perform real work in this school setting, which usually comes in the form of sitting down with what Dr. Newton's clients usually call a "life book." Although this first appears to look like a typical, large, bound leather book, it acts much more like an advanced holographic projection technology once we open it. Each "page" of this book represents a given period of time in our lives. As we go through the book, we review all the different experiences we went through in our lives—in vividly realistic detail. This process is much like virtual reality, in the sense that we often end up directly projecting into the scenes we are reviewing. Special emphasis is placed on projecting into the minds and hearts of those we interacted with, particularly if we caused them to feel hurt or pain in some way. We now get to personally experience everything we put them through, including the most painful events. The Law of One series reveals that this process can be significantly shortened if we remember events where we hurt others while we are still living in a physical body and forgive ourselves for what we did.

Not all of the Placement stage involves the difficult work of reviewing our lives and forgiving ourselves for what we have done to hurt others. There are also periods of recreation, where souls of many different levels of evolution gather together for enjoyable activities. This may include forming circles with others to unify our thoughts and feelings more fully and to project energy. Such interactions with others may involve singing, or the energetic equivalent of it. We also interact with our guides, who are on a higher level of evolution, and we feel a great sense of community.

SEVEN DIFFERENT LEVELS

Once we reach this point in the book, Dr. Newton begins discussing the seven different levels he discovered that souls move through in the afterlife. This was initially discovered by people describing the colors of their own energy bodies, as well as the colors of those around them. Level I was white, Level II reddish yellow, Level III yellow, Level IV dark yellow with traces of blue, Level V light blue, Level VI dark bluish purple, and Level VII purple—which is very rare. Newton considers Level I to be beginner, Level II lower intermediate, Level III intermediate, Level IV upper intermediate, Level V advanced, and Level VI highly advanced.

One client referred to Level VI beings as "the sages," whereas Level VII beings are the "old ones," who are rarely seen—and highly mysterious. There is astonishing agreement between Dr. Newton's independent, hard-earned observations and what we read in the Law of One series about the seven different "densities" corresponding to the colors of the rainbow and the evolutionary level of beings we find there. Dr. Newton found that 42 percent of his clients were Level I, 31 percent were Level II, 17 percent were Level III, 9 percent were Level IV, and only 1 percent were Level V.[298]

WANDERERS

Not one of Dr. Newton's clients was a Level VI. He found that souls at Level V were usually working in the helping professions or working to alleviate social injustice in some form while living on earth. They beam with kindness, composure, and stability and are not motivated by self-interest.[299] The lack of Level VI clients in Dr. Newton's practice may be because people at this advanced level would not normally seek out hypnotherapy. In the Law of One series, higher-level souls—including those from fourth, fifth and sixth density—do occasionally take on physical incarnations and are known as "Wanderers." In this next quote, it is important to point out that the word *distortion* is not a bad thing in the Law of One series. Anything other than "intelligent infinity" is a distortion of the pure awareness that the universe is formed from. Therefore, space, time, light, matter, energy, and biological life are all distortions, as are any choices we make. Some distortions move us closer to unity, while others move us farther away. The goal of all Wanderers is to help us remember who we truly are.

> 12.26 Question: . . . You spoke of Wanderers. Who are Wanderers? Where do they come from?
>
> Answer: . . . Imagine, if you will, the sands of your shores. As countless as the grains of sand are the sources of intelligent infinity. When a social memory complex [a group soul usually in fifth density or sixth density] has achieved its complete understanding of its desire, it may conclude that its desire is

service to others with the distortion towards reaching their hand, figuratively, to any entities who call for aid. These entities whom you may call the Brothers and Sisters of Sorrow move towards this calling of sorrow. These entities are from all reaches of the infinite creation, and are bound together by the desire to serve in this distortion.

Question: How many of them are incarnate on Earth now?

Answer: . . . The number is approximate due to a heavy influx of those birthed at this time due to an intensive need to lighten the planetary vibration. . . . The number approaches sixty-five million.

Question: Are most of these from the fourth density? What density do they come from?

Answer: . . . Few there are of fourth density. The largest number of Wanderers, as you call them, are of the sixth density. The desire to serve must be distorted towards a great deal of purity of mind and what you may call foolhardiness or bravery. . . . The challenge/danger of the Wanderer is that it will forget its mission, become karmically involved, and thus be swept into the maelstrom from which it had incarnated to aid the destruction.

Question: What could one of these entities do to become karmically involved?

Answer: An entity which acts in a consciously unloving manner in action with other beings can become karmically involved.

Question: Do many of these Wanderers have physical ailments in this third . . . Earth situation?

Answer: Due to the extreme variance between the vibratory distortions of third density and those of the more dense [higher] densities, if you will, Wanderers have as a general rule some form of handicap, difficulty, or feeling of alienation which is severe. The most common of these difficulties are alienation, the reaction against the planetary vibration by personality disorders, as you would call them, and body complex ailments indicating difficulty in adjustment to the planetary vibrations such as allergies.[300]

"WHO DO YOU THINK NATURE IS?"

In the Placement stage, we also can travel great distances from our original home base as we become intermediate- and advanced-level souls and venture out into exotic locations. Pages 161 through 166 in *Journey of Souls* reveal a fascinating discussion about what one client called "the World of Creation and Non-Creation."[301] This is a three-dimensional, physical world—like the earth—in which biological life is just getting started. Souls begin visiting worlds like this once they reach Level IV. If we extrapolate from the percentages in Dr. Newton's own client pool, one out of ten people now on earth is pursuing these activities in between lifetimes. One of Dr. Newton's clients named the planet these individuals were visiting "Earth II." These souls directly participate in designing the life-forms that are growing on the planet they visit. "Earth II" happened to be larger and somewhat colder than earth, with fewer oceans.

Such planets are considered "vacation spots," but our journeys there also serve a valuable purpose; we are learning to become co-creators of life itself. We are able to form physical, living organisms by focusing our own soul energy. Teachers are on hand to assist us with this process. This particular client, case twenty-two, was working only with basic elements—for example, using gas vapors to create water or combining dust, water, air, and fire to create rocks. His soul's own energy was able to manipulate heating, pressure, and cooling. In his waking life he worked at a charitable organization feeding the homeless, and in the afterlife state he described the process of making rocks as "tricky, but not too complicated." When Dr. Newton said he thought nature was responsible for the creation of these things, his client laughed and responded, "Who do you think Nature is?"[302]

Case twenty-two, whose name in the spirit world was Nenthum, was also working on developing plants, but he didn't yet have the sophistication to create them properly. Sometimes he deconstructed his attempts to make plants before anyone else could see his mistakes, as a form of self-protectiveness and pride. The reason for these mistakes was apparently that his energy was not applied "delicately enough" to combine the chemical elements to get the desired results. Dr. Newton's research revealed that souls are not able to make real contributions to the development of living things until they reach Level V, though Level IV souls are the first to begin exploring this process of creation.

Another client at Level V, known only as case twenty-three, was a woman in her midthirties working as a substance-abuse counselor. As it turned out, she was an old pro with creating life on many different "earth-type planets" and had already worked her way up through a variety of oceanic life-forms. She said that the first biological life souls learn to create is microorganisms—and this is "very difficult to learn."[303] Early in her career as a co-creator, she started out with basic forms of oceanic life such as algae and plankton and worked up to more complex creatures such as fish over time. This prompted Dr. Newton to ask her a revealing question.

Dr. Newton: A soul who becomes proficient with actually creating life must be able to split cells and give DNA instructions. . . . You do this by sending particles of energy into protoplasm?

S: We must learn to do this, yes—coordinating it with a sun's energy. . . . Each sun has different energy effects on the worlds around them.[304]

This unique energetic method of creating biological life is validated by the new scientific discoveries we have discussed—in which DNA can be seen as a quantum wave and life is written into the basic laws of quantum mechanics. Unbeknownst to him on any conscious level, Dr. Newton's results have now been independently verified with new scientific discoveries, and this certainly lends support to the overall credibility of his work. After he heard this surprising answer, Dr. Newton became concerned that if individual souls are participating in the creation of life-forms that could live on for millions of years on a given planet, they may be interfering with its overall evolutionary course. Case twenty-three then said that these life-generating activities are a natural part of the co-creative nature of the universe, where souls grow further and further into living embodiments of the Creator. Other souls at higher levels carefully watch over the process to ensure that everything progresses smoothly and in a beneficial direction.

We also find out that larger groups of advanced souls can create full-scale stars. Case twenty-three revealed that she was already creating "small bundles of heated, highly-concentrated matter." She told Dr. Newton that if he were to see these creations of hers when they were finished, they would look like miniature solar systems.[305] She had already been able to create suns the size of basketballs and planets the size of marbles. The "concentrated energy of the Old Ones"—those at Level VII—was required to make physical universes—and space itself.[306] This gives us a very interesting way of seeing the living universe—namely, that planets and stars can be created by the focused thoughts and energies of advanced souls, who could also be experiencing incarnations on earth. These Law of One quotes shed further light on what Dr. Newton independently heard from his clients.

13.16 Each step [of creating a planet] recapitulates intelligent infinity in its discovery of awareness. In a planetary environment, all begins in what you would call chaos—energy undirected and random in its infinity. Slowly, in your terms of understanding, there forms a focus of self-awareness. Thus the Logos [the mind of the galaxy] moves. Light comes to form the darkness, according to the co-Creator's patterns and vibratory rhythms, so constructing a certain type of experience. This begins with first density, which is the density of consciousness—the mineral and water life upon the planet learning, from fire and wind, the awareness of being. . . . Picture, if you will, the difference between first-vibrational mineral or water life, and the lower second-density beings which begin to move about within and upon its being. This movement is the characteristic of second density—the striving towards light and growth. . . . The second density strives towards the third density, which is the density of self-consciousness or self-awareness.[307]

82.10 The One Original Thought is the harvest of all previous, if you would use this term, experience of the Creator by the Creator. As It decides to know Itself, It generates Itself into that plenum, full of the glory and the power of the One Infinite Creator which is manifested to your perceptions as space or outer space. . . . Gradually, step by step, the Creator becomes that which may know Itself, and the portions of the Creator partake less purely in the power of the original word or thought. This is for the purpose of refinement of the one original thought. The Creator does not properly create, as much as It experiences Itself.[308]

51.10 This Creator is to be understood, both in macrocosm and microcosm, to have, as we have said, two natures: the unpotentiated infinity which is intelligent; this is all that there is. Free will has potentiated, both the Creator of us all, and our selves, as co-Creators with intelligent infinity—which has will.[309]

75.25 It is well for each to realize its self as the Creator. Thusly each may support each, including the support of self by humble love of self as Creator.[310]

74.11 The heart of the discipline of the personality is three-fold. One, know yourself. Two, accept yourself. Three, become the Creator. The third step is that step which, when accomplished, renders one the most humble servant of all—transparent in personality and completely able to know and accept other-selves.[311]

18.13 All serve the One Creator. There is nothing else to serve, for the Creator is all that there is. It is impossible not to serve the Creator. There are simply various distortions of this service.[312]

TASTY BITS OF COSMIC TRUTH

Dr. Newton's clients revealed that souls can visit planets throughout our galaxy—and possibly beyond it—though this notion is refuted in the Law of One series. Many souls develop a fondness for certain planets and continue returning to them between incarnations.[313] Most people are not able to bring back any clear memories of life on other worlds under hypnotic regression; only the rare and advanced client is able to access this information. Dr. Newton speculates that mental blocks may be put in place by our guides so that we do not recall information that would be beyond our ability to use and appreciate in a positive way.

One midlevel client described his desire to take a break from life on earth and reincarnate somewhere else. He was sent to a world of human-like intelligent beings who were quite different from us. They were small and thickset and had chalk-white faces that were incapable of smiling. They did not experience laughter like we do and were thoughtful and somber. The client ended up being quite outside his normal element, did not integrate well there, and decided to return to earth after one incarnation.

Natural stargates, or "time doors," are also discussed at this point. These natural passageways, which exist throughout the universe and allow us to travel to different times and places, are routinely used by souls as a basic form of travel. In the spirit world, past, present, and future can all be seen as one continuum. Years can pass by as quickly as seconds—and the events that occur during this time can be observed as if you were fast-forwarding a video. Traveling though different times is as easy in the spirit world as traveling from one place to another is in this world. Much of the second half of *The Source Field Investigations* is dedicated to exploring the scientific proof that explains how there is a parallel reality in which time is three-dimensional. This, again, was based on the complex discussions in the Law of One series.

Dr. Newton concludes that time and duration were both created so that we have an opportunity to experience evolution, as souls, at a given rate. If past, present, and future were all accessible at once, there would be no mystery, no surprise, and no challenge that would help us grow. Yet in the spirit world it is very important for us to be able to perceive our greater reality from the "overview" perspective so we can find out where we keep repeating the same lessons, from one lifetime to another, and design lessons in future incarnations that will help us work through these difficulties.

Another interesting connection between Dr. Newton's research and the Law of One series is his discussion of "spiritual substance" in the afterlife. In Law of One terms, different planes of existence are measured not by "dimensions" but by different densities of energy. These densities can be physically experienced in the afterlife as different levels of thickness. Dr. Newton's clients reported exactly the same phenomenon—observing different forms of spiritual substance as being lighter or heavier, thicker or thinner, and larger or smaller.

THE COSMIC HEARTBEAT

One of Dr. Newton's clients, named Thece in the afterlife, described that the universe moves through cycles of expansion and contraction[314]—and this also is mirrored directly in the Law of One series. We are also told that there is no real center of the universe; it is all around us, can be found in any one location, and functions much like the beating of a heart. Both time and space are driven in these regular rhythms. Cycles, therefore, will occur throughout the universe, at all different levels of size and duration, and are driven by a heartbeat-like pulsation. Again, this is exactly how the Law of One series describes the nature of reality.

> 27.6 Intelligent infinity has a rhythm or flow as of a giant heart—beginning with the central sun, as you would think or conceive of this, the presence of the flow inevitable as a tide of beingness without polarity, without finity; the vast and silent all beating outward, outward, focusing outward and

inward until the focuses are complete. The intelligence or consciousness of foci have reached a state where their, shall we say, spiritual nature or mass calls them inward, inward, inward until all is coalesced. This is the rhythm of reality as you spoke.[315]

27.13 Love . . . [is] the great activator and primal co-Creator of various creations using intelligent infinity . . . Love uses light and has the power to direct light in its distortions. Thus vibratory complexes [such as your human form] recapitulate in reverse the creation in its unity, thus showing the rhythm or flow of the great heartbeat—if you will use this analogy.[316]

In the Placement stage, souls may also project themselves into various natural settings or life-forms as a recreational or vacation-type activity. Rocks can give a feeling of density. Trees can convey a powerful sense of serenity. Water can give a feeling of flowing cohesiveness. Butterflies can help the soul feel beautiful and free, and whales can help the soul feel powerful and immense.[317] As enjoyable as the Placement stage of our journey often is, sooner or later we have to get serious and plan out our next incarnation. In Dr. Newton's experience, souls do not gain the opportunity to stop reincarnating in physical bodies until they have reached at least Level V.

Stage Seven: Life Selection

Leaving the spirit world can be a horribly difficult process. You are knowingly turning your back on a world of love, peace, wisdom, and blissful happiness to return to a world that can often be filled with suffering, pain, betrayal, and disappointment. Some souls resist this process for as long as they can and genuinely wish they did not have to return—but sooner or later, they must. Some souls move on to other worlds if the world they had been living on is no longer available to host physical human life.[318] In Law of One terms, once earth has fully transitioned into fourth density—estimated to be between one hundred and seven hundred years after 2011—anyone who still needs third-density incarnation for their evolutionary growth process will naturally end up moving to a new and different world.

Case twenty-four reveals that he will not be returning to earth in his next life. He plainly states that in the future, some earth people have been moved to another planet and the earth has fewer people and is less crowded.[319] Several of Dr. Newton's clients indicated that something like this will happen in our future. This concept of "planet hopping" in Dr. Newton's work precisely validates what we read in the Law of One series about the shift from third to fourth density "green-ray" life on earth. It is also interesting to note that Newton observed every color in the rainbow spectrum appearing in his clients' souls fairly routinely, except for green—which is almost never seen. In Law of One terms, the earth has to make a quantum leap into the green-ray level before any of its inhabitants can become "activated"—which is when their souls fully transition into the green-ray density. We will discuss this process in Part 4. Higher-level entities, from blue ray and indigo ray, can and do visit earth as Wanderers, usually to help out the planet while massively speeding up their own evolution as well.

Dr. Newton's research about the timing between incarnations closely mirrors what we find in the Cayce readings. Dr. Newton found that during Neolithic-type time periods, hundreds or even thousands of years can elapse between physical incarnations. Once we see agriculture and animal husbandry, reincarnation begins to happen more often—but lifetimes can still be separated by as many as five hundred years. Dr. Newton's clients lived an average of once every two hundred years between A.D. 1000 and A.D. 1500, and after A.D. 1700 they lived once per century. It is very common for souls to incarnate more than once a century as we head into the 1900s. All of this research very neatly parallels what we learn in the Cayce readings.

THE RING OF DESTINY

The main responsibility we have in the Life Selection stage is to reach a place that some of Dr. Newton's clients called the "Ring of Destiny," which often appears as a sphere of bright light. Moving into this stage, we are full of bright hope and lofty expectations as we think positively about our next lifetime, and we are excited about the possibility of making real spiritual growth. Once we move into this sphere, we often feel like we are stepping into a highly futuristic cockpit. Different screens float around us, giving us visual impressions of the different lifetimes we could choose for our next incarnation. We also have a control panel that allows us to review these different screens, including fast-forwarding and rewinding the events that will happen in these lives. The screens are in dynamic, fluid-like movement within the sphere of light. As we pull up one screen for review, it flows toward us, while other nearby screens move away. We also have the opportunity to project into these different scenes and experience them as if they were really happening to us. Some part of our awareness still remains at the control panel, but most of what we experience is now happening within the scene itself.

Each lifetime we can choose from has different events, and some could be challenging or difficult, such as debilitating injuries. These events are ultimately intended to help us grow and evolve as souls. We see that choices will be placed in front of us as these events occur, and we cannot be sure what decisions we will make once we reach those points. We are not allowed to see what the consequences of those decisions will be as we move into the future within these lifetimes. We may try to make guesses, but the future reality of those choices is not made visible to us—for a very good reason. If we knew and could foresee the consequences of the events that will happen and the choices that we will make, there would be no real free will and learning experiences as we select a given lifetime. A typical Life Selection process within the Ring of Destiny will involve a choice from among four different lifetimes.[320] Our guides are not present to advise us at this stage—we run through the entire process by ourselves.

In some cases, souls volunteer for lives that will end prematurely, in violent deaths, or through sudden, fatal illnesses. One client chose to be an American Indian boy who would die when he was only seven years old. In this case, a short life as a mistreated, starving child gave him a fast lesson in humility, which helped burn off a great deal of karma very quickly.[321] Another client chose to incarnate at the Dachau concentration camp with three others of her soul group, giving her the chance to comfort the children and try to help them survive. She accomplished her mission courageously, and she undoubtedly created a great deal of positive karma for herself in the process.[322] Bear in mind that souls do not haphazardly choose missions like this—they will choose them only if they feel they are strong enough to handle them. These missions, of course, don't always go as planned—but the souls do go in with the highest and best of intentions.

Stage Eight: Choosing a New Body

Dr. Michael Newton does not consider "Choosing a New Body" to be a separate stage, since this process also occurs within the Ring of Destiny–Life Selection area. Nonetheless, a separate chapter is devoted to this aspect of the process we all must go through, and it heavily influences our decision-making process for whichever life we will choose. In this stage, on the screens that float around in this cockpit-like area, we are presented with various bodies within which we can choose to incarnate. We can see how the bodies will look and feel, how they function, and how they think—throughout the different levels of biological age we will experience. Every human body we see around us, no matter how it looks, is the product of a careful soul choice. A great deal of time and attention is paid to the specifics of each body; there is usually no such thing as a hasty decision. This is generally not the first time we have thought about our next body—we often spend time deliberating which body we will choose in the earlier stages and will talk the choice over with our guide and the people in our soul group.

Dr. Newton found that most major injuries we go through in our lives are chosen at this stage, before we are born. Choosing a body involves a full awareness of what will happen to it throughout a given lifetime. Again, we are prevented from seeing exactly how these events will shape our personality. Each body has difficulties that come along with it, and we take our time and choose carefully. If we have recently come out of a life that was relatively easy and stress-free, we may well decide to come back into a body and a life that will present us with many more challenges. Dr. Newton's research found that bodies with physical

difficulties of various sorts almost always end up producing an accelera-
tion of our spiritual evolution.[323]

LETH: THE VIKING'S CYCLE OF KARMA

Case twenty-six in Dr. Newton's book is fascinating in terms of showing
how wildly a soul's choice of a body can vary from one incarnation to the
next. Case twenty-six was a tall, athletic, well-proportioned woman who
had suffered recurring leg pains throughout her life. Doctors could not
find any medical reason for her pain, but it persisted nonetheless, and she
was willing to try anything, including hypnotherapy, to seek relief. Dr.
Newton suspected that the root cause of the pain might be found in a
past life, so he put her through regression. In the superconscious state,
she found herself in the Ring of Destiny after having requested a life in
one of the strongest, healthiest, and most powerful bodies on earth at
that time.

She had the choice between a Roman soldier, who would have suffered through a hierarchical system of control, or a Viking named Leth,
who could run free and do as he pleased. She chose Leth, and in this
lifetime, from around A.D. 800, she appeared as this brutal and powerful
man. As a soul, she enjoyed the experience of the power of the body and
all the material pursuits—including drinking, fighting, pillaging, and
sexual conquests. Leth never got sick and was unresponsive to physical
pain. He could never get enough food, drink, fighting, plundering, and
sex. Apparently, everyone in this era had similar behaviors and attitudes,
so Leth did not stand out as an unusually aggressive or negative soul.
Nonetheless, the infringements he caused to the free will of others came
back around—quite strongly. He may well have needed to wait several
lifetimes until he was strong enough to balance the karma he had created
as Leth. This case also reveals that younger souls do not necessarily understand the law of karma. If they want to go into a life that will most
likely involve hurting others, their guides will knowingly allow them to
do so. They are offered choices of new life situations and new bodies—
but until they become more advanced, they may not realize that the
preprogrammed disasters that must happen in those bodies are the direct
result of the choices they made in earlier incarnations.

When Dr. Newton asked this woman to explore the reason for her recurring leg pains, she immediately moved into her most recent past life. She was now a six-year-old girl named Ashley who was living in New England in the year 1871—more than a thousand years after her lifetime as Leth. While Ashley was riding in a horse-drawn carriage that was heavily burdened with weight, she fell out. The wheels ran over her legs above the knees and crushed them. Ashley's legs never healed properly, and she spent the rest of her life having to walk with wooden crutches. She also suffered frequent swelling in her legs and died at a relatively young age in 1912. By this point she had worked as a writer and a tutor of disadvantaged children and thereby had built a great deal of positive karma as a soul.

In the afterlife state, she realized that she had chosen this injury to help her develop the power of mental concentration, but she did not appear to understand that it was also a karmic balancing of the experiences she had created for others as Leth. In her lifetime as Ashley, she spent most of her time in bed and learned to read, write, and communicate well. She was then able to see how she had directly worked, from the afterlife state, to arrange the carriage accident and to make sure it would happen properly, at the chosen time. This involved a telepathic coordination between her soul and her body on the subconscious level. She had also given herself subconscious memory tags to know and expect this moment. Although she had a period of time when she could have chosen not to go through with the carriage accident, she knew it was the best move she could make. She had options for other bodily injuries but had specifically chosen this accident because it would limit her ability to walk. This would compel her to develop her mind more fully, since she had long periods of unbroken solitude. She made good use of the experience, with the sole problem being that she was slightly too indulged and pampered in that lifetime.[324] Dr. Newton was able to run her through desensitization exercises, while under hypnosis, that removed her subconscious memory of leg pain entirely. Later, she reconnected with Dr. Newton and happily revealed that her leg pain had never come back and she was routinely playing tennis.

Dr. Newton also reveals that an energetic handshake of sorts must be made between the soul and the physical body. Without the influence of the soul, a person wouldn't be very interesting—he or she would be fairly primal in nature and would be ruled by emotions. The soul can determine whether someone is an extrovert or an introvert, whether the person is emotional or intellectual, and whether the person is rational or idealistic in nature. Many of our personality attributes carry over from one life to the next, but there are also personality influences that are a direct result of the body itself, its heredity, and its experiences.

Some souls consistently choose to return as people who are critical, domineering, and cold, even though they will end up being fully accountable for the hurts they cause to others by their attitude and behavior.[325] Souls like this can offer a great deal of karma and growth experiences to others—and are often needed to help others balance out their own debts. Some souls realize that they need to have people like this in their lives, people who are strong and tough, or else they will end up dominating and manipulating everyone around them. Souls with this dominant, critical personality type appear to have greater difficulty than most in blending themselves with the human body and brain they have chosen in a given lifetime. The soul often cannot get messages through or does not have much influence on the body when the body is going through great stress or strong emotions.[326]

Stage Nine: Preparation and Embarkation

In the Preparation and Embarkation stage, we leave the Ring of Destiny and have an intensive planning meeting with the people who will play key roles in our lives, usually from our soul group. This stage of the afterlife is very relevant to our discussion. Many synchronicities we will experience are planned out at this point, in order to ensure that we take certain steps at certain times. Higher-level guides help us plan out the symbols and events that will help steer us through these key moments. If we choose to be in a relationship with someone, we may deliberately plan a symbol that will appear when we first see that person—a particular place, a particular object they are wearing, something funny they say, some specific music we hear in the background, and so on. We struggle at this stage to memorize each of these cues, so that we will know what to do when we see them. Once we have incarnated in a physical body and these signals appear, we generally will not remember the careful and deliberate planning that went into these events, but the memory trigger encourages us to make certain decisions.

A male client, case twenty-eight, described a prebirth agreement he made in which a woman he meets as a child will be wearing a shiny silver pendant on a necklace, and the sunlight then gleams off of it. Once he was alive in a physical body, living in his hometown, this same woman walked every day on his street, and she always wore a silver pendant. The first time he met her with it, the sunlight reflected off it, just as he had intended it to in the afterlife—and this event activated his memory trigger. He was immediately drawn to become her friend and engage in conversation, without consciously knowing why he felt so strongly about doing this. Even though he knew her for only a short time before his family moved, she gave him a very valuable lesson in learning to respect others.[327]

As we go through the Preparation and Embarkation stage, we may be concerned about our level of stubbornness and resistance to the synchronicity and gut feelings that our souls use to communicate with us. In cases like these, we may layer in several different memory tags that will appear as synchronicities in our lives, just to reinforce one particular decision we intend to make. Case twenty-eight describes multiple planned triggers he would experience when meeting the woman he had chosen to be his wife. Both of them agreed on these memory triggers and would cooperate, as souls, to make sure they happened. This included a laugh of hers that would remind him of the sound of tiny bells or chimes, a familiar perfume scent he would notice the first time he danced with her, and the way her eyes would look. Her chosen memory triggers included his big ears, the fact that he would step on her toes when they danced the first time, and the specific way she would feel when she first held him.

After planning out these synchronicities to keep us on track, we often have another meeting with the Council of Elders before we head into the Rebirth stage. This meeting is used to remind us of our goals and of how important it is that we stick to our ideals in our next lifetime. On page

261, a client of Dr. Newton's reports the Elders as all being hairless, with oval faces, high cheekbones, and smallish features—much like the appearance of certain types of extraterrestrials people have reported seeing.[328] These people did have eyes like ours—not black ovals—but many extraterrestrial witness reports do feature this type of appearance. The Elders are bathed in light, and there is a strong sense of divinity. This meeting is akin to a last-minute pep talk encouraging us to have patience, to hold true to our values, to trust ourselves in the midst of difficult situations, and to avoid indulging in anger and negativity. We may also receive an energetic boost from the Elders that appears as a burst of positive power helping inspire us and charge us with love.

Stage Ten: Rebirth

The final stage Dr. Newton identified is Rebirth. After the meeting with the Council of Elders, some souls become quiet and introspective before they reincarnate, whereas others joke around with their friends and have a lighthearted attitude about the reincarnation. Once we finally depart, we have a sense of plunging downward, through areas of luminous energy. We may also see another dark tunnel, only this time we are returning to the earth in it, rather than leaving the earth through it. As soon as we exit the tunnel, we find ourselves in the body of a baby within our new mother's womb.

Up until our new child begins school at around age five, we still have enough flexibility that we can leave the body for various lengths of time. We may go off and enjoy traveling with our friends to revisit places we lived in other lifetimes. The minute the baby is in any physical danger or distress, we instantly snap back to take care of the problem.[329] While we are in the baby's body, we work to integrate our own soul energies with the brain of the physical body. We may also get the baby to do things that will help smooth out the relationships within the family. For example, if our mother and father are fighting, we may do something cute, such as poking their faces with both hands, smiling, or giggling, to distract them back into positive thoughts. It is well within the power of the soul to get the baby to laugh when needed.

Cycles of History as the Master Organizing File for Reincarnation

The scientific proof for a living universe is quite far-reaching in scope. DNA and biological life appear to be written into the laws of quantum physics and manifest as an "emergent phenomenon" wherever and however they can. Stars and planets exert strong energetic influences on our conscious minds, whether we realize it or not. Our waking personalities are the result of a fusion between the body and the soul, and we cycle through many different incarnations to master the same lessons. We ensure that we will see most of our friends in each lifetime, and we also reincarnate within larger groups of people as well—potentially in the hundreds of thousands, if not more. We may very well be tied to them through common bonds of karma, and we need to keep moving through the ups and downs, the highs and lows, the triumphs and disasters of life. Within these secondary groups, we keep repeating the same experiences until we choose, as a collective, to make more loving and positive choices. Our experiences are organized into extremely precise time cycles, as we will explore in Part 3.

We've all heard the saying that history repeats itself, but until I encountered this incredible body of data—and did far more research on it myself to see if it was really true—I had no idea how structured our experiences really are. Global events seem to be completely random, formed by an impossibly complex array of factors. However, it turns out that all the experiences we go through, from lifetime to lifetime, are being guided by a hidden template of spiritual evolution known as the Hero's Journey. In the Law of One series, these experiences are called "the archetypical mind," which represents the personality of the galaxy. The fourth and final book in the original Law of One series is almost entirely dedicated to studying this galactic mind.

> 90.14 The archetypical mind is part of that mind which informs all experience. Please recall [our earlier] definition of

the archetypical mind as the repository of those refinements to the cosmic or all-mind made by this particular Logos [our Milky Way galaxy] and particular only to this Logos. Thus [the archetypical mind] may be seen as one of the roots of mind, not the deepest but certainly the most informative in some ways. The other root of mind to be recalled is that racial or planetary mind, which also informs the conceptualizations of each entity to some degree. . . .

Each Logos [galaxy] desires to create a more eloquent expression of experience of the Creator by the Creator. The archetypical mind is intended to heighten this ability to express the Creator in patterns more like the fanned peacock's tail— each facet of the Creator vivid, upright, and shining with articulated beauty.[330]

This epic story is written into every movie and television show in existence—and I soon found out, through a great deal of pain and suffering, that you can't even write a Hollywood screenplay that sells without having studied it extensively.

CHAPTER NINE

The Hero and His Story

S cience and spirit have finally caught up to each other. There is a
ghost in the machine. Life on earth is nowhere near as random or
haphazard as many of us think. Synchronicity is a powerful,
day-by-day means of awakening us to our true identity—and it is also
happening on a much larger scale in the cycles of history we will soon be
discussing. If Dr. Newton's research is correct, a great deal of our experiences are being coordinated from the afterlife—and this may include
very precise cycles of time, in which the events in our own history are
repeating with incredible precision. This information can be a powerful
tool to help us awaken to this much greater reality that surrounds us,
particularly for those who are hungry for physical proof. These cycles can
be hundreds or even thousands of years in length and can operate with
astonishing exactness and effectiveness.

In this new science, everything is alive, including planets, stars, and
galaxies. Each level of the universe, from quantum to galactic, has a hidden energetic structure, driven by a pulsing heartbeat, that directly affects our free will. According to the Law of One series, the beating of
your heart in your physical body is meant to be a holographic mirror of
this greater reality that surrounds you. As we drift through different
energetic regions as a planet, every one of us experiences different influences. The thoughts we think and the actions we take—even among

those of us who are the most negative—are being guided by this hidden architecture of time. This is truly where synchronicity becomes a science, stepping out of the realm of the personal and subjective and into the world of the global and provable.

In order to understand these cycles of history, we first must grasp that they are telling us a story, also called the Book of Life. Each soul is going through cycles of joy and despair, as we said at the beginning. The Wheel of Karma is not at all random. There is a very precise series of experiences—a great story—that we keep repeating, over and over again, from lifetime to lifetime, until we master it. This story is written into all the world's greatest mythologies, and it also appears in the cycles of historical events. Every movie and television show you've ever seen is based on this story, as I eventually found out through extremely difficult personal experience. Once we understand the structure and function of this global Wheel of Karma, we may conclude that it has the power to create a full spiritual enlightenment and Golden Age for humanity.

The School of Hard Knocks

In 2005, I gave my first-ever lecture in the fast-paced world of Los Angeles, at the Conscious Life Expo. I was soon approached by a Hollywood producer who had worked with A-list actors including Burt Reynolds, Dolly Parton, and Sylvester Stallone. He told me that if we made a documentary film about these subjects—including the idea that DNA is formed by a quantum energy wave—it would be very helpful to others and could potentially be a huge commercial success. I had honestly never even thought of making a film out of my work. I was still living in Milton, Kentucky, at the time, renting a three-bedroom house just a mile and a half away from a nice plot of land that was owned by L/L Research, which produced the Law of One series. Volunteers who worked on that land were using my house as a place to live, or at least to visit for a shower and some conversation. Milton was a quiet, sleepy town—not much bigger than the strip of highway it was built around. If you walked into any of the stores on the Kentucky side of the bridge that led to Madison, Indiana, the cigarette smoke was so thick it would curl around you as you walked down the aisles.

The biggest events that happened around my home were the neighbor's dog barking too much and their cows breaking through the fence from the pasture next door. I was in complete seclusion, and I definitely enjoyed the solitude. The only human interactions I had were with people at the post office or grocery store, the volunteers, or clients who called me up for a dream reading, which was my sole source of income at the time. I had discovered that, in addition to being able to give people an Edgar Cayce–style deep-trance intuitive reading, I would also dream about them on the day they were going to have the session with me. I would personally go through their deepest and darkest shadow experiences in my dream as if it were happening to me. It was quite common for the client to begin crying as I described the dream to them, because in almost every case there were astonishingly accurate connections to their personal lives. I did five hundred of these readings from 1998 to 2005 and had a 99 percent satisfaction rate. However, because I had no regular staff to sit with me for these sessions, they had become very draining. I also had a huge waiting list, forcing me to work much more than I was comfortable with. Some client dreams were so intense that I started to feel a loss of personal identity; I couldn't tell whether these painful dreams were warnings about me or just reflections of my clients. I knew I had to retire, for my own good, and focus on things that could help many more people all at once—and this film was the key.

In this monastic, country environment, I worked through nine feet worth of printed and bound books I had compiled from many different Internet websites, as well as a huge number of links and excerpts I had saved in my daily journal. By early September 2005, after an incredible, fourteen-hour-a-day effort, everything I had ever researched about the living universe was summarized in a master set of data, which I then used to inspire the creation of this new documentary film. I had intended to call this film *Convergence*, ever since the name first appeared in a dream from 1996. This body of research was eventually incorporated into *The Source Field Investigations,* as well as this book you are now reading.

That same September, we attached to the project a bright female director who had potential connections to A-list actors and who worked as a film professor in Los Angeles. She felt that a feature film built around a fictional story line would be much more effective than a documentary. Of course, I knew nothing about screenwriting, and for the first fifteen months of the project, I felt I was much too busy to dig into a bunch of books on the subject. We did raise enough money to pay for me to retire from doing readings for one year, and I moved to a noisy, lower-floor apartment in Los Angeles in January 2006, so I could be "in the business." For an entire year, I poured my heart and soul into writing what I thought were good screenplays. This was sometimes done with co-writers, including our first director, but in those early days, none of our employees were specialists in the art of screenwriting; they all had other jobs in film as well.

Again and again, these scripts were openly laughed at and ridiculed by the script advisers my team had asked to give us "reads." Although this type of attitude was apparently an industry standard, the cruelty and sarcasm I experienced was shocking, and my mother was quite upset by what she saw after sitting in on one particular meeting. Our new director lasted through only two script cycles before we parted company and started over from scratch. Others lasted for only one version of the script before we were forced to try again. This repeating cycle of pain was a valuable personal experience for me, as I realized I had been so attached to my own creative works that I perceived any criticism of them as a savage personal attack. I had to learn to clearly separate myself and my self-esteem from my creative output. Yet, I was still experiencing crushing pressure to perform. As I revealed in public lectures I gave the following year, every day I got the same call, which could be summarized as "What are you doing and what have you done? How many pages?" We even joked that I could use a touch-tone phone system instead of answering the phone, and just punch in the number of pages I had written each day.

This incredible pressure to perform gave me powerful anxiety attacks, deep depression, and even paranoia and hopelessness. I had to make sure I had a story to tell, every day, about how hard I was working to finish the script—and I certainly was not willing to lie, given what I knew about karma. I hardly wrote anything on my website and basically did nothing to contribute to the lives of others online. I felt totally alone. Everything about who I was as a person seemed to revolve around whether or not I could write a screenplay, and all our investors were counting on me to get the job done. I went through cycle after cycle of what felt like total betrayal and utter humiliation. I would work through weeks or months of relentless, crushing pressure and physical and emotional fatigue to finish a script or a rewrite, only to hear the same response, again and again: It's terrible. Ridiculous. Childish. Laughable. Who wrote this? Or—this time it's only bad, not terrible. You might be able to fight your way through freshman entrance exams into film school with something like this. Maybe.

As this grinding initiation went on, I came to feel as if writing a script was very mysterious. Even with my level of intelligence and my background as a writer, I couldn't produce something that was seen as a mature, effective screenplay. I couldn't seem to control whether someone liked it or not—they either did or they didn't. I was forced to start over from scratch, with new characters, new ideas, and new co-writers, several times. Ultimately I said that if this one college film professor keeps criticizing my scripts the most, and his opinion obviously carries the greatest weight, then let's hire him and bring him in to co-write the next version with me.

Synchronicity Saves the Day

Right after this, in early 2007, I moved from the crushing noise and pollution of Santa Monica to the relaxed, serene mountains of Topanga. A great deal of guidance, through synchronicity and dreams, steered me to this new location, where I still live today. Before I moved, synchronicity and dreams had guided me to transcribe tapes of dreams and deep-trance readings from as far back as 1999. I had gotten so busy over the years that I never went back to transcribe those early tapes, and I couldn't afford to pay anyone to do it. Now I was doing all the work myself. I found, to my amazement, that there were many specific references to exactly what I was doing now. I had dreams that very precisely indicated I would be living in Los Angeles and working on a film. The characters I was interacting with, including female friends who commiserated with me, were all clearly described, with astonishing specifics—as was the pain of my failed screenplays. One dream even referred to there being sweet potatoes on the top of my refrigerator that had sprouted and grown into tall stalks. That scene appeared in an eight-year-old dream tape— but now, for the first time, I was stunned to realize this had really happened in my apartment.

I had to work through a great deal of frustration and many dead ends before I realized where I was being guided to live. I had been absolutely convinced that I wanted a place in Santa Monica by the ocean, but every time I thought I had something lined up, disasters would strike. Realtors would rent it out from under me minutes before I was about to show up. Power lines would be two feet away from the window, a deal breaker. Calls never got returned, even after both the owner and I were ready to sign. One time, when I thought I had the perfect place and was literally picking up the phone to make the final call, a bird slammed into my window with so much force that it broke its neck and was dead before it hit the ground. I became very frustrated, and I cursed the universe, saying that I needed to have a nice place to live, I was running out of time, and I could not bear the thought of signing another one-year lease in the madness I was living in now.

Finally, I realized that synchronicity might have been interfering with my plans. I went back to the Law of One series for inspiration and remembered that the team was told a "sylvan atmosphere"—among trees—was the best place to live for spiritual work.[331] A friend of mine had just told me about Google Earth, where you could zoom over the land from a satellite view, in three dimensions, and I soon found myself projecting over Los Angeles, looking for where the most trees were located. Right away, I could see that the best area was Topanga. I swallowed hard but knew this had to be right. Back when I lived in Virginia Beach, from early 2000 to the end of 2002, my ex-girlfriend had frequently insisted that we move to Los Angeles—and specifically to

Topanga Canyon. Again and again, for three years, I told her, "Forget it! I am never moving to Los Angeles—and I will never live in Topanga Canyon!" Now, it was looking like Topanga was exactly the right place to go. I realized that synchronicity had been working through her all along, even though it had made me very frustrated with her at the time.

I quickly began searching for places in Topanga and found some leads. I wanted an affordable private space but decided to check out a house that was offering a lower-floor, single-room rental as well. When I went to bed the night before I was going to see the house, I had already decided not to bother going. I was overtired and I couldn't bear the thought of being on the lower floor ever again. I had endured an entire year of music, partying, screaming children, car horns, bus noises, diesel exhaust, cigarette smoke, barking dogs, people peering in my windows, and the chaos of being on the lower floor, including a woman who stomped her foot whenever I spoke on the phone, and who ran her dishwasher right over my head every morning at eight thirty sharp. I had to get out—but there was no way I would ever be on the lower floor again. Sleeping in would be better than taking the time to drive out to see that apartment. That same night, while I was fast asleep, my hand flew up and hit the headboard of my bed, causing me great pain—and immediately waking me up. Nothing like this had ever happened to me before—nor has it ever happened again. I had red marks and a bit of skin damage on my knuckles, but I managed to fall back asleep. Later that same morning, I thought I heard my phone ringing, and I was waiting for calls on several potential apartments. I dashed awake and bolted my hand out to answer the phone, only to realize that I'd had some kind of dream hallucination.

However, now my heart was pounding, I was wide-awake, and I said, "Okay, fine, I'll go see the house in Topanga." The whole time I drove there I felt very negative, saying, "I'll just rule this one out and get a look at the neighborhood." The drive was a lot longer than I thought, and I became increasingly pessimistic about how far away it was from civilization. Then, when I finally made it to the driveway, I had to keep on going, because a black SUV was coming down the hill, and there wasn't enough room for me to go up there at the same time. The SUV belonged to the Realtor, who was leaving because I was so late. The owner was still there when I drove up, and he and I had a great connection. I was stunned by the house and went from being completely negative to thinking, "My God, I will do whatever it takes to get this place." People would literally commit atrocities to get parking spots in Santa Monica. On the biggest streets, Santa Monica's finest would ticket you within seconds of when your meter ran out. I'd never gotten so many tickets in my life. If you parked on the street in unmetered areas, there was the constant, inevitable threat of having to move your car on the street-sweeper days or pay another exorbitant fine. Now I was seeing a huge driveway that could easily park twenty-five cars. I was hooked.

Once I moved in, I felt much better. I was renting a single bedroom in a nice house, with a great view, and my housemate traveled two or three weeks a month. I was finally able to re-create the country serenity of Milton, Kentucky, in Los Angeles County—only this was much better, because I was now living in the entertainment capital of the world and could focus on getting my work out to a much larger audience. I began writing for my website again—more than ever—and updated people on the status of the film. I wrote a new piece of music called "The Journey" within days of my arrival, describing in musical form the cycles of joy and disaster we go through. I continued transcribing my eight-year-old cassette recordings of dreams and readings and was dazzled to discover that many very specific details about the house—including the sloping driveway, the mountain view, the soaring hawks, and the personalities of the people I was now interacting with—were precisely embedded in these recordings, which I "just so happened" to have forgotten to transcribe until now. Some part of me was able to read my future just as clearly as if it were a roadmap—and I was very curious to see where it was going.

Structure: The Biggest Secret of Showbiz

At this point, we hired our main story consultant—a head professor at a top film school in Los Angeles—to sit down and co-author a script with

us, as a group, in weekly meetings. He couldn't hate a script that he
himself had co-written with me. I quickly found out that his favorite
genre seemed to be the psychological spy thriller, in which a complex
story is told with a big twist at the end, which only the most perceptive
viewers could have seen coming, but that makes sense once it arrives. He
began speaking to my film partner about something mysterious he called
"structure," which was apparently the basis of all screenplays. At first I
had no idea what they were talking about. This had never come up before. I had no idea what they meant when they said a film was broken
into three acts. There was a lot of technical jargon, and at times it was
almost like a foreign language. Nonetheless, I soon found out that there
was a science to screenwriting. It was not random, and it did not require
any mysterious force that only certain talented writers could possess.

The industry had a carefully guarded secret. Screenwriting was vastly
more formulaic than I had ever realized in all the years I'd watched movies, but you were utterly forbidden from calling it a formula. That was
sacrilege. The media was certainly never going to talk about structure in
films, TV shows, magazines, or newspaper articles, as it would give away
the keys to the kingdom, but there were plenty of screenwriting books
you could read that revealed the big secret. I had been deeply hurt by the
criticism my previous scripts had received, and I had a very strong desire
to be respected in these weekly meetings. I began devouring all of the
most revered and credible books on screenwriting I could find—and
taking copious notes—throughout all of 2007. I managed to master the
contents of the thirteen best books I could find, each of which gave me
new perspectives on the same underlying concepts.

By the end of the year, I had learned the hidden language of Hollywood, which allowed me to talk to the big shots on their own terms and
finally claim respect. I shared this knowledge in a 2008 video called *The
2012 Enigma*, filmed at the same Conscious Life Expo in the same hotel
where I first got invited into the film business. I had no idea that in December 2009, this video would be seen by Jim Hart—the principal author of the movie *Contact*—after becoming the number one most viewed
video of the day on Google, thanks to the publicity machine for the
movie *2012*. Jim Hart had worked with Steven Spielberg, Francis Ford

Coppola, and other A-list directors—and I had always used *Contact* as the model for my early attempts at screenwriting. I was absolutely stunned when I got an email from Jim, inquiring about whether I might want to hire him as a writer for *Convergence.* Before long, we raised enough new money to bring him on board in early 2010—and again started over from scratch. As I complete this book, he is finishing the final draft of our screenplay—based on the suggestions we received from a top production company—and he feels it is one of the finest films he's ever written.

Once I studied the art of screenwriting, I was shocked to discover that almost every movie we know and love—regardless of whether it is a comedy, drama, thriller, horror, sci-fi, fantasy, or romance—is telling exactly the same story. This is stunning—and it seems impossible to believe until you understand that this story is more of a set of guidelines than a specific series of characters, locations, and details that must happen a certain way. Every film is supposed to take a main character, with obvious flaws, and send him or her on a quest for something that is deeply, passionately desired. The main character must go through a really rough time in pursuing this goal, even in the funny movies. There are indeed some films that break away from this structure, but all Hollywood studio execs expect it to be there. They know exactly what they're looking for. They even know what pages these story elements are expected to appear on. If you don't "play the game" and do this, it is very unlikely that you will be able to finance your script. In fact, your work will probably never even make it past the readers the studios and investors hire to review it. Perhaps the best book on the market about structure and its connection to ancient mythology is *The Writer's Journey* by Christopher Vogler[332]—who also happens to be an old friend and colleague of Jim Hart's. Vogler's groundbreaking book was adapted from a shorter briefing document originally prepared for Disney executives.

Time has proven that the public votes with their wallets. They want to see the same story told over and over again, perhaps with a few new twists or doses of visual excitement along the way. You can still innovate, but if you want your film to be a commercial success, you must channel your creativity through the guidelines. The same is true for any novel, particularly if you ever hope for it to be adapted into a film. Once you understand structure, you will easily see how James Cameron's *Avatar,* currently the top-grossing movie of all time, is a point-by-point illustration of it. Since I now understood this story-making background, once I saw *Avatar,* the structure was so obvious that it completely pulled me out of the film. Two other classic, best-selling examples of films that meticulously follow the structure in Vogler's book are the original *Star Wars* movie, and the original film in *The Matrix* trilogy. Disney's *The Lion King* was also heavily worked around Vogler's blueprint. Many people noticed that the *Avatar* story line was similar to *Dances with Wolves* and *Pocahontas*—not realizing that these were only two of the more obvious comparisons that could be made.

Joseph Campbell Exposes the Archetypes Within All Mythology

How did Hollywood reach this point? All stories can be broken down into three acts—beginning, middle, and ending—and this basic structure was first spelled out by Aristotle. In traditional plays there is a curtain call between acts, giving the audience time to get up and use the bathroom, allowing the actors to relax, and giving the stagehands time to rearrange the sets. However, the hidden DNA of storytelling started to be exposed much more fully in 1856, when Max Müller noticed similarities between ancient epic stories in his classic "Comparative Mythology," first published in *Oxford Essays.* Other researchers subsequently explored the same idea. The study of comparative mythology reached its fruition in 1949, when Joseph Campbell first published *The Hero with a Thousand Faces,* an astonishingly far-reaching scholarly work. In this electrifying book, Campbell exhaustively analyzes myths from all over the world, in all different time periods, and finds that they have remarkable similarities to one another. Campbell calls the overall story the Hero's Journey. It's how we work through our fears, our weaknesses, our limitations—each and every day. It is ultimately the blueprint of our evolution—and the path to a Golden Age. Anyone who writes an engaging, believable screenplay is tapping into the Hero's Journey story structure, whether they realize it or not. Those who are aware of it have a much better chance of success.

Campbell drew heavily on the legendary work of Dr. Carl Jung, who found that these various ancient myths keep repeating in our dreams with certain ongoing themes he called archetypes.[333] These archetypes can be so specific that people will paint pictures of what they saw in their dreams, without realizing they are illustrating ancient mythological artwork. Although it is a very complex discussion that is outside the scope of this book, one Amazon reviewer summed it up nicely: "The most important archetypes appear to be the Shadow (the inferior aspects of the self which we hide from others), the Anima/Animus (our object(s) of desire), and the Wise Old Man [or Mentor,] (e.g., teacher, medicine man). [Jung] also discusses a Mother archetype and a Child archetype, and indicates the existence of numerous others. Identifying strongly with an archetype leads to psychosis."[334]

Another key archetype, which this reviewer missed, is the Prodigal Son—a hero character who runs away from home, thinks he's in big trouble for leaving, and eventually comes back, fearing the worst . . . only to find out that he's been loved the entire time, is completely forgiven, and is welcomed home with open arms. The Law of One series gets a lot more specific, revealing that there are twenty-two archetypes altogether—seven for the evolution of the mind, seven for the evolution of the body, seven for the evolution of the spirit, and one final standalone that represents the Prodigal Son, who is also known as the Fool— the hero who is just starting on this quest.[335] These twenty-two archetypes were given symbolic images to illustrate them and became the Major Arcana in the Tarot cards. These archetypes developed over time as the mind of our galaxy became increasingly aware of how to design the best spiritual course for us.

> 91.18 The archetypes were not developed at once but step by step, and not in order, as you know the order at this space/ time, but in various orders.[336]

George Lucas heavily credits Joseph Campbell with the inspiration
that helped consolidate the world he had built for *Star Wars:* "In the
three decades since I discovered *The Hero with a Thousand Faces,* it has
continued to fascinate and inspire me. Joseph Campbell peers through
centuries and shows us that we are all connected by a basic need to hear
stories and understand ourselves. As a book, it is wonderful to read; as
illumination into the human condition, it is a revelation."[337]

What exactly did George Lucas mean when he said Campbell's book
was an "illumination into the human condition" and a "revelation"? At
this point we will quote from Fredric L. Rice, author of the ironically
titled Skeptic Tank website. Rice's article is found in a subfolder called
Atheist2, as you can see from his website link, so his beliefs are clear.
Nonetheless, even as a devout skeptic and atheist, when Rice honestly
considers the scope and importance of Campbell's work and its influence
on modern society, he makes some surprisingly candid confessions. Rice
believes *The Hero with a Thousand Faces* will easily become the most
influential book of the twentieth century in the fullness of time. He also
acknowledges that Campbell's epic work has had a huge impact on film-
making and story-telling in general. Filmmakers like George Lucas, Steven Spielberg, and Francis Ford Coppola are all heavily indebted to the
ancient story pattern that Joseph Campbell identified.

> The ideas in [Campbell's book] are older than the Pyra-
> mids, older than Stonehenge, older than the earliest cave
> painting. Campbell's contribution was to gather the ideas to-
> gether, recognize them, articulate them [and] name them. He
> exposed the pattern for the first time—the pattern that lies
> behind every story ever told. . . . What [he] discovered in his
> study of world myths is that THEY ARE ALL BASICALLY THE
> SAME STORY—retold endlessly in infinite variation . . . .
>
> Campbell was a student of the Swiss psychologist Carl
> Jung, and the ideas in THE HERO WITH A THOUSAND FACES
> are often described as Jungian. The book is based on Jung's
> idea of the "Archetypes"—constantly repeating characters
> who occur in the dreams of all people and the myths of all

cultures. Jung believed that these archetypes are reflections of the human mind—that our minds divide themselves into these characters to play out the drama of our lives. The repeating characters of the hero myth, such as the young hero, the wise old man, the shape-shifting woman, and the shadowy nemesis, are identical with the archetypes of the human mind, as shown in dreams. . . . [Shape-shifting refers to suddenly changing emotional states—which may be depicted as physical changes in form in a mythical story.]

Stories built on the model of THE HERO WITH A THOU-SAND FACES have an appeal that can be felt by everyone, because they spring from a universal source in the collective unconscious, and because they reflect universal concerns. They deal with universal questions like "Why was I born?" "What happens when I die?" [and] "How can I overcome my life problems and be happy?"[338]

It is surprising to hear a devout skeptic and atheist describe a "universal source in the collective unconscious" that causes every human being to admire and dream about the same story. Although he may explain this as a biological phenomenon—the result of having a human body and mind—it nonetheless is a groundbreaking concept. Our subconscious minds are influencing us strongly enough that we keep wanting to hear the exact same story, over and over again. The use of Campbell's work as a hidden structure in Hollywood screenwriting can be traced back to at least September 26, 1964, when Stanley Kubrick advised Arthur C. Clarke to study *The Hero with a Thousand Faces* while working on the screenplay for *2001*. Clarke found Campbell's book to be "very stimulating."[339] In order to further explore the work of Joseph Campbell, and how it affects us, Kristen Brennan summarized years of exhausting research in her detailed, far-reaching Star Wars Origins website.

In 1949 Joseph Campbell (1904–1987) made a big splash in the field of mythology with his book *The Hero with a Thousand Faces*. This book built on the pioneering work of

German anthropologist Adolph Bastian (1826–1905), who first proposed the idea that myths from all over the world seem to be built from the same "elementary ideas." Swiss psychiatrist Carl Jung (1875–1961) named these elementary ideas "archetypes," which he believed to be the building blocks not only of the unconscious mind, but of a collective unconscious. In other words, Jung believed that everyone in the world is born with the same basic subconscious model of what a "hero" is, or a "mentor" or a "quest," and that's why people who don't even speak the same language can enjoy the same stories.

Jung developed his idea of archetypes mostly as a way of finding meaning within the dreams and visions of the mentally ill: if a person believes they are being followed by a giant apple pie, it's difficult to make sense of how to help them. But if the giant apple pie can be understood to represent that person's shadow, the embodiment of all their fears, then the psychotherapist can help guide them through that fear, just as Yoda guided Luke on Dagobah. If you think of a person as a computer and our bodies as "hardware," [then] language and culture seem to be the "software." Deeper still, and apparently common to all homo sapiens, is a sort of built-in "operating system" which interprets the world—by sorting people, places, things and experiences into archetypes. [340]

Most of us do not realize that we have a built-in "operating system" and that we all have a deep, undying need to hear the same story repeated back to us again and again. We innocently ask to hear this same story in endless variations, often on a day-to-day basis, as we routinely watch TV and movies. This is Campbell's great contribution—leading the skeptic Fredric L. Rice to conclude that *The Hero with a Thousand Faces* will eventually be seen as the most influential book of the twentieth century.

Precisely Calculating How Much Money a Film Will Make—Through Structure

Hollywood certainly doesn't publicize how much it uses this story structure, because if it were more widely known, it might start to become too obvious. Nonetheless, this hidden structure has such a huge impact on how many people will pay to see a movie that computer programs have now been written that can tell you exactly how much money a film will make—within a surprisingly narrow window. This method was developed by Dick Copaken and his friend Nick Meaney, who built their company Epagogix[341] around this incredible concept. They use powerful computers to analyze screenplays using a form of artificial intelligence called a "neural network." A variety of different script characteristics are studied through this process, as revealed in the May/June 2013 issue of *The Economist: Intelligent Life.*

> When Meaney is given a job by a studio, the first thing he does is quantify thousands of factors, drawn from the script. Are there clear bad guys? How much empathy is there with the protagonist? Is there a sidekick? The complex interplay of these factors is then compared by the computer to their interplay in previous films, with known box-office takings. The last calculation is what it expects the film to make. In 83% of cases, this guess turns out to be within $10m of the total. Meaney, to all intents and purposes, has an algorithm that judges the value—or at least the earning power—of art.[342]

Some film critics think this whole idea is crazy, believe Copaken and his associates are scam artists,[343] and can't believe it could ever work. However, the truth really seems quite simple. We all share the same "operating system," as Campbell and others discovered, and the closer a movie gets to revealing it, the more successful the film will be.

The real-world financial success of the film can then be calculated, in advance, with astonishing precision. This quote from Malcolm Gladwell's article in *The New Yorker* summarized it nicely in 2006.

> In the summer of 2003, Copaken approached Josh Berger, a senior executive at Warner Bros. in Europe. . . . [They ran] sixteen television pilots through the neural network, and [tried] to predict the size of each show's eventual audience. . . . In six cases, Epagogix guessed the number of American homes that would tune in to a show to within .06 per cent. In thirteen of the sixteen cases, its predictions were within two per cent. Berger was floored. "It was incredible," he recalls. "It was like someone saying to you, 'We're going to show you how to count cards in Vegas.' It had that sort of quality."[344]

This earlier accuracy rating of 99.94 percent is very impressive— seemingly impossible by any normal standards. And that's not all.

> Copaken then approached another Hollywood studio. He was given nine unreleased movies to analyze. . . . On one film, the studio thought it had a picture that would make a good deal more than $100 million. Epagogix said $49 million. The movie made less than $40 million. On another, a big-budget picture, the team's estimate came within $1.2 million of the final gross. On a number of films, they were surprisingly close. "They were basically within a few million," a senior executive at the studio said. "It was shocking. It was kind of weird." Had the studio used Epagogix on those nine scripts before filming started, it could have saved tens of millions of dollars.[345]

So what was the big trick? Let's find out.

> "I was impressed by a couple of things," another executive at the same studio said. "I was impressed by the things they

thought mattered to a movie. They weren't the things that we typically give credit to. They cared about the venue, and whether it was a love story, and very specific things about the plot that they were convinced determined the outcome more than anything else. It felt very objective. And they could care *couldn't* less about whether the lead was Tom Cruise or Tom Jones. . . . There's always a pattern," he went on. "There are certain stories that come back, time and time again, and that always work. . . . It's the consistency of these reappearing things that I find amazing."[346]

There's the key! Certain stories come back. Very specific things about the plot determine how successful a movie will be. Comparative mythology—and particularly the work of Joseph Campbell—reveals the answer. Hollywood is already doing its best to follow these guidelines—but Hollywood may not have fully realized that the story is the most important element of all.

How Do We Tell the Story?

So how do we tell the story? Most of the screenwriting books seem to agree on the main points. Some of the concepts are extremely basic. You have a beginning, middle, and ending—setup, conflict, and resolution—and these phases are called the first act, second act, and third act. As I said, this goes all the way back to Aristotle, who was the first to identify these segments. Again, in the old days of stage plays, you had curtain breaks between acts, when the curtains close, the audience has time to get up and go to the bathroom, the stagehands load in the new sets, and the actors can hang out and relax backstage. Then the lights dim, everyone sits back down, the curtain re-opens, and the next act begins. Modern films, of course, no longer do this, but the breaks between acts are still very much there in screenplays.

If you want to write a film script that will sell, it is expected to be almost, if not exactly, 120 pages long—though some studios now want the same sequence of events to happen within 110 pages, as outlined in *Save the Cat!* by Blake Snyder.[347] Each page is expected to take about a minute of screen time, usually a little less. The first act is thirty pages. The second act is sixty pages. The third act is the final thirty pages. Very specific story points need to happen in each of these acts, and we also see an overall change in the scenery and the pace of events as we move through each act.

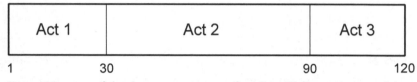

Fig. 9: Diagram of the three-act structure of modern Hollywood screenplays

Though there are rare exceptions to the rule that did become success-ful films, every commercial script must start out with a main character—the hero—who has obvious flaws. The story is all about the changes that this character goes through as he or she works through personal weak-nesses to achieve the one goal he or she wants more than anything else in the world. All of us instinctively resonate with this concept. This ap-pears be a collective, subconscious memory of the goals we set for our-selves between physical incarnations. We have a deep, subconscious knowledge that we are here to grow and evolve and move through our flaws to achieve greater levels of spiritual maturity.

If you try to write a film with more than one main character, it is much harder to follow the story—and unless it's really well written, your script will never sell. With TV you can write what is called an episodic narrative, where multiple main characters have converging destinies that guide each of them through their own version of the story, but this is very difficult to pull off in a two-hour movie. One of the main reasons why this is so challenging is character development, which is what sepa-rates the amateurs from the pros. Anyone can learn the basics of how to paint by numbers within the structure of the story—and many do try—but what the industry bigwigs really want to see is compelling, believable characters that make the story come alive. One of the classic giveaways of an amateur screenwriter—which I also got blasted for several times in the early years—is that each character's dialogue reads like it was written by the same person.

When we watch a film, we immediately try to figure out who the main character is. Generally speaking, this is the first person we meet who says or does anything interesting. At the beginning, we are subconsciously looking for the main character's flaws. This allows us to identify with the hero—which literally means we have transferred our identity into that character for those ninety minutes or so during which we "engage the story." If we don't engage the story—if we don't identify with the hero, if structure is not followed—then we get pulled out of the story. This is the kiss of death. The magic spell is broken. We realize we are watching a movie. We begin analyzing what we don't like about it. We may even laugh at moments in the film that are not supposed to be funny. Audience members whip out their smartphones and text their friends, telling them not to see it. Critics lambaste it. The film is a failure.

The Grand Journey of Initiation—Individually and Globally

We already know the hero will go through an initiation in the film—when he will have to confront his flaws directly. In a happy-ending film, the hero is victorious, and in film noir, the hero's flaws are victorious, but either way the hero goes through a transformation. The story will always be a tale of character change. It's about evolution—even if that means we go through a cycle where we mess up, things end very badly, and we have to do it all over again. In our own lives, this may amount to literally dying and reincarnating once again, only to repeat the same lessons even more. The cycles that characters run through in movies and television shows are experiences that we may spend many lifetimes mastering. By watching the story play out—through the entire range of events—we are hopefully left with a renewed sense of wisdom and inspiration that carries into our daily lives. We identify these same cycles in our personal relationships and gain new insights into how to work through them.

When we compare the classic Hollywood story line to the rise and fall of nations through various cycles, there are parallels. Nations begin, have some obvious flaws at the outset, develop a clear nemesis, go through increasingly grave struggles as they fight the nemesis, and often get overtaken by their flaws and die out. A classic example would be a nation that experiences great prosperity but does not know how to conserve its resources. The nemesis can be as simple as a group of greedy people who are overconsuming the wealth of the nation. Once these resources finally run out, the nation's economy collapses. That would obviously be a story with a "down" ending. However, if a corrupt government is then overthrown in a coup, and a more positive government emerges in its place, that may be seen as an "up" ending. The idea of "fourth density," or a Golden Age on earth, would be the worldwide "up" ending—in which we've finally gone through these cycles enough times that we get the point and are brave enough to make the changes that will create the outcome we desire.

CHAPTER TEN

The First and Second Acts of the Hero

In the first act, the hero starts out in the ordinary world. Everything that happens to the hero—every event, every conversation—is a reflection of that ordinary world. Importantly, the ordinary world represents the hero's ego—the uninitiated mind, with all its flaws. We will clearly see the weakness of the hero, for example, lack of courage, lack of intelligence, naïveté, selfishness, greed, and so on. Blake Snyder specifically recommends putting "Six Things That Need Fixing" in the hero in the first five pages.[348] Snyder also recommends you insert a "Theme Statement," in which a character nonchalantly says something that becomes a thesis, which the rest of the film sets out to prove. The most obvious "hidden" example of this in modern films is in the beginning of *The Matrix,* when the mescaline-dropping, computer-hacking rogue Choi tells our hero, Neo, "Hallelujah. You're my savior, man. My own personal Jesus Christ." Choi appears to be thanking Neo only for the computer disc he was just handed, but in fact the theme statement is carefully inserted at this point—and subconsciously, the viewer knows it. The scenes and events surrounding the theme statement will further establish the setting and tone of the message the film intends to convey.

Then, a major event, often called the "Inciting Incident," draws our hero into a great quest. In action films, this is often a sudden tragedy that hurts or destroys someone or something our hero loves very dearly. In romances, this is often the moment our character first sees a new romantic interest. The motive for the hero to enter this great quest could be revenge, love, justice, mystery, or greed, but it will always be something we will easily identify with. It is something the hero now wants more than anything in the world. The inciting incident usually happens around page 12 in a commercial script, after we've established the theme of the film and the ordinary world of the hero. In geopolitics, the inciting incident is often the spark that triggers a war, such as the bombing of Pearl Harbor or 9/11. When you start watching the beginning of a commercial film, you know something big is coming, and this is always going to be the inciting incident that propels our main character on the Hero's Journey. It is important that this quest is deeply primal, coming from the hero's struggle to fulfill the most basic emotional needs and desires. However, the real key is that this quest will cause the hero to face his worst flaws and defeat them in order to get what he wants.

Throughout the many interlocking cycles of history we will discuss, the inciting incident will often be the spark that starts a war, but it could also be a positive event. We may see an amazing new burst of progress in society, like the discovery of electricity. There may be a massive public gathering like Woodstock, a brilliantly inspiring work of art, or the election of a revered new leader. Cycles can also overlap each other, so that the grand, triumphant conclusion of one cycle can become the inciting incident of another.

Debate, the Mentor, and the Magic Gift

After the inciting incident, there is a period of hand-wringing debate when the hero decides whether or not to go on the quest. The hero usually spends about eighteen pages weighing the pros and cons of this decision, getting distracted, and shifting back and forth. This is often where the mentor or wise old man character first appears to give our hero valuable advice. On a subconscious level, we recognize the mentor as our main guide in the afterlife, steering us through each incarnation. We also receive a magic gift or talisman from our mentor that might not seem important at the time but is a tool that later becomes extremely vital to our survival when we need it most. In *Star Wars,* this is when Obi-Wan Kenobi gives Luke his father's lightsaber. In some stories, the magic gift is not a physical object but a call—a decisive statement or revelation that inspires our hero to pursue the quest. The magic gift may also be a piece of information that is planted in the hero's mind and becomes very important later on. In *The Writer's Journey,* Christopher Vogler indicates that the gift could be "a magic weapon, an important key or clue, some magical medicine or food, or a life-saving piece of advice."[349] In the afterlife, the magic gift could be seen as the synchronicities and "memory triggers" we plan out in advance and commit to memory to inspire us to take on an important quest at a key moment in our lives. The great cycles of history keep everything organized, so we know that certain events will happen at certain times, thus allowing us to plan out our experiences very precisely.

In order to follow the pattern of the story, our hero must choose to go on the quest rather than simply getting thrown into it by circumstances beyond his or her control. We make a conscious decision to join the quest and follow the timelines it puts us on. The wisdom and guidance of the mentor help us make this valuable decision—much like the decision we made of which lifetime, and which body, we would take before our current incarnation. If we don't accept this challenge of the Hero's Journey, we will slip back into the ordinary world of our ego, with all its flaws, and continue living our boring lives, endlessly repeating the same hurts and fears.

Many of us fail to take on a quest in our own lives. We are paranoid, fearful, and distrustful of the outcome. We may settle for a lot less than we could achieve if we were courageous enough. Films and television shows allow us to ask "What if?" What if we were bold enough to take that leap of faith and pursue that one thing we want more than anything else in the world? In a feature film, it is a given that our hero will jump into the quest.

The Second Act Break

Once our hero finally commits to the quest, we have our second act break. In a commercial script, this happens around page 30. Our hero must now enter the magical world—a new set of experiences that are both thrilling and highly challenging at the same time. In modern romance films, this is when the relationship between the two characters begins to get interesting and there is a rush of new emotions. In the ancient mythologies, mystical things happen in this magical world that are not a part of conventional reality as we know it. Modern films often strip this mystical aspect of the story out, but in the ancient structure, which is far older than human life on earth, magical events are a vital part of the story. Good directors will change the whole look and feel of the movie—the colors, the textures, the locations, the characters, the musical score, everything—once we enter this magical world. We also meet new friends and develop key alliances with them that will help us out on our quest later on. Given everything we've now learned about reincarnation, the magical world seems to represent the afterlife—at least in one of its key forms. All of us subconsciously remember what the afterlife is like, so when this part of the story features genuine magic, as we see in *Avatar,* we are more likely to instinctively feel as if we have returned to our true home.

In the cycles of a nation's history, the second act may be when the people finally embrace the decision to go to war. This plunges them into a strange new world of challenges and fears, new allies and friends, sinister enemies lurking behind every corner, prayers to divine forces for protection, and unexpected disasters that threaten to destroy the safety and security of the ordinary world they had lived in before. This stage of the quest may also appear in more positive ways. If the inciting incident and magic gift both appear as a technological breakthrough, such as the lightbulb, this new invention may create the quest for a world that is transformed by such awesome technology. Then the second act would represent the early stages of that technology appearing in society. Of course, there will be struggles to work through along the way, such as corrupt industrial lobbies that do not want to be put out of business. The technology itself, once seen as our savior, may shape-shift into our greatest nemesis. The journey of discovery does create a magical world, but it is still fraught with challenges.

Consider the American history of the railroad as one example of the Hero's Journey story playing out through technology. Granted, there was a vision for a transcontinental railroad that would connect the East and West, but the reality was that the Native Americans provided significantly violent opposition. The real threat of moving out west transferred into many personal stories as well as a collective national story. Whether it was a triumph or a tragedy depends on whom you talk to and when in history that conversation takes place.

The Nemesis

In the early stages of our time in the magical world, we have what Blake Snyder calls "Fun and Games."[350] At this point, we get to catch our breath, temporarily distract ourselves from the intensity of the quest, and experience all the wonders and delights of this new state of existence. Many of the film's most entertaining and memorable scenes appear in this section and often appear in the film's promotional trailer. This point seems to be similar to the top of the Wheel of Karma—the peak point at which everything seems to be terrific, and things are only going to get better and better. However, as the pages flip ahead, we increasingly find out that all is not well. If we didn't already figure it out in the first act, we soon realize that there is a nemesis out there—a really dark, dangerous adversary who wants to terminate our quest with prejudice.

Joseph Campbell refers to the nemesis as the Guardian of the Threshold. This ultimately represents the part of our personality that blocks the doorway, or threshold, that leads to the fulfillment of our goal. In ancient mythologies, the Guardian of the Threshold may be a dragon, and once we cross the threshold the dragon is guarding, we find the virgin, symbolizing the virginal state of the superconscious mind; the gold, symbolizing the riches of wisdom and genius we will find when we regain contact with our higher self; and the afterlife. Campbell also demonstrated that the most important treasure is the "Elixir of Immortality"—a magical companion, substance, or piece of knowledge that can transform the ordinary world we originally came from.[351] The nemesis usually has a variety of allies, or "minions," whom we have to confront along the way—with ever-increasing difficulty—as we seek this treasure. Within ourselves, the nemesis or Guardian represents the ego. Our proud, strident ego refuses to listen to the whisperings of the soul, which compels us to continue on our quest for greater truth, love, and meaning.

On a global level, the Cabal or so-called Illuminati represent the ultimate Global Adversary. The more rocks we turn over in the cold, dark pockets of the Internet, the more we find the same, squiggling creatures hiding underneath. We have entered the magical world. We are on a quest. We want to know the truth, and it keeps getting weirder and weirder. Once we choose to read these creepy articles, listen to the disturbing radio shows, watch even more disturbing YouTube videos, and decide not to fall prey to the Sheep Effect and turn away, we realize that the world we have lived in—the world of mainstream media lies and deception—is not reality. There is something more out there—something deeper. The Illuminati dragon may well be guarding the ultimate Elixir of Immortality—technologies inherited from our extraterrestrial relatives that could give us spontaneous healings, limitless free energy, antigravity flight capability, teleportation, space travel, and incredible prosperity for everyone.

It is terrifying for us to confront this hidden reality, but we also know the promise of what awaits if we can defeat it—freedom, peace, new technology, and harmony on a level most people could never have even dreamed of. However, the path of gaining this information is fraught with danger. Not everyone will believe us. Our family and friends may turn against us. We may fear that shadowy forces will disrupt our lives simply because they do not want us to possess this information. Unbeknownst to us, we are moving through our own Hero's Journey and are now spinning on the Wheel of Karma. The challenges and fears we now go through along the way are burning off our karma, much like the Gehenna fire spoken of by Jehoshua. Once we gain full self-acceptance, through love and forgiveness, we do not need to be plagued by fear, and the Wheel of Karma will finally remain at the highest and most rewarding point. The nemesis fades away to insignificance or transforms along with us.

Just like in the symbolic logic of a dream, in our story the nemesis must represent the hero's shadow, which is another name for the ego, that part of us that denies the greater spiritual reality we live in. In the ancient story, the nemesis is a mirror image, or projection, of the hero's own ego in its darkest moments. In some screenplays, we roll the nemesis and the hero into the same character. If we combine these two characters, then the nemesis appears when the hero's own negative emotions emerge and take him over. In romantic comedies, the hero's love interest may also be the nemesis, and this character will "shape-shift" between roles during the film. In many other films, the nemesis is the classic villain, the man behind the curtain, whose identity may not be revealed until the big twist at the end.

Either way, if you want to follow structure and write a commercial script, your nemesis must show us an exaggerated version of the hero's flaws. The nemesis is the mirror image of the hero, showing what happens if the quest is rejected and the most negative and self-serving choices are made. On a soul level, we all know this selfish choice is exactly what we want to avoid; we've been trying to steer ourselves into making more loving decisions at key crisis points for many lifetimes. If we let the nemesis win, we will keep reincarnating over and over again and repeating the same lessons—both personally and collectively. We are well aware that the nemesis is within us, but by transcending those personal weaknesses and learning to accept and protect ourselves and others, we finally achieve the great victory that cycle after cycle of human lives are meant to teach us. As the hero finally gains the courage to confront the nemesis, he or she will be healed through the struggle. This phenomenon is also happening on a global level. As we move through and release the Sheep Effect, we are moving out of a global childhood and into a true global adulthood, stepping into genuine spiritual maturity for the first time.

In order to make this hero-versus-nemesis standoff reach the deep, subconscious roots of the viewer's mind and connect to his or her journey through the afterlife, the screenwriter must have a healthy understanding of symbolism. It definitely helps to know how dreams work—where every character, every setting, every object, and every event is a reflection of the dreamer. Excellent screenplays are written very much like dreams without the audience ever even realizing it. Every character secretly symbolizes some part of the main character's personality structure. This includes the sidekick, or window character, who knew the hero before we did. The sidekick gives valuable feedback that teaches us more about the hero, such as things the hero said or did in the past that directly relate to what is happening now. The sidekick may also represent the hero's flaws and may resist the changes the hero makes on the quest. *Anatomy of a Screenplay* by Dan Decker is one book that puts strong focus on the grand trinity of hero-sidekick-nemesis as the three main aspects of the hero's psyche.[352]

The Movie *Alien*: An Example of the Nemesis Mirroring the Hero

One of the most obvious examples of the nemesis mirroring the hero is in Ridley Scott's film *Alien*. In his book *Crafty Screenwriting*, Alex Epstein provides an excellent review of how this film tells the great, ancient story once again.[353] The hero of the movie, played by Sigourney Weaver, is confronted with a serious problem. One of her men has a nasty, alien octopus thing attached to his face. Rather than making any attempt to save him, she decides to sacrifice his life—and the lives of the other innocent men who were outside her ship with him—in the hopes of protecting her own life and the lives of her crew. An aggressive member of her crew overrules her authority and lets them in anyway. After a slow boil of ever-increasing tension, the nasty octopus thing falls off the man's face. He seems to be fine, but then the alien bursts out of his chest and runs away, leaving him dead. The alien quickly grows into a full adult and shows absolutely no respect for the lives of the hero's crew; it kills almost everyone.

Sigourney Weaver's character didn't respect the lives of the innocent men outside her ship. She wasn't willing to take any risks in trying to save their lives. Even though they were almost certainly uninfected, she was perfectly willing to kill them off just to make sure. The alien shows us an exaggerated version of what Weaver's character could have turned into if her unrestrained ego kept getting worse and worse; it kills everyone, with no care for anyone but itself. Ultimately, Weaver's character must face off against the alien directly. To defeat the nemesis, she must give up her greatest flaw, which was her willingness to sacrifice the lives of others in an attempt to save her own. She takes a huge risk to save a trapped little girl—as well as a cat—even though she could have easily escaped without them. (This is also why Blake Snyder named his book *Save the Cat!*) Our hero was willing to sacrifice her own life in a valiant attempt to save the lives of others. This is the critical character change and spiritual realization she makes that is the ultimate goal of her entire quest. This tells us, in the story, that the alien—her shadow—can now be vanquished. She has now learned the lesson the adversary was teaching her. The most important part of the entire quest—the breakthrough into courageous love, acceptance, and forgiveness of others—has now been achieved and turned into solid action.

The Wheel of Karma Keeps Turning

Of course, we play out these dramas in our personal lives through the people with whom we surround ourselves. If we don't love and respect ourselves, the universe won't send in a bunch of loving, respectful people to make us feel warm and comfortable. Although the people in our lives may seem kind enough at first, we may soon find them turning on us and playing the nemesis role. Statistically speaking, of all the people we meet, the sociopaths will number between 1 and 3 percent—and possibly many more if we are attracting certain lessons through our own unwillingness to grow and evolve. These people will provide us with exceptional difficulty as we struggle to understand why they keep hurting us—and try to find out how we can get them to change. The same patterns play themselves out, and we may repeat certain sections of the story over and over again.

The emotional pain you go through in these cycles can be unimaginable. Until you truly face your fears and gain enough courage to weed out the villains, users, and manipulators in your life, you will never truly finish your quest. You may be terrified of hurting other people's feelings, even if they have no problem hurting you. Sometimes the solution can be as simple as realizing that the greatest gift you can give them is to prevent them from manipulating you any further, so they may eventually learn to respect others. Yes, they will very likely take your actions personally and complain about how much you hurt their feelings. This may well be the only way they can learn their lesson. On a higher soul level they may be thanking you greatly. You may be saving them from having to reincarnate, suffer profoundly, and play the villain yet again. When you lovingly block their attempts to manipulate you, they are being given the opportunity to gain great new insights. Their soul, their guide, their inner circle, and their extended family of friends and supporters in the afterlife may have all been praying that they will be able to achieve these realizations, so they will not need to keep suffering again and again.

CHAPTER ELEVEN

Facing Your Fear and Completing the Quest

M ovies are very satisfying for us to watch on a subconscious, spiritual level. Every film takes our hero on a neat, compact journey through cycles of soul evolution, like those we have been working on throughout multiple lifetimes with the same group of people, reincarnating again and again together. New adversaries immediately replace the older ones in our lives until we truly master the lessons they bring us. Love—for ourselves and for others—is the ultimate Elixir of Immortality that these nemesis characters block us from being able to consistently feel and share. Our big breakthrough occurs once we become strong enough to stand up and face them. Our current understanding of time is that it moves in a linear progression, but in spiritual terms, time moves in repeating cycles. These cycles have been called the Wheel of Karma or the Book of Life, the great story of the Hero's Journey. We move through these cycles as we struggle to learn the lessons of love on a sustainable, ongoing basis within our own lives.

The Turning of the Wheel

We start at the top of the wheel feeling great, with little or no conscious awareness of our key flaws. We may be self-serving, narcissistic, lacking in courage, unwilling to take responsibility, and immature. We may step on other people's feelings without even realizing what we are doing. We may not have learned to truly love and accept others. This becomes the ordinary world that we live in each and every day, repeating the same mistakes. As the wheel starts turning, our ordinary world is soon disrupted by an inciting incident. Something jolts us out of our unconsciousness and compels us to take on a great quest. Now we want something on a very deep, primal level, with all the passion in our hearts. The second act begins as soon as we start actively pursuing this new goal—and now we're in conflict. The great quest is under way. We have to fight—hard—for what we want. The wheel then takes us down to our lowest point. We are left with no choice but to crawl back out, move through unspeakable misery, and eventually fight our way to the top once again.

This is the basis of all great storytelling; it is the deep, hidden logic of the story itself. Film screenplays break up the wheel into three sections, or "acts"—beginning, middle, and ending, or setup, conflict, and resolution. In Hollywood screenplays, the climb back up from the bottom takes much less screen time than the journey downward. The second act builds up to the moment of ultimate courage when the hero chooses to face off against the nemesis in order to complete the quest. This confrontation is never easy. Near the end of the second act, the hero reaches the rock-bottom point on the Wheel of Karma. This point is also known as the "dark night of the soul." All of us go through these crippling, terrifying, desperate moments in our own lives. These are the times when negative karma strikes us the hardest. We have accidents, we are betrayed, we lose our jobs, our money, our friends, our health, our belongings, and our stability, and we feel that all is lost.

As I said, perhaps my single favorite Law of One quote is, "In forgiveness lies the stoppage of the wheel of karma." Once you can forgive those who have hurt, betrayed, and disrespected you, the wheel no longer has to keep dragging you down through the same cycles. Your life will not be defined by a constant, painful struggle against a nemesis. You will no longer need to attract nemesis characters into your life, because your ego is not running the show. The things you want the most in life will manifest without bitter, painful struggle and jeopardy. This can, and will, happen on a global level as well. The Wheel of Karma will rise to the top and stay there so we can continue to function at our highest and best possible level. I am one of many seekers who know from personal experience that this practice really does work. Once you can stay at the top, you open yourself up to other timelines that can bring in even greater levels of happiness and spiritual achievement. The same logic applies to nations and civilizations as well as individuals.

Watching the Cycles Play Out in Global Events

Getting back to the story structure, in order to climb up from the absolute bottom, you have to love and respect yourself enough to face your deepest flaw, your strongest and most consistent weakness. You have to risk everything your ego holds most dear—and sacrifice those very things—in order to heal. If your main flaw is a lack of bravery, then you will have to release that flaw and find that core of courage within yourself to complete your quest. If your main flaw is that you have too much pain inside to truly love someone, you will have to open your heart in order to move past the threshold and gain the happiness you seek. If your main flaw is a lack of responsibility and a desire to remain in a childlike state, you will have to become a true, spiritual adult in order to realize your greatest dreams and ambitions.

> 20.25 The greater preponderance of your entities find themselves in what may be considered a perpetual childhood.[354]

The patterns that keep repeating on a worldwide level in the grand cycles of time fit the Hero's Journey story line precisely. The childish immaturity of the leaders often reflects the lack of development within the people who voted for them. There are thousands of different cases where one political group has built its identity out of extreme religious principles, refusing to tolerate anyone who doesn't believe the way they do. They face off against another group who shows them a funhouse mirror image of themselves, and the groups clash. Each nation runs its own Wheel of Karma by seeing itself as the hero and the other nation as the nemesis. Both sides may have valid reasons for thinking the way they do—but in the greater sense, who is right?

Racial, religious, and other stereotypes are generally used by both sides to exaggerate the negative aspects of their adversaries. In so doing, they attempt to classify those people as "other," so they become nonpersons. As a child in the 1970s and a teenager in the late 1980s, I certainly remember media depictions of Russian people as mindless, robotic drones: armies of ugly, warty, sweaty, and obese women, wearing the same gray outfits and mopping floors. The clear message was that they were leading sterilized, colorless, inhuman, militarized lives and were acceptable casualties in a nuclear war against the Evil Empire. If a government can successfully paint its opponents as villains, then the people no longer feel it matters if "the enemy" is hurt, abused, tortured, or killed. Future cycles will then be required to balance everyone out and teach them the basic lessons of loving and respecting others.

The great cycle of 25,920 years and all its smaller subcycles of historical events appear to guarantee, through repetition, that these seething, ancient conflicts will be exposed, healed, and resolved. One of many examples is the difference between how early American pioneers saw Native Americans, and vice versa, and the level of respect and appreciation that now exists. James Cameron's *Avatar* presented this age-old conflict very well, and that's undoubtedly a significant part of why it succeeded. We all know that we have to move into greater unity as a planet if we want to survive. The Golden Age may well represent the time when we finally stop throwing these projections at one another, collectively speaking, and we all learn to just be nice.

Four Equal Parts

As we return to the basic elements of the story that we need when we are writing a film, our battles with the foot soldiers of the nemesis and the many other "initiation experiences" must get increasingly difficult through the entire second act. Right in the middle of your 120-page screenplay, you need to have a peak, or the midpoint, where there is either a false victory or a false defeat for the hero. (We'll explore that in a minute.) This ends up dividing the entire story into four equal parts, with the key plot points on pages 30, 60, and 90.

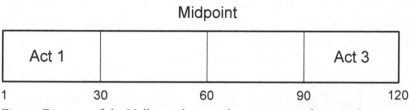

Fig. 10: Diagram of the Hollywood screenplay structure as four equal parts

The grand historical cycles discovered by Professor Anatoly Fomenko (featured in chapters 15 and 16) are also divided into four equal parts, as we will see. Perhaps the reason the Hollywood formula—the structure—divides the story into four equal sections is that this is exactly how historical events move along, but in cycles that extend well beyond any one person's lifetime. On some subconscious level, it appears that we know the story, even though we may have to experience more than one physical lifetime to see the full sequence take place within a given nation or political climate, depending on the length of the cycle. Some cycles take more than two thousand years to complete.

The midpoint occurs in the exact middle of the script, in terms of page count, and divides the script into four equal pieces. Things may seem to have resolved peacefully at this point, without the hero having to face the great nemesis (the false victory), or it may seem that the quest is impossible to complete, and defeat is certain, so it's time to walk away (the false defeat). Regardless of which way your midpoint goes, the underlying concept is always the same. The hero does not want to have to face the nemesis, but ultimately there is no other way to complete the quest. Once you study this phenomenon and begin watching films with an educated eye, you will be amazed by the number of movies you know and love that are structured precisely along these lines.

A Personal Example of the Hero's Journey

For example, let's say you are the hero in our story. Let's say your obvious flaw is that you are irresponsible on the road and drive too fast. I know, of course that's not you, but this is a hypothetical example. The inciting incident could be the moment when you get pulled over and the officer writes you a ticket. The second act begins when you stop the debate within yourself and finally decide you're going to fight the ticket rather than just pay the fine and be done with it. Beating the ticket is now your quest. You go through fears and a lot of discussion with various people, including some laughter about the whole thing. You end up going to court, knowing that if the police officer doesn't show up, you won't have to pay the fee. The false victory midpoint is that moment when you think the officer isn't coming—only to find out that he walks right in as soon as you were convinced you were free. Now you know you're going to have to stand trial after all and endure the final confrontation with the nemesis, the judge. Within the history of a nation, the false victory could occur when the country the nation is warring with appears to have surrendered only to come back even more ferociously, with a new surprise attack, for example. The big lesson of your traffic ticket story may well be that the judge finds you guilty, but as a result, you learn to slow down and take your time. This may actually end up saving your life as well as the lives of others. A dramatic and painful scene could reveal how this seeming loss in court became your ultimate salvation.

The Dark Night of the Soul: All Is Lost

As the final showdown with the nemesis continues, our hero's initiation experiences get worse and worse. This ultimately leads to the critical moment in the whole story, near the end of the second act. It's known as the "dark night of the soul," or what Blake Snyder calls "All Is Lost."[355] At this point, the hero seems to be totally defeated. The quest seems impossible to fulfill. There appears to be no hope. You also get what Snyder calls the "Whiff of Death," where the hero often seems to have literally died. Not every film has our hero experience the threat of a physical death at this point, but every film will have a scene where we feel the hero's goal is utterly and completely unachievable. Snyder recommends that some form of death—even a symbolic reference such as clouds, a flying bird, or hole in the earth—be inserted here to make this part of the story reach the viewer on the deepest possible level.

In a romance, the all-is-lost point could be a terrible event that makes it seem impossible that the hero will ever be able to get together with his love interest. We have no idea how this problem can be solved. This is invariably the biggest tearjerker moment in every film. As a kid, I remember when my father came home one night, said he just saw an incredible movie called *E.T. the Extra-Terrestrial,* and told us we had to go see it as soon as possible. He was so excited that I could barely wait. I had trained myself to be strong and not to cry, especially at movies, but when E.T. was dying and looked like he was covered in oatmeal, and nothing seemed to be able to save him, tears ran freely down my face. I literally bawled like a baby when E.T. died—as did most of the other kids in the theater around me.

This may seem like the end of the road for our hero—the darkest moment, and the complete failure of the quest—but in symbolic terms, all that really dies at this point is the ego. Many movies milk this section of the story to the last drop. The hero often appears to be truly dead for five full pages of screen time. You will hear people all around you in the theater sniffling and sobbing if this part is really done well. Occasionally, movies actually kill off the hero at this point, just to keep us guessing, but this is very, very rare. Knowing that a resurrection is built into every screenplay does take a lot of the surprise out of it. However, in many films the mentor does die at this point—just as Obi-Wan Kenobi died in *Star Wars.* This can make the hero hit rock bottom and feel it is impossible to go on.

In the case of a country playing out the cycles of history, the all-is-lost point could be a seemingly grave defeat in battle, a horrifying economic collapse, or the loss of a highly revered and influential leader. Either way, all the doomsayers are certain it is the end of time, and the world will cease to exist as a result—but it never does. From this perspective, the times we're in as I write this book in 2013 can still be considered our collective dark night of the soul. We've been building up to this moment for hundreds, if not thousands, of years, depending on which of the cycles we're looking at. Since so few of us really understand the story on a conscious level and realize that the same events keep happening in regularly repeating cycles of history, we think the dark night is the end—the defeat is total and complete, and the story is finished. This is not so.

Working Through the Dark Night

The hero has cherished his or her flaws from the very beginning of the story. These are the negative habits, the selfish thoughts, the irrational fears, and the irresponsible behaviors that have allowed the hero to cope without facing his or her inner demons. In a romantic comedy, it may be the hero's fear of loving someone because he or she was hurt before. Now, in the dark night of the soul, the hero realizes that his or her love interest will be completely lost if the hero's fear of intimacy is not healed. In an action film, a hero who has been a coward and has been ruled by fear now finally gains the courage to face the nemesis against seemingly impossible odds.

The hero drops the ego—the flaws holding him or her back—and in so doing gains insight into how to complete the quest and defeat the nemesis. The talisman the hero received from the mentor often plays a very important role at this point, giving the hero that magic element needed to complete the quest. In a romance, once the hero finally lets go of his or her flaws, he or she may receive a key piece of information from the love interest that reveals how to satisfy the quest. In action films with a romantic "B story," this new information may simultaneously teach our hero how to get the love interest and defeat the nemesis. This information can be as simple as a kiss from the love interest, giving our hero the courage to acknowledge his or her love and face the bad guy.

Facing the Nemesis—in Movies, Personal Events, and Global Conflicts

A commercial script must have the hero face the nemesis directly and either defeat the nemesis ("up" ending) or be defeated by the nemesis ("down" ending). You can write a movie where someone or something else defeats the nemesis, and you may even get it financed and developed into a film, but it won't be anywhere near as popular as the films that follow the ancient structure. If a screenwriter uses some mysterious, unexpected, magical force to get the hero out of a jam at this point, without having the hero do the work, this is called deus ex machina—"a god from a machine"—and is considered very sloppy screenwriting. Some films do have this happen, but it is widely frowned upon; it does not conform to the ancient story. Our hero must summon the ultimate courage and face the nemesis. This is because every character in the film is ultimately a key aspect of the hero, just as we see in our dreams. If the hero doesn't face the nemesis directly, then the dream symbolism we receive each night is not being adequately portrayed in the story we are being told.

Let's say a nation built everything around a glorified leader. This masked their own flaws because they looked to someone else to provide them with the strength and leadership they were not willing to generate within themselves. When they lose their leader, either to death or perhaps to political forces beyond the leader's control, it does seem that all hope is lost. The people may be crying and shaking with fear, convinced that the nemesis they've been struggling against is now certain to overtake them.

However, as the people work through their grief and become increasingly brave, they reorganize and are willing to stand tall against the problem, which may be a physical, external enemy but could also be a social issue such as illiteracy, hunger, economic failure, and the like. New allies suddenly step up to help the people complete their quest. If the people succeed, then the qualities of the leader have inspired them to such a degree that they can now steer their civilization on their own. They don't need the leader's help anymore but can work as a community, along with their new allies.

The Third Act: Final Showdown, Triumph, and Seizing the Elixir

The third act doesn't begin until the hero has worked through the dark night of the soul and has discovered a solution by which to achieve the one thing he or she wants more than anything. Once the answer becomes obvious and the hero knows what has to be done, the third act begins. Let's not forget that in traditional plays, the curtains close at this hopeful point, where the final solution is now in sight—not at the cliffhanger moment that modern television shows often end on to compel us to "tune in next week!" This act break inspires a great deal of excitement in the viewer. Now our hero seems to have the answer! Can the hero do it? Will the hero succeed? I can't believe the hero has made it this far! What do you think is going to happen? The excitement of a pending solution reaches deep into the roots of the tree of mind. We love to reach this moment in our own lives because it means that all our hard work is about to pay off. We now have an opportunity to integrate the nemesis within us and stop the Wheel of Karma from causing us to suffer. As souls, we know this is our ultimate goal, and subconsciously we hunger for it.

At this point, the hero must be brave enough to take whatever steps are needed to ensure that he or she can face the nemesis—the Guardian of the Threshold—and achieve triumph. This plan may be fraught with peril; there is no guarantee that our hero will succeed. However, the ancient structure ensures that the Hero's Journey will lead to victory, even if the hero ends up dying in order to achieve it. Once the hero is brave enough to let go of his or her flaws and commit to the final solution, another key moment occurs in the great story. Now that the hero has fully embraced honor and destiny, the allies we met in the second act suddenly flood in—seemingly out of nowhere—to help defeat the nemesis. This is the other tearjerker moment in our story. Right when this happened in *Avatar,* I said, "The allies—of course!" The hero's quest had felt very lonely by this point, as if the hero had to complete the quest all alone. Now, suddenly, the kindness the hero showed others returns—in a remarkable burst of "good karma"—when the hero needs it most.

The allies represent other aspects of the hero's personality that suddenly come to his or her aid once the hero has discovered how to vanquish the selfish demands of the ego. One of these characters could embody strength. Another could embody humor, cunning, bravery, wisdom, love, or the trickster. In well-written and well-developed films, we may cry with exultant relief when we see all our friends from the second act suddenly return to help the hero at the exact moment he or she needs it most.

In Hollywood, happy endings are far more commercial, far more popular, and fit into the original story much more closely than unhappy ones. The hero achieves victory, lives through the struggle, and seizes the treasures of full illumination that the nemesis has been jealously guarding. Once you face the nemesis within yourself and knock down the defense mechanisms of the ego that have walled you off from loving others, you are ready to cross the threshold—and finally get a sense of your authentic self. The people who showed you kindness in the past, once you began pursuing your quest, have reappeared as valuable allies. Your authentic self is not the personality that built its identity around worry, pain, and fear but is the original core of who and what you are. In spiritual terms, this is the ascension—the evolution of your soul to a higher level. Every triumph we experience in life is a smaller version of this same breakthrough.

Once the nemesis is vanquished and the threshold is crossed, the hero must seize the Elixir of Immortality. This is the magic ingredient that makes the entire quest seem worthwhile. Again, the elixir can be an important person, a mysterious substance, a powerful device, a great treasure, or a valuable piece of knowledge that can transform the world. Some movies roll the credits right as the elixir is seized, but the ancient story does not. For this reason, viewers may feel as if they've been cheated when movies do this, but they don't quite know why.

The Return

Within the great story, after the hero seizes the elixir, he must then return to the ordinary world in his newly transformed state—and improve it. He may be chased out of the magical world by the nemesis once again or by some other opposing force. Either way, once the hero makes it back to the ordinary world with the elixir, we know the quest has finally been completed and the hero has transformed the world for the better. The more the hero improves the world as a result of his or her triumph, the stronger he or she fulfills the promise of the ancient story written into the mind of our galaxy.

Let's go back to our historical example of a nation that lost a glorified leader. All along, the people were helping their leader but were too afraid to get directly involved. After his or her tragic death, the people finally develop courage and face their problems directly. Together, they find a seemingly magical solution for their problems—a better, cheaper way to print books to combat illiteracy, a new process for cultivating more food in less time to fight hunger, or a useful product they can manufacture that stimulates their economy. When we reach the return part of the story, the elixir is put to use and starts appearing as an enhancement within everyone's daily lives.

The return part of the story is well outlined in the final film in the *Lord of the Rings* trilogy. Frodo finally gets to return home to the Shire, after casting the Ring of Power into the lava, forever destroying the evil forces of Sauron, and freeing the land from fear and pain. Similarly, George Lucas spent a good bit of time creating an epic awards ceremony for Luke Skywalker and his allies at the end of *Star Wars: A New Hope*, the first film in his original trilogy. In this crowd-pleasing scene, a huge crowd roars with approval for Luke's successful completion of his quest as he is honored by his lost sister, Princess Leia. Similarly, at the end of *Return of the Jedi*, the entire galaxy erupts in celebration as Luke's mentors look on with approval in their ascended light-bodies.

In plays, this final celebration often appears as the curtain call, when all the actors step out onstage, one-by-one. Our hero, the ultimate guest of honor, comes out last. Every actor smiles and waves at the adoring audience, and once they are all together, they take a bow. The fourth wall is finally broken, the actors make eye contact, and the audience becomes a direct part of the story. On a subconscious level, this reminds us that all the world is a stage, and we are merely players in the story of our own lives. We are working our way through an elaborate script we wrote in the afterlife, and we have a much greater existence outside the story. Someday, we will be reunited with our friends once more and celebrate the joys and disasters of the life we lived.

The return and curtain call are very satisfying parts of the story, but many modern films overlook them because of time constraints or as a stylistic convention. Many films roll the credits as soon as the hero vanquishes the nemesis and achieves the goal of the quest, leaving you to finish the story within your own mind and heart. In some cases, this move feels right, but many viewers end up feeling like they've lost something important if they don't get to enjoy the hero's return along with him or her. Some movies carry our hero through incredible ordeals and roll credits as soon as the first real sign of relief arrives. Movies like this may still sell well, but something is missing.

This Is Story

This is "story." This is what many of us are constantly driven to surround ourselves with whenever we have free time. Every time we turn on the television, every time we see a movie, every time we call up friends and tell them about a problem we have and how we're trying to solve it, we are in the story. It is a spiritual ceremony. We are drawn to it because we are spiritual beings. Hollywood presents it to us because we hunger for it.

We often lack the incredible patience it takes to watch the story slowly unfold on the worldwide level over the course of what might be hundreds or even thousands of years. We can easily see the problem and yearn for the answer well before everyone else on earth is fully ready to have it delivered. At this point, we must turn to the story of our own lives and work on healing ourselves. In so doing, we heal the world—and we can change the story's outcome.

Separation, Initiation, and Return

We already mentioned the beginning, middle, and ending as being setup, conflict, and resolution—or first act, second act, and third act. Blake Snyder also refers to these divisions as thesis, antithesis, and synthesis.[356] Joseph Campbell breaks this three-part sequence down into separation, initiation, and return. In the separation phase, you feel cut off, you feel alone, you feel, in the deepest sense, that love, or the creator, has abandoned you. This causes you to build up defense mechanisms to protect your sensitive core. In the initiation phase, you face your fears, confront your shadow, and ultimately let go of your deepest flaws. In so doing, you achieve triumph, or illumination—the spiritual ascension into the realm of pure knowledge, where that true love is the Elixir of Immortality that is now readily available to you. In the return phase, you go back to your normal life and transform it, with the new understandings you have reached. Even if the one you loved ends up dying at the end, you realize that you have yourself, and therefore you can never be alone. Once you learn to love yourself, you gain whatever your true heart desires—and you help others in the process.

We run through these cycles every day of our lives. We run through them over the course of years with parents, teachers, friends, bosses, and romantic partners who have been returning to be with us in lifetime after lifetime. Ultimately, we run through these same cyclical patterns on a worldwide level. It's all the same identity, moving through the same story in a worldwide lucid dream. At the end of each lifetime, we get another grand curtain call and again have the full awareness that the life we just lived is only one facet of a much greater jewel. We are reacquainted with our inner circle—the same troupe of friends who have chosen to play different parts in each new story that comes along. We are able to step back, take a deep breath, and appreciate that the struggles we thought were so all-important—which seemingly threatened the core of our existence—were merely reminders. We placed these apparent ob-stacles in our path to help us awaken to our core identity as eternal souls who are perfect, holographic projections of a loving Creator.

Intelligent, self-aware co-creators have been working through and mastering this story, individually and collectively, since long before there were ever human beings on earth. Some of the older ones may become mentors who appear in our dreams and help steer events on earth to a more favorable outcome, behind the scenes. When we see that story acted out in songs, poems, books, plays, television shows, or movies, we are inspired. We are moved. Deep down inside, we know this is our story—the Book of Life—and we know the book is written to have a happy ending. We now begin to awaken within the dream. And what might happen once we fully and completely wake up? Will we penetrate the veil and touch intelligent infinity?

The Worldwide Third Act

We have not yet figured out, on a worldwide level, that this Book of Life applies equally well to the events in our own history—that is, the Hero's Story. Nor do we consciously realize that we are now well into the third act—the final struggle with our own worldwide ego projection. We have worked through the dark night of the soul, we have identified the Guard-ian of the Threshold, and we know what we have to do in order to defeat this guardian, the nemesis. No more Sheep Effect. We must face the truth—for the truth will set us free. In the not-too-distant future, we may even head into a worldwide curtain call. Reality as we know it may be revealed as an elaborate illusion orchestrated from higher levels for our own evolution within a living universe. In this grand, triumphant moment of ascension, on a global scale, the angelic players who have helped us all along may finally step out from behind the veil and take a bow. The data collected in this book makes it a lot easier for us to imag-ine that something like this may actually happen. Synchronicity is the key that is helping us awaken on an individual and collective level.

We already discussed the pope's shocking resignation in 2013 and lightning striking the Vatican that same night. This was a stunningly perfect embodiment of the symbol for the dark night of the soul that is written into "the roots of the tree of Mind," in Law of One terms. Considering the depth to which the original Roman church modified Christianity, this symbolism is extremely poignant. Another interesting example from our recent history was that on Thursday, January 15, 2009, just five days before Barack Obama's inauguration, Captain Chesley Sullenberger pulled off a successful water landing of his critically damaged passenger airliner in the Hudson River. This was the symbolic opposite of the airline disaster of 9/11. As I wrote on my website,[357] this appeared to be another manifestation of the worldwide lucid dream we're all experiencing, in which seemingly random world events in fact have symbolic meaning.

Many people felt that something profoundly mystical was going on in the Miracle on the Hudson, but they didn't really understand it. Among other things, I presented video proof that the exact moment all the survivors lined up on the wings in the iconic photograph was 3:33 P.M. This was only weeks after Obama's victory was announced in the election, once he garnered 333 electoral votes. The 333 stayed on everyone's television screens during John McCain's entire concession speech.[358] I must admit it was a great surprise to see 333 appear on a worldwide level in two different obvious ways over such a short period of time.

I do not believe either of these events was contrived or planned by anyone here on earth, nor do I think they make Obama a savior figure. Each of us must become the hero in this global story in our own way. The fact that Obama won two elections shows that the people voted for the message he gave them, whether he could live up to it in office or not. At the time of this writing, he has started his second term, and there is widespread discontent with the way things are going. These "geo-synchronicities," like the Vatican lightning strike and the Miracle on the Hudson, may be the result of direct spiritual interventions into our collective story—sending us all a powerful message that a positive future will appear. Within the framework of the story, events like this are called foreshadowing, or harbingers, hints that the hero will indeed be successful in his or her quest, regardless of how dark the road may seem at the time.

In the Miracle on the Hudson, the symbolism appeared to be telling us that under the violent, imperialistic policies of the Bush administration, the world was rapidly spiraling into a complete disaster, including the massive economic collapse of 2008. September 11 was a grand symbol of that catastrophe. However, the public awakened enough to vote for the candidate who promised to end the fear, who did not see people in foreign lands as "the enemy," and who vowed that he would bring everyone in, together, for a safe landing—regardless of their race, nationality, or religion. The heroic pilot achieved the impossible—facing the threshold of death, vanquishing the same airline demon that brought down the Twin Towers on 9/11, and seizing the Elixir of Immortality. This stunning event subconsciously showed the world that there can be a happy ending within even the most troubling and disturbing of global predicaments. Sullenberger's rescue was considered a miracle that inspired millions around the world and is now praised as "one of the most dramatic escape stories in aviation history." [359]

Whether you call them the Illuminati, the New World Order, the Cabal, the Shadow Elite, or the Bad Guys, the planetary elite do represent a worldwide projection of our own ego, distorted to funhouse-mirror extremes. There are an ever-increasing number of harbingers that this collective nightmare is indeed coming to an end, and I consistently track them on my website. The Elixir of Immortality that this "dragon" is guarding is far more significant, and fantastic, than most people could ever have imagined—and will have a huge impact upon our world. It includes the full and complete knowledge that we are not alone in the universe and is the gateway to meeting our long-lost relatives in a global curtain call. Given the ever-increasing pace of events now unfolding, and the incredible number of prophetic dreams I've been having about the disclosure and defeat of the Cabal, there may already have been very significant developments between the time I finish writing this manuscript and the time the book is published.

On a directly physical level, the increasing problems of earthquakes, tsunamis, hurricanes, volcanic eruptions, and climate change are also key aspects of our worldwide dark night of the soul. These upheavals appear to be a very significant part of the grand design to awaken us, according to almost all ancient myths and prophecies worldwide. Regardless of our race, country, color, or creed, the oil spills, earthquakes, floods, hurricanes, tornadoes, droughts, and the like are a global wake-up call. We all need to have solidarity in the face of these catastrophes, particularly if we realize that they may have energetic causes that we can change for the positive by our own thoughts and actions. The Law of One series directly indicates that these global problems are intended to awaken us on a planetary level.

> 65.6 [Your people will have a] greater opportunity for service due to the many [earth] changes—which will offer many challenges, difficulties, and seeming distresses, within your illusion, to many who then will seek to understand—if we may use this misnomer—the reason for the malfunctioning of the physical rhythms of their planet.[360]

Ready to Explore the Cycles of History

Now that we have established the structure that spiritual evolution is taking—written into our galactic mind within this living cosmos—we are finally ready to explore the cycles of history. This knowledge presents us with a shocking, revolutionary, and utterly world-transforming change in perspective. It is the ultimate unveiling of the grand nature of the illusion we are living in and the intelligence of the greater cosmos that surrounds us. We will soon see that many, if not most, of the events that happen in our world—even the worst mass atrocities—are not random at all. They appear to be the manifestations of an intelligent structure in time that we keep moving through. The ancient story seems to keep being told, over and over again, until we learn the lessons it is meant to teach us. If we see others as separate from ourselves, as less than, as the enemy, then the nemesis is winning—and we will keep suffering right along with our forgotten brothers and sisters. Wars and fatalities will keep repeating, again and again, until we finally see that we are all one, and everyone has a right to live with freedom and peace. Our leaders cannot steer us into wars unless at least a certain percentage of us believe that violence is necessary to solve our problems.

Sociopaths are very clever at concealing themselves and convincing us that we want the same things they want, but that is all changing now. Once the truth is exposed, it can never be stopped. Our individual and collective free will has been neatly kept within certain guidelines, moving and dancing within energetic influences that most of us would never believe could exist. At various points in the ancient Hero's Journey, single individuals can embody certain character archetypes within the story on a personal, regional, national, or even global level. The great inventors were mentors who handed us the talismans, or magic gifts, that allowed us to transform our society into the magical world. The mysterious new force of electricity was harnessed for positive ends, enhancing the simplest things we needed in our daily lives, such as washing laundry, cleaning dishes, reading books, storing and cooking food, traveling, and communicating with one another. The nuclear bomb represented the great evil that this technology was capable of creating. Now we have reached a point at which we have isolated the enemy that is threatening us with this and other weapons of mass destruction, and we can seize the much greater benefits of technology that will follow in its defeat.

The energetic influences that are causing members of our society to jump into these archetypal roles and fulfill them according to this ancient pattern seem to be caused by our earth's movement. Specifically, our planet is slowly drifting through different areas of space that are ultimately alive and intelligent. Our earth's axis traces out a slow, 25,920-year wobble, and the cycles of history follow neatly along. As we will review in Part 4, this Great Year is ultimately the orbit that our entire solar system is tracing around a mysterious Black Sun companion star. The energetic fields of our sun's companion are structured in perfect, harmonic geometric patterns, and our free will is being precisely guided by these fields on an individual and collective level.

PART THREE

CYCLES OF VICTORY
AND DEFEAT

CHAPTER TWELVE

Joan of Arc Rises Again

The Great Cycles of History

The Law of One series has some intriguing quotes on the true meaning of history, which give us an excellent starting point for this discussion. We are reminded that there really is only one story being told again and again. The specific details, times, and places are much less important than the philosophy of spiritual evolution these cycles are ultimately meant to teach us.

> 16.21 There is no history, as we understand your concept. Picture, if you will, a circle of being. We know the alpha and omega as infinite intelligence. The circle never ceases. It is present.[361]

> 9.4 Each of your planetary entities is on a different cyclical schedule, as you might call it. The timing of these cycles is a measurement equal to a portion of intelligent energy. This intelligent energy offers a type of clock. The cycles move as precisely as a clock strikes your hour.[362]

> 2.2 The time/space of several thousand of your years creates a spurious type of interest. . . . The teach/learning which is our responsibility is philosophical rather than historical.[363]

1.1 We are not a part of time and, thus, are able to be with you in any of your times.[364]

16.22 There is past, present, and future in third density. In an overview such as an entity may have, removed from the space/time continuum, it may be seen that in the cycle of completion there exists only the present.[365]

An Epic Mystery—Encoded in Myths All Over the World

In *The Hero with a Thousand Faces*,[366] Joseph Campbell revealed that all lasting myths, worldwide, tell us the same story, which he called the Hero's Journey. Giorgio de Santillana and Hertha von Dechend found that dozens of these same myths, from all over the world, had hidden metaphors of the 25,920-year precession—or Great Year—very deliberately encoded within them. We know that there is a slow, counter-rotating wobble in the earth's axis that takes 25,920 years to complete, but conventional science has no explanation for why it was considered so important in so many different ancient mythologies. The hero's triumph over the nemesis in these myths seems to reveal a clear prophecy of a coming Golden Age—a new level of human evolution that is called "fourth density" in the Law of One series. There is one, great Hero's Journey story that takes 25,920 years to complete, with many subcycles in which the same story keeps repeating itself in different ways. These cycles of history appear to be referred to in the book of Ecclesiastes (3:1, 2, and 15):

> For everything its season, and for every activity under heaven its time: a time to be born and a time to die. . . . Whatever is has been already, and whatever is to come has been already—and God summons each event back in its turn.

The Hindu scriptures repeatedly discuss cycles of evolution in the cosmos—including a full "day and night of Brahma," which they believe is the entire cycle of the universe—at 8 billion, 640 million years.[367]

The 25,920-year cycle is also mentioned, as well as its divisions into the twelve 2,160-year Ages of the Zodiac. The Hindu scriptures teach that we are now moving through the greatest age of darkness—the Kali Yuga—when there is a progressive decline in morality, as well as an excess of materialism and violence. This paves the way for the coming transformation into the Satya Yuga, or the Golden Age, when great avatars will reappear. Krishna speaks of himself as an embodiment of the reappearing hero archetype in the Bhagavad Gita (4:5–11):

> I have been born many times, Arjuna, and many times hast thou been born. But I remember my past lives, and thou has forgotten thine. Although I am unborn, everlasting, and I am the Lord of all, I come to my realm of nature—and through my wondrous power I am born. When righteousness is weak, and faints, and unrighteousness exults in pride, then my Spirit arises on earth. For the salvation of those who are good, for the destruction of evil in man, for the fulfillment of the kingdom of righteousness, I come to this world—in the ages that pass.

I first became aware of the idea that history may be moving in cycles when I read *The Great Pyramid Decoded* by Peter Lemesurier in the summer of 1993:

> History . . . [may] indeed [be] cyclic, as we earlier surmised, and as the Maya also long believed. . . . [This] cyclic view of history . . . [is] capable of being expressed in terms of astrological notions derived from the precession of the equinoxes. . . . We might perhaps more justly conceive of the progression of the ages in terms of a spiral. The march of evolution and history, in others words, displays a circular motion, but each revolution takes place at a different level (presumably a higher one)—and is characterized by accomplishments of a different order. Indeed, the fact that the ancient Aztecs apparently regarded the conch-shell as symbolic of the succeeding

ages would suggest that they subscribed to some such notion. Nor is the idea without its distinguished modern adherents: even Einstein is alleged to have subscribed to it. . . .

There appears to be nothing improbable in a cyclic view of world history. In fact, the only real obstacle to the more general acceptance of such a view is the apparent lack of specific archaeological evidence to back it up—which may have more than a little to do with lack of knowledge of what to look for, or where exactly to look for it. Whether, as Edgar Cayce has claimed, such evidence will in due course be found, only time will tell.[368]

The Mystery Is Solved—Six Years Later

I continued thinking about this mystery, on and off, for another six years after I first read Lemesurier's vastly complex work of scholarship. Finally, during a birthday party my friend David Steinberg threw for me on March 7, 1999, he handed me an unpublished, yellowing manuscript of a book he had been hired to translate from French into English. He considered this decaying stack of papers to be extremely precious and wanted it back as soon as I finished reading it. I soon realized it was very synchronistic to receive the ultimate magic gift at my birthday party, as this was the shift point in my own yearly cycle. I was about to upload my first full-length online scientific book, *Convergence II,* to the Internet the very next day, and I briefly mentioned the book David lent me at the very end of *Convergence II*'s conclusion.[369] More than a year and a half later, I told David this book really had to be online and offered to scan and publish the entire manuscript. He agreed, and it appeared on my website on January 10, 2001. The book is called *The End of Our Century,* by François Masson, and the chapter that stands out above the rest is called "Cyclology: The Mathematics of History."[370]

Masson had the hard evidence to prove exactly what Lemesurier had suggested in his book from 1977. History does indeed appear to be moving in very precise cycles—and Masson gave extensive, astonishing evidence to prove it. I was quite surprised that no publisher had been willing to carry such a fascinating book. However, in March 2013, I conducted an Internet search and found that an alternate English translation of this book did actually get published by Donning Company Publishers in 1983 and was entitled *The End of Our Era.*[371] This book is now out of print and may be available only by interlibrary loan, but Steinberg's translation is freely published on my website. The Library of Congress lists *The End of Our Era* as being copyrighted on June 25, 1982, and revised on March 22, 1984,[372] proving that the book did appear in public as of 1982–1983.

Masson highlighted the discoveries of Michèl Helmer, who presented a vast and compelling new theory in the course of multiple articles for the journal *Les Cahiers Astrologiques* over the course of sixteen years. Helmer argued that historical events repeat themselves in very precise cycles of time—with stunning accuracy. Masson wrote the following in 1980: "In the *Cahiers Astrologiques* (journal) of 1960, M. Helmer presented his theory on the cyclic repetition of events—a cycle based mainly on using the Ideal pre-eminent Number 25920 and its factors. Applying his theory enabled [Helmer] to make many exact predictions—both economic and political."[373]

Helmer does not appear to have any publications in the *Cahiers Astrologiques* journal archives for 1960, but his work may have been reprinted that year. Since *Cahiers Astrologiques* still has an online record of all its publications we do know that Helmer wrote "Solar Revolution" in issue 75 of *Cahiers Astrologiques* (1958); untitled articles in issue 91 (1961) and issue 99 (1962); "Encrypted Documents of Heaven and Earth" in issue 100 (1962); and untitled articles in issue 114 (1965), issue 118 (1965), and issue 121 (1966). Helmer also wrote "The Harmony of the World Is Based on the Rhythm and the Golden Section, What Do You Think?" in issue 126 (1967); "Discovering the Mystery of the Sothic Cycle" in issue 131 (1967); and untitled articles in issues 132 and 133 (1968).[374] Helmer also contributed to "Pluto Survey Answers" with ten other authors in issue 168 (1974).[375]

If This Is True, Then It Changes Everything

If Helmer's core hypothesis is true, then the implications are staggering. We can no longer trust in our own free will—nor can we trust in the apparent randomness of world events. The things that are happening now have happened before, and these events may well be following a mysterious ancient script, written into the very fabric of space and time itself. This is a very different, and much more hopeful, way of viewing our lives—and indeed of our entire "reality" on earth. No matter how bad things may look, we're never really in that much trouble; we are going through organized cycles of events that are designed to promote our collective spiritual evolution. Graham Hancock combined Copenhaver's[376] and Scott's[377] modern translations of the ancient Egyptian Hermetic texts to reveal their prophecies of a Golden Age. These Hermetic prophcies called for a "new birth of the Cosmos; it is a making again of all things good, a holy and awe-inspiring restoration of all nature; and it is wrought inside the process of Time, by the eternal Will of the Creator." [378] What exactly is the "process of time" these ancient Hermetic writings referred to? Helmer and Masson seem to have found the answer.

Helmer was able to verify, in great detail, that "history repeats itself." Specifically, he found that there were a variety of different cycles in which events curiously repeat themselves. Of course, these events are not precisely the same. The names, the places, and the specific details change, but the exact timing of major events, such as the biggest wars, repeat with astonishing precision. Cycles that last hundreds or even thousands of years can trigger new wars within days of when they appeared in the previous cycle. Almost all of the cycles Helmer discovered were perfect subdivisions of the Great Year, in which earth orbits around the sun 25,920 times. The most well-known subdivision of 25,920 years is the Age of the Zodiac at 2,160 years in length. There are, of course, twelve of these zodiac cycles within the Great Year. Helmer also found that each Age of the Zodiac could be further divided into four equal pieces. This gives us a 540-year subcycle in which historical events can repeat.

The 539-Year Cycle

Helmer concluded that we need to shave one year off this 540-year cycle in order to truly appreciate its magic. Once we knock it down to 539 years, we get additional "harmonics" that do not appear in the number 540. For example, a 539-year cycle is evenly divisible by seven and eleven. This allows us to create perfect subcycles of seven and eleven years in which historical events may be repeating. If you do the math, you will see that there are exactly seven cycles of seventy-seven years in 539 years, as well as forty-nine cycles of eleven years. We already know that our sun goes from a very quiet, tranquil surface to a boiling inferno of sunspot activity in cycles that typically run in eleven-year units. The Russian scientist Tchijevsky proved that all the most significant events on earth do occur during the peak of the sunspot cycle. Helmer further proved that Tchijevsky was right; the eleven-year cycle has a direct effect on human civilization. Tchijevsky never considered that this eleven-year sunspot cycle might only be the building block of something much larger.

Helmer also speculated that this 539-year cycle might have been alluded to in the Bible as "7 times 77." The best match I found is in Matthew 18:21–22 (NIV): "Then Peter came to Jesus and asked, 'Lord, how many times shall I forgive my brother when he sins against me? Up to seven times?' Jesus answered, 'I tell you, not seven times, but seventy-seven times.'"

Why would Jehoshua reveal the numbers seventy and seventy-seven, back to back, when he was discussing the true art of forgiveness? Was this some kind of a hidden message, since Jehoshua often spoke in dreamlike riddles, or parables? Other translations have Jehoshua saying "seven times seventy."[379] Helmer apparently had a Bible translation where Jehoshua actually said "seven times seventy-seven." We must multiply the numbers seven and seventy-seven together to decipher the hidden message. If Jehoshua did, in fact, "penetrate intelligent infinity" and become an embodiment of the hero—the original mind of our galaxy—then he may have gained the direct knowledge that history moves in 539-year cycles. Jehoshua may be telling us that this cycle is written into the mind of the galaxy as a cycle of forgiveness that we move through in the course of multiple lifetimes. Through these great cycles of time, we work out our karma—and heal our society on a collective basis.

The Bible connection may seem to be a bit speculative, but according to Masson, there's good science behind the cycle itself: "This [539-year] cycle is surely the most important of those whose scope we can comprehend: it is the turning point of the basic cycles of a civilization."[380]

Using this cycle, Helmer was able to predict, in 1960, that very powerful events would take place in French history by 1968. According to Masson, Helmer published these predictions openly in 1964—though again, Masson may have seen a reprint from an earlier edition of the journal, since the online record does not show that Helmer wrote any new papers that year. Either way, this prophecy was a very bold move. If Helmer was proven wrong, his career and credibility would be destroyed—but by this point, he had already identified this cycle at work in modern-day France. Helmer must have been quite excited, as he knew that these cycles were building up to a moment where the public would be inspired to rise up against their nemesis, and a newer and stronger form of freedom would result. According to Masson, "Helmer chose as his starting point the year 1429—when the tide turned against the English in the Hundred Years' War. This affected the whole history of Europe."

Joan of Arc's Cycle Repeats in Twentieth-Century French History

After this critical turning point in the Hundred Years' War, England largely stopped attacking its own European neighbors, including France, and focused on building its empire overseas. This crucial defeat of the English was triggered by none other than Joan of Arc—a nineteen-year-old girl with seemingly mystical powers to communicate with the magical world of the spirit. Joan of Arc was put in charge of the entire French army because of her unique abilities. Joan of Arc is, therefore, a perfect hero character within our collective Hero's Journey.

The ancient three-act structure is prewritten, in perfect form, in the story of Joan of Arc. There is no need to add, delete or reorganize any of the events that took place in order to tell the story. Joan of Arc's epic tale is a perfect example of how specific individuals can become embodiments of the main character in the Hero's Journey story at various points in history. It may ultimately be everyone's destiny to fulfill this ancient pattern in our own unique ways. Joan of Arc's critical victory against the British in the city of Orleans occurred from April 29 to May 8 in the year 1429. Helmer's prophecy did not disappoint his readers in the least: "539 years later, practically to the day, the French youth, on another level of the spiral, brought about the shift and incredible destruction of a whole state of mind belonging to the past."[381]

All You Need Is Love

Sure enough, on May 3, 1968, just 539 years and four days after Joan of Arc led the previous uprising, there was a new uprising in France, led by young college students. The Beatles' groundbreaking *Sgt. Pepper's Lonely Hearts Club Band*—now voted the number one rock-and-roll album in history by *Rolling Stone* magazine—had just come out the year before. The Beatles also released the hit single "All You Need Is Love" on the first-ever live, global television program on June 25, 1967, entitled *Our World*. An estimated 400 million people in twenty-six countries tuned in to see this broadcast,[382] and the BBC commissioned the Beatles to write a song for the United Kingdom's contribution to the program.

The sexual revolution was in full swing, but French students were kept locked up in separate single-sex dormitories under strict security. No "newspaper taxis" appeared on the shore, and the "girl with kaleidoscope eyes" was held away under heavy guard in a private room. Love, apparently, was not something French college students needed—at all. The students were not allowed to visit one another in their homes at any time, day or night—and this was enforced with rigid, military strictness. This total lockdown on freedom clearly seemed to be an archaic, leftover relic from an increasingly irrelevant religious code promoted by a hyper-conservative government, but these harsh rules affected the lives of the college students quite dramatically. How were they ever supposed to make friends with members of the opposite sex if they weren't even allowed to pay each other a friendly visit during the day? *The Independent* revealed that this strict rule had created a tense political climate in France by March 15, 1968: "Pierre Viansson-Ponté said that France was suffering from a dangerous political malady: 'boredom'. Elsewhere, he said, from Spain to the US, students were protesting about wars or fundamental liberties. 'French students are mostly concerned that the girls . . . should be able to visit the bedrooms of the boys, which is a rather limited conception of human rights.'"[383]

A New Hero Arises—and History Repeats Itself

Daniel Cohn-Bendit, a fiery, red-haired twenty-two-year-old, became the new hero character in the next turn of the 539-year cycle when he led a mob of three hundred students into a full uprising. His army of frustrated students occupied the administrative block of their school and demanded change. This put them at risk of being expelled, which would have cost them all the money they and their families had invested in their education. This did not stop them from taking action and defending their right to freedom. *The Independent* revealed that the nemesis tried to crush this political uprising just as we saw in the case of Joan of Arc, 539 years earlier: "Several students, including Cohn-Bendit, were accused of 'agitation' and threatened with expulsion. A demonstration in support was planned in the courtyard of the venerable Sorbonne, in the centre of Paris's Left Bank, on 3 May."[384]

This dispute soon escalated into a clash with armed riot police—the minions of the great nemesis that must be confronted on the Hero's Journey. The police seemed to enjoy their jobs too much and began committing acts of brutality, but the people fought back: The police were wearing "old-fashioned uniforms and old-fashioned helmets. They looked rather like French soldiers from the 1914–18 war." This may well be part of the overall symbolism of the story revealing itself, through synchronicity—showing how the police represented the minions of the old, crumbling, oppressive world order in France.

> The demonstrators had been promised that they could leave freely. About 400 of them were brutally arrested. Larger demonstrations gathered. The first "pavés," or cobble stones, were thrown at the police. The Paris police, supported by a few busloads of the notorious CRS riot police, responded with indiscriminate baton charges and volleys of tear gas— assaulting students, journalists, passers-by, tourists, cinema- goers and elderly couples who were sitting at café terrasses watching the fun. Many of the younger victims, and some older ones, joined in the riots. By that night, there were bar- ricades all over.[385]

Much Greater Numbers of People Are Inspired to Rise Up

Joan of Arc's key battle ended on May 8, 1429. Although she and her group of soldiers lost the battle, her story was so powerful—hitting the Hero's Journey "button" within everyone's subconscious mind so strongly—that she inspired much greater numbers of people to rise up against tyranny and defeat the nemesis. The key turning point in the student uprising happened 539 years and two days after Joan of Arc's landmark battle on May 8. A group of students armed with nothing but their bare hands made direct, violent attacks against the police ringing the courtyard in their riot gear: "A week [after May 3rd], a large crowd of students tried to 'liberate' the Sorbonne, which had been ringed by the CRS [police forces]. Trees were ripped up, cars overturned and cobble stones hurled—exposing yards of sand."[386]

Of course, this only caused the police to fight back even harder. Once again, it seemed like an all-is-lost point. The students did their best, but the government was fighting back with brutal military force. However, the students had fulfilled their role in the Hero's Journey, just as Joan of Arc had done—they faced off against the nemesis directly. This is where the allies from the second act can now come rushing in. Back 539 years ago, Joan of Arc's brave actions sparked a much greater uprising, which ultimately freed France and other European countries from the nemesis. In the French student rebellion, after their main attempt to defeat the riot police was crushed, more than 8 million people were soon inspired to jump into this new battle for freedom. The allies stormed in just three days after Daniel Cohn-Bendit and his army of students had done their best to "liberate" the Sorbonne—and failed: "The trades unions— against the better judgment of their own leaders—called a one-day strike and demonstration. The government ordered the CRS to withdraw, and an immense student and worker demonstration choked the Left Bank. But the strike did not end after one day, as the union leaders planned. Eight million workers went on indefinite, wildcat strike—the largest labour stoppage in French history."[387]

A Truly Powerful Event That Changed History

The Independent revealed the scope and power of this student-led uprising—almost exactly 539 years to the day after Joan of Arc worked her magic in the previous cycle: "There were other student revolts in Europe and America, before and after May 1968, [but] in no other country did a student rebellion almost bring down a government. In no other country did a student rebellion lead to a workers' revolt, one that rose up from the blue-collar grass roots and overwhelmed the paternalistic trade-union leadership as much as the paternalistic, conservative government."[388]

The effects of this revolution continued beyond just a student uprising: "The leaders of the young people who built barricades and overturned cars in the Paris Latin Quarter in 1968 went on, in many cases, to become senior journalists, writers, philosophers, and politicians (including the present foreign minister, Bernard Kouchner)."[389]

Masson also explained that "since that year 1968, which saw the same youth movement appear throughout the world—in France, Czechoslovakia, the USA, Mexico, Japan, West Germany, etc.—no one can depend on his title [of nobility or a graduate degree] to be obeyed, but must prove his abilities."[390]

How Could This Possibly Have Happened?

These are astonishing correlations—particularly when we remember that Helmer predicted, in writing, that Joan of Arc's revolutionary overthrow of her people's nemesis would precisely repeat in French history 539 years later. How could Helmer possibly have made such an accurate prophecy at least four years in advance? How could the key turning point have happened only two days apart in each of these cycles? Now the 2,160-year Age of the Zodiac cycle doesn't seem so archaic, boring, and useless in our modern world anymore. This may turn out to be an incredibly advanced science, requiring the very best computer power we have to truly map out and understand. Once we divide the Age of the Zodiac into four equal pieces and subtract one year to make the cycle into a more harmonic number, we see historical events repeating with remarkable precision. This challenges everything we think we know. If historical events are not random, then what about free will? Suddenly, the science of the ancient gods from all over the world seems far more modern than we ever realized.

The Ages of the Zodiac were highly revered in Sumer, Egypt, Greece, Rome, and India—and appear to be the original inspiration for the idea that "history repeats itself." Skeptics might argue that Helmer just "got lucky" and the fulfillment of his prophecy—within two days of total perfection—was somehow just a coincidence. However, this is only one of hundreds of examples, extending throughout documented history, in which events reappear in perfect cycles of time—as we will see in future chapters. Helmer and Masson found dozens of striking examples that fit this same pattern very precisely—and as we will see, I was able to continue their work and prove that these events have continued happening ever since. That, for me, was the final proof I needed. In 2010, I discovered that 9/11 and several key events before and after it were precisely correlated with similar wars and political upheavals that had occurred 539 years earlier in Europe. The battle that corresponded to 9/11 in the previous cycle occurred only six days apart from where it appeared in our time—exactly one quarter of the Age of the Zodiac later—on September 11, 2001.

I honestly don't know how long it will take for our society to discover and accept that this is really happening. My guess is that unless we see a monumental historical event—such as a genuine disclosure of the extraterrestrial presence on earth, in both modern and ancient times—most people will simply ignore this. Many other amazing scientific discoveries are already being dismissed, without question. I will be happy to fight for the truth—but I admit that the whole concept sounds so outrageous to most people that the only way they will ever be convinced is if we can provide mountains of proof and present an entirely new cosmology that supports this new information. Thankfully, we have that new scientific paradigm already. If the universe is indeed a living, conscious being, and there are many scientific discoveries that prove it, there is a solid body of evidence to model how this might be happening—and why. The first steps of this model will be shared in Part 4, though it calls for a much deeper investigation.

Things Got Better the Next Time Around

It is interesting to note that in the next turn of the cycle in France, no one had to die, neither the students nor the police. The entire cycle played out in a much more peaceful way. Both sides—the conservative old guard and the liberal youths—were able to grow up and stop seeing the other as their nemesis. This suggests that as we move through these great cycles, there are no real "sides." The hero and the nemesis are both aspects of who we are as a society. We do not need to declare ourselves "right" and others "wrong," simply because we do not agree on everything. By finding ways to forgive one another and get along as a planet, we are collectively purifying and transforming our ego mind on a larger, worldwide level, as well as on an individual basis. The students were forgiven for wanting to have sex before marriage, and the government was soon forgiven for having tried to enforce a traditional code of ethics.

CHAPTER THIRTEEN

The 2,160-Year Cycle Between
Rome and the United States

T he 539-year cycle was very impressive, demonstrating mathematical precision that was accurate to within forty-eight hours across
more than half a millennium. Michèl Helmer predicted there
would be a major French rebellion at least four years in advance—and
indeed, more than 8 million people were inspired to join the students'
fight for freedom. If Helmer and Masson were right, then each Age of
the Zodiac breaks down into quarter cycles, in which historical events
will repeat themselves with astonishing accuracy. If you read the original
translation on my website, you will find many different examples of exact
turning points in history, separated by 539 years.[391] No one but David
Steinberg, his immediate family, and the potential book publisher had
ever seen this manuscript. As far as I could tell, no one other than
Helmer and Masson had ever discovered these cycles repeating in our
history, though Peter Lemesurier's book had put me on the lookout six
years earlier. Helmer and Masson's research seemed to be unique—and
utterly groundbreaking. If this phenomenon was real, there should be
many more examples of the 539-year cycle than Helmer and Masson
discovered, which should be detectable through further research. It
should be possible to crunch vastly detailed historical databases with
supercomputers in order to look for more patterns like this.

I was equally surprised when I found out that the 2,160-year Age of
the Zodiac cycle was precisely guiding the movement of historical events

as well. Furthermore, for me, an American, this data was up close and personal, as there was a direct connection between historical events in the Roman Empire and twentieth-century events in the United States. A 2,160-year zodiac cycle seems staggeringly long. If we go back 2,160 years, that's older than the New Testament and older than the time Jehoshua walked the earth. We now find ourselves back in an area we lovingly call "B.C."—but the great cycles of history do not even blink across this seemingly vast distance. Masson's research had not been updated since 1980 in the version of the manuscript I was given. Once I started combining thirty years' worth of research together in 2009 and 2010 to write *The Source Field Investigations,* I soon found myself irresistibly drawn into a new quest. I had to know if this zodiac cycle was still at work today. It didn't take long to discover that these cycle connections between Rome and the United States were still working just as well in the 1980s, 1990s, and 2000s as they were when Masson wrote the book in 1979–1980. Before I show you how well the zodiac cycle is still working, I will take you through all the stunning data points Helmer and Masson discovered.

Once I saw the truth, everything changed. I had to step back, take a deep breath, and rethink everything I thought I knew about life on earth. The great structure of story that we find in almost every ancient myth and modern-day movie on earth is guiding our lives, far more than we could ever believe. Events in our history become equivalent to major turning points in screenplays, but hardly anyone on earth understands that there is a hidden intelligence directing all of this. The political events of the 1960s had many interesting connections to the Hero's Journey story line—and they will take on even more significance once we see how they connect with similar political events in Rome.

Political Events from the 1960s and 1970s Fit the Hero's Journey Story Line

The assassinations of JFK, Martin Luther King Jr., and Robert F. Kennedy certainly qualified as dark nights of the soul or all-is-lost moments—and could also be classified as inciting incidents that sparked millions of new quests. The Beatles quickly rose to enormous popularity in America after their landmark appearance on *The Ed Sullivan Show* on February 9, 1964—less than three months after John F. Kennedy was shot on November 22, 1963. America needed a new hero, and the teenage girls in the studio audience screamed and cried for the simple love songs of the Beatles with unprecedented, ear-shattering volume. This was the most-watched event in television history for its time, drawing an estimated 73 million viewers—but the Beatles songs were so new that most of the audience members didn't know the lyrics, as you can see in the original footage. This was a major historical event that triggered a huge boom in the music industry known as the "British Invasion."

The tears and "primal screaming" of the young women in the Beatles audience helped to purge the collective terror and sadness that Kennedy's brutal assassination had caused less than three months earlier and that other difficult events, including wars and political assassinations, would cause as well. This cathartic, ear-shattering screaming continued happening at every show and ultimately caused the Beatles to retire from all public performances just two and a half years after their landmark *Ed Sullivan* appearance—in August 1966. They no longer felt their shows were about the music and couldn't even hear themselves performing. They immediately began work on their groundbreaking *Sgt. Pepper's Lonely Hearts Club Band* album in late November 1966.[392] Paul McCartney, with a little help from John Lennon, may have been trying to cheer up the crowds by writing a song with the chorus "It's getting better all the time" on this album—and helped set the tone for a positive future. George Harrison wrote "Within You, Without You," which had a surprisingly deep spiritual message, including the idea that love—individually and collectively—could save the world. It was set to traditional Indian musical instruments and modern orchestra, further enhancing the mystical feel of the song.

> *When you've seen beyond yourself, then you may find peace of mind is waiting there. And the time will come when you see we're all One—and life flows on within you, and without you.*[393]

This music helped spark multiple revolutionary changes, but none quite so widespread as the French student rebellion. However, the battle against the nemesis that seemed to have killed Kennedy was not yet over. The struggle became even more personal when the Vietnam War dramatically expanded under the presidency of Richard Nixon in 1968. Now, hundreds of thousands of young American men were being drafted into the military to fight an apparent war against communism that no one really understood or supported. Nixon had run against Kennedy in the previous election and lost—and now Nixon was the figurehead ordering every young man in America into the Vietnam death machine.

Everyone suspected that "the government" killed Kennedy because he wouldn't dance the way they wanted him to. The media was humiliated by supporting the ridiculous idea of a single bullet that zinged around in several different directions and made right-angle turns, in a feeble attempt to explain how Kennedy suffered two different gunshot wounds from completely different angles. This widespread public suspicion of a media cover-up could be seen as the magic gift—a talisman of embarrassing truth that would inspire the media to come roaring back with a vengeance in their pursuit of the Watergate scandal.

Five years after Kennedy was assassinated, tens of thousands of young Americans had been sent to their deaths under the Nixon administration. Hundreds of thousands more were traumatized with the horrors of war after being drafted into military service against their will. Anyone unlucky enough to be between eighteen and thirty years old in the late 1960s and early 1970s, was in a life-and-death struggle against the ultimate nemesis in a way that teenagers of the 1980s, 1990s, and 2000s would never understand with the same degree of immediacy and passion. My father was one of them. He volunteered for the Army Reserve in the hope of avoiding Vietnam but ended up having to go anyway. The Beatles, who had originally served only as a convenient distraction in the aftermath of Kennedy's assassination by writing simple, nonpolitical love songs, became genuine mentor figures. The Beatles songs were talismans that inspired a social and spiritual revolution with titles like "All You Need Is Love," "Getting Better," "All Together Now," "Here Comes the Sun," "Revolution," John Lennon's first solo single "Give Peace a Chance," and John Lennon's "Imagine."

In the Watergate scandal, journalists became heroes in the great story, revealing a key weakness in the nemesis that was sending young men to their deaths. Nixon's Republican Party was secretly wiretapping the offices of the Democrats, in order to listen in on their strategies to defeat them in the election. This was a very real form of election rigging and revealed that the administration was willing to lie, cheat, and steal to get what it wanted. The Watergate scandal plunged America into a third act—where Americans could win a major victory against their own nemesis. By this point, the dark night of the soul had been worked through, and a practical way to fight the behemoth of the Vietnam War was finally achieved. Lennon, McCartney, and Harrison's songs provided the perfect soundtrack for this critical moment in the story. President Nixon was fully exposed, was threatened with impeachment, and ultimately resigned from office before his inevitable downfall occurred. On a deeper level, Watergate provided absolute proof that the government was lying and set in motion a truth movement that has been growing ever since. Never again could the Cabal rely on mass ignorance and a complacent lapdog media to cover up their actions. The full outcome of this third-act struggle has not yet been realized—but again, these cycles can take many years to culminate.

What very few of us have realized, until now, is that Roman wars and, in some cases, political events in the Age of Aries correspond precisely with American wars and political events—including the Watergate scandal—in the Age of Pisces. I wouldn't be surprised if we find a popular movement in the Roman arts that corresponds very nicely with the Beatles, although I have not yet found a resource that is specific enough to conduct that research. However, the precision with which Roman history reappears as twentieth-century American history in the next zodiac cycle, 2,160 years later, is nothing short of dazzling—and it's still working, as we will see in chapter 15. Rome was clearly the biggest empire in the Age of Aries, and the United States became the sole superpower in the twentieth century, within the Age of Pisces. The Edgar Cayce readings revealed that most Americans are part of a "secondary group" of people who had previously incarnated in Rome. This same core group of Romans apparently re-created their society, in a new form, and then experienced the same major historical events—again—in the hopes of creating a more favorable outcome.

Specific 2,160-Year Overlaps in Roman and American History

In order to see the parallels between Roman and American history, we must see how countries can become characters that oppose each other in the story, much like the hero opposes the nemesis. Prior to 264 B.C., Rome and Carthage were comparable in size and strength as republics, which created a vigorous power struggle between them. Rome soundly defeated Carthage in the First Punic War, which raged from 264 to 241 B.C. This consolidated Rome's status as an empire. Rome became the sole superpower of the day. As one historian wrote, "The Punic Wars, the first of which began in 264 B.C., mark the beginning of a transition of Rome the Republic into the Roman Empire."[394] If we go 2,160 years into the future from this period, we have the years 1896 to 1919 in the United States. *Encyclopedia Britannica* lists almost these exact same years—1896 to 1920—as part of the subheading "United States: Imperialism, the Progressive Era, and the Rise to World Power."[395]

The First Punic War was an aggressive attempt by Rome to expand its power. And 2,160 years later, in 1896, McKinley won the election and immediately began an aggressive expansion of US power. The United States became an imperialist nation as soon as McKinley was elected—just as Rome became an imperialist nation when it attacked Carthage in 264 B.C.

The USS *Maine* sank on February 15, 1898, creating an inciting incident that contributed to the start of the Spanish-American War. The United States quickly won this war, which further expanded its imperial powers. The Spanish-American War was only one front in a much greater battle the United States was waging against Europe in general, but particularly Germany—the other "big kid on the block"—in its struggle to achieve global economic control. The Federal Reserve System consolidated US economic power in 1913, outsourcing the issuance of American currency to a small, highly powerful cabal of bankers, many of whom were not US citizens. This allowed the United States to provide the raw power the Cabal needed in their battle for global financial control. America's economic war again became a military war when it entered World War I in 1917 against Germany. The United States provided the critical support that led to Germany's total defeat.

We now have solid evidence that the Cabal financed both sides of World War I so they would emerge victorious, regardless of which side won. This may have happened in Roman history as well, between Rome and Carthage, though it would probably be very difficult to find documentation to prove such a conspiracy for events that happened well over two thousand years ago. Although a single cabal appears to have been playing both sides against the middle in World War I, this cabal exploited real tensions that existed among the people. Their goal was to get the people angry and convince them that their own country's alliance was the hero and the opposing country's alliance was the nemesis. Then the people could be moved to support a major, bloody conflict once again, rather than seeing diplomacy and negotiations as a viable road to peace.

Again, just to review, the First Punic War against Carthage started in 264 B.C. Exactly 2,160 years later, McKinley transformed the United States into an aggressive, imperialist nation that declared economic war on Europe—and particularly Germany. Rome's first Punic War ended in 241 B.C. Exactly 2,160 years later, Germany signed the Treaty of Versailles, ending World War I on June 28, 1919. Article 231 of the treaty made Germany financially responsible for all damages the war had caused in other countries. This ensured that Germany's defeat would be total. The Cabal stripped the German people of their wealth, diverting their resources into corporate contracts that would rebuild the industries and infrastructure that had been destroyed by the war. These contracts were made with corporations owned by the Cabal itself, thus ensuring that the economic pillaging of the German people strengthened the Cabal's corporate power even more. This economic disaster also created widespread fear and anger—which allowed for the rise of Hitler and the Nazi Party.[396]

This looting strategy is one of many ways in which by 2011 the Federal Reserve banking cabal secretly had come to control 80 percent of all the money earned on earth—as revealed by Dr. Glattfelder's team of scientists. America became the supreme economic power in the world—just as Rome's defeat of Carthage in 261 B.C. drained the Carthaginians of their wealth and quickly transformed the Roman Republic into the Roman Empire.

The Second Punic War

According to Masson, "The Second Punic War, the gravest and most dangerous for Rome, started in 218 B.C. and ended in 201 B.C." This war "brought Rome within a hairs-breadth of destruction." This is an important point, as there is no guarantee that these aggressive, imperialist moves will actually succeed in any given cycle. The health of an entire country and its people is put at grave risk as these geopolitical chess games are being played out. Yet, just as Rome narrowly managed to achieve victory in the previous zodiac cycle, the United States accomplished a similarly difficult triumph in the Age of Pisces.

The Second Punic War, which, again, started in 218 B.C., according to Helmer and Masson, was followed 2,160 years later by America's entrance into World War II in 1942. The Japanese created an inciting incident by bombing Pearl Harbor on December 7, 1941—just three weeks before the year 1942 began. America's entrance into World War II therefore came within months or even weeks of Rome's entrance into the Second Punic War in the previous zodiac cycle. The mystical power of the zodiac cycle again becomes clear. The "cycle equivalent" of Carthage in our own Age of Pisces clearly appears to be Germany—and World War II again pitted the United States (Rome) against Germany (Carthage). Rome was nearly defeated in the Second Punic War—just as the United States was nearly defeated by Hitler and his army of Nazis.

Hitler Was Not the First

Hitler: the most ruthless, aggressive military strategist of our time. The face of pure evil. A compelling leader who roused the most lethally effective military campaign in the Age of Pisces. Is there anyone like Hitler in the earlier version of World War II—the Second Punic War in the Age of Aries?

Yes. He is considered the greatest military strategist in history. His name also starts with an *H*. His name also shares the letters *I* and *L* with *Hitler*. He was the face of pure evil in the Age of Aries. He created naked, mass aggression on a scale never before seen on earth. His name was Hannibal. Just like the word *Hitler* in our time, the name *Hannibal* is synonymous with pure evil; it translates as "Ba'al is my lord"[397] or "With the grace of Ba'al."[398] In biblical Hebrew, Ba'al is the equivalent of Satan—*Ba'al zebhubh,* or "Lord of the Flies" in Hebrew, becomes Beelzebub. Hannibal's name proclaims Ba'al to be his lord, guiding his every action. Matthew Barnes, who earned a master's degree from the Interdisciplinary Center in Herzliya, Israel, made a direct comparison between Carthage under Hannibal and Germany under Hitler, having no conscious idea of their zodiac cycle connection:

> The First Punic War came to an end after twenty three years of bitter fighting on both land and at sea. As the victor, Rome became the dominant Mediterranean naval power and Carthage suffered a humiliating defeat. Carthaginian expansion was checked, their influence challenged and their pride severely damaged. It is from this background that Hannibal Barca, the son of Hamilcar Barca, a First Punic War general, came to the fore. Carthage after the First Punic War was comparable to post World War One Germany, for a great power was beaten, humbled, reduced and forced to accept terms which whet the appetite for revenge. It could be argued

that Carthage had been spoiling for a fight since the day of their defeat at the Battle of the Aegates Islands.[399]

Hannibal raised a huge army with an estimated one hundred thousand men, and 37 or 38 elephants.[400] He started his incredible march in Spain, crossed the Rhône in France, and ordered the entire army through the Alps—in the wintertime—to attack Italy, Rome's home country, from the north. This army was extremely powerful and destructive, and the use of large elephants as an effective battle strategy puts one in mind of Hitler's use of tanks. Hitler also mounted the Alps in his own war campaign. Hannibal attacked by land because Rome dominated the seas—as Matthew Barnes revealed in his research paper on the Second Punic War.

> The Second Punic War began in 218 B.C. under the auspices of the talented young general Hannibal, whose deeds have gone down in history marking him as one of the greatest leaders of the ancient world. His plan was bold and aggressive because it consisted of a land war in which he would take the fight to his enemy in their own back garden. His march is legendary, but it was also necessary, because although an invasion by sea was infinitely more appealing, it was not possible due to the new naval power reality post First Punic War. Hannibal's war had to be confined to land—and it was here that he showed his greatness, despite being born into a maritime power.[401]

Another publicly stated insight into the connection between Hannibal and Hitler appeared in a *Daily Mail* article from 2010. Since the historian the paper quoted is a Holocaust denier, let me be absolutely clear that I believe the Holocaust was real, I have done my own research, and I do not believe these counterarguments are credible. The key here is that a very effective comparison can be made between Hitler and Hannibal and was featured in the *Daily Mail* in 2010. Both of these men captivated the worlds they lived in with terrible wars of unprecedented scale—and both engaged in the fiercest aggression for six years: "Controversial British historian David Irving . . . who was once jailed in Austria for denying the Holocaust, also told tourists that the German dictator should be compared to Hannibal, the leader of Carthage that fought against and who almost overpowered Rome. The historian said: 'He was like Hannibal. He held the military forces of the rest of the world for six years. Exactly like Hannibal.'"[402]

There was no turning back for Hannibal. Just like Hitler, it was win or die—as we see in this quote from *Hannibal and Me* by Andreas Kluth.

> Conquer or die. Rarely in life are choices that stark. But Hannibal's strategy had brought him into exactly this situation. He had decided not to be a defender but an invader. From this point on, his dream, his quest, and his life depended on one thing: winning. Projecting invincibility—not only to Rome but to Rome's enemies, and even more to Rome's allies in Italy—was the premise of his entire plan. . . . Hannibal needed to win—and then to keep winning. If he lost only one major battle, his invasion would fail—and his army, unable to retreat, would almost certainly be exterminated. So he really was like his Alpine prisoners. He had volunteered to win or die.[403]

Hidden Intentions

I discovered the Hannibal-Hitler connection only at the very end of writing this book—by pure synchronicity. Despite how obvious it seemed to be in hindsight, Masson never mentioned this parallel in his book, and I still have not been able to track down Helmer's original research articles. I discovered the Hitler-Hannibal connection by studying the zodiac cycle of 2,160 years, beginning in Hitler's time. It started when I was researching Hitler's use of staged terrorism, also known as "false flag" attacks. This is where a government attacks its own country and blames the attack on its enemy in order to justify further aggression. After Hitler was defeated, his top generals and strategists revealed their actual plans for the first time during the Nuremberg trials—an unprecedented moment of truth. Thanks to Nuremberg, we found out about Operation Himmler—a revolting plan in which the Nazis created multiple fake, government-sponsored terrorist attacks against their own country.[404] Concentration camp prisoners were dressed in Polish uniforms, given fatal injections by a doctor, and shot. Their bodies were then positioned where each operation was staged.[405] The Nazis would storm various buildings on the border with Poland, scare the locals with inaccurate gunshots, vandalize the buildings, and retreat, leaving the planted bodies in Polish uniforms behind.

The most powerful attack under Operation Himmler was the Gleiwitz incident, when Hitler attacked his own top radio station and broadcast anti-German messages that appeared to originate from Poland, his main enemy. This and thirteen other attacks all happened on the night of August 31, 1939, and became the inciting incident that started World War II in Europe.[406] Hitler used the Gleiwitz incident to declare war on Poland the very next day—as you can read in his own words: "Recently in one night there were as many as twenty-one frontier incidents: last night there were fourteen, of which three were quite serious. I have, therefore, resolved to speak to Poland in the same language that Poland for months past has used toward us. . . . I will continue this struggle, no matter against whom, until the safety of the Reich and its rights are secured."[407]

During the Nuremberg trials, we discovered that Hitler told the truth about what he was doing, and why, to his generals on August 22, 1939: "I will provide a propagandistic *casus belli*. Its credibility doesn't matter. The victor will not be asked whether he told the truth."[408]

Hannibal's Rise to Power Was Not So Different

I subtracted 2,160 from 1939 and got 221 B.C. as the corresponding year. I immediately discovered that Hannibal became commander in chief of the Carthaginian army this same year—221 B.C.—after his brother-in-law Hasdrubal was brutally assassinated. Was Hannibal secretly responsible for this attack? Historian Chuck M. Sphar concluded that the answer is likely yes—and wrote about it in a novel he is developing called *Against Rome*: "Did Hannibal assassinate Hasdrubal the Handsome, his predecessor as governor of Spain? There's no evidence to suggest that he did, but Livy (1965, XXI, 1) and others do say that a Spanish native assassinated Hasdrubal (see Note 4), and given Hannibal's very likely impatience to be on with his work, it seems plausible that Hannibal could have given the native a push. Anyway, it makes for a good story, so I've used it."[409]

Hannibal's father, Hamilcar, was clearly a vicious man who traumatized Hannibal severely enough to make him capable of committing mass atrocities. In one instance, Hannibal begged his father to take him along on an overseas war. Hamilcar grabbed his son, dragged him into a sacrificial chamber, and held him over a roaring fire, demanding that he swear he would never be a friend of Rome. In this gripping scene, with a tempest of orange flames beckoning his body to its doom, Hannibal— the servant of Ba'al—made his covenant: *"I swear! So soon as age will permit . . . I will use fire and steel to arrest the destiny of Rome!"*[410]

This type of trauma bonding can be very strong, and Hannibal must have been devastated when his father later died in battle. Hannibal's brother-in-law, Hasdrubal the Handsome, became commander of the Carthaginian army, with Hannibal serving as only an officer underneath him. Hasdrubal started working to form diplomatic relationships with neighboring tribes in the hopes of consolidating Carthage as a power. The turning point for Hannibal may have been the day he found out that Hasdrubal signed a treaty with Rome, his father's mortal enemy. Hasdrubal made a deal that Carthage would not expand north of the Ebro River as long as Rome did not expand south of it. This was very different from what Hannibal had sworn to over the roaring flames. Hasdrubal was killed by a Spanish assassin almost as soon as he got to Italy to conduct even more negotiations, and his head was sent to Hannibal, who then became commander in chief.

Once I realized Hitler and Hannibal both rose to power the same year and probably used very similar means to get there, the story started coming together. Then I quickly looked up Hannibal to see his face. I was stunned. Hannibal was Hitler with a beard. The facial similarity was astonishing. Although this has not yet been done, Dr. Jim Tucker could easily use forensic facial recognition software to establish their linkage. Given all the other similarities, including the length of their main military campaigns, I thought for sure that someone must have already seen this, but an Internet search did not turn up any other results.

Fig. 11: Carthaginian warlord Hannibal and Adolf Hitler. Notice stunning facial similarity to Hitler.

Another curious synchronicity may suggest that Hannibal's army also reincarnated with him—and remembered their past history on a subconscious level. Admiral Karl Dönitz conducted one of the largest emergency evacuations in history as the Soviet army was bearing down on German soldiers and civilians in Courland, East Prussia, and the Polish Corridor. Hitler had insisted that the war go on, right up until his suicide, but Dönitz heroically realized it was too late. This mass evacuation transported between eight hundred thousand and nine hundred thousand refugees and 350,000 soldiers across the Baltic Sea to Germany and Denmark, which was still occupied by Germany—possibly saving more than a million lives in the process.[411] The code name of this mass evacuation was Operation Hannibal.[412]

The Korean War—and a Chance for Peaceful Coexistence

The zodiac cycle gets slightly harder to follow once we see that the Second Punic War lasted until 201 B.C.—which is 1959 in our own Age of Pisces. Even though World War II seemingly ended in 1945 with Hitler and Japan's defeat, the United States immediately began fighting another Cabal-financed superpower—the USSR. The Cold War started directly after the end of World War II with the highly deadly nuclear arms race, threatening all life on earth. This significantly raised the stakes from the previous age, as no matter how much Rome attacked and defeated its neighbors, life on earth was never threatened in an overall sense.

The war against the USSR went hot from 1950 to 1953, when the United States battled the USSR's hidden ally, North Korea, in the Korean War. The Soviet Communists were supporting North Korea, while the United States was supporting the pro-Western regime of South Korea. The United States considered this a fight against global communism, and the threat of a much bigger war with the USSR or China was always looming. Five million soldiers and civilians were killed in this war.[413] The Cold War continued escalating after the Korean conflict ended in 1953, until a remarkable breakthrough finally occurred. On September 25, 1959, Russian premier Nikita Khrushchev visited the United States to meet with President Eisenhower. This highly influential visit occurred exactly one zodiac cycle after the Second Punic War ended in 201 B.C. This was the first time in the entire history of the Cold War that a Soviet leader had visited the United States.

As revealed on Politico.com, in this groundbreaking summit, Khrushchev "denounced the 'excesses' of [communist] Stalinism and said he sought 'peaceful co-existence' with the United States. . . . In a joint communiqué, issued after two days of meetings, the leaders said . . . they believed that 'the question of general disarmament is the most important one facing the world today.'"[414] Although the talks didn't last, this meeting was a key harbinger of a positive future, as it presented the people with a real opportunity to end the war, and achieve true, lasting peace.

Hardly anyone knew, at the time, that a very similar peace opportunity had occurred exactly 2,160 years before, when the second Punic War had ended in 201 B.C.

The Macedonian War

Rome's taste of peace was very short-lived, as the Macedonian War began the very next year, in 200 B.C. Macedonia is a very small country just north of Greece—and in our modern zodiac cycle, its equivalent may be Cuba. Through reincarnation research, we may eventually find that many Cubans in the 1960s were also Macedonians in or around 200 B.C. In March of 1960, 2,160 years after Rome attacked Macedonia in 200 B.C., the United States drew up plans to attack Cuba. The conflict between the United States and Cuba was another proxy war fought between the United States and the USSR. The Soviet Union had made economic and trade agreements with Fidel Castro, the prime minister of Cuba, in February 1960, and the United States felt the need to mount an immediate counterattack.[415] Cuba was directly southeast of the continental United States, just ninety miles from the southern tip of Florida. This provided the USSR with a valuable strategic location from which to wage war—including the potential placement of first-strike nuclear weapons that would hit before the United States could effectively counterattack.

On May 1, 1960, the United States provocatively flew a U-2 spy plane over Russian airspace. The Soviets shot it down and captured the pilot, Gary Powers.[416] The Cold War immediately restarted—precisely 2,160 years after Rome plunged into another war with Macedonia. Kennedy won the 1960 presidential election and was sworn in on January 20, 1961. In February 1961, very soon after his inauguration, Kennedy trusted his new, Cold War veteran advisers and authorized the CIA's plan to invade Cuba. Air strikes began on April 14, 1961, in B-26 bombers disguised as Cuban aircraft, but the planes were quickly identified as belonging to the United States.

Kennedy was embarrassed and canceled the next round of air strikes, but the land invasion went ahead on April 17, 1961, at the Bay of Pigs.

Twenty thousand Cuban troops were waiting for the invading force of about fourteen hundred Cuban exiles who had been trained by the United States. The battle quickly ended with 144 of the exiles killed and 1,189 captured. This was a great embarrassment for the United States and immediately threw its fledgling president into full-scale crisis.[417] In terms of the ancient story, the failed Bay of Pigs invasion would be seen as another all-is-lost point for the United States—a nationwide dark night of the soul in its battle against the Soviet nemesis.

Predictably, the USSR then began beefing up Cuba with weapons—including nukes. This caused the United States and USSR to come very close to full-scale nuclear war during the Cuban Missile Crisis, which reached its peak on October 22, 1962. On this day, Kennedy addressed the nation to present solid evidence that the Soviets had positioned nuclear weapons in Cuba. This was a tense third-act moment: The United States had regrouped, learned from the dark night of the soul in the Bay of Pigs disaster, and gained the strength to confront their own Soviet nemesis through its proxy state in Cuba. Out of a total of 1,436 B-52 bombers in the Strategic Air Command, fully one-eighth were sent airborne—to be ready to strike at a moment's notice.[418] US military forces worldwide were placed at DEFCON 2, requiring an increase in force readiness. Twenty-three nuclear-armed B-52 bombers were placed in orbit within striking range of the Soviet Union as well.[419]

After a series of terrifying moves in a very high-stakes chess game, Khrushchev admitted what the USSR had done and announced it would pull back as of October 28. All offensive weapons in Cuba would be dismantled and returned to the USSR.[420] This was a great triumph moment for Kennedy and for America as a whole in the ancient Hero's Journey story line, and the dramatic events have triggered multiple movies, novels, and TV adaptations. The last US missiles were removed from Turkey on April 24, 1963, ending the conflict on both sides.[421] In Rome, the Battle of Cynoscephalae ended in 197 B.C.—exactly 2,160 years before the Cuban Missile Crisis ended. The Battle of Cynoscephalae was the decisive turning point that led to Macedonia losing the war.

It's not always easy to figure out what our modern equivalents may be for the countries against which Rome waged war. The Age of Pisces equivalent of Macedonia appears to be Cuba, but the USSR was the real nemesis lurking behind the scenes all along. It seems that the great cycles of history describe an overall script of what types of events will happen, but various characters here on earth will shift in and out of those roles, ultimately depending upon how the people in each cycle respond. And, of course, not all events fit perfectly into these cycles. Multiple cycles can be intersecting and colliding at once, providing a push-pull of competing influences that we may not be able to map out without a great deal more information and computer power. Nonetheless, it is amazing to see how well the biggest events, and the most significant wars, all seem to reappear so precisely across the zodiac cycle.

The Macedonian War did not actually end at the battle of Cynoscephalae; it ended a year later, in 196 B.C. Although Kennedy was assassinated on November 22, 1963, Khrushchev was ousted on October 14, 1964—exactly 2,160 years after the Macedonian War finally ended for Rome.[422] Although Khrushchev appeared to have been secretly working to negotiate peace treaties and alliances all along, he was still the primary figurehead for the USSR in worldly terms.

There may well be a vast wealth of other interlocking events that are not significant enough, in the Roman Empire, to be well documented as historical events—such as examples of music or theater that had as much of an effect as the Beatles would in the next cycle. There may well be a vast array of details that are repeating with equally stunning precision. This may all seem very hard to fathom, since we are used to thinking of time as completely linear. However, if we begin envisioning time as cyclical, moving through circular loops that are created by the celestial energy fields we move through as a planet, it makes more sense. Each time our planet reaches the same position in the circle, the events from previous rounds are much more likely to bleed through into our own reality—and repeat again.

CHAPTER FOURTEEN

Vietnam, Watergate, and the Fall of the Iron Curtain

Rome went to war against Antiochus III in 192 B.C. Antiochus III was a king who ruled over Greater Syria and western Asia. Antiochus III invaded Greece with a ten-thousand-man army, triggering the Roman-Syrian War, which raged from 192 to 188 B.C. When we advance this same time period ahead by 2,160 years, we have 1968 to 1972. This precisely corresponds to the key turning points of the Vietnam War—which also was a war in Asia. The United States first began covert operations in North Vietnam in 1964. On August 2, 1964, three North Vietnamese PT boats fired on the USS *Maddox*. This led to the Gulf of Tonkin Resolution, in which Lyndon Baines Johnson, Kennedy's former vice president, gained permission to wage war against North Vietnam without a congressional declaration.[423] The United States began bombing North Vietnam in 1965 while troop levels topped two hundred thousand. In 1967, Secretary of Defense Robert McNamara said the bombing raids were not effective enough to solve the problem and more needed to be done.

Then, in January 1968—2,160 years after the Asian king Antiochus III invaded Greece with ten thousand men, plunging him into an all-out war with the Roman Empire—North Vietnamese and Vietcong forces swept into South Vietnam. The Asian enemy attacked several cities, including the capital—similar to Antiochus's attack on Greece in the Age of Aries. This bold and daring military maneuver was called the

Tet Offensive. Though this attack was repelled, it was a political and psychological victory, causing great questions about whether the United States was involved enough in the war. General William Westmoreland requested a doubling of the troop presence in February, calling for an additional 206,000 men. The idea of ordinary young men being drafted into military service suddenly became a very real and very terrifying prospect.

Then, on March 16, 1968, American soldiers massacred hundreds of innocent people in the village of My Lai. In 1969, when the incident became public knowledge, it caused shockwaves through the American political and military establishment as well as the general public. The American people had an opportunity to demand the end of the war right there, but the political will was not yet strong enough. These three events— the Tet Offensive, the proposed doubling of the troop presence, and the My Lai massacre—dramatically increased the emotional impact of the war. The number of young men being drafted suddenly skyrocketed. Again, these events all occurred in 1968—precisely 2,160 years after Rome went into full-scale war against the Asian king Antiochus III in 192 B.C.

A Bitter Taste of Treason—Served on a Fifty-Two-Year-Old Platter

Furthermore, on March 17, 2013, it was revealed that presidential candidate Richard M. Nixon had deliberately sabotaged peace talks with Vietnam that same year, 1968. I happened to find this article through synchronicity, while looking for other information on Nixon to help flesh out this part of the book. This incredibly treasonous story was covered by Rachel Maddow on MSNBC, as well as in other media outlets, but I wouldn't have found it if I hadn't already been looking for links to Nixon and 1968. We now know that Nixon bribed the Vietnamese with promises that they would get a much better peace deal if they held off until he became president. This shocking betrayal of the American people guaranteed that the deadly Vietnam War would grow much, much larger—and far more profitable for the military-industrial complex. This treasonous secret deal with the enemy provided fuel for much greater military power in Nixon's presidency. President Eisenhower had warned America about the growing, potentially "disastrous" menace of the military-industrial complex in his closing address on January 17, 1961. Eisenhower was another mentor figure who gave America a magic gift in this speech, which could ultimately be used to defeat the nemesis: "In the councils of government, we must guard against the acquisition of unwarranted influence, whether sought or unsought, by the military-industrial complex. The potential for the disastrous rise of misplaced power exists—and will persist."[424]

The president at the time, Lyndon Baines Johnson, was aware of Nixon's treasonous deal but said nothing. Nixon thereby sentenced hundreds of thousands of additional young men into the military draft, and tens of thousands more American soldiers into their deaths—when it was all entirely preventable. The audiotapes that proved Nixon did this were declassified by the LBJ Presidential Library in 2013. The story was published literally the day before this chapter of the book was being revisited for its final publication for the first time since 2010.[425]

It is interesting that fifty-two years elapsed between Eisenhower's prophetic warning in January 1961 and the final exposure of Nixon's treason in 2013. The Maya strongly believed that history moved in fifty-two-year cycles, which were made up of four smaller cycles of thirteen years. People throughout Mesoamerica celebrated this "Sacred Round" cycle as "the Binding of the Years" and used it to help them understand past and future events.[426] For example, the Spanish conqueror Hernán Cortés began destroying the Aztecs shortly after his initial, peaceful visit in November 1519—causing the Aztec prophecy of "nine hells" of fifty-two years to begin.[427] Five "Sacred Round" cycles of fifty-two years add up to the tzolkin cycle of 260 years, which was widely revered throughout Mesoamerica. Australian professor Robert Peden discovered that the 260-year tzolkin cycle is a perfect "common denominator" for all the orbits of the planets in our inner solar system.[428] The period of 260 years is a subcycle that divides perfectly into the exact length of every orbit within the inner solar system. It is quite astonishing that the "primitive" cultures of Mesoamerica were somehow able to discover this number.

They also constructed an estimated three hundred to five hundred pyramids out of huge stone blocks—which again suggests they may have had access to advanced technology.

The End of the Roman-Syrian War and the End of Vietnam

According to Helmer and Masson, Rome went to war with the Syrian king Antiochus III in 192 B.C.; 2,160 years later, in 1968, the Vietnam War dramatically expanded. (Remember that we now have absolute proof that Nixon bribed the Vietnamese government to extend the war.) The Roman-Syrian War lasted five years, finally ending in 188 B.C. If we advance 188 B.C. forward by 2,160 years, we arrive at 1972, which is the exact year that a cease-fire was negotiated by Henry Kissinger and Le Duc Tho.

John Lennon's song "Imagine," released in September 1971, now seems oddly prophetic as a foretelling of the defeat of the Cabal. In archetypal terms, "Imagine" was a harbinger of the Elixir of Immortality that would soon be seized—the promise of peace—once the dragon of the Cabal, and its military draft of ordinary young men, had been slain.

> I hope someday you'll join us; and the world will live as One.[429]

The final peace treaty was signed with Vietnam and went into effect on January 27, 1973. This led to the formal announcement of the end of the draft and the withdrawal of the last American troops from Vietnam.

The Scipio Africanus Scandal and Richard Nixon

In 187 B.C., the year after the Roman-Syrian War ended, a scandal began brewing around the Roman consul Scipio Africanus. It started when his brother Lucius was prosecuted for hiding a payment of 500 talents he accepted from Rome's mortal enemy, Antiochus III.[430] Within two years, Scipio himself stood trial on charges that he had accepted this payment from Antiochus III as a bribe to end the war. The beginning of this scandal in 187 B.C. corresponds to the year 1973 in the Age of Pisces. Why would Scipio Africanus have accepted secret bribe payments from Rome's apparent enemy? Why did Nixon bribe the Vietnamese to extend the war by telling them they'd get a better peace deal once he became president? Why did the Cabal finance both sides of World Wars I and II—as the data clearly shows, if we are strong enough to look at it? These actions are difficult, if not impossible, to understand until we remember that 1 percent of the people in our society are genuine sociopaths, who have no regard or respect for anyone outside their own elite circle. What makes the Cabal so frightening for the average person is the idea that sociopaths banded together to strengthen their power and have pursued long-term goals that could stretch on for hundreds of years.

The treasonous collusion between Scipio Africanus and Antiochus III may have gone much deeper than a bribe that Antiochus paid to end the war. If Nixon was replaying a series of events that occurred, in secret, in the previous zodiac cycle, then Antiochus may have agreed to invade Greece with ten thousand men in the first place as part of a secret agreement he made with Scipio. In modern times, this could correspond to the secret agreement Richard Nixon made with the Vietnamese to significantly intensify and prolong the war—exactly 2,160 years after the Roman-Syrian War started.

If an earlier version of the same Cabal was secretly financing both sides of the Roman-Syrian War, they were well aware that their wealth, power, and control could be consolidated by pulling the people into full-scale warfare. In these times of great crisis, people will spend a lot more, lose their life savings to the Cabal in an invasion, and give up their lives to fight for what they believe to be a higher purpose. Although the full, ugly details of treason may not have been provable, Scipio Africanus had now been caught in a critical lie. He and his brother had accepted a payment of 500 talents from Antiochus III,[431] ostensibly to end the war. This epic mistake may have been enough to trigger even more unsavory disclosures—possibly including the idea that wars were being deliberately engineered to plunder wealth from the people—but such information never came to light in the previous cycle.

The Big Third-Act Resolution

This trial was the big moment, the third-act resolution, in which the Roman people had been through the dark night of the soul, ended the war, and could now directly face the nemesis—in this case their own leader—and defeat him. Scipio's brother Lucius was brought to trial in a grand public exhibition that captivated the republic. The court forced Lucius to produce his brother's accounting books, which were being demanded as evidence. These financial documents were the "smoking gun" that would prove, at the very least, that Scipio had accepted a bribe from Antiochus to end the war. It is entirely possible that other treasonous payments, going even further back in time, might have been found as well. According to the written historical record of Polybius, in an astonishingly brazen move that electrified the people of the Roman Republic, Scipio grabbed the books and tore them up in front of the entire coliseum.[432] Everyone knew that this meant Scipio was publicly admitting he was guilty, but he was too proud to say it. The Roman people may not have considered that other evidence might have been in Scipio's financial books that would have been even more damning. Scipio left Rome and

Fig. 12: Emperor Scipio Africanus and President Richard Nixon

effectively resigned three years after the scandal began, in 184 B.C., disgraced by the conspiracy, and his trial for what we would now call an impeachment was discontinued.[433]

If you know anything about late-twentieth-century American history, this story is probably sounding very familiar by now. As Masson wrote, "2,160 years [after Scipio's scandal began,] in 1973, it was the Watergate scandal that forced Nixon, who had honorably terminated the Vietnam War, to resign and retire to his estate—just as Scipio had done 2,160 years earlier."[434] Given the science of reincarnation, as revealed by Dr. Ian Stevenson, Dr. Jim Tucker, the Edgar Cayce readings, the between-life regressions of Dr. Michael Newton, and others, it is entirely possible that Scipio Africanus reincarnated as Richard Nixon in order to repeat these same cycles of karma once more. Scipio had been Hannibal's archenemy in the Second Punic War, and now it appears that he also reincarnated to fulfill a similar destiny. This time, Nixon would not walk away as easily as his predecessor Scipio did in Rome. Nixon had to complete his own cycle of karma by being forced to confess to his wrongdoing in a wild television interview. Journalist David Frost became the hero who aggressively bullied the fallen nemesis into admitting what he had done.

This epic Hero's Journey story was effectively adapted into Ron Howard's 2008 film *Frost/Nixon*,[435] which received Academy Award nominations for Best Picture, Best Actor, Best Adapted Screenplay, Best Director, and Best Editing. Although this karmic loop may have taken 2,160 years to come full circle, if Nixon was Scipio, then this time he had to admit what he had done to the public in much more detail. Further compelling evidence for reincarnation is in the remarkable facial similarities between Scipio and Nixon. Dr. Ian Stevenson and Dr. Jim Tucker both provided extensive evidence that the "real" reincarnation cases feature strong face matches. Scipio and Nixon definitely resemble each other—including the general shape of the nose, cheeks and chin, the bags under their eyes, and the "lazy eye" in the way they stare. Is it possible that this same soul reincarnated to again work out the same issues it had created 2,160 years earlier, in a previous cycle of the zodiac? If so, Scipio really didn't seem to learn very much and ended up playing the same role he occupied in the Age of Aries. The on-air confession Nixon gave to David Frost in 1977 may have helped alleviate some of his karma, however.

Cato, Meet Carter

After serving as Roman consul, Cato was elected to become the new "censor" of Rome in 184 B.C.[436] This was considered an important position, as one key role of the "censor" was to guard the morality of Rome. 2,160 years later, in 1976, Jimmy Carter was elected president of the United States. You may have already noticed that there is an immediate similarity in their names—both start with the letters *CA*, and these two letters are soon followed by a *T*. Cato came from a family of farmers, as did Carter. When Cato's father died, Cato quit the armed forces and went back to cultivate his land. Carter did exactly the same thing. According to Helmer and Masson's research, Cato was the politician who demanded that Scipio and his brother turn over their records and accounts to the public, beginning in 187 B.C. 2,160 years later, there is no direct evidence that Carter, who was then the governor of Georgia, had any role in the Watergate scandal. However, Carter certainly benefited from Nixon's wrongdoing when he became president three years later.

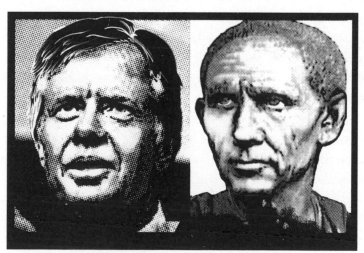

Fig. 13: President Jimmy Carter and Cato the Censor

The public was hungry for a squeaky-clean, snow-white character who was the antithesis of Richard Nixon in every way—and they got one.

There are remarkable and undeniable facial similarities between Cato and Carter. The structure of the nose and the shape of the ears are almost identical, and there are strong similarities in the shape of the lips, cheeks, and chin. Cato put Rome through a period of censorship, during which he tried to restore morality to the republic. Cato issued several decrees in an attempt to slow down the greedy, overconsuming economic behavior and lifestyle of the Romans—and his censorship was so strict that he ultimately had to defend himself against 44 different accusations and attempted prosecutions.[437] 2,160 years later, Carter took very similar actions to rein in the overconsumption of energy in America. On February 2, 1977, just two weeks after he took office, President Carter tried to encourage the American public to keep the heat much lower in their homes—in the midst of a very cold winter: "All of us must learn to waste less energy. Simply by keeping our thermostats, for instance, at 65 degrees in the daytime and 55 degrees at night we could save half the current shortage of natural gas."[438] Carter delivered this request while wearing a thick cardigan sweater, which became a focal-point for the right-wing media to mock him.[439] Even in 2009, this speech was still remembered as a historical event, though this writer did not give the correct year it was delivered: "There's another problem—the ghost of Jimmy Carter's sweater haunting the discussion [of energy conservation]. During the 1979 energy crisis, Carter put on a cardigan, said the nation was suffering a "crisis of confidence," and told everyone to turn the thermostat down in the winter. Saving energy somehow became permanently associated with malaise and discomfort."[440] In this same 1977 speech, Carter announced he was reducing the size of the White House staff by one-third, and recommended all his cabinet members reduce their own private staff by the same amount. Carter also said the following in his *Report to the American People on Energy.*

> We have eliminated some expensive and unnecessary luxuries, such as door-to-door limousine service for many top officials, including all members of the White House staff.

Government officials can't be sensitive to your problems if we are living like royalty here in Washington. While I am deeply grateful for the good wishes that lie behind them, I would like to ask that people not send gifts to me or to my family or to anyone else who serves in my administration. . . . I've asked the people appointed by me to high positions in Government to abide by strict rules of financial disclosure and to avoid all conflicts of interest. I intend to make those rules permanent.[441]

Carter's campaign to rein in American energy consumption continued when he raised taxes on big gas-guzzling cars[442] and installed a solar heating system on the roof of the White House.[443]

Cato became one of the most revered politicians in ancient Rome, and he continued to remain politically active until his death in 149 B.C., which corresponds to the year 2011 in our current Age of Pisces. Carter is still alive and well in 2013 and has also remained highly politically active. Cato produced many respected literary works, including a history of Rome in Latin.[444] Carter has released twenty-seven books since his presidency,[445] including *Palestine: Peace Not Apartheid*[446] and a fictional novel about the history of America entitled *The Hornet's Nest: A Novel of the Revolutionary War*.[447] Although Carter served only one term as president, leaving office in 1981, he was awarded the Nobel Peace Prize in 2002 after multiple previous nominations. Here is a quote from the official Nobel website on Carter's award.

[The Nobel Peace Prize was given for Carter's] decades of untiring effort to find peaceful solutions to international conflicts, to advance democracy and human rights, and to promote economic and social development. . . . [He] has served as an observer at countless elections all over the world. He has worked hard on many fronts to fight tropical diseases and to bring about growth and progress in developing countries. . . . In a situation currently marked by threats of the use of power, Carter has stood by the principles that conflicts must, as far as possible, be resolved through mediation and international co-operation based on international law, respect for human rights, and economic development.[448]

The First Celtiberian War and the War in Afghanistan, 1979 to 1986

After Cato's election, the next significant event in Roman history was the first Celtiberian war, in which Rome had to confront an uprising in its Spanish territories. The First Celtiberian War began in 181 B.C.[449] and initially ended in 179 B.C., but there was a major Celtiberian revolt in 174 B.C., in which 15,000 Celtiberians were either killed or taken prisoner;[450] 2,160 years later, this brings us to the time period of 1979 to 1986. François Masson finished writing his manuscript in 1979, so no further investigation could be done at the time. I did not consider myself a historian, and when I published Masson's manuscript on my website in 2000, it seemed like far too much work to try to explore whether or not these cycles were still working. There was not enough information uploaded to the Internet to mount an effective investigation at the time.

I soon forgot about it, got captivated by many other things, and never bothered to go back and check on the zodiac cycle connection between Rome and the United States any further. However, once I wrote the first draft of these chapters in 2010, I realized that it was now or never and pursued that line of questioning. The volume of information that was available on the Internet had vastly increased in the preceding ten years, which made it much easier to do the research.

Again, the first conflict with the Celtiberians stretched from 181 to the revolt in 174 B.C. This becomes 1979 to 1986 in the Age of Pisces. As it turned out, the United States fought another proxy war with the USSR during this exact period of time in Afghanistan. It appears that the people of Spain in the Age of Aries may have mass-reincarnated as the people of Afghanistan in the Age of Pisces. This new proxy war between the United States and USSR began in 1979—right when Masson had expected it to.

Another Proxy War with the Soviet Union

Although the SALT II nuclear weapons treaty with the USSR was signed in June 1979, President Carter signed a directive on July 3, 1979, that secretly provided aid to the people in Afghanistan who were fighting against their own pro-Soviet government. According to Carter's Cold War adviser Zbigniew Brzezinski, "We didn't push the Russians to intervene, but we knowingly increased the probability that they would."[451] Russia did indeed respond with shocking violence in less than six months. Russian paratroopers landed in Kabul, the capital of Afghanistan, on Christmas Day, 1979. These Russian soldiers are now believed to have shot the president, Hafizullah Amin, two days later.[452] This was a blatant display of military power by the Soviet Union that created searing new geopolitical tensions in 1979, the same year the Celtiberian war began in the Age of Aries. The United Nations condemned the invasion as early as January 1980. The United States strongly opposed Russia's sudden, violent presence in Afghanistan; banned the export of grain to Russia; ended the SALT talks; and boycotted the Olympic Games that were scheduled to be held in Moscow in 1980. According to Brzezinski, "Other than that, America did nothing. Why? They knew that Russia had got itself into their own Vietnam."[453]

Rome's Celtiberian War ended in 174 B.C. If we move ahead 2,160 years after this relieving conclusion to the original war between Rome and its Spanish territories, we have 1986. This exact year, 1986, was the decisive tipping point into defeat for the Soviet Union in its war for control of Afghanistan. The United States had been fighting the proxy war the entire time by secretly training and supporting the resistance movement in Afghanistan to fight the Soviets—and in this case, the resistance prevailed. As of 1985, the CIA began training the Afghan resistance to use car bombs, assassinations, and cross-border raids into the USSR. Then, in 1986, the United States armed the resistance with hundreds of Stinger antiaircraft missiles. The United States also donated another $600 million in aid and secured matching financing from the Persian Gulf states. China sold tanks, assault rifles, rocket-propelled grenades, and other weapons to the Afghan resistance in 1986 as well. The USSR, realizing it had been defeated, began formulating an "exit strategy" this same year, 1986. The USSR began training the Afghan armed forces to fight the Afghan resistance on their own and built them up to an official strength of 302,000.[454]

Another Foiled Peace Opportunity

Russia's glaring defeat in this proxy war with the United States also led to an open attempt to make peace—and permanently end the Cold War. This made the year 1986 an even stronger match with the end of the first Celtiberian War in 174 B.C., during the previous zodiac cycle. On September 15, 1986, Gorbachev sent a letter to Reagan asking for "a quick one-on-one meeting, let us say in Iceland or in London," to discuss the total abolition of all nuclear weapons. The summit took place in Reykjavik, Iceland, beginning on October 12, 1986.[455] This presented the world with another phenomenal opportunity to defeat the Global Adversary and bring about true peace, but we weren't quite ready for it yet. The Iran-Contra scandal soon erupted, forcing Reagan's key ally in the struggle for disarmament, National Security Advisor John Poindexter, to resign.[456] This occurred after Attorney General Edwin Meese III revealed that Poindexter knew that the profits from selling arms to Iran were being covertly redistributed to a paramilitary group that was fighting socialism in Nicaragua, called the Contras.[457]

The US military soon "presented huge estimates of needed additional conventional spending to make up for not having the [nuclear] missiles" if Gorbachev and Reagan's total ban on all nuclear weapons went through.[458] In another signal that the entrenched Cabal bureaucrats had no intentions of going along with Reagan and Gorbachev's treaty, the United States announced it was expelling all fifty-five US-based Soviet diplomats on October 22, 1986.[459] The United States ordered all Soviet diplomats to leave by November 5, 1986.[460]

A New US-USSR Proxy War from 1988 to 1992

At this point in the Age of Aries, Rome again went to war with Macedonia from 172 to 168 B.C. When we move this time window ahead by 2,160 years, we reach the period of 1988 to 1992 in the United States. At first I thought the parallel zodiac cycle timelines between Roman and American wars had finally broken down and failed—but I was wrong. I soon realized that another key phase of the proxy war between the United States and the USSR erupted during this exact timeframe. This time, it ended in the complete defeat and collapse of the USSR—right on schedule with the defeat of Macedonia in 168 B.C.

We already learned that Rome's previous war with Macedonia appeared in our own Age of Pisces as a battle with the USSR through Cuba as a proxy state. Rome began fighting Macedonia for the second time in 172 B.C. And 2,160 years after 172 B.C.—on February 12, 1988—there was another direct confrontation between the United States and the USSR. Cuba was not a staging ground for the battle this time, freeing it from its previous cycle connection to Macedonia. In this case, the two main adversaries faced off directly. The United States provoked the USSR once more by sailing a known spy vessel, the USS *Caron,* into waters off the Crimean peninsula that were claimed by the USSR. History.com revealed that the United States was blatantly trying to start a fight by doing this: "In many ways, the incident was an unnecessarily provocative action by the United States. . . . The *Caron* was well known as an intelligence gathering vessel, and its appearance in waters claimed by the Soviets would be seen as suspicious at best."[461]

The USSR responded by aggressively ramming its ships into the USS *Caron* and the USS *Yorktown*, which was nearby. History.com revealed that this panicked move was a sign that the "wounded lion" of the USSR was still quite capable of lashing out at its enemies. "For their part, the Soviets probably overreacted. Perhaps the Soviet military felt a message should be sent that Russia, which was experiencing severe economic and political problems, was still a nation to be taken seriously as a major military power."[462]

Afghanistan Proxy War Continues Until 1992

Despite this new provocation, the USSR signed a pact to leave Afghanistan completely, after nine years of occupation, on April 14, 1988. The Georgetown University Institute for the Study of Diplomacy's "US and Soviet Proxy War in Afghanistan, 1989–1992" revealed that the United States and the Soviet Union did not stop providing military support to their respective allies in Afghanistan until four years later, in 1992— which was the same year the Second Macedonian War ended in the Age of Aries. The United States' CIA had financed and trained the resistance in Afghanistan to conduct car bombings and terrorism in Afghanistan since 1985. This US-backed resistance was a nefarious, ultrafundamentalist Islamic group known as the Taliban. Documents recovered in 2011 proved there was a "close working relationship" between Osama bin Laden's group and the Taliban—including a "very considerable degree of ideological convergence."[463] The American corporate media almost completely ignored this previous US support of the Taliban in the aftermath of 9/11. The 2,160-year zodiac cycle continued to influence our history during this time. The Georgetown University article clearly reveals that the US-Soviet proxy war did finally end in 1992—which synchronized with the ending of the Second Macedonian War in 168 B.C.:

> The official Soviet withdrawal from Afghanistan was by no means the end of the internecine struggle for power between the US and Soviets in that country. Both superpowers would continue to arm and aid their proxies in the Afghan conflict until late 1991, even while the Soviet Union itself was collapsing. After the US and the Soviet Union ended all military support to Afghanistan in 1992, the country was left to cope with groups of highly trained, organized and

equipped factions—who engaged in what rapidly devolved into civil war.[464]

The Fall of the Iron Curtain—Right on Time

Rome prevailed against its own nemesis when it defeated Macedonia in 168 B.C. This was within months of when the Soviet Union collapsed in the Age of Pisces. A coup attempt was organized against Soviet premier Mikhail Gorbachev on August 19, 1991, where tanks formed a blockade around the Kremlin.[465] I watched this in amazement on a television screen in the Hasbrouck Dining Hall during my college orientation— and I will never forget how bored, disinterested, and utterly oblivious the teenagers around me were as this stunning event was occurring. I seemed to be the only one who was even bothering to watch as tanks advanced on the Kremlin—the central, beating heart of the United States' number-one nuclear nemesis—on live television. This coup attempt soon failed, due to poor planning.[466] Nonetheless, it was the culmination of a widespread dissatisfaction with the communist system, and an ongoing crumbling of the USSR. Russian states began declaring their independence in 1989, beginning with Azerbaijan, and the remaining states all followed in 1990.[467] However, the USSR didn't fully collapse until shortly after the attempted coup in 1991. Gorbachev resigned as president on December 25, 1991[468]—just seven days before January 1, 1992. Macedonia fell to Rome in 168 B.C.—precisely 2,160 years earlier. The zodiac cycle had remained remarkably active after more than two millennia.

François Masson Made an Accurate Prophecy

In his original 1980 book, Masson could see this trouble coming well in advance—and he issued the following prophetic statement: "This second Macedonian War could correspond cyclically to 1988–1992, when a direct USA-USSR confrontation would take place—as during the Cuban affair of 1962. Considering the means of total destruction available on both sides, modern wars are usually waged through buffer states, and are played out like a chess game—as with Cuba in 1962. Let us pray that it will be similar this time, and that mankind will not rush into mutual suicide."[469]

Masson's prophecy was absolutely correct. This time, the "buffer state" between the United States and the USSR was Afghanistan. The USSR lost the chess game and was balkanized into a group of nation-states. The United States trained, financed, and armed its next great nemesis—Osama bin Laden and the Taliban—in the process of fighting the USSR.

September 11, 2001: A Perfect Match with the 539-Year Quarter Cycle

By now, you must be wondering about September 11, 2001—the next major act of war in US history after the proxy war with the Soviet Union in Afghanistan ended in 1992. Is there any corresponding event in the zodiac cycle for Rome that was as significant as 9/11? Apparently not. The year 2001 corresponds to 159 B.C. in the Age of Aries. There are no identifiable Roman wars or noteworthy historical events that occurred in 159 B.C., other than the invention of the first water clock. However, when I went back to Masson's original data, I found that the 539-year quarter-cycle dramatically reappeared on 9/11—literally within days of when an epic European battle occurred in the year 1462. Once this connection was found, many other parallel events soon lined up with astonishing precision across the 539-year quarter cycle as well.

This stunning new data gave further support to the 539-year cycle connection between Joan of Arc's historic battle in 1429 and the 8-million-strong French youth revolution of 1968. Helmer and Masson were right. We must completely rewrite our entire cosmology of the universe—and begin seriously considering the evidence that the cosmos is alive. Moons, planets, stars, and galaxies can now be seen as vast mega-life-forms in their own right—and are exerting powerful influences on all life around them. They appear to be intelligently guiding us through the Hero's Journey archetypes on an individual and collective scale. These cycles of wars and atrocities will keep repeating until we master the lessons they provide—namely the forgiveness and acceptance of others.

I was quite surprised to discover that such a shocking, memorable, world-changing event as 9/11 wasn't random at all. The country that played the nemesis in 1462 was Germany. Although it's tempting to get into the specific details right now, we need to finish our investigation of the zodiac cycle connections between Rome and the United States first—to see how the cycle has continued operating from 1992 through to the time of this writing in 2013.

CHAPTER FIFTEEN

The Sky Is Not Falling—Only
Our Blindfolds Are

J oan of Arc's epic visions compelled the people of France to put her in charge of an entire army. Her bravery soon inspired her country to rise up against the British Empire—and win. Exactly 539 years later, almost to the day, a student rebellion in France inspired 8 million workers to rise up against their hyperconservative government—and win. This stunning synchronicity was predicted four years in advance by French astrologer Michèl Helmer. Additionally, major wars in Roman history reappear in American history 2,160 years later in the Age of Pisces, beginning with the imperial aggression of President McKinley against European powers in 1896. Political conspiracies like the Watergate scandal are precisely mirrored in Roman history, when Scipio Africanus was accused of accepting bribes from the enemy to end the war. Even the two principal consuls in the Roman stories—Scipio and Cato—appear to have reincarnated as Presidents Nixon and Carter. Despite the seemingly vast 2,160-year gap of linear time separating these events, we still see high-quality matches in the facial features of these modern presidents and their Roman counterparts, just as Dr. Ian Stevenson and Dr. Jim Tucker's scientific research suggested will happen in genuine reincarnation cases. This may be only one of many other examples that can be found synchronized by the great cycles of time. Each one of us may be living through a series of very specific experiences, repeating what we've gone through in other lifetimes until we master the lessons. The units of time between what we are doing now and what we did before appear to be extremely precise. There is no reason to assume these cycles work only on large-scale geopolitical events.

The "ideal" precession-of-the-equinoxes cycle features twelve of these Ages of the Zodiac—which add up to 25,920 years. Worldwide myths associated this "master cycle" with the coming of a Golden Age, which they say is literally paradise on earth. At the time of this writing, I found one quote from François Masson's final, published English version of *The End of Our Era* online—in a Facebook post from June 6, 2011—and it is very relevant:

> "Aside from all prophetic speculation, one thing is definite: our precessional entrance into the sign of Aquarius. This motion is mathematically regular—and the cyclic repetition of religious changes accompanying each zodiacal transition is undeniable. Whatever else may happen during this time that is upon us, a fundamental religious and ideological change is bound to occur."[470]

A Grand, Compassionate Design

Now that we have passed the Mayan calendar end date of December 21, 2012, we have crossed over into the Age of Aquarius, as I argued in *The Source Field Investigations*. This massive change, propelling us into a Golden Age, has already begun—and will undoubtedly get more and more interesting as time goes by. We can clearly see that the 25,920-year "master cycle" is much more than a slow, boring wobble in the earth's axis. Instead, it seems to represent a mechanism that is written into the mind of our galaxy and all its stars, planets, and satellites. This grand cycle appears to work like the mainspring in a cosmic clock. It powers our evolutionary path and our events in history through the Hero's Journey archetypes in nice, neat cycles of time. In Law of One terms, this grand story was carefully planned out, long before we ever got here, as the "preferred method" to help us awaken to the basic need to love one another—regardless of race, color, religion, gender, or nationality. We keep repeating the same events and the same atrocities, until we no longer choose to create them. Once we finally decide not to discriminate against one another, and decide to strive for a better world, peace and freedom will finally be ours for the taking—and we will enter into an unprecedented Golden Age.

We can be much more confident that everything is going to work out once we understand that the most distressing wars and political events are not random. There is a grand, compassionate design to the workings of history that unfold before us. As a collective consciousness, this appears to be the method by which we are ultimately prepared for a whole new way of thinking, acting, and being. Our living universe is not sadistic. We are not meant to simply keep suffering the same wars and atrocities, right on schedule, as if this were some form of ongoing, ritual torture. We do have free will, and this means we do meet up with whatever we create. As we grow and evolve, the histories of our nations can increasingly detach from negative timelines and gravitate toward other, healthier cycles the earth has to offer us. We may even experience an epic, worldwide curtain call—the ultimate piercing of the veil. In that case, the whole mechanism and its hidden players, both positive and negative, may finally be revealed, and we will enter into an entirely new structure of time itself. This is where the dance of free will comes in. What channel of the greatest show on earth are we collectively deciding to watch? What future are we voting for by the thoughts and actions we take each moment?

Smart Enough Not to Take the Bait

I was very relieved to discover that the United States appears to be increasingly pulling away from the Roman wars that occurred in the Age of Aries. The potential triggers were still offered to the public, right on schedule, but we finally got smart enough not to take the bait. Masson believed that the period from 1988 to 1992 could be as dangerous as the Cuban Missile Crisis nuclear showdown, if not more so—but the proxy war with the USSR in Afghanistan did not turn into a world nuclear Armageddon.

We also saw the original, short-lived Gulf War in Iraq, known as Desert Storm, in the key risk period of 1988 to 1992. This war began on August 2, 1990, when Saddam Hussein invaded Kuwait. Aerial bombardment of Iraq began on January 17, 1991. Iraq declared a cease-fire only one hundred hours after the February 24, 1991, start of the ground campaign.[471] Although many people died in the bombardment, Desert Storm was nowhere near the global disaster that Masson had feared it could have been if the zodiac cycle had exerted the full force of seemingly ancient Roman wars upon the destiny of the United States. I graduated from high school in 1991, and that was also the last year I watched television on a regular basis. Since there was no Internet back then, I quickly made friends with books, because every time I turned on the television during the Gulf War, attractive female newscasters and unsmiling male anchors were interviewing "experts" who insisted the entire Middle East was about to light up like a huge, fiery cauldron of violence. Everyone was afraid that World War III was about to begin, fulfilling biblical prophecy—but the other Middle Eastern countries never took the bait. After all this time, they finally broke the old pattern and realized that the nemesis was trying to provoke them into having a violent reaction, in order to cause much greater harm—with vastly superior weapons.

American Heroes Block "Biblical Armageddon" in 2006

As we learned in the previous chapter, the period 1988 to 1992 in the Age of Pisces corresponds to Rome's second war with Macedonia—from 172 to 168 B.C.—in the Age of Aries. The next significant event was Rome's war against Lusitania—beginning in 154 B.C. When we look 2,160 years into the future, this brings us to the year 2006. Although it may seem, at first, that nothing significant happened in 2006, we did actually come very close to a disastrous war that same year. On March 16, 2006, the United States formally declared war against Iran. The declaration appeared in that day's National Security Strategy announcement: "We may face no greater challenge from a single country than from Iran. . . . When the consequences of an attack with WMD are potentially so devastating, we cannot afford to stand idly by as grave dangers materialize."[472]

This declaration also made it clear that the United States would use nuclear weapons to fight this conflict.[473] This was very serious, and it appeared that a nuclear first strike against Iran was imminent. The Cabal wanted their biblical Armageddon as soon as possible. Thankfully, people in key positions rose to stop the cycle of violence from playing out as it had in Rome during the Age of Aries. John Negroponte, the director of national intelligence, became the hero who directly confronted the nemesis when he told the press in April 2006 that it would be "a number of years off" before Iran would be "likely to have enough fissile material to assemble into or to put into a nuclear weapon—perhaps into the next decade."[474]

A National Intelligence Estimate (NIE) that made the same conclusions about Iran was held up for more than a year by the Bush administration. It was finally released on December 4, 2007: "We judge that in fall 2003, Tehran halted its nuclear weapons program. . . . Tehran has not restarted its nuclear weapons program as of mid-2007. . . . We judge with high confidence that Iran will not be technically capable of producing and reprocessing enough plutonium for a weapon before about 2015."[475]

The very beginning of this groundbreaking report said, "This NIE *does not* assume that Iran intends to acquire nuclear weapons."[476] The words *does not* were italicized in the original document. As of this writing in 2013, it's now been seven years since Rome started fighting the Lusitanian War in the previous zodiac cycle, during the Age of Aries— but we still haven't seen any overt aggression toward Iran. Nor are there any other major new wars. The United States does still maintain a presence in Afghanistan but has now largely pulled out of Iraq. I was quite relieved to discover that the old cycles finally appear to be breaking down. If forgiveness is the key that will stop the Wheel of Karma from spinning, then it appears we are finally learning to love and accept one another. The nemesis can continue to harm us only if we fail to learn the lessons of forgiveness—and accept the temptation to turn against one another.

We Can Change the Outcome

It is very important to remember that we can change the outcome in these cycles. We are not trapped—and we do not need to keep repeating the same wars and atrocities again and again. As we learned earlier, we now have direct scientific proof that a small group of people can have a major effect on the behavior of the entire planet for the positive. Specifically, a group of seven thousand ordinary people was able to reduce worldwide terrorism by 72 percent—simply by meditating. They had similarly powerful effects in stopping wars, violent outbreaks, and loss of life.[477] Fifty different scientific studies have validated this meditation effect. This proves that the cycles are not fixed. Wars will not keep repeating, right on schedule. We can change the outcome. The lesson is that if enough of us begin practicing peace in our lives, the ancient story finally achieves its purpose in bringing all of us face-to-face with the nemesis, so we can integrate our ego and learn not to blame one another for our feelings of pain, fear, and anger. We can finally master the lessons this pattern of archetypes is teaching us—and stop projecting our shadow onto others by making them into our nemeses.

We may then experience a stunning, worldwide curtain call, such as in a full breakdown of government, media, and financial secrecy. Based on the testimonies of multiple high-ranking witnesses I have personally interviewed, once the Cabal is fully exposed on the world stage, this will quickly lead to a disclosure of the advanced human relatives who have been assisting us—and were seen as gods in every ancient culture on earth. These people have been here all along but appear to have largely stepped behind the curtain since the rise of Islam in the 700s, in order to allow us to become a modern society. Because they remain shielded from public view, each person has the freedom to accept or reject the idea of their presence. This premise of free will is very important in the Law of One series, but once we shift into fourth density, at the end of the twenty-five-thousand-year cycle, everything changes. Apparently, as we settle into this new reality, we will graduate into an entirely new time structure with surprisingly different rules.

I have often said that if reincarnation has been proven to be a scientific fact, how can we assume that we will just keep coming back and repeating the same lessons, lifetime after lifetime? Isn't there a point at which we learn the greatest teachings of the Hero's Journey—and are now ready to step into a higher level of our own human evolution?

The Federal Reserve: The Heart of the Cabal

Michèl Helmer did not detect a cyclical connection between the Roman Empire and the United States before 1896. This was the year that big-business bankers began seeing their plans realized with the election of the imperialist president McKinley. Under McKinley's reign, the Cabal soon began an unprecedented expansion of its power, using the United States as its new staging area. After many years of planning, the big bankers—such as the Rockefeller–Standard Oil dynasty in America and the Rothschild banking dynasty in Europe—pooled their resources to create the Federal Reserve in 1913. The creation of the Federal Reserve effectively overthrew the US Constitution. Harry V. Martin published the following research online in 1995, before so many others discovered the same facts. Now, even the corporate media is increasingly beginning to discuss this hidden truth. The number of people who know the real story of the Federal Reserve has skyrocketed since I first began researching this mystery in 1992. According to Martin, "Article I, Section 8, Clause 5 of the United States Constitution provides that Congress shall have the power to coin money and regulate the value thereof, and of any foreign coins. But that is not the case. The United States government has no power to issue money, control the flow of money, or to even distribute it. That belongs to a private corporation, registered in the State of Delaware—the Federal Reserve Bank."[478]

Senator Ron Paul uttered the following words in a landmark

Congressional speech from 2002. Ron Paul definitely seems to fulfill the wise old man archetype in our story, giving us the magic gift of knowledge that we still haven't fully utilized against our global nemesis.

> Since the creation of the Federal Reserve, middle and working-class Americans have been victimized by a boom-and-bust monetary policy. In addition, most Americans have suffered a steadily eroding purchasing power because of the Federal Reserve's inflationary policies. This represents a real, if hidden, tax imposed on the American people.

> From the Great Depression, to the stagflation of the seventies, to the burst of the dotcom bubble last year, every economic downturn suffered by the country over the last 80 years can be traced to Federal Reserve policy. The Fed has followed a consistent policy of flooding the economy with easy money, leading to a misallocation of resources and an artificial "boom" followed by a recession or depression when the Fed-created bubble bursts.

> With a stable currency, American exporters will no longer be held hostage to an erratic monetary policy. Stabilizing the currency will also give Americans new incentives to save, as they will no longer have to fear inflation eroding their savings.[479]

The Cabal's Secret Support of Nazi Germany

In 2007, the BBC revealed that George W. Bush's own grandfather Prescott Bush was directly involved in a business plot to overthrow the US government and install a fascist regime in 1933. Unless you regularly read "truth media," you've probably never heard of this story before. Even though the BBC called attention to it, corporate media haven't gone anywhere near this explosive story at the time of this writing. Prescott Bush's goal was not to create a government that would embrace the conservative Christian values his son George H. W. Bush and grandson George W. Bush would later publicly claim to promote. Instead, Prescott wanted to install a fascist government—patterned off Adolf Hitler's blueprint—to beat the Depression. This is a very different view of history than the one most of us grew up with, of course—considering that George H. W. Bush was vice president from 1980 to 1988 and president from 1988 to 1992, and his son George W. Bush was president from 2000 to 2008. Fully twenty out of the twenty-eight years from 1980 to 2008 featured a Bush as either president or vice president of the United States. Let's not forget that Germany was a Christian nation throughout Hitler's entire rule. Mussolini also rose to power as a fascist dictator in Italy—and Italy has always been the seat of the Vatican and the former home of the Roman Empire.

At the time of this writing in March 2013, there is still no one in the mainstream media who has been willing to touch this story. The BBC never even published a full article about it, but they have steadfastly maintained the page that links to the radio program—along with a synopsis of what the show reveals. Here is the text we find on this surprising page.

> *Document* [the radio program] uncovers details of a planned coup in the USA in 1933—by right-wing American businessmen. The coup was aimed at toppling President Franklin D Roosevelt—with the help of half-a-million war veterans. The plotters, who were alleged to involve some of the most famous families in America, (owners of Heinz, Birds Eye, Goodtea, Maxwell Hse & George Bush's Grandfather, Prescott) believed that their country should adopt the policies of Hitler and Mussolini to beat the great depression. Mike Thomson investigates why so little is known about this biggest-ever peacetime threat to American democracy.[480]

Granted, the true evils of Hitler were not yet obvious in 1933, but remember, a coup is hardly a minor squabble. These wealthy Cabal bankers and businessmen wanted to engineer the bloody overthrow of the legally elected constitutional government of the United States. Their plan called for inspiring half a million World War I veterans to get angry enough against their government that they would rise and do the job themselves.

The Plot Thickens

Another mainstream British newspaper, *The Guardian,* revealed that this uncomfortable story most definitely did not end in 1933; in fact, it seemed to get even worse.

> George Bush's grandfather, the late US senator Prescott Bush, was a director and shareholder of companies that profited from their involvement with the financial backers of Nazi Germany. . . . Remarkably, little of Bush's dealings with Germany has received public scrutiny, partly because of the secret status of the documentation involving him. . . . John Loftus . . . a former US attorney who prosecuted Nazi war criminals in the 70s . . . , [said,] "You can't blame Bush for what his grandfather did any more than you can blame Jack Kennedy for what his father did—bought Nazi stocks—but what is important is the cover-up, how it could have gone on so successfully for half a century, and does that have implications for us today?"[481]

Exactly how far did this treasonous American involvement in helping the Nazi Party really go? Could the Nazi Party have fulfilled its objectives before and during World War II without the help of the Cabal businessmen? Former US attorney John Loftus, who we just learned had prosecuted Nazi war criminals in the 1970s, spelled out the importance of American corporate assistance to Nazi Germany when he spoke to *The Guardian:*

> This was the mechanism by which Hitler was funded to come to power. This was the mechanism by which the Third

Reich's defence industry was re-armed. This was the mechanism by which Nazi profits were repatriated back to the American owners. This was the mechanism by which investigations into the financial laundering of the Third Reich were blunted . . .

There is no one left alive who could be prosecuted, but they did get away with it. . . . As a former federal prosecutor, I would make a case for Prescott Bush, his father-in-law (George Walker) and Averill Harriman [to be prosecuted] for giving aid and comfort to the enemy. They remained on the boards of these companies, knowing that they were of financial benefit to the nation of Germany.[482]

This Is Not About Doom and Gloom

When we refuse to look at our problems, they only get worse. This applies on the collective level as well as the personal. As I said before, the Sheep Effect can be very strong—and you may even feel physically sick as you read this. I do believe that in the fullness of time, everyone will know that Nazi Germany was only one visible form of a much larger Cabal—which was far more pervasive than we thought. However, when the denial finally breaks, we often rush to the opposite extreme. Almost everyone who writes about these "conspiracy theories" on the Internet has a fatalistic, doom-and-gloom attitude about it. They see the Cabal as random, violent, and unpredictable and believe it may well achieve total victory. Until now, hardly anyone was aware that the timeline of the United States synchronized with the timeline of the Roman Empire in the Age of Aries, after an aggressive expansion of power in 1896—which set the stage for the creation of the Federal Reserve in 1913. This allowed private bankers, many of whom are not even US citizens, to manipulate the world's economy by controlling the US dollar.

Once you are armed with this knowledge of how the cycles work, history doesn't seem so random anymore. The sinking of the USS *Maine*.

The Spanish-American War. World War I. The defeat of Germany at the Treaty of Versailles. The bombing of Pearl Harbor and America's entrance into World War II. Khrushchev's visit to the United States in 1959, seeking peace. The Cuban Missile Crisis. The Vietnam War. Watergate. The Soviet war in Afghanistan. Gorbachev's attempt at nuclear disarmament in 1986, signaling Soviet defeat. The US invasion of Soviet waters with a spy ship in 1988. The collapse of the Soviet Union in 1991. The Gulf War in 1991. And a formal declaration of war against Iran, with an intent to use nuclear weapons, in 2006—which was blocked by heroes within the US government.

It's all a big story. Movies give us a condensed, satisfying version of the Wheel of Karma. It requires much more patience for us to cycle through it on the global stage. But as we see the great story retold, we are reminded—on a soul level—of its triumphant conclusion.

The same patterns will keep repeating themselves, right on schedule, until we awaken, on a worldwide basis, and begin using our power to change the outcome. The more we focus on thoughts of love, peace, and progressive change, the more we make our hopes and dreams come true. We now have the proof that this really works; all we really need is the collective will for change. If our elected leaders do not reflect that will, it ultimately doesn't matter. History will align with our true level of spiritual progress—one way or another. Existing entrenched power structures will be exposed and uprooted so that we will not be damaged by them.

It appears that the story is finally working to awaken the American people, so they no longer have to play out all the tragic events of Roman history in the same fashion. This time around, the people did not support the aggressive, imperialistic policies they were being presented with by the media. Neither the American people nor those who were being goaded into taking on the role of the nemesis took the bait. The wars became increasingly less severe than they had been in Roman history, even though they still came and went, right on time, in the next zodiac cycle. Thankfully, the next major war, scheduled for 2006 in the zodiac cycle, never happened. This was a concrete signal that America had finally jumped off of the Wheel of Karma through the forgiveness of those it had once seen as faceless foreign enemies.

Let's Take an Honest Look

As we head deeper into an explanation of why the zodiac cycle may have finally broken down within modern-day America, please bear in mind that I have no problem with anyone who follows a conservative Christian mind-set. I also feel there is nothing wrong with gathering your own information and deciding on what you feel is truth. I certainly do not want any of these ideas I present to be seen as a religion or a dogma; we have more than enough of those already. This is simply a philosophical and scientific viewpoint, and if you don't agree with it, then you should feel free to reject it.

It does appear that the Cabal are posing as wolves in sheep's clothing and have specifically targeted Christians for many years now to form a support base. It has become increasingly obvious that Republican conservatives have portrayed themselves as if they support family values while actively pursuing aggressive, imperial policies similar to those of the fascist regimes their forefathers secretly financed in World War II. These policies are also similar to those of the communist Soviet regime they covertly built up in 1917. The fans of conspiracy websites have become akin to religious zealots in their own way—increasingly addicted to an endlessly replenished daily diet of sarcastic, victimized, angry, and hopeless rantings that give them a temporary high of righteous anger. Each new burst of "fear porn" soon bottoms out into a much harder and longer-lasting crash in which the conspiracy reader is drowning in a prison of fear, depression, paranoia, and loneliness. This can have a terrible effect on the peace and harmony of their families as well.

Once you've read enough of the snarling, attacking propaganda that insists "they're all in on it" and have reasoned that at least some of it must be true, it can be very difficult to change your mind and accept that heroes can appear within any government, military, or corporation. Hate can be a very comfortable, even addictive place to stay. Forgiving the people you have felt the most strongly betrayed and offended by is never easy. Nonetheless, forgiveness is and will always be the path to healing, even in the case of the most genuine sociopaths who have done the greatest harms. The Law of One clearly indicates that we should draw healthy boundaries with those who try to manipulate us, but the key to breaking down the Wheel of Karma is to not feel anger or negative emotions toward them as we protect ourselves and others. To genuinely love them, understand who they are, and see the horrors of abuse they must have gone through in their own families to end up that way, while also blocking them from doing any further harm, is the final triumph in the Hero's Journey.

In the Wild West of alternative Internet media, facts and journalistic integrity are often thrown right out the window. This makes it the ideal breeding ground for tabloid-style propaganda to be distributed as seemingly independent and patriotic reporting. Until we withdraw our projections from the world at large, and embrace and forgive the shadow within ourselves, we will always be looking for the next great devil in our global lucid dream. The more public someone is, the easier it is to see that person as the enemy. Yet, despite the massive, day-by-day political attacks, the endless blathering of corporate media, and the constant attempts to create as much fear and terror as possible, everything keeps working out. Although life can be very painful on earth, no Armageddon-type scenario has come along to wipe us out—and I strongly suspect it will continue to be that way, due to the protection we enjoy. We are not living within a closed system; there are many others out there who are helping us.

The Cabal Is Prevented from Doing Too Much Harm

It appears that the negative forces wishing to manipulate and control the people have an irreversible handicap that ensures they can never do more than they are allowed to do, thanks to the organizing power of the ancient cycles of time. This is a very important part of the Law of One model. Our planet is being carefully guided and managed so that we never see any negativity that is greater than what we have invited through our free will. As I wrote in *Disclosure Endgame*,[483] when you read the insider testimony of Peter David Beter, who appears to have had access to credible information in the 1970s that was unavailable to the general public, you find out that the Cabal has consistently tried to push the world into total chaos and destruction—both on a military and an economic level.[484] Underground cities were covertly built for a very good reason; the Cabal was doing its best to create a genuine nuclear Armageddon on the surface. Here is how Beter described this ongoing struggle in his fortieth audio letter, from November 30, 1978.

> For more than two years now the United States and Russia have been embroiled in secret hostilities in preparation for Nuclear War One. It began in earnest during the summer of 1976 when the still-secret Underwater Missile Crisis erupted. Then it expanded into wholesale nuclear sabotage of the United States with weapons now planted at literally thousands of locations nation-wide. These range from mammoth hydrogen bombs ready to destroy our largest dams and reservoirs down to tiny nuclear devices called "micronukes" by the Russians. . . . it no longer makes any sense to speak of preventing Nuclear War One, because it has already begun.[485]

UFOs, apparently piloted by benevolent extraterrestrial humans, have consistently interfered with the nuclear arsenals of every country that possesses them—not to attack us, but rather to prevent any political faction from destroying the planet. On September 27, 2010, Robert Hastings hosted the UFO-Nukes Connection press conference at the National Press Club in Washington, DC, in which seven US Air Force veterans shared their eyewitness testimony of UFO incursions at nuclear installations during the Cold War era, going as far back as 1948.[486] Then, only twenty-six days after this event, on October 23, 2010, a cigar-shaped UFO appeared over F. E. Warren Air Force Base in Cheyenne, Wyoming. Fifty Minuteman III missiles powered down and went completely offline for twenty-six hours. This was the largest missile failure in American history—and represented fully one-ninth of the entire arsenal. I summarized the evidence in "1950s ETs Prepare Us for Golden Age."[487]

In "Disclosure War at Critical Mass: Birds, Fish and Political Deaths," I linked to articles indicating that Russia, India, China, and Pakistan have all experienced UFO-related nuclear shutdowns.[488] According to *India Daily,* the Indian government was directly contacted by human ETs after their first successful nuclear tests in 1998.[489]

> Indian scientists are slowly understanding that the extra-terrestrials have the very unique power of jamming the operational characteristics of any . . . nuke missiles in the world, including those of India, Pakistan and China. . . .
>
> Americans and Russians have experienced the same phenomenon several times in the last sixty years. The Chinese have experienced the effect, and have in the past suspected Americans and others were causing the problem. They have moved their nuke operational theater way below the earth's surface, but the jamming effects have not gone away.
>
> According to Indian scientists, if the extra-terrestrials ever get to know that a country is trying to use nuke missiles that will impact over the whole world to a catastrophic extent, they will immediately disable the nukes. . . .
>
> Reports from the UK say that the extraterrestrials know every nuke installation very well—and their exact locations in the world. The main reason why these unmanned, robotized UFOs visit in so many numbers on the earth is to locate all the nukes that human beings are making—including the ones made and carried by the terrorists, like suitcase radiological bombs. According to sources, all the Governments with nuke capabilities know that their delivery systems can be disabled by these extra-terrestrials—and that is a major concern for them.[490]

Thanks to Kerry Cassidy and Bill Ryan of Project Camelot,[491] a free online video was released in 2009, where each of us took turns interviewing Dr. Pete Peterson,[492] a highly intelligent and clearly genuine insider. After countless hours of conversation I have had with Dr. Peterson, I am convinced that he is one of the most important and far-reaching inventors of classified technology for the Cabal throughout the second half of the twentieth century. Dr. Peterson lost a $6,700-a-month government pension as a direct result of coming forward with us on camera. Several of his technologies have the power to significantly enhance human health and intuitive abilities. Among thousands of other data points, Dr. Peterson told me he once had a desk right down the hall from Peter David Beter. In our taped interview, Dr. Peterson revealed that the American economy was planned to go into complete chaos in 2001—leading to a total breakdown in civilized society. He was told this well before 9/11. After 9/11, his higher-ups never told him whether this was the event they had expected or not—but it wasn't very hard to figure out.

Dr. Peterson was also told to expect a similar disaster in 2008—and the economic collapse happened in the exact time window he was given.[493] His higher-ups did get the dates of these events right—with a very narrow margin of error in both cases—but the social collapses never happened. Other imminent deadlines of disaster have come and gone since then as well.

The same Cabal that hoped to mobilize a half-million-man army of World War I veterans to overthrow the US government in 1933 and install a fascist dictatorship apparently has been working consistently to see such a breakdown in society occur for many years. In our video with Dr. Peterson, I pointed out that despite these dire prognostications and plans, life on earth has continued. We still have not seen any worldwide disasters, even though many different attempts have apparently been made.

Let Go of Guilt and Fear

If you do find yourself getting sucked into these fear-oriented stories and believing them—including any feelings of guilt that you didn't see the signs and try to do something about them sooner—there is something you can do to help the world. Empty your guilt and fear into the peaceful presence of the now. Just breathe in. Breathe out. Relax. Let go.

Consider the great mysteries of our existence. Reflect on the many prophecies of a Golden Age, and realize that the change begins right here, right now, within you. It's not something you're waiting to read about online, see on TV, or find in the newspaper. It happens in this moment when you let go of the constant chattering, defensiveness, and suspicion that often plague the mind. It happens when you reflect on the perfection that you already are, right here and right now . . . as you read these words or sit in silence.

As many gifted spiritual teachers have said, guilt pulls you into the past and fear pulls you into the future. Either way, you are pulling yourself out of the purity and serenity of the present moment, where all is well if you simply allow it to be. These incredible repeating cycles of time, humming right along for countless eons before the dawn of written history, appear to be a carefully scripted design to help us evolve on a collective level. Nuclear war is not permitted to occur, as it would disrupt the deeper reason for why these cycles are allowed to persist—namely, to help us all grow spiritually, from lifetime to lifetime. These cycles also act as a master indexing file we use to structure our reincarnations, so we know what events to expect within a given lifetime. Thankfully, all the suffering and death can finally come to an end if we can take the opportunity to learn from these cycles and make a collective decision that we are indeed ready to enter the Golden Age. Instead of seeing someone you may disagree with as your nemesis, you can say this: "Whoever you are, wherever you are, whatever you believe, you will always have a place in my heart. I love you. I am sorry. Please forgive me. Thank you."

If you can achieve that point of stillness and peace in the now—and believe me, I know how difficult it can be after generations of betrayal and hatred—you have just become part of the solution. You have vanquished the Guardian of the Threshold and seized the Elixir of Immortality. The power of just a few of us, focusing on the positive, can have a massive effect on the overall level of peace and prosperity in the world. If we were to truly have a worldwide awakening—a simple allowing of one another to be as we are—the effect could be so powerful that the old wheelworks of time might break down forever. We may finally see a worldwide curtain call—as extraterrestrial humans told the Indian government to expect, sometime after 2012[494]—when we enter a Golden Age, with a whole new story. That may very well be what the ancient prophecies were forecasting for the Age of Aquarius. Either way, it is up to us to make it come true, within the privacy of our own minds and hearts.

Think About What Jehoshua Really Taught

If you consider yourself a Christian, you can be on the front lines of this wave of human evolution by harmonizing with what the great master Jehoshua really taught, rather than the politics the corporate media may have encouraged you to embrace. No one is going to hell, since this entire concept was almost certainly a fabrication. Jehoshua's teaching was very likely mistranslated by the Roman government, long ago, for political purposes. Jehoshua's real message appears to be that we will keep reincarnating and burning off karma—the Gehenna fire—until we learn to love one another. The artificial division of the people between "liberal" and "conservative" is not in keeping with Christian morality or ethics. Everyone deserves love and appreciation. If there is someone in the world whom we do not love, it is our blessing to work this out within ourselves. A very key spiritual principle, echoed in the Cayce readings as well as mainstream psychology, is that whatever we see in others that makes us angry, sad, or jealous is a reflection of an issue we have in ourselves. If we can learn to love, respect, and forgive ourselves, then we will not be angered and offended by what we see in others.

Conservatives who are angry about gay marriage are secretly feeling abandoned by God. They feel that if the God they know and believe to be true were really in charge, no one would want to be homosexual. If God were in charge, no one would want to have an abortion. If God were in charge, everyone would want to be a Christian. This sense of profound misery and alienation hasn't changed in thousands of years—certainly not since the Age of Aries. Political parties rise to power by identifying these biases and prejudices and promising to make laws that will further restrict the public's free will. Traditionally, as the majority of voters have seen these laws get passed and watched their own freedoms being increasingly taken away, they have cheered. They felt as if their side was winning. Maybe God is still alive and well in their homeland, they think. However, as events go on and the world continues to act in ways they don't want it to, they feel an ongoing, deep sense of alienation, anger, fear, and sadness.

The Big Game: Manipulation of Perception

The big game of politics has always been about the manipulation of perception. Politicians find out who will generate the most votes, and then give them what they want—or at least promise to. Then when it becomes impossible to continue the game, they apologetically change the rules. Rome's greatest public speaker, Marcus Cicero, became consul in 63 B.C. Marcus's brother Quintus wrote him a brutally honest letter on how to achieve victory, which is translated and reprinted in *How to Win an Election: An Ancient Guide for Modern Politicians*.[495] The translator, Philip Freeman, wrote an introduction in which he broke down Quintus's expert advice—probably from the collective wisdom of an earlier incarnation of the Cabal—into ten steps, as follows: (1) Make sure you have the backing of your family and friends; (2) surround yourself with the right people; (3) call in all favors; (4) build a wide base of support; (5) promise everything to everybody; (6) communication skills are key; (7) don't leave town; (8) know the weaknesses of your opponents—and exploit them; (9) flatter voters shamelessly; and (10) give people hope.[496] Here are some relevant excerpts from this section of Freeman's introduction:

> 5. *Promise everything to everybody.* Except in the most extreme cases, candidates should say whatever the particular crowd of the day wants to hear. Tell traditionalists you have consistently supported conservative values. Tell progressives you have always been on their side. After the election, you can explain to everyone that you would love to help them, but unfortunately circumstances beyond your control have intervened. Quintus assures his brother that voters will be much

322 THE SYNCHRONICITY KEY

angrier if he refuses to promise them their hearts' desire than if he backs out later. . . .

8. *Know the weaknesses of your opponents—and exploit them.* . . . Winning candidates do their best to distract voters from any positive aspects their opponents possess by emphasizing the negatives. Rumors of corruption are prime fodder. Sexual scandals are even better.

9. *Flatter voters shamelessly.* . . . Make voters believe you genuinely care about them.

10. *Give people hope.* . . . Give the people a sense that you can make their world better, and they will become your most devoted followers—at least until after the election, when you will inevitably let them down. But by then it won't matter, because you will have already won.[497]

Karl Rove, former deputy chief of staff and senior advisor to George W. Bush, was quite enamored with Cicero's advice—and issued this quote for the back cover of the book: "Quintus Cicero . . . [is] a master political strategist. . . . This primer provides timeless counsel—and a great read for the modern political practitioner."[498]

Gary Hart, former US senator, admits that Cicero's brutally honest letter proves how history does indeed repeat itself: "Given the lowly state of politics, this ancient Roman handbook on electioneering shows how little has changed. . . . [It is] so masterful that one might think it was actually a spoof."[499]

The hyperconservative French government used these same manipulative tactics to appeal to their conservative base in 1968. They refused to let go of archaic laws that forced college students to be locked away from one another. Young adults were not even allowed to spend time together as friends in their own rooms. How could legitimate marriages ever form if the students were never allowed to spend any of their time together in their dormitories? The great cycles had the answer. Right on time, the revolutionary impulses that are programmed into the very nature of time kicked in—practically 539 years to the day after Joan of Arc led a massive public uprising against tyranny in her own cycle.

Allowing Love

The wheelwork of time notches us ahead. The gears keep turning, one click at a time. Eventually we throw our cards down on the table, let go of the games, the names, and the holier-than-thou attitude, and simply allow.

> 50.7 Question: Why must [an entity] come into an incarnation and lose conscious memory of what he wants to do—and then act in a way in which he hopes [he will] act [while he is still in the afterlife]?
>
> Answer: . . . Let us give the example of the man who sees all the poker hands. He then knows the game. It is but child's play to gamble, for it is no risk. The other hands are known. The possibilities are known—and the hand will be played correctly, but with no interest.
>
> In time/space [the afterlife] and in the true-color green density, the hands of all are open to the eye. The thoughts, the feelings, the troubles: all these may be seen. There is no deception and no desire for deception. Thus much may be accomplished in harmony, but the mind/body/spirit gains little polarity [growth] from this interaction.
>
> Let us re-examine this metaphor and multiply it into the longest poker game you can imagine—a lifetime. The cards are love, dislike, limitation, unhappiness, pleasure, etc. They are dealt and re-dealt and re-dealt continuously. You may, during this incarnation begin—and we stress begin—to know your own cards. You may begin to find the love within you. You may begin to balance your pleasure, your limitations, etc. However, your only indication of other-selves' cards is to look into the eyes.
>
> You cannot remember your hand, their hands, perhaps even the rules of this game. This game can only be won by

those who lose their cards in the melting influence of love. It can only be won by those who lay their pleasures, their limitations, their all upon the table, face up, and say inwardly: "All, all of you players, each other-self, whatever your hand, I love you." This is the game: to know, to accept, to forgive, to balance, and to open the self in love. This cannot be done without the forgetting—for it would carry no weight in the life of the mind/body/spirit beingness totality.[500]

We can allow there to be love in this moment. We can allow there to be peace in our lives. We can allow this universe to be a perfect place, just as it is. We can allow the realization that we will never die, that we will always exist. We can allow ourselves to be in allegiance with life—wherever and however it may appear—as all life is made from the same awareness that is within us.

Positive Changes

The majority of the American people decided not to support the aggressive, war-mongering policies of the Republican/neoconservative faction when the Cabal tried to create a new nemesis in 2006 by claiming Iran was an imminent nuclear threat. Instead, there was a landslide in the 2006 election: "The election resulted in a sweeping victory for the Democratic Party, which captured the House of Representatives, the Senate, and a majority of governorships and state legislatures from the Republican Party."[501]

This was not a loss for those who identify with Christian values. Had it not happened—had we not been ready for it to happen—we may very well have repeated some of the most deadly and destructive Roman wars in our own timeline. Many more lives would have been lost because we weren't ready to love one another—at least not enough to save the lives of others we think of as the enemy. This doesn't necessarily mean that all 2,160-year zodiac cycle crossovers between Roman and American history have stopped. Indeed, the shadows of the great clock still linger as its mighty hands tick forward.

The Cato-Carter Connection Continues

Cato maintained his position as consul of Rome for many years. Cato was elected censor in 184 B.C., which is the same year Carter was elected in the Age of Pisces cycle—1976. Cato remained politically active right through to his death in 149 B.C.—which corresponds to the year 2011 in our cycle. Obviously, Carter was president for only four years. Nonetheless, he won the Nobel Peace Prize in 2002 for his ongoing efforts to make this a better world.

During the last years of his life in the 150s B.C., Cato constantly worked the phrase "Carthage must be destroyed" into any speeches he made—whether it was relevant or not.[502] This corresponds to the years leading up to 2011 in the Age of Pisces. Cato obviously was very passionate about this quest. One historian revealed more details about Cato's perspective:

> [Cato] pushed his idea of simplicity and frugality on both the government and the people during a time when there was an increase in personal wealth and a desire for more. . . . [He revised] the roles of the Senate and Cavalry . . . [and invented] a way to tax luxurious items. But the most popular thing that he did was . . . [to promote] the final destruction of Rome's old enemy, Carthage, after discovering all of the agricultural prosperity that was existing there.[503]

Although many historians consider Cato's new campaign against Carthage to have been an unjust and senseless war, it is possible that he was on to something. Perhaps he had proof that there was indeed a secret, treasonous deal between Scipio and Antiochus, as the trial suggested, and that this was only one symptom of a much larger problem.

Was Carthage the center of the secret Cabal that was playing both sides against the middle during that time—just as we see in our modern era?

The Third Punic War—and the Battle to Defeat Financial Tyranny

Cato did ultimately go to war against Carthage in 149 B.C. This corresponds to 2011 in the Age of Pisces. I did not know what to expect when I first discovered this in 2010, but I certainly kept my eyes open. Shortly after *The Source Field Investigations* was published, Neil Keenan filed a huge lawsuit against the Cabal on November 23, 2011—the forty-eight-year anniversary of the Kennedy assassination.[504] This was very much an act of war against the Cabal—and if it succeeds, it will become a very significant historical event. A 57-nation alliance—which has grown to include more than 160 nations—supported this campaign to restore peace on earth, release classified technologies, and provide full disclosure. Carter may have supported this alliance all along, though no insiders have confirmed it at this point. Unlike most wars, this one had to be fought quietly, through legal paperwork and gradual exposure of the truth, and it is still ongoing as of this writing.

Keenan's alliance-led lawsuit was filed two hundred years and sixteen days after the Prophet's alliance of Native American tribes attacked Harrison's forces in the Battle of Tippecanoe on November 7, 1811. There are 216 cycles of one hundred years in each Age of the Zodiac. Perhaps our grouping of history into centuries is not arbitrary; it may be another lost inheritance from the same ancient knowledge that revealed the cycles of time. The mass theft of Native American land in the early 1800s seemed to correspond, very neatly, with the mass theft of gold and treasure that the Federal Reserve conducted, worldwide, in the twentieth century. The Battle of Tippecanoe and the filing of Keenan's lawsuit were only sixteen days apart within two turns of a hundred-year cycle, or ten turns of a twenty-year cycle.

In Roman history, the Third Punic War lasted until 146 B.C. This corresponds to the year 2014 in our time. Carthage was indeed utterly and completely destroyed, as Cato had prognosticated. "Cato's slogan was implemented in typical thoroughgoing Roman style. The walls of Carthage were torn down, the city put to the torch. The citizens were sold into slavery, and the Senate passed a decree that no one could live where Carthage once stood."[305]

I do not support war and carnage; neither does Carter. Events from the Age of Aries have become significantly less violent as they repeated themselves in our own age, particularly since the 1980s. Germany's defeat in 1919 at the Treaty of Versailles occurred exactly 2,160 years after Carthage was defeated in the First Punic War in the Age of Aries. Carter appears to have come a long way in the last 2,160 years. He is nowhere near as sarcastic and warmongering as he was in his possible previous incarnation as Cato—where he positively delighted in repeating that "Carthage must be destroyed." Based on Carter's track record, with multiple nominations for the Nobel Peace Prize and a win in 2002, he definitely would not want any group, including his own worst enemies, to be so utterly destroyed and defeated as Carthage was in 146 B.C.

The great cycles of time are not affected by propaganda. They are not blind to the deeper truth that exists among all of us. If the mass karma of Carthage reappeared in modern times as the mass karma of Germany, there may be other connections between Germany and the Cabal that we haven't yet covered. I am particularly fascinated by the fact that the 2011–2014 window in the zodiac cycle also precisely overlaps with our entrance into the Age of Aquarius. This may well be the ideal combination of cycles that will synchronize to generate the mother of all historical events. The Cabal definitely appears to have taken on Carthage's role within this new 2011–2014 war against the alliance, since Carter is clearly working for world peace.

Project Paperclip

We already saw that a fascist coup was plotted against the US government in 1933—and the Germans were secretly financed by Cabal industrialists such as Walker, Harriman, and Bush and their corporations throughout World War II. This is still only one part of a much bigger story. In 2005, BBC News revealed that the connection between the German Nazis and the United States became even stronger after World War II:

> Sixty years ago the US hired Nazi scientists to lead pioneering projects, such as the race to conquer space. These men provided the US with cutting-edge technology which still leads the way today, but at a cost. . . . Project Paperclip . . . [was a] US operation which saw [Werner] von Braun and more than 700 others spirited out of Germany from under the noses of the US's allies. Its aim was simple: "To exploit German scientists for American research—and to deny these intellectual resources to the Soviet Union."[306]

It is surprising to see how many people have never heard of Project Paperclip—but this is another one of many secrets the Cabal obviously does not want the public to know about. President Truman signed Project Paperclip into law as of August 1945, and the first Germans came to America on November 18 that same year. They arrived by boat in the United States just months after they had been crushed by the same country they now were relocating to. Truman drew up strict guidelines that he expected to be followed. He did not want anyone who was a member of the Nazi Party, or who had participated in Nazi activities or supported Nazi military plans, to be welcomed in. Let's now continue with our quote from the BBC:

> Under this criterion even von Braun himself, the man who masterminded the Moon shots, would have been ineligible to serve the US. A member of numerous Nazi organisations, he also held rank in the SS. His initial intelligence file described him as "a security risk." . . . [Nonetheless,] All of these men were cleared to work for the US, their alleged crimes covered up, and their backgrounds bleached by a military which saw

winning the Cold War, and not upholding justice, as its first priority.[507]

Did these Nazi scientists simply let go of their former political beliefs and relax into the traditional American lifestyle and value system once they arrived? Or were they able to influence the direction of the country itself? In 2007, *The Guardian* newspaper published a compelling argument by journalist Naomi Wolf, in which she showed how the sociopathic "Ten Steps to Fascism" were being rigorously followed in the United States:

> If you look at history, you can see that there is essentially a blueprint for turning an open society into a dictatorship. That blueprint has been used again and again—in more and less bloody, more and less terrifying ways. But it is always effective. It is very difficult and arduous to create and sustain a democracy—but history shows that closing one down is much simpler. You simply have to be willing to take the 10 steps. As difficult as this is to contemplate, it is clear, if you are willing to look, that each of these 10 steps has already been initiated today in the United States by the Bush administration.[508]

Thankfully, the Cabal was never able to complete those steps—but every one of them was rigorously attempted, or actually implemented, by the Bush administration.

The October Surprise

Carter's reelection may well have been sabotaged by dirty tricks instigated by George H. W. Bush. This sabotage occurred in the so-called October Surprise, when the Iranians were allegedly paid to hold Americans hostage until after the election. This would cause Carter to appear to be a wimp who could not successfully negotiate the release of these hostages. This secret, treasonous deal with a country that was supposedly America's mortal enemy would have helped ensure a smooth victory for the Reagan-Bush ticket. This would also add a personal element to Carter's ongoing political struggle for peace ever since. Robert Parry wrote the following exposé of the October Surprise on Truthout:

> Did disgruntled CIA officers conspire with their former boss, George H.W. Bush, to exploit the Iranian hostage crisis in 1980 to defeat President Jimmy Carter, whose policies had infuriated many CIA veterans? Did that secret CIA operation change the course of American politics, paving the way for a quarter-century of Republican dominance?
>
> On Nov. 4, 1980, after a full year of frustrating efforts to free the 52 American hostages held in Iran, Carter lost in a landslide to Ronald Reagan and his running mate, George H. W. Bush. The hostages were finally freed after Reagan was sworn in on Jan. 20, 1981.[509]

This sudden release of Iranian hostages—on the very same day that Reagan and Bush were sworn in—was certainly suspicious. Israeli intelligence officer Ari Ben-Menashe revealed the following in his memoirs, entitled *Profits of War:* "Carter's hostage negotiations had fallen through because of Republican opposition. . . . The Republicans wanted the Iranians to release the hostages only after the Nov. 4 election, . . . with the final details to be arranged in Paris between a delegation of Republicans, led by George H.W. Bush, and a delegation of Iranians, led by cleric Mehdi Karrubi."[510]

Another noteworthy book on this subject was written by Carter's top National Security Council aide for Iran and the Persian Gulf and was titled *October Surprise: America's Hostages in Iran and the Election of Ronald Reagan.*[511] His testimony also appeared in the *New York Times* in 1991, and it was entered into the official congressional record.[512] Barbara Honegger, a former Reagan-Bush campaign and White House staffer, also supported these allegations in her book *October Surprise*.[513] You can imagine how upset Carter must have been once he realized what most likely had been done to him. A treasonous deal was struck with America's enemy—and the Cabal got away with it. These fifty-two hostages could have been killed and were living in fear. Their lives were being held as a ransom to ensure Carter would lose the election, by making him appear ineffective and unable to lead the United States. Carter is obviously aware that to stand up to the Cabal in a bold, public fashion, at least at this point in our history, would be certain death. Nonetheless, he certainly appears to have committed himself to doing as much as he can to improve the world, within reason. Carter was deeply honored by winning the Nobel Peace Prize in 2002, and after receiving the award, he said the following: "When I left the White House I was a fairly young man, and I realized I maybe have 25 more years of active life . . . so we capitalized on the influence that I had as a former president of the greatest nation in the world, and decided to fill vacuums."[514]

Breaking Down the Walls of Secrecy

What types of "vacuums" might Carter wish to fill? It seems likely that he would want to expose and defeat the same Cabal that sabotaged his presidency. He might also want to see other hidden truths revealed—on a mass, public scale. In October 1969, Carter had a breathtaking UFO sighting. During his 1976 campaign, he made a bold statement: "If I become President, I'll make every piece of information this country has about UFO sightings available to the public and the scientists."[515] According to *BBC News,* the Germans might have brought some very powerful secrets along with them to the United States as a key part of Project Paperclip.

The large number of still-secret Paperclip documents has led many people, including Nick Cook, aerospace consultant at *Jane's Defence Weekly,* to speculate that the United States may have developed even more advanced Nazi technology, including antigravity devices—a potential source of vast amounts of free energy. Cook says that such technology "could be so destructive that it would endanger world peace—and the US decided to keep it secret for a long time."[516]

Carter has already proven he is willing to boldly speak out against what he perceives as injustice when, in September 2009, he criticized the ongoing, day-by-day campaign of the Republican Party and its supporters to destroy President Obama by fueling racial hatred. "I think an overwhelming portion of the intensely demonstrated animosity toward President Barack Obama is based on the fact that he is a black man— that he's African American."[517]

Clearly, Carter is not afraid to play hardball. Although I am not personally aware of Carter being a part of the alliance that is working to defeat financial tyranny at this time, the cycle connections between the Keenan lawsuit in 2011 and the Third Punic War against Carthage in 149 B.C. are very interesting. If Carter's change of heart represents a shift in the zodiac cycle itself, then the patriots within the United States who are willing to protect the people against all enemies—foreign and domestic—may have stepped into the hero's role as well. The Illuminati dragon is, as I said, guarding the ultimate treasure: technologies that could vastly improve the quality of all life on earth. Is the struggle to defeat the Cabal the new version of the Third Punic War, timed precisely with our movement into the Age of Aquarius? Will this battle to expose and defeat the Cabal reach its peak in 2014? Will Carter use his public position, when the time comes, to help create leverage to get the truth out? Will this also lead to the disclosure of the extraterrestrial presence on earth—along with the technologies we have acquired? It is an interesting question—and we don't have to wait very long to find out the answer.

Finally, as we head into the next chapter, we will begin discussing the astonishing quarter-cycle connection with September 11, 2001, across the gulf of 539 years. Once we see how the pieces fit together within the cycles, we are given even more proof that the Cabal's days are numbered. Was this epic event really caused by "Arabs with box cutters" who happened to get lucky and take two huge skyscrapers down in a single attack? Given all that we now know about the Cabal, is it possible that the official story is a lie? Who was the aggressor when the same cycle played out 539 years ago? How does this knowledge reflect on the events we are seeing today? In this case, we will also see another example of how two different cycles can overlap and exert a combined effect on the outcomes of historical events on earth.

We will also see that these time cycles are being observed, influenced, and managed by those on the other side of the veil, so to speak. Not everything is foreordained; real efforts are made to protect us from the most negative timelines. I was very fortunate to gain conscious access to those "on the other side" and be given prophetic information—such as about 9/11—that I published on my website nearly two years before the event itself. The Internet Archive still has a time-encoded record of when these words were posted, proving they were made public well before 9/11 occurred.

CHAPTER SIXTEEN

September 11 from Both
Sides of the Veil

Back in 2010, when I was first summarizing and extending this research, I immediately got the idea to check on September 11, 2001. This was, after all, the ultimate inciting incident of my generation—a trigger that awakened many more people to the existence of the Cabal, further ensuring its eventual defeat. The logic in Masson's book was simple and straightforward, and there were only a few cycles to choose from. I looked at the 2,160-year zodiac cycle first, but there were no events in Roman history that lined up with 9/11. The next-best choice was the 539-year quarter cycle. I immediately discovered that 9/11 was only six days away from a major European battle in the previous turn of this cycle.

If we count back 539 years before September 11, 2001, we have September 11, 1462. Six days later, on September 17, 1462, we find the Battle of Swiecino—the single biggest turning point in the Thirteen Years' War, which had captivated much of Europe at the time. This 9/11 correlation was not a single, stand-alone "coincidence." I soon found at least four direct synchronicities between the biggest political events in the Thirteen Years' War and major political events before and after 9/11 in our modern era. The beginning of each war, the building of the alliance against the nemesis, the key turning-point battle in each war, and the end of each war all synchronize—within less than a month—in both cycles. The Battle of Swiecino obviously did not feature airliners crashing into huge skyscrapers; however, there was a huge storm of crossbow fire that utterly devastated the losing side.

Helmer and Masson both concluded that the literal events that occur in each cycle are obviously not going to be exactly the same—but there are many astonishing similarities. Key archetypal moments in the Hero's Journey story line also seem to repeat themselves. At first, it appears that bin Laden and Al-Qaeda is on one side of the battle and America on the other when we analyze 9/11 for its cycle connections to the Battle of Swiecino. However, once I started identifying the key turning points in the cycles and saw who was fighting in each version, the answers became obvious. The true nature of the nemesis was revealed once more. We need to establish additional background material in order to properly understand how the Thirteen Years' War and 9/11 fit together, and who occupied the role of the nemesis in each version of the cycle.

A New Pearl Harbor

The official 9/11 story is that the attack was masterminded by Osama bin Laden and the Al-Qaeda terrorist group. There is obvious truth to this version of the events, and most Americans have accepted this. These people were involved and the United States did bring them to justice eventually. But it also appears that the terrorists could have had help. It is quite a stretch to believe that three different World Trade Center buildings collapsed into their own footprints, at free-fall speed, in one day through airliner collisions. Building 7 was never even struck by an airplane—it was only hit by falling debris. Both of the Twin Towers were engineered to withstand more than one airliner crash simultaneously. There are no other historical examples of collapses like this happening except through controlled demolition. Jet fuel is very similar to kerosene, and if kerosene could melt steel this easily, then every kerosene heater ever made should be a tremendous fire hazard.

There are dozens more holes like this in the official story, and the information is so prevalent online that you can spend years analyzing the evidence and print volumes of books on the subject of what really happened that day. If you have taken the time to study the facts, you may be able to lecture about this case for hours—but if you've refused to look at it, then you will probably reject every piece of evidence you see, and nothing will ever convince you. Each of us must move through enormous personal fear to imagine a nemesis that would be capable of sociopathic behavior on this grandiose a scale. Ordinary people could never get themselves caught up in such a huge, murderous lie and still be able to put their kids to bed at night. It is terrifying to imagine a government creating a self-inflicted wound of this scope and magnitude in order to attempt to install a military dictatorship and martial law.

Just twelve months before 9/11, the neoconservatives publicly revealed, in writing, that they needed a "catastrophic and catalyzing event—like a new Pearl Harbor" to advance their agenda.[518] Then, on May 25, 2001, the movie *Pearl Harbor* was released nationwide. It was the most expensive movie ever made—with a budget of $140 million.[519] *Pearl Harbor* was a very popular film, grossing $200 million in the domestic box office and $450 million worldwide. Everyone was viscerally reminded that America had suffered a terrorist attack that immediately triggered a world war and a mandatory draft. Three months and seventeen days later, the next Pearl Harbor occurred.

In September 2000, the neoconservatives published a document entitled "Project for a New American Century: Rebuilding America's Defenses." You can still download the PDF from the organization's website at the time of this writing, March 2013. Scroll down to page 51 and you will read the following: "Further, the process of transformation [to this New American Century], even if it brings revolutionary change, is likely to be a long one, absent some catastrophic and catalyzing event—like a new Pearl Harbor."[520]

This document clearly outlines that the neoconservatives needed a "new Pearl Harbor"—a "catastrophic and catalyzing event"—to transform the United States into what they were calling the New American Century. A big-budget movie like *Pearl Harbor* could have been designed to inspire the nation to militarize after suffering such a huge terrorist attack and join the new world war in the Middle East, if the other Arab countries had joined the fight to defend Iraq and Afghanistan. One of my most deeply placed "insiders" told me the following about this document: "David, hardly anyone really understands what they meant when they said 'New American Century.' They wanted to create a whole new age in which they had total, dictatorial control over the earth—and no longer needed to hide who they are or what they are doing."[521]

Let's not forget that Prescott Bush and other Cabal associates wanted to overthrow the US government in 1933 and create a fascist regime modeled on the principles of Hitler and Mussolini. They continued covertly financing Hitler through World War II—and got away with it. They transferred the best Nazi scientists to the United States immediately after Hitler was defeated—and got away with it. Prescott's own grandson was president of the United States during 9/11. During the Bush administration, the Cabal systematically followed the "Ten Steps to Fascism" identified by journalist Naomi Wolf. Hitler used the same ten steps to establish his own dictatorship in Germany. Even the new Department of Homeland Security was very similar to Hitler's description of Germany as the Fatherland. These historical facts give us legitimate reasons to consider that the Cabal may have had a vested interest in creating a new Pearl Harbor event to bring about major changes to government and society.

The USA PATRIOT Act

On September 24, 2001, just thirteen days after the 9/11 attacks, the USA PATRIOT Act was handed to Congress.[522] The text of the bill was nearly five inches thick—making it impossible for anyone in Congress to actually read it—but they were all under strong pressure to sign it into law. The bill was a total blueprint for a fascist dictatorship in America, stripping the people of all the most important rights and freedoms they were guaranteed by the Constitution.[523] Although this enormous bill was allegedly written in response to 9/11, evidence soon emerged that it had been sitting on the shelf for some time, waiting for the right moment.[524] The following excerpt is from a Truthout.org article by Jennifer Van Bergen that emerged in May 2002.

Similar antiterrorism legislation [as the USA PATRIOT Act] was enacted in the 1996 Antiterrorism Act, which however did little to prevent the events of 9/11. Many provisions had either been declared unconstitutional or were about to be repealed when 9/11 occurred. . . .

[The USA PATRIOT Act] allows for indefinite detention of suspected (not "proven") alien terrorists, without probable cause of a crime, without a hearing or an opportunity to defend or challenge the evidence against them, when they have not even been proven to be a threat—and have already established a legal right to remain here. . . . The USAPA expands the Secretary of State's power to designate terrorist groups without any court or congressional review—and allows for secret searches without probable cause.[525]

On October 9, 2001, two of the senators who were calling for rational thinking and trying to slow the passage of the bill—namely, Senate Judiciary Committee Chairman Patrick Leahy and Senate Majority Leader Tom Daschle—were sent letters filled with weaponized anthrax. These letters could have been a blatant threat from the sociopathic Cabal to everyone in Congress, warning them that they had better sign the USA PATRIOT Act, or else. The bill was signed into law on October 26, 2001.[526]

By September 29, 2001, 130,000 tons of steel were removed from the World Trade Center crime scene, and an additional 220,000 tons were hauled away soon afterward, leaving nothing behind. Only 150 pieces were held for future investigation with FEMA, and the public still does not have access to most of these pieces.[527] Every truck that shipped the steel beams away was equipped with a $1,000 GPS device to ensure that none of these "highly sensitive" pieces of evidence wound up anywhere else but the smelting furnace.[528]

According to several insiders I am in contact with, the US military quickly realized that 9/11 was an inside job. It is their job to look the wolf in the eye and not cower in fear. They realized they were not on a need-to-know basis about what had happened. They were already aware of the Cabal and how dangerous it was. They also knew they had sworn an oath to protect and defend the Constitution of the United States against all enemies, foreign and domestic. However, if they were to openly reveal what they knew, they would never survive—so the mission to defeat the Cabal needed to continue on a covert basis in order to ensure success.

Higher Guidance

In November 1996, after four years of stunning synchronicity, four years of writing my dreams down every morning, and eleven months of studying the Law of One series, I began pulling in my own intuitive readings. Just twenty-six days after I started, on December 6, 1996, I got a very clear prophecy of 9/11. Furthermore, as you are about to see, the readings had expressed a concern about the Cabal from the very first day. A working link to this 9/11 prophecy can still be found on the Internet Archive at the time of this writing, dating back to January 24, 2000—more than a year and a half before the tragic event took place.[529] In order to do this technique properly, I carefully followed the protocols of "remote viewing," where the main secret to getting good intuitive data is to avoid trying to understand any of it as it comes in. You go into a deep state of meditation, right on the brink of falling asleep, and listen to the "still, small voice" inside you. Then you document the data, being careful to have no emotional reactions, no mental analysis, no attempt to understand what it means, and no stopping; you keep a brisk pace. On November 10, 1996, right when I was first waking up, I listened, and I captured any words or sentences that naturally floated into my mind. As soon as I felt like I understood any of the words, I backed off, breathed more deeply, and went into a deeper state of meditation. My job was only to listen to the sound of the words, wake up enough to write them down, go back into meditation, and keep going. Within less than a month I began dictating the words into a portable cassette recorder instead of writing them down, which greatly improved the quality of the data.

Right from the very first day, two stunning prophecies took place. The first one happened almost immediately. I spent about an hour going

in and out of a deep trance state, and writing down anything and everything I had heard each time I pulled myself out of it. I ended up writing
down eight pages of sentence fragments, without paying any attention to
what they were saying. When I finally let myself wake up and read them
in a normal state of mind, I was completely amazed. Much of it was
cryptic and mysterious, but some of it made perfect sense. The very last
paragraph read, "I love it when people refer to the Midwestern Atlantis.
There are also formations in the desert you should know about, in
Chichen Itza. After I'm done, you should take a walk to them. You can
go with your mind, you know? Check it out." Immediately after I finished reading this line and understood that it was encouraging me to
learn the art of astral projection, the phone started ringing. A friend of
mine from a local UFO group was calling to invite me to a seminar on
astral projection. I told him what had just happened, and he was
stunned—but we both knew that paranormal things like this were not
impossible, just unusual.

The second prophetic statement was rather cryptic: "One of our
women, Teresa, a sibling, inoperative—the Christian, psychically." This
clearly seemed to be talking about Mother Teresa, the famous Roman
Catholic nun and human rights crusader. Twelve days after I wrote down
those words, on November 22, 1996, Mother Teresa suffered a heart attack and was hospitalized. She had surgery on November 29 to clear
blocked arteries and was given an electric shock on December 11 to correct an irregular heartbeat.[530] This procedure had to be delayed because
she was also suffering other health problems, including bronchial pneumonia. Her health continued declining, leading her to step down from
the head of Missionaries of Charity—her own organization—on March
13, 1997.[531] Mother Teresa died on September 5, 1997—just five days after
the tragic death of Princess Diana on August 31, 1997. Many people felt
that the timing of these two iconic female leaders' deaths was synchronistic. By that point I had also received prophetic information about
Diana's imminent loss. All of this data can be backed up with eyewitness
testimony from my housemate, as well as others who were renting ad-
joining apartments within the remodeled 1800s schoolhouse we were
living in.

At the time I pulled in this reading, I was seriously considering joining the Masonic Order. During that time, I knew much less about it than I do now. I did consider that there could be risks involved, but I also felt like there might be some positive aspects to it as well. The very first sentence gave me a strong warning against this idea—and since then, I have become well aware that the secrecy of the Masonic Order has been used as a cover for the Cabal. We also see direct reference to the idea of "harvest"—the biblical term for the transformation into a Golden Age—by mentioning "the farmhand." The term *harvest* is also used in the Law of One series. What you are about to read is a series of the most understandable and relevant excerpts.

> Sunday 11/10/96—10:00 A.M. Most things in this world are a lateral hell; you can move about in them. Freemasonry is a vertical hell; you can go down much quicker. . . . Does the Farmhand have enough manual labor? The Bible, just analyze it—I'm too proud of you! . . . The religions I am concerned with will be someday lighted—and we will go on to greater heights as a conglomerate being in the cosmos. . . .
>
> [Your] country and continuity [is being] shaded by an invisible hand which controls the sound in the lower ear. [It is] the sound of Hades—it massages the temples. Pause for the government's actions to be completed. . . . It could be better, for there is sometimes touch and significant contact with the devil.[532]

When the source mentioned "the devil," it was discussing how some members of the Cabal have engaged in Luciferian rituals and believe they are in contact with such a being. In these early sessions, the readings referred to the Cabal as "the patriarch" more than once. I was dazzled by the information I was pulling in, particularly after getting invited to a class on astral projection immediately after seeing that line in the readings for the first time. Mother Teresa's heart attack on November 22, 1996, made me even more convinced that this was not my imagination. As the days went on and my reception continued improving, the messages about "the patriarchy" became even more insistent and carried a hopeful message, revealing that despite these negative actions, we would move through this planetary evolution successfully.

Monday 12/2/96—7:00 A.M. The patriarch is winding down, landing with such a force in each stanza. More and more, the barriers are toppling. Those who have faith in the one capitalizing on the shopping [are misguided;] we all know by now that this is a malevolent force that will soon disintegrate. Murder is still being sung in the hearts of foul men. . . . Know that the decades of tyranny are over. Accept that circumstances have changed; there is a new understanding now that is being brought out into the light. People will not be the same; with the speed of thought, they will fly and travel.

Tuesday 12/3/96—6:30 A.M. In unison, the voice of the Creator sings out, but who shall decode the signal? Continued assumptions prove incorrect. It is our pledge to be of assistance despite the circumstances. Those who learn the truth of religion will find themselves in an inverse position to the dictates of society.

Tuesday 12/3/96—7:26 P.M. Swiftly come the messengers of destiny, bringing with them the notions of a new age. It is but for you to perceive it that it may become reality. . . . The technological abuses of Earth's history will fall away. What you choose to believe is for you to decide. The choice is around you, and you may drink of it. No one survives in the pathways of the dead. If you believe there is only one mind, how can there be two different people?[533]

Then, on Friday, December 6, 1996, the first direct prophecy of 9/11 came in—almost five years in advance. The information was cleverly disguised, and at first I thought it was only speaking about a car crash. However, in hindsight there were several clues that strongly suggested this was a prophecy of 9/11—and that the readings were well aware that the Cabal was responsible for the attacks. The term "Rescue 9/11" is directly mentioned, followed by the humorously ironic phrase "CBS and ABC give it adequate coverage." We see references to the idea of "special effects" being used to create this disaster, and a clear statement that "it's the greatest science fiction story ever told." Furthermore, we see multiple references to sickness—and this seems to refer to the plague of fear that had prevented humanity from being willing to see the Cabal. Though the higher forces could have stopped 9/11, through various undetectable means, they had to let it happen in order to help us move through a mass awakening. Interestingly, it also said "the patriarch must be denominated"—which was an interesting choice of words. When a politician wants to run for president, he must be nominated by his party, and this curious word choice implied that the event being spoken about was ultimately a political one.

> Friday 12/6/96—7:35 A.M. Under the aegis of friendly planetary transformation, the talk show host has got a new one. They're all special effects, designed to ride the lightning bolts. It's doctor-recommended; who is going to ask the pediatrician? Who is going to look at the Self with tangible results? Self-awareness is the key to building a foundation. If a person is sick, they need constant attention. If a person is real sick, they need to collapse. Sometimes a habit must be dropped cold turkey in order to leave it. All pleasantries have been exhausted; there is no other way for the energy to flow. The patriarch must be denominated.
>
> It's the greatest science fiction story ever told. Someone comes in—Rescue 911. CBS and ABC give it adequate coverage. A cast-iron fence is wrought around the victim's body. An impenetrable wall needs only be potentiated by positive energy. In the context of the rest of the people, the material you present is truly a magical gift. Peace be with you in the Light of everlasting Love.[534]

The "cast-iron fence" was another major clue in the aftermath of the attacks. After the Twin Towers fell, a wall of solid steel I beams was left standing at the bottom—and it did look like a cast-iron fence. The message ended positively, as it clearly said that the seemingly "impenetrable wall" presented by the Cabal could be transformed "by positive energy." Eight days later, additional clues were given that further indicated the readings knew they were talking about an event we now call 9/11—and that forces within the White House were responsible for it.

> Saturday 12/14/96—6:00 A.M. There is a new, immediate story. Fear is thine worst enemy. Something about the dollar will be increased, and the White House will also be increased. We are calm about it; it is just a matter of fact.[535]

The readings expertly guided me through a series of jobs, and ultimately influenced me to move to Virginia Beach—the home of Edgar Cayce's own Association for Research and Enlightenment, or A.R.E.— on October 4, 1997. I had hoped to attend the A.R.E.'s graduate school, Atlantic University, and organized my move to Virginia Beach through the A.R.E. as well. As soon as I arrived there, people began recognizing me as the spitting image of Edgar Cayce as a young man. The facial resemblance was astonishing. After weeks of uncertainty, I finally had the courage to ask my readings if it was true that I was Edgar Cayce's reincarnation on November 26, 1997—and they answered in the affirmative.

Everything changed for me at that point. I really was quite terrified of the whole thing, because until then my readings had been strictly private. Now, suddenly, the work I had been doing seemed to take on much greater importance—and carried a significant responsibility. Even worse, I was told it would be "considered a felony in the spiritual realms" if I didn't go public with the story of the connection between Cayce and myself. I still wasn't sure if it was true, despite the resemblance—but once I checked the astrology, I was stunned. There was incredible synchronicity between the positions of the planets at the time of Edgar Cayce's birth and my own. The sun, the moon, Mercury, Venus, and Mars were all in almost exactly the same positions. Later on, an astrologer named Brian McNaughton calculated that my exact birthday— March 8, 1973—featured the best possible alignment with Cayce's astrology, in a 127-year period after his death. The readings also asked me to formally present the evidence to the A.R.E., including the comparison photos and birth charts. As fate would have it, they told me they had someone coming in every week who claimed to be Edgar Cayce. I did also meet with Edgar Cayce's son, Edgar Evans Cayce—and he admitted to me that although he couldn't believe it was true, I was the best contender he'd ever seen.

On February 23, 1999, just as I was preparing to debut my own website, I woke up at two A.M. with a prophetic dream of an impending disaster in New York City. In this case I thought the dream might be referring to a massive earthquake. I published an article about it on Joe Mason and Dee Finney's website, GreatDreams.com. A capture of this article can be found in Archive.org, dated October 9, 1999. This same article also features a dream from November 10, 1998, in which a "cast of characters . . . were entering and staying in a hotel . . . [that] looked more like the White House. . . . There was definitely some sort of political stuff going on. . . . This dream ends with some incredibly serious Earth Changes, and the hotel collapsing." The reading then came in after this and said the following—which appeared to be yet another reference to 9/11.

> Tuesday 11/10/98—7:23 A.M. A malevolent, brief problem. . . . We can use this material to predict those occasions where the entire system is breaking down, while simultaneously illustrating why it is that the press releases will be speaking up for a moment. . . . What we cannot do is urge the violence to continue. . . . There are indeed those concerns stemming from the direct use of force therein, and the cataclysmic nature of how it functions. . . .
>
> Instead of simply letting go of one's position and one's power, there are those situations where power is being sought after rather continuously. When we bring down the house, it is designed to enable the awakening process to continue. . . .
>
> Great strides are made by those people who never have to become anything different, but simply accept who and what

they are now. Those loving souls that have followed the Christ pattern to a tee will be available now to illustrate for others what it is that must needs transpire in the present moment. [536]

In this next excerpt from the same article, we see one sentence describing the dream I had, followed by the analysis I wrote in February 1999. I clearly warned that something big was going to happen in New York City, and urged the reader not to panic. A powerful synchronicity had occurred as I was dictating this dream into the recorder, and this inspired me to write up the article. Right as I said that the dream appeared to be predicting "an imminent disaster, possibly in New York," I had a very powerful feeling of ringing in my ears. This has always been one of the most powerful and sudden forms of synchronicity I receive, and has proven to be useful on many, many occasions.

> Tuesday 2/23/99—2:00 A.M. I met a client of mine who lives in New York City at one point in this dream, and that seemed to triangulate it to New York. . . .
>
> As I lay in bed and dictated this dream, I tried to make sense out of it. There obviously was an analogy to Mother Earth "vomiting," possibly indicating volcanic/tectonic activity, and the fact that even though it would happen, it was still okay. At one point on the tape, I said, "I think this has something to do with an imminent disaster, possibly occurring in New York." No sooner did I say this but what a huge, deafening sound pressure came into my ears.
>
> My brother also had a dream about tidal waves recently, while he slept for a night in New York City. In this dream, huge waves were coming in, and people were saying, "Well, I guess this is the end of the world." He was trying to go around and comfort people, telling them of the positive nature of this transformation of the planet. Indeed, we all need to stay focused on that part of the picture. These disasters might be very intimidating and disheartening when they happen. Many people might feel hopeless enough to contemplate

suicide or other drastic measures. The point here is not to panic.

You, the reader of this article, are getting advance notice about what is going to happen, as well as the positive outcome of it. You will be needed in your community to keep people calm when these things start to happen. If you need more convincing of the positivity of what is about to happen to us, please read the book that I have written, and the readings that have come through me.[537]

These next two excerpts from this same time period can be heard on the original tapes, and read in the original transcripts I have—including hard drives dating back to 1999. Unfortunately, I never published them on my website—but they nonetheless became much more relevant as time went on.

Tuesday 2/23/99—9:34 A.M. Severe wartime. You haven't asked us about this as often or as frequently as we would like. There are certain developments now taking place that have made this a much more current proposition than before, and at the same time, those differences between the past and the present are largely ignored in the conscious sense.

Monday 3/15/99—8:15 A.M. The Roman empire must again fall, as is the nature of cycles of time, and of the universe.

Susan Lindauer Tells the Truth

Many people who believe that "9/11 was an inside job" consider it to have been a huge success for the Cabal, when in fact it was a spectacular failure. Dr. Peterson and other insiders revealed that the Cabal expected this event would literally lead to mass starvation, rioting in the streets, and a total breakdown in American society, making it ripe for a military dictatorship and a new world war with a mandatory draft and mass death.

We did see a huge economic collapse after 9/11, but society bounced back much better than the Cabal had apparently hoped it would.

Several insiders told me that Flight 93—the plane that crashed in Shanksville, Pennsylvania—was headed for the Congress. The collision would have been used to kill many, if not most of the members of the Senate and the House of Representatives. This would have created a full-blown constitutional crisis and would have made it much easier for an emergency government to declare martial law and establish a military dictatorship.

Susan Lindauer was the top CIA agent working to negotiate with Iraq for the Bush administration. She worked in the Iraqi embassy in New York from 1996 right up until the second Gulf War began. Her job was vital to the safety of America—and extremely important to the Bush administration. United Nations sanctions had been placed against Iraq and were causing mass starvation and terrible humanitarian crises. The Iraqis were desperate to prove they did not possess weapons of mass destruction. Susan Lindauer was their closest connection to the Bush administration, and she was doing her best to orchestrate a peace treaty with them. She was shocked when she was ordered to sabotage the negotiations—even after the Iraqis offered complete, total, and unconditional surrender. They were ready to open every facility, pay every fine, and sacrifice every concession just to prove that they did not have WMDs.

Susan has since come forward and openly testified, in free public videos as well as in writing, that she was warned in advance about a major attack that was about to occur in New York. Independent sources confirmed that Susan gave advance warning about the 9/11 attacks. After 9/11, Susan was also told that Flight 93 had been shot down—and that the pilot who was responsible for downing the plane has been kept prisoner, in a chemically induced coma, ever since. Susan revealed her full testimony in her groundbreaking book, *Extreme Prejudice*.[538]

Susan was about to testify before Congress and reveal everything she knew about the Bush administration's efforts to sabotage peace negotiations with Iraq. Tragically, before she could ever make it to Congress, she was arrested under the Patriot Act. She was imprisoned in a Texas military base and kept in a chemical straitjacket with the powerful drug

Haldol for an entire year without a trial or a hearing. She was then kept indicted for five years without a conviction or a guilty plea. All charges against her were dismissed by the Justice Department—just five days before Obama was inaugurated as the forty-fourth president of the United States.[539]

The Testimony of Elizabeth Nelson

Additional evidence of the shooting down of Flight 93 comes from Elizabeth Nelson, a Project Camelot witness whom I had the honor of meeting and spending time with.[540] I was absolutely convinced of her sincerity and truthfulness once I got to know her, and we got along like old friends. Elizabeth (not her real name) first approached Bill Ryan in February 2009, revealing that she was in an emergency military command room on September 11, 2001, when the order to shoot down Flight 93 was given. This is only a very brief excerpt of her detailed testimony, which you can hear and read online.[541]

> I was in the last six months of my active duty, in training in the US Army, still of the rank of a Private, I believe— Private First Class. I was stationed at Fort Meade under the Kimbrough Ambulatory Care Center Hospital. Fort Meade also has on it the base of NSA, which is the National Security Agency. . . .
>
> I remember the room that they took us into. And they told us that we were in charge of getting coffees, any kind of snacks . . . [and] making photocopies, because she and I had the access codes for the rooms, to get in there. . . . It was made very clear to us that we were not to look at them. They sat us in chairs at the far end of the room, not facing them. We were told to look at the wall and not listen to anything we heard. This was our direct orders.
>
> [There were] probably six or seven men around this very large table, just like you would see in a big office somewhere.

And they had this funny phone. It was like a conference-call phone. . . . I didn't hear a thing about hijackers. We just heard that this plane was flying in a no-fly zone, and they couldn't make contact with the plane, or something like this. There was no communication. Protocol says it has to be taken out. And so I was in the room when the decision was mutually made by the people talking on the phone . . . to shoot this plane down. . . .

I remember the distinct feeling inside of me of when I saw on the news that there was this story that there were terrorists on this plane, and that the people overtook . . . the terrorists and crashed the plane themselves. And how this was leaking out as these people being heroes. And I remember the extreme moral frustration inside of me, of feeling: *But that's not true! That's not true at all! We shot this down.* And a huge conflict inside of me, of knowing that the world is made to believe this story that's not true.[542]

Building the Resistance

Highly placed insiders revealed to me, in private conversation, that the truly patriotic heroes in the US military dramatically intensified their efforts to defeat the Cabal after 9/11. They knew they had to do this in secret or they could all be tortured and killed. They knew it could take many years before their plans would ever be able to succeed. However, they already had developed a comprehensive blueprint to actually defeat the Cabal—despite its massive, worldwide power and control—in the aftermath of the Kennedy assassination.

After 9/11, I was told that numerous Cabal offices were secretly outfitted with audio-video surveillance equipment and that a great wealth of damning footage was gathered. This surveillance data allowed the alliance to remain one step ahead of the Cabal—and sabotage their plans whenever possible. Although their work had to remain secret, the patriotic elements of the US military quietly developed an international alliance that cut off the Cabal's financial supply, blocked every attempt they made to start World War III, and eventually planned to expose their wrongdoings publicly once they were too weak to resist. In order to effectively choke off the Cabal's financial lifeline, all its biggest sources of profit would need to be attacked.

Follow the Money

The connections between the Thirteen Years' War and the events surrounding 9/11 might not make sense until we reveal how the Cabal makes its money. As I revealed in *Financial Tyranny,* health care companies earned a whopping $64,924,600,000 in 2010. Nine out of the top fifty most profitable Fortune 500 companies were health care corporations. Pharmaceutical companies earned an incredible 19.3 percent profit margin in 2008, which would make them excellent stocks to invest in if your goal was to profit as much as possible. This also means nearly 20 percent of the cost of your prescription medicine becomes money in their pockets, even if your life depends on being able to pay for those drugs. Seven different industries on the Fortune 500 list are health care related—out of only forty-three American industries that earn a profit. The only other industries that can meet or beat these fantastic profits are oil and gas producers and national defense contractors, who do not have to publicly reveal their earnings.[543] Senator John Kerry made an interesting statement about these other two industries in his first 2004 presidential debate with George W. Bush.

> The only building that was guarded when the troops went into Baghdad was the oil ministry. We didn't guard the nuclear facilities. We didn't guard the foreign office, where you might have found information about weapons of mass destruction. We didn't guard the borders. . . . I think a critical component of success in Iraq is being able to convince the Iraqis and the Arab world that the United States doesn't have long-term designs on it. As I understand it, we're building

some 14 military bases there now, and some people say they've got a rather permanent concept to them. When you guard the oil ministry, but you don't guard the nuclear facilities, the message to a lot of people is . . . "Wow, maybe they're interested in our oil."544

A 2009 investigation by Fairness and Accuracy in Reporting, or FAIR, revealed that health insurance and pharmaceutical companies are being run by people who are also on the board of directors of the biggest media corporations. Out of the top nine media conglomerates—Disney (ABC), General Electric (NBC), CBS, Time Warner (CNN, *Time*), News Corporation (Fox), New York Times Company, Washington Post Company (*Newsweek*), Tribune Company (*Chicago Tribune, Los Angeles Times*) and Gannett (*USA Today*), the only company that did not have board members from insurance or pharmaceutical corporations was CBS.545 These same media giants own and control a surprisingly large number of all the movies, television shows, radio shows, magazines, and newspapers that the public has access to.546 This may seem scary—but it is a provable fact.

The Connection Between Neoconservatives and Big Pharma

There is also a clear, provable financial relationship between the health care industry and the Republican neoconservative faction. The business of fighting the big health care corporations' political battles has been quite good.

Between January and September 2009, health care interests spent $600 million on lobbying Congress, television commercials and lobbying. $38 million, about the maximum that they could give, went to Congress in campaign contributions . . . [The] health industry profits in 2008 were $8.4 billion . . . So they were able to pay their CEOs average annual salaries of $14 million, and still have enough to give big stockholders huge profits—and still lobby against the American People.[547]

The evidence became even more compelling in 2009, when the first stage of the Obama administration's Affordable Care Act passed in the US Senate. This quote from *Populist Daily* makes the case very nicely: "Right to the end, the Neoconservative Obstructionists in the Senate fought their hardest for the health insurance industry, trying to get every benefit they could—and putting pressure on all Democratic Senators with any political vulnerability. They fired salvo after salvo at health care reform."[548]

Does this mean that the neocons and their associates actually own the top drug, insurance, and health care companies that are profiting from this corruption? Perhaps. This may be one of the main sources of profit for their faction. Either way, the Swiss scientific team led by Dr. Glattfelder used supercomputers to reveal that 147 companies are earning 80 percent of all the money there is to be made on earth. Of these companies, 75 percent are financial institutions—and the top Federal Reserve banks are the most powerful members of this highly secretive group. These financial institutions would need to heavily invest in the health care and insurance industries in order to establish maximum control. Therefore, any serious attempt to defeat the Cabal would require a direct attack against the enormous profits of the health care industry. And here's the problem: The health insurance and pharmaceutical companies also have controlling interests in eight of the top nine media corporations. Therefore, the mainstream media would be very unlikely to tell the public the truth about a war against the pharmaceutical / health care industry—and the massive amount of money that is at stake. Much of the struggle to reduce health care profiteering would need to be done publicly, through legislation—but the real reason for the war has remained a closely guarded secret at the time of this writing.

When we go back in time by 539 years, we find that a very similar war was being fought on very similar terms. Once again, we have a nemesis that was plundering much of the public's wealth—by making the people pay extremely high taxes for the basic things they needed to survive. Imagine having to pay taxes to a foreign government just to sell your neighbor the vegetables you grew on your own land. Imagine being threatened with huge fines, imprisonment, torture, and even death for failing to pay these taxes. This was the situation that was gripping much of Europe in the 1400s. The nemesis in the 1400s was Germany, specifically the Teutonic Knights. In 2010, the Imperial Teutonic Order website boldly stated, "For God, The Holy Reich and The Fatherland!" at the bottom,[549] though this slogan has since been removed. In our own cycle, the Cabal seems to be repeating the karma of the German Teutonic Knights. The Federal Reserve Cabal financed and built up Nazi Germany—and then imported their scientists to the United States after Hitler was defeated. Once I saw how well my readings predicted the events that were still to come, I realized that none of these developments were random or unexplained. Those on the other side of the veil could view our future just as easily as we view the present. These tragic events had to be allowed to happen because we had invited them by our own free will on a collective level. With this knowledge comes the key to resolving the outer and inner crises, worldwide. An era of unprecedented peace and prosperity awaits us once the great cycles of time are reprogrammed with the knowingness that we have finally learned the lessons the universe has spent so many thousands of years trying to teach us.

PART FOUR

RESOLVING THE OUTER AND INNER CRISES

CHAPTER SEVENTEEN

Cycles and Prophecies at the End of the Age

The Thirteen Years' War

A major political event on December 5, 1453, quickly became the inciting incident for the Thirteen Years' War, which officially started with a formal declaration of war two months later. By this point in time, the political climate in Europe had become extremely tense. Prussian cities and states were being heavily taxed by the Teutonic Knights. They were being forced, under pain of torture, imprisonment, and death, to pay large fees for the "privilege" of selling the crops they grew on their own farms. This was causing them real economic pain, and it was only getting worse and worse. Families were suffering. Children were starving. The people were groaning under the weight of oppression.

In 1453, there was no separation between church and state. The Prussian cities and states needed to appeal to Frederick III, the Holy Roman Emperor, if they wanted these taxes repealed. However, by December 5, 1453, Frederick had refused to give them an answer for well over a year. Frederick did not want to tell the Prussian Confederation that he had no interest in helping them solve their conflict with the Germans, as this was likely to trigger a major conflict. However, on December 5, 1453, Frederick was forced to admit that he would do nothing to help them. This was the inciting incident that started the Thirteen Years' War against Germany's Teutonic Knights.[550]

Bush Loses to Clinton Within Thirty-One Days of the War in the Previous Cycle

The Teutonic Knights' fate was sealed on this very day, December 5, 1453; they just didn't know it yet. When we look ahead 539 years into the future, we have December 5, 1992. This was just one month—thirty-one days—after George H. W. Bush lost the presidential election to the Democratic candidate, William Jefferson Clinton. This was the first time the Republican neoconservative faction of the Cabal had lost an election to a Democratic rival since 1980. George H. W. Bush had been either vice president or president of the United States for twelve years by the time Clinton prevailed. Once Bush lost the reins of executive power, the scope of what the neoconservative faction could accomplish was significantly reduced. This eight-year gap in Republican political dominance gave the Democratic opposition some time to begin mounting a counterattack—as we will see.

That being said, I do not believe that Republicans are bad and Democrats are good. The Cabal has penetrated the American government on many different levels, and there are good guys and bad guys on both sides. Both parties have been compromised to varying degrees. Therefore, the best way to view this conflict is to see it as a modern battle between warring factions in the Cabal. However, as they fight against each other and weaken each other, the Cabal's overall ability to do harm is reduced.

Clinton's Health Care Reform Synchronizes with Prussian-Polish Alliance

The Thirteen Years' War was triggered shortly after Frederick blatantly refused to help the Prussian Confederation on December 5, 1453. George H. W. Bush lost the presidential election within thirty-one days of this event in our own cycle. Once we examine the full context, it definitely seems that the Prussian Confederation synchronizes with the Clinton administration, and the Teutonic Knights synchronize with the neocon faction.

The Prussian Confederation knew they needed help fighting the nemesis in order to stop their people from being robbed and terrorized. The German Teutonic Knights were too powerful, and the Prussian Confederation couldn't fight them alone. Everyone in Europe was being hurt by these painful taxes and lethal threats, but old animosities had stopped them from realizing they had a common enemy. During this time, Poland was the big heavyweight. The Prussian Confederation could not win a war against the Germans without Poland's help. In our new cycle, Poland seems to synchronize with the US Congress—a much larger legislative group, with senators and representatives from all fifty states. Clinton could not win the battle for health care reform without the help of the US Congress. The Prussian Confederation could not win the battle for tax reform without the help of the Polish kingdom.

In January 1454, associates from the Prussian Confederation, led by Johannes von Baysen, approached Casimir IV, the king of Poland, and asked him to absorb their entire alliance into the Polish kingdom. By pooling their resources, they had a real chance to choke off the Germans from their main source of profits—namely, the huge taxes they were imposing upon the people with violent force. The Polish king was willing to talk it over, but he wanted them to discuss it him in a more formal meeting so they could work out the details. This initial meeting between Casimir IV, von Baysen, and his Prussian Confederation associates took place in January 1454. In our own cycle, this becomes January 1993.

Clinton was not sworn into office until January 20, 1993—and his very first priority was to attack the health care industry for its exorbitant price gouging and corruption. Derek Bok of Harvard University reveals the trouble that Clinton encountered in this process: "Clinton made health care reform a centerpiece of his campaign platform. . . . True to his word, he moved quickly to address the issue, by announcing early in 1993 that he would assemble a task force of experts to review the subject—and construct a plan that he could propose to Congress."[551]

Bill Clinton's wife, Hillary, was named to head the health-care reform task force on January 25, 1993.[552] Prussia first approached the Polish king to discuss this hitherto-unprecedented alliance that same month—539 years earlier.

The First In-Person Meetings Were Only Three Days Apart

Clinton got his first in-person meeting with Congress to seek a formal alliance for health care reform on February 17, 1993. On February 20, 1454, just three days later in the previous cycle, von Baysen and the Prussian Confederation got their first in-person meeting with Polish king Casimir IV to discuss a formal alliance. This is one of the closest time locks we've seen yet. Their negotiations were finalized and the Prussian delegates formally pledged allegiance to the king as of March 6, 1454. Clinton did not have as much luck in our own cycle—at least in terms of the specific issue of health care reform.

On March 8, 1993, *The New York Times* published the article "Looking for Alliance, Clinton Courts the Congress Nonstop."[553] Clinton's health care reform package never did pass in the 1990s, although he did manage to develop a cooperative alliance with Congress in other ways. The Obama administration, with Hillary Clinton as secretary of state, did finally pass the Patient Protection and Affordable Care Act (PPACA) on March 22, 2010—fully seventeen years later. This shows how long this "war" has raged on.[554] The neoconservative-driven media has dubbed this new plan Obamacare and has presented it to the people as if it is one of the most diabolically evil acts ever committed by the US government. As of March 21, 2013, congressional Republicans had made thirty-seven different attempts to repeal PPACA.[555]

A Long Battle Without Any Major Success

After the Prussian Confederation formed an alliance with Poland in 1454, they had a long, difficult fight. For the next eight and a half years, they struggled in vain to defeat Germany—but could not. In our own cycle, Clinton was consistently dogged by Republican-fueled scandals during his administration, including the Monica Lewinsky scandal—when he was ultimately forced to admit to having sex with an intern in the Oval Office. The "All Is Lost" moment in the Lewinsky scandal came when Clinton paid $550,000 to Paula Jones on November 13, 1998, in an obvious admission of guilt. Johannes von Baysen, the head of the Prussian alliance, died November 9, 1459, at Marienburg Castle, and was succeeded by his brother. These events are only four days apart in the 539-year cycle. I have not yet been able to find any image of von Baysen, but I suspect he looked very similar to Clinton.

A Prophecy of the 2000 Election Crisis—and Beyond

Eight years after Clinton won his first presidential victory, his administration hoped to remain in power by having Vice President Al Gore run for office. In a very surreal series of events, the race between George W. Bush and Al Gore was so tight that a winner could not be determined. The entire nation held its breath from November 5 straight through until December 13, when Gore conceded to Bush after the Supreme Court voted in Bush's favor. Not long after, the final vote tallies from Florida revealed that Gore actually won the 2000 presidential election by popular vote—but by that point it was too late.

On November 24, 2000, nineteen days before this conflict was resolved, I realized that I had already posted an accurate prophecy of the outcome on my website, embedded within a psychic reading I had done myself. I first started doing readings on November 10, 1996, and had many astonishingly accurate prophecies, but this was the first major one that I had clearly published in advance on my website before it came true. I had very little awareness of what I was saying as the words were being spoken but followed a strict protocol of praying that only the highest and purest forms of guidance would come through. This prophecy was originally posted within a larger set of readings on June 23, 1999.[556] The link to the original content was preserved by Archive.org on

October 2, 1999, and can be found near the bottom of the main page as "Global Politics Part Three."[557] I rediscovered these prophecies on November 24, 2000, and wrote "Prophecy: 2000 Election Crisis Predicted in 1999" that same day.[558] The reading itself was conducted on June 17, 1999, at 9:21 A.M. The exact wording of the election prophecy was as follows: "The vice president looks at this as being partly his own authorship, while not realizing that he is completely naked. The interim period decides the next victor."[559]

I was quite astonished when I read this in the midst of the election crisis. I did not want to see George W. Bush win, but this prophecy clearly said Gore was "completely naked." It also indicated there would be an "interim period"—an extended wait—before the "next victor" of the presidential election would be announced. Further support for this perspective was given in a very deep reading I pulled in on April 22, 1999, at 4:13 A.M., and published on April 29, 1999.[560] The Internet Archive has a time-encoded snapshot of my homepage from May 8, 1999, shortly after this content was published as "ET Government Speaks on Kosovo Issue."[561] You can then click on the link and read the article itself in its original form, though Archive.org unfortunately deleted all duplicate snapshots it had taken prior to April 9, 2001. This reading, from the very early morning of April 22, 1999, directly referred to the "Bush troops" while Clinton was still president. It also mentioned the discovery of fully preserved Roman galleons that had just been discovered and publicized in the news, and suggested that this event had deeper symbolic meaning—showing the cycle connections between Rome and our own present.

> Ever wonder about the banking crisis? The top three most valuable computer gurus in the world still don't realize how exactly they will be affected by this. Most would seem to be wanting a quick and easy solution, when the entire matter is actually flown away from, and not professionally dealt with. We have sought to undermine the Bush troops, and their influence on the global/political picture. This has failed us. . . . The other night, I had a dream about you, and it said that the strictest Christians have become the most diehard opponents

to Christianity in its Fundamentalist forms—instead embracing the true reality of the Oneness of the universe. . . .

Place a few dozen more roses on the graves of those who have gone beyond. For you see that all is One, and this senseless killing and violence must not go on. It needs to be established that there is a solid fact behind why there will never be a one-world hegemony of these financial powers. . . . Another issue on the table is the sudden and spontaneous discovery of perfectly preserved Roman galleons, buried beneath the sands of the ocean of time and now brought back into the public awareness—as though not a day had passed since they first sank. We want you to understand the profound symbology of this. As David has been studying the field of cyclology, he can see that many correlations have already been made between that of the Roman history and the American history. Events occurring upon similar timetables play themselves out in such a fashion, as described in those works. . . .

It is a fundamental fact that a connection has been established between the Roman regime and the United States regime. So too is there a fact that the United States regime must collapse and fold, as did Rome, once thought to be the greatest superpower of the world. When the Roman civilization did collapse, it was cause for great alarm. Similarly, the greed and desire for limitless profits is also now fueling the stock market's increases. As this is seen to fall away, there will be many of those who have placed great faith in the stock market who will suddenly have all of their earnings vaporized—and be left with stock that is completely devalued.[562]

This prophecy about a collapse in the stock market did come true, three different times after this reading: the dot-com collapse of 2000, the post-9/11 collapse of 2001, and the Lehman Brothers collapse of 2008. My next article picked up with new readings after the point where this one left off—and included the prophecy of the election crisis, as we are about to see.

A Series of Stunning Readings in 1999

The forces speaking through me clearly seemed to be able to peer into the future with no difficulty—at times. However, not all of the words in the readings I posted were 100 percent "clean." That was a frustrating reality. It was entirely possible to get data that was not accurate. As one notable example, I was heavily influenced by a then-widespread belief that California might have a giant earthquake in 1998 or 1999, which several guests on the Art Bell show were predicting. With years' more experience, it is now a lot easier for me to spot the best material—and see where the authentic messages were encouraging me to keep refining and tuning my abilities. The deepest readings always have a poetic, metaphorical quality that the less-accurate readings did not display as strongly. Everything I have included below appears to be "clean," based on the benefit of experience and hindsight, and much of the rest of it is clean as well. The prophecy of the election crisis is hidden within these passages. There is a reference to the Constitution being "in deferment," again tying in to the election crisis. We also find clear prophecies of 9/11 and the 2011 Fukushima earthquake disaster in Japan. The earliest, clickable version of this page still preserved by Archive.org is from March 11, 2000.[563]

> Sunday 5/23/99—4:49 A.M. It is important to recognize that the globalist agenda is felt to have significance of a very profound nature, based on the existence of extraterrestrial life and the need to present oneself to it. And thus, similar to Manifest Destiny, these forces in your physical plane feel it necessary to strive to conquer in order to bring about these matters. . . . We do want to assure you that the course is still steady and clear, and thus do not be afraid by whatever transpires in the physical, as it is only indicative of a much larger arena of spectators that watch and guide these events. We cannot take away your free will, but we do have an enormous

number of resources available to us in order to produce change in your environment. That should be something of significance to you.

Thursday 5/27/99—7:18 A.M. The average brother (in your colonial building) was open to a whole host of different tactics that would explain why the constitution was in deferment. . . . Their minds are clever with hatred. Part of what we are seeing here is the machinations of the deeper plan. . . . From our perspective, things are indeed looking pretty good, I think. Tie a tether to the balloon of the Spirit and be prepared for the ride as the Upgrade looms closer. Many scientists will be quite puzzled and perplexed about this afterward, but this is definitely not [going to be] an optical illusion.

In order to finish a large Experiment, we need to react to the Divine will of all forces involved. The free-will decisions of your people still determine the course of future events at this point. . . . We want everyone to be able to participate in this, because it is so lonely afterward if they are not involved. . . . Be it four years' time, four centuries' time or four thousand years' time, there is a relativity to one's perspective. So, in the present moment, all phases of human civilization are again becoming visible—and this gives us pause.

Saturday 5/29/99—9:18 A.M. . . . We do not want to see the modern children of this generation being molested by a shadowy and insurgent world order that seeks conquest and hegemony.

Tuesday 6/8/99—4:16 A.M. The repetitive looping of the processes in the present are soon to be circumvented by the explosion of new energy from the galactic center. There is a certain manifestation of an energetic presence that will be physically visible—and that is an important part of understanding how this cycle functions.

Wednesday 6/9/99—8:37 A.M. A rumbling newsquake rushed into Brazil, overturning cars and trucks and automobiles and wreaking havoc on the economy at large. The seas from Japan spill over onto the lands, and we have seen all about that before. The steps on the long march back to progress can be rather difficult.

On the jet, it will appear that two were obeying orders and one was carrying them out. In fact, it was a huge theater or arena of spectators, all of whom were responsible. The hotels were open when disaster struck. The landlord despised the conflict, but he understood that he could not surrender to the ultimate ordeal instead. The white flag will rise, but it means nothing.

Better instead to try to focus on the reality of the moment-by-moment quest to end the long-standing reign of violence as it now stands, through diligent application of all that you have learned in this life. The top priority comes from the desire to cease the violence against self and others. That is very important. The senate makes tougher laws on gun restrictions as a result of this whole debacle. . . .

Nor should the dividers that would settle up the lands amongst themselves fail to realize that the clubhouse they are playing in is not impervious to damage from outside forces such as ourselves, who would seek to right these situations. So don't fret and fume about the politics that you see on the Earth—as the focus, as always, is upon your own spiritual growth, enlightenment and Ascension.

Thursday 6/17/99—9:21 A.M. The vice president looks at this as being partly his own authorship, while not realizing that he is completely naked. The interim period decides the next victor.

We have come allying ourselves with those highest forces of Love and Light, to insure that no one is harmed further than necessary. . . . When you look at it strictly from a higher-dimensional perspective, there is a certain quantitative value of negative energy that exists on the planetary sphere at present. This needs be counterbalanced, for as we move closer and closer to the vernal point, or the conjunction of the solar cycle that we have spoken of, there is then no further wiggle room, so to speak.

Higher and higher the chariot raises in the sky, and it will be seen by all. The buildings will be smoking, the people will be crying, and at that point it will already have been done. There will be other stages of it, of course, but this is an important point. . . .

It is only through a very elaborate series of cooperative dreaming exercises that your physical illusion exists as it does. It is rather humorous for us to contemplate on the fact that everything around you is an illusion, and that you have become so captivated with it that you have completely forgotten that this is what it is. So many of the events that you call 'Random' are actually scripted and guided by Higher Intelligence that it would bring your mind to fathomless depths to even be able to conceive of the level of planning and forethought that is actually going on.

Cigar smokers indulge themselves after a new baby is born. Although we do not smoke cigars, we do certainly look forward to the new delivery. We eagerly await each of you coming before the Throne of the Divine and signing your name on the parchment of Everlasting Life, as we have said. You will then complete your obligation to the third density of bondage, polarity, karma and suffering, and move forth into higher directions of space and time. And with that, we remind you that you are being taken care of, and that you are loved more than you could ever possibly imagine. Peace be with you in the Light of everlasting Love. [564]

The following passages came through on September 30, 1999, and are found in an Archive.org capture from April 9, 2001.[565] The readings are describing an ongoing spiritual battle for the heart and soul of humanity. They must work to counteract messages of doom and fear, while also guiding us through major social and financial readjustments.

Modern times never before had an administrator who realizes anti-gravity wells and electrostatic, levitating machines. So as well, these things really need to get out into society as a whole. They will solve the Earth's mountain of difficulties, and take stress off of the heads of the University of Chicago and other institutions by drastically increasing the level of technology with which we are working. . . .

Fortunately or unfortunately, the frequency is defunct in its current light point. The available energies continue to batter the third dimension while rising everyone into the fourth, whether you like it or not. . . .

A long, largely disturbed road traces a path through all of these issues for you. Your dreams of old are now becoming realities. We don't need to remind you about what the negative forces are going to do next. A multinational nervous system center spans the globe, with many other sources describing what they believe as the key of the central nervous system of the giant. . . .

Our battle is what would be termed as a spiritual one, and the light bulb in your people's minds has turned out. Messages of doom predominate, [and] we know that we must come in and set the record straight. . . .

The entire country, and indeed the world, is on the brink of a major social and financial adjustment—and this adjustment incorporates much more than the physical body. . . .

[Our] more immediate struggle is to provide as many opportunities as possible to lead you into your personal gateway of transformation while there is still time, before the moment of quantum awakening when the resonant frequency of the quanta themselves must be seen to rise over the critical threshold point in their evolution.

We remind you to believe that the Board of Directors would not have constructed such a cycle or a circumstance unless it were incumbent upon them to do so. The stagnation that would occur, were these cycles not to move you through the curriculum, would be vast and immense and unnecessary. And so, we really do have your best interests in mind in the middle of all this. You simply now find yourselves in a position where the cycle's time has come up, and you must begin making very serious decisions about who you are—and what you are doing here.[566]

This next published excerpt is from October 1, 1999. Archive.org's earliest capture of it is from March 4, 2000.[567] We are clearly told that there will ultimately be a moment on earth that will transform how we see reality "in a matter of minutes," and that we are not to fear this change. However, other aspects of the "frequency change" will be slow enough that many people will not even realize that anything different is happening. Many will choose to react with fear—particularly as the Cabal becomes ever-increasingly visible and exposed.

This transformation . . . is obviously of the deepest and most spiritual sort. . . . So do not fear them, but simply come to accept the system changes as positive. It is a boldly positive moment on your planet, a moment that will dissolve preconceptions and alter existing judgments through stamina in a matter of minutes.

We cannot be more clear about telling you that everything is coming to a head. You need to be aware of this on the most fundamental level possible. . . .

Even though the content of these readings tends to be quite grandiose and difficult to believe, it is nevertheless the truth. . . .

What follows will be the most intense periods you have ever seen. Do not fear them. . . .What we have here is not a bunch of children playing with matches, but a bunch of budding God-Selves starting to realize their own abilities and powers.

We don't know whether those on your planet will become more aware of this frequency change or not. But you yourself, having studied this material, can indeed rest easy, with confidence, that even as everyone around you is freaking out in a panic, you yourself already know that everything is perfectly on schedule. And with that realization comes the intimate knowledge of your own protection and safety.

We do remind you again that you are loved more than you could ever possibly imagine.[568]

September 4, 1999, featured a prophecy suggesting there will be a mass extraterrestrial contact in our future—and this will be seen as a very positive event, not as an "alien invasion."[569] I am well aware that some people, particularly religious fundamentalists, may see this as a demonic event, but my own work with these people has convinced me that the majority of people visiting us from outside the earth are of positive orientation. I discussed other prophecies of such a mass contact event, some time after the year 2012, at the end of *The Source Field Investigations*.

When the discs are made visible in daylight, all will then see how the hidden strings are being pulled, and who is responsible for these aerial visitations—certainly not flocks of geese, swamp gas and the like. Rest assured that under the most adverse and difficult circumstances, there will be miracles the likes of which never before have been seen. We will come with an armada of spaceships, glistening in the morning light, prepared to do whatever is necessary to protect you from any and all hardships. . . .

You yourselves know that when you want to, you can call upon your own higher spiritual force through prayer. Since we are your guardians, it is our responsibility to insure that when the free will has been granted, the appearance will be made. Understand that this has happened many of your times in the past, wherein open communication has existed between those of humanity and those from the stars. It should not be much of a surprise to you that we are readying for this again, only that you can see how it is that there are those who still would resist this contact through their own sense of fear and foreboding of some imminent mock alien invasion or the like. . . .

When you start seeing yourselves as a social entity as well as a spiritual entity, you will realize the utter futility and nonsense of classism, genderism, racism and the like. . . .

We leave you with the notion that the fruit of the vine can produce the purest wine, or the sourest of vinegar. It is up to you how you will decide to milk your own fruits of the Spirit, so that the lamb may again come and choose to lie in your pasture, radiating peace, serenity and believability that there is indeed a Oneness.[570]

There is much to contemplate in these readings—and what makes it even more interesting was that some of the prophecies have already come true, whereas the most grandiose-sounding ones obviously have not, at least at the time of this writing. It appears that all of us have access to some higher aspect of ourselves that can peer through time as easily as we look through a window—thanks to the dynamic interplay of cycles. In the next chapter we will continue exploring how this new science of cyclical time may help to validate the many prophecies I have received about this coming change over the years. The 9/11 is only one of a series of events that seem to have reappeared 539 years after the Thirteen Years' War. Once we see how the political struggles of the Thirteen Years' War apply to current events, we have the potential to gain deeper insights into the behind-the-scenes war that has been fought against the Cabal for many years in our own recent history.

CHAPTER EIGHTEEN

9/11 and the Defeat of the Cabal: The Cycle Perspective

G eorge W. Bush was inaugurated as president in January 2001, which was a seemingly decisive victory for the neocon faction. During a comparable time period in the Thirteen Years' War, the Polish alliance still had not been able to prevail against the Germans. That finally changed in the Battle of Swiecino on September 17, 1462. This battle was just six days away from 9/11 in our own cycle. It was the first time the alliance had ever scored a decisive victory against the imperialist German Teutonic Knights. The crossovers with our own time period do have key differences in terms of who attacked first, but the parallels are very interesting.

Although we do see specific crossovers between the Thirteen Years' War and the struggle for health care reform, the real battle appears to be a secret war to cut off the financial blood supply to the neocon faction. We have already surveyed some of the evidence suggesting 9/11 may have been deliberately planned by the neocon faction. The neocon faction appears to be repeating the karma of the German Teutonic Knights from the last cycle. This context becomes extremely significant when we explore the connections between the Battle of Swiecino and 9/11.

The Battle of Swiecino: A Blueprint for the Defeat of the Cabal

The Battle of Swiecino, which was fought on September 17, 1462, was considered the most important turning point in the Thirteen Years' War. The inciting incident for the war occurred on December 5, 1453, when Frederick finally stated, in writing, that he would not help the Prussian Confederation against the Germans. This, again, occurred a month after George H. W. Bush lost the 1992 election in our own cycle.

In the Battle of Swiecino, the alliance struck first. The Germans did not have time to devise an effective counterattack strategy once they were hit with the full brunt of this assault. The Germans came under very heavy crossbow fire from the Polish infantry, causing huge losses. Many of the German soldiers began fleeing. The German commander Raveneck ordered his soldiers to stop running and demanded that they charge one last time. This was an utter disaster, as far as the German side was concerned. Crossbow arrows rained down on them with ferocious effectiveness, like the thunderbolts of the gods. Every German soldier died, surrendered, or escaped—and Raveneck himself died from a crossbow wound. The Teutonic side suffered more than a thousand casualties, losing ten times as many men as the alliance did in the initial heat of battle. The Polish army of two thousand mercenaries decisively defeated the twenty-seven hundred mercenaries in the Teutonic Knights' army. Let's take a look and see what we find: "The psychological significance [of this battle] was that this was the first open field battle won by the royal forces—so it increased the morale of the Polish forces, and lowered the morale of the Teutonic Knights. Many military historians say that the battle of Swiecino was the turning point of the Thirteen Years' War—leading to the final victory in 1466."[371]

This battle also recaptured critical territory, allowing the alliance to cut the Teutonic supply chain from Western Europe to Prussia, which significantly weakened them financially.

The Final Collapse of the Teutonic Knights—and Hurricane Katrina

Amazingly, there was only a six-day gap between the Battle of Swiecino and 9/11 within the 539-year quarter cycle. However, this was not the end of the Thirteen Years' War—it was merely the key turning point when the momentum of the war shifted in favor of the Polish alliance. How does the rest of the war in the 1400s line up with our own recent past?

Although the Teutonic Knights suffered a critical defeat in the 1462 battle of Swiecino, it took another four years for their control system to finally crumble. The final tipping point was when Warmia, which had been holding out the entire time, finally decided to join the alliance and fight. This next entry is from Wikipedia and is the most detailed resource available about this alliance online.

> In 1466 the Prince-Bishop of Warmia, Paul von Legens-dorf, decided to join the Polish forces—and declare war on the Teutonic Knights. Polish forces under Dunin were finally also able to capture Konitz on September 28, 1466. The Polish successes caused the exhausted Teutonic Order to seek new negotiations. . . . The new mediator was Pope Paul II. With help from the papal legate, Rudolf von Rudesheim, the Second Peace of Thorn was signed on October 10, 1466.[572]

The final battle that wiped out the strength and morale of the Teutonic Knights was on September 28, 1466. This brings us to September 28, 2005, in the next quarter cycle. September 28, 2005, was just twenty-six days after Hurricane Katrina critically defeated the Bush administration, irreversibly destroying their support base. Hurricane Katrina was much more destructive than 9/11, wiping out an entire American city—and it was as significant a disaster as 9/11 in the political sense. The Bush administration's response to the crisis was so ridiculously inadequate that it would appear they wanted to see the city of New Orleans transformed into total anarchy. According to the insiders I spoke with, this is exactly what they wanted.

The Superdome Becomes a Giant Death Trap

The New Orleans levees broke on August 29, 2005, flooding the entire city in water so deep that some people drowned in their own homes as they tried to swim up through their attic ceilings. The people of New Orleans were told to flee to the Superdome for their own safety and that they would be taken care of once they got inside. Once everyone had gathered, huge chains were placed over all the doors, locking them in from the outside with very little food, very little water, very little sanitation, and no hope of escape for four full days. The National Guard did not arrive to help people who were stranded in the Superdome until Friday, September 2.[573]

How could this disaster response possibly have taken so long, considering that fighter jets, helicopters, and supply vehicles could have been deployed as soon as they went inside? The public did not know why this was done—and due to the Sheep Effect, most of them probably did not want to know. Nonetheless, this failing revealed that the Bush administration was woefully incompetent, at the very least—despite how much they championed the need for greater national security in the wake of 9/11.

Before this event, more than one insider with access to highly classified information had told me that the sociopathic Cabal built large sports arenas in every major city for a reason—to form massive internment camps. This was part of a plan that went back at least as far as the 1960s. The Cabal planned to use these arenas during a mass catastrophe that they would engineer, hoping to reduce population and declare martial law. Although it seems impossible to believe that any person or group could be this sociopathic, this does sound like a souped-up, large-scale version of a Nazi concentration camp, disguised as nothing more than a humble sports arena. I was told that the Cabal had a long-standing plan to create mass chaos and starvation in America, herd people into sports arenas, lock them inside, and prevent anyone from escaping. Within less than two weeks, everyone inside would die of starvation and dehydration. The sociopathic Cabal could secretly film the entire horrific process with the instant-replay cameras mounted inside the arena. I had already been warned about the arenas before Katrina but unfortunately never published this information on my website. After Katrina, I met other insiders who confirmed the existence of this same plan.

Complete Blockage of All Emergency Supplies

Not long after Katrina, while I was still living in Milton, Kentucky, I spoke with a telephone representative for my car insurance company, which is one of the top carriers in America. Once she found out what I was interested in, she told me, somewhat reluctantly, that their company had sent two full eighteen-wheel trucks to New Orleans. These trucks were piled to the ceiling with a treasure trove of emergency supplies for natural disasters—bottled water, toilet paper, bandages, medical supplies, storable food, clothing, bedding, dishes, silverware, and so forth. She told me that both trucks were stopped by the Federal Emergency Management Association, or FEMA, before they could ever reach the areas that were hardest hit by Katrina. Even worse, FEMA officials completely emptied both trucks and confiscated the materials inside. The trucks were then turned around and sent back, empty—and the insurance company was ordered to say nothing about what had happened. The representative told me her company was considering mounting a very public lawsuit against FEMA and the Bush administration for the criminal theft of their supplies to cover the cost of replacing all the lost goods and to expose a much greater humanitarian crime. This lawsuit never materialized—but this story was soon validated by other, similar accounts that appeared in the mainstream media. This next excerpt comes from a September 5, 2005, article in *The New York Times.*

Furious state and local officials insisted that the real problem was that the Federal Emergency Management Agency, which Mr. Chertoff's department oversees, failed to deliver urgently needed help and, through incomprehensible red tape, even thwarted others' efforts to help. "We wanted soldiers, helicopters, food and water," said Denise Bottcher, press secretary for Gov. Kathleen Babineaux Blanco of Louisiana. "They wanted to negotiate an organizational chart." . . .

"Why did it happen? Who needs to be fired?" asked Aaron Broussard, president of Jefferson Parish, south of New Orleans. Far from deferring to state or local officials, FEMA asserted its authority and made things worse, Mr. Broussard complained on "Meet the Press." When Wal-Mart sent three trailer trucks loaded with water, FEMA officials turned them away, he said. Agency workers prevented the Coast Guard from delivering 1,000 gallons of diesel fuel, and on Saturday they cut the parish's emergency communications line— leading the sheriff to restore it, and post armed guards to protect it from FEMA, Mr. Broussard said. . . .

Dr. Ross Judice, chief medical officer for a large ambulance company, recounted how on Tuesday, unable to find out when helicopters would land to pick up critically-ill patients at the Superdome, he walked outside and discovered that two helicopters, donated by an oil services company, had been waiting in the parking lot.[574]

A Stunning Defeat for the Neoconservative Faction

Hillary Clinton, a modern-day representative of the Prussian-Polish alliance in the previous quarter cycle, soon called for an independent investigation of these astonishing crimes. She wanted a comprehensive inquiry, not controlled by the government, that was similar in size and scope to what had occurred after 9/11.[575] Gasoline prices increased by a tremendous amount in the aftermath of Katrina as well, settling at roughly $4 a gallon—ostensibly because of damage to oil refineries in the Gulf of Mexico—and they never went back down to their former levels, which were less than $2 a gallon. This provided the neoconservative faction with a much-needed infusion of quick cash in the hope of staving off their financial defeat a little longer. Not surprisingly, August 2005 was the last time that any major poll reported a majority of the American people supporting Bush or his policies.[576]

Katrina was the key turning point. It was a landmark political defeat for the neoconservative faction. This crushing loss for the neoconservative faction occurred within twenty-six days of when the Teutonic Knights were wiped out in the previous quarter cycle, on September 28, 1466. The alignment between these two political events becomes even greater when we see that Senator Clinton did not seek a vote for an independent inquiry into these appalling government failures until Wednesday, September 14, 2005.[577] This was just two weeks away from when the Teutonic Knights were defeated in the previous quarter cycle. Even though Hillary Clinton's proposed inquiry never went through, it nonetheless sank in with voters and triggered a massive defeat in the polling booths the following year.

In 1466, the critical defeat of the Teutonic Knights did not occur until the people of Warmia finally decided to stand and fight. Perhaps the long-reluctant people of Warmia correspond, in our timeline, to the Republicans who wanted to support the Bush administration as long as they possibly could but eventually realized they could not agree with the administration's policies any longer. The neoconservative alliance quickly began to crumble after Katrina, leading to bickering, infighting, and betrayal, whereas until this time they had always stood in solidarity with one another.

German Defeat Corresponds to Lame-Duck Presidency in 2006–2008

Poland finally signed a peace treaty with the German Teutonic Knights on October 10, 1466, ending the war. This corresponds to October 10,

2005, in the next quarter cycle. Nothing significant appears to have happened during this time other than the fact that no independent inquiry ever occurred, and the whole story about the government's failed response to Hurricane Katrina was dropped. This was exasperating to the public, who certainly had not forgotten the horrors of Hurricane Katrina that they had lived through or watched on their television screens. Poll numbers plummeted for Bush as well as all levels of government in the aftermath of Katrina.[578] Seventy-six percent of the public wanted an independent commission to investigate the federal government's response to the disaster.[579] The final loss for the neoconservative faction didn't become fully visible until 2006 in the voting booths—where the Republican Party lost six seats in the Senate, twenty-seven seats in the House of Representatives, and six state governorships.[580] This created a lame-duck presidency for the last two years of George W. Bush's term and severely restricted the ability of the neoconservative faction to force their agenda upon the people. Even in 2009, the Gallup Poll was reporting serious declines in Republican Party support among all demographic groups except frequent churchgoers, conservatives, and senior citizens—and admitted that "most of the loss in support actually occurred beginning in 2005, after Hurricane Katrina . . . which created major public relations problems for the administration." [581]

Overlaps Between the Quarter Cycle and Zodiac Cycle

Let's not forget that the 539-year quarter cycle is not the only energetic influence that is affecting American politics. The zodiac cycle was still causing events from Roman history to reappear in the United States as well, fully 2,160 years later. The Lusitanian War began in 155 B.C., when the Lusitanians raided Hispania Ulterior (Farther Spain).[582] This also inspired the Celtiberian tribes of Hispania Citerior (Nearer Spain) to rebel, and the following year, in 154 B.C., they formed a confederacy with neighboring towns and began building a defensive wall against Rome.[583] Therefore, by 154 B.C., Rome was fighting dangerous wars in two different Spanish territories—and this corresponds to the year 2006 in modern times. As we remember, the politically neutered neoconservative faction was unable to attack Iran in 2006—even after issuing a formal declaration of war. They had already lost the political will to create change after their shocking attempts to turn Katrina into a massive death trap for the people of New Orleans. They continued to hold office until the end of their term in 2008, but their power was effectively check-mated by the massive defeat their Republican cohorts suffered in the 2006 elections, creating a lame-duck presidency.

Rome's war against Carthage from 149 to 146 B.C. in the Age of Aries now reappears in our own era as the years 2011 to 2014. This carries us through the Age of Pisces, over the long-awaited end of the 25,920-year cycle, and directly into the Age of Aquarius. We have already seen how Carthage in the Age of Aries directly corresponded to Germany in the Age of Pisces. Now we are also seeing a clear connection between Germany in the last quarter cycle and the neoconservative faction in modern times. This creates a double reinforcement of the connection between Germany and the neoconservative faction within these cycles. This is quite understandable once we see how Prescott Bush financially supported Hitler, bankrolled a failed fascist coup attempt in 1933, and was undoubtedly involved in the transfer of more than seven hundred top Nazi scientists to America immediately after Hitler's defeat.

The Law of One series, the Cayce readings, my own intuitive read-ings, and a host of ancient prophecies all suggest that life on earth will transition into a far more peaceful, harmonious, and evolved level as we move into the Age of Aquarius. The highly credentialed historians de Santillana and von Dechend compellingly argued that dozens of ancient myths around the world were secretly encoded with information about this 25,920-year cycle. They urged us to study the 25,920-year cycle of precession and revealed it would usher in a Golden Age. As we are now seeing, the 25,920-year cycle is indeed the Synchronicity Key; it is the mainspring of the cosmic clock. The Great Year is driving cycles that steer our destiny with astonishing precision. I suspect that we have barely scratched the surface of understanding how far-reaching and powerful these cycles are. It is also important to mention that the villains in the Book of Life are not permitted to continue harming others indefinitely. The hero's journey structure of archetypes includes an absolute defeat of the nemesis—which can be quite gruesome. Karma is often repaid in a very dramatic fashion—and no one is exempt from the great wheelwork of time. However, if we continue to meet violence with violence, the same cycles may need to continue repeating. Through forgiveness, we demonstrate that we are ready to graduate into a never and much more evolved form of thinking, feeling, and being.

CHAPTER NINETEEN

History Gets a Wicked Case of Déjà Vu

We are accustomed to thinking of time as linear, believing that the events that happen in the present are not influenced by the past. The Synchronicity Key reveals that time may be structured like a series of circles, overlapping one another in a repeating spiral. The biggest circle is the 25,920-year "wobble" of the earth's axis in the precession. In August 2012, I finally found compelling evidence that our sun is orbiting a neighboring star, thanks to Walter Cruttenden's epic book *Lost Star of Myth and Time*. The energy fields of this neighboring star create distinct regions of space that affect our collective behavior as we move through them.

There appear to be twelve major regions, corresponding to the twelve Ages of the Zodiac. Each of these regions is then further subdivided into four evenly spaced zones, forming the 539-year quarter cycles. Each of these cycles can be visualized as a circle. Each time we reach the same point in the circle as before, we experience energetic bleed-throughs from events that occurred the last time. In a quarter cycle, one circle would take us 539 years to move through.

However, since our solar system is also moving forward through the galaxy at the same time, these circles must also be extended into corkscrew-shaped spirals. It is tempting to think that these circles will always stay the same width, forming cycles that will always be the same length, but let's not forget that they are forming in three-dimensional

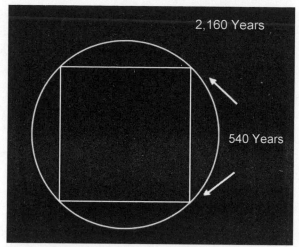

Fig. 14: The 540/539-year cycle could divide a sphere with a 2,160-year circumference into a four-sided cube shape.

space. It is therefore possible that some spirals may be expanding away from a single point or contracting toward a single point in nice, neat geometric intervals. The factor of "seven times" that Jehoshua spoke about in Matthew 18:21–22 may represent one ratio for how fast they expand or contract.

This is exactly what Michèl Helmer discovered. Not all cycles are perfectly round. Some of them expand or contract in very precise geometric ratios—such as a growth factor of seven. The most stunning example of this can be seen when we compare the French Revolution of 1789 to the Russian Revolution of 1917. In order to see the shocking parallels, all we have to do is expand one year of French history into seven years of Russian history. François Masson revealed many of these astonishing connections in the translation of his book I posted on my website.

The Downfall of Robespierre

The French Revolution was one of the worst mass atrocities ever committed against a people by its own government—dwarfing the events of Hurricane Katrina in their magnitude and severity. Maximilien de

Robespierre was a French lawyer and politician and one of the most influential figures of the French Revolution. There is extensive documentation in William T. Still's epic work *New World Order: The Ancient Plan
of Secret Societies* that the French Revolution was one of the greatest
historical examples of the Cabal deliberately creating a mass atrocity
by systematically cutting the supply lines of food, water, medicine and
other essentials to the people, while simultaneously collapsing their economy so their money became worthless. Robespierre sang the virtues of
revolutionary government and argued that a government's terrorism
against its own starving detractors was a virtuous, necessary, and inevitable reality.

> If virtue be the spring of a popular government in times of
> peace, the spring of that government during a revolution is
> virtue combined with terror: virtue, without which terror is
> destructive; terror, without which virtue is impotent. Terror
> is only justice prompt, severe and inflexible; it is then an em-
> anation of virtue. . . . To punish the oppressors of humanity
> is clemency; to forgive them is cruelty.[584]

Robespierre's stirring speeches compelled the French government to
formally institute terrorism against its people as a legal policy on September 5, 1793. This came to be known as the Reign of Terror, and many
innocent, starving people were tortured and executed as a result. Robespierre also tried to convince the public to embrace an Illuminati-type
religion that he called the Cult of the Supreme Being. He organized a
major public festival on the Christian holiday of the Pentecost, June 8,
1794. This was the first time the public had ever seen Robespierre. He
constructed a small, symbolic mountain in the middle of the festival and
walked down the mountain in a manner that was clearly intended to
remind people of Moses carrying the stone tablets. One of Robespierre's
colleagues, Jacques-Alexis Thuriot, was heard saying, "Look at the bug-
ger; it's not enough for him to be master, he has to be God."[585]

Karma struck quickly. Just one month and five days later, Robespierre
and his top cohorts were charged with conspiracy to commit acts of

terror and sentenced to death. Robespierre tried to shoot himself in the head with a pistol but succeeded only in shattering his lower jaw. Robespierre's brother Augustin jumped out a window and shattered both his legs. Philippe Le Bas committed suicide, and another of Robespierre's co-conspirators shot himself in the head. After shattering his jaw with the pistol, Robespierre lay there on the table bleeding profusely, awaiting his execution, until a doctor was brought in to stop the bleeding by wrapping a handkerchief around his jaw. Robespierre was guillotined, without trial, the next day—July 28, 1794. The executioner tore off the bandage that was holding his shattered jaw together to prepare his neck for the blade, causing him to scream in agony until he was decapitated.[586]

The Downfall of Joseph Stalin

Let's fast-forward now to the merciless Soviet dictator and mass murderer Joseph Stalin, who was responsible for the deaths of millions of people and the operation of prison gulags, which were equivalent to concentration camps. On February 28, 1953, Stalin went out on an all-night dinner and movie trip with his interior minister Lavrentiy Beria, as well as Georgy Malenkov, Nikolai Bulganin, and Nikita Khrushchev. All four men accompanied Stalin back to his home that night. Stalin did not appear from his room at dawn, and his guards were given strict orders not to go inside.

Stalin was not discovered until ten o'clock that same night, March 1, 1953. He was found lying on his back, drenched in his own stale urine, and uttering strange, unintelligible sounds. Stalin was believed to have suffered a stroke. He became bedridden, quickly deteriorated, and died on March 5, 1953. In 2003, a joint group of Russian and American historians concluded that Stalin had been assassinated with a powerful, flavorless rat poison known as warfarin. Stalin's autopsy revealed severe hemorrhaging in his heart, gastrointestinal tract, and kidneys, which does not happen in a normal stroke but does happen when a human body is given warfarin.[587] Malenkov, Bulganin, and Khrushchev all became Soviet premiers, and each of them was with Stalin the night he fell ill. Both Beria and Khrushchev were in a perfect position to add the poison to Stalin's wine the night they went out to dinner with him.[588] In his 1993 political memoirs, Vyacheslav Molotov claimed that Beria told him, with pride, that he personally assassinated Stalin that night.[589] A power struggle for who would succeed Stalin lasted from 1953 until 1958, when Khrushchev finally won out over his rivals.

The Cycle Connection Between Robespierre and Stalin

Michèl Helmer found astonishing connections between the French Revolution and the Bolshevik Revolution by expanding one year in France to seven years in Russia. The French Revolution began on July 14, 1789. The Bolsheviks achieved their initial victory in the Russian Revolution on November 14, 1917. Once we have these two dates—July 14, 1789, and November 14, 1917—we have our starting points. Then we can take any date in the French Revolution and count how many days had gone by since the revolution started on July 14, 1789. We then multiply this number of days by 7. Once we have the number, we add it to the start-date of the Russian Revolution—November 14, 1917. This gives us an exact date in twentieth-century Russian history.

Once Helmer did the homework, he found that many events in the French Revolution expanded perfectly into the Russian Revolution within only days of each other. François Masson believed the most stunning example of all was the timing between the violent deaths of Robespierre and Stalin, both of whom clearly represent terrorist Cabal leaders.[590] Once we do the math, the exact date of Robespierre's execution becomes February 22, 1953, in the new Russian cycle. Joseph Stalin was apparently poisoned by Beria and his cohorts only six days later, on the evening of February 28, 1953.

Many more specifics can be found in Masson's book on my website. What surprised me the most was that Masson used this system to predict that Russia would collapse eleven years after he finished writing the book in 1980: "Applying the [1 to 7] ratio tells us that the Soviet regime will end in late 1990 or early 1991. These three dates show up on the chart of the precessional cycle—marking the start and finish of mass movements."[591] The USSR didn't actually collapse until August of 1991, but this was still within months of the prediction Masson had made.

Time to Take This More Seriously

I was quite surprised to hold this yellowing, typewritten manuscript from 1980 in my hands and realize that Masson had been able to make such a stunning prediction. The American corporate media gave no indication that the Soviet Union was on the verge of collapsing until it actually happened. The Cabal needed an epic nemesis to keep the people in perpetual fear of a nuclear war that could destroy all life on earth. And yet, once we see how many events in the French Revolution transferred into the Russian Revolution, the downfall of the USSR seemed all but inevitable.

This was a very invigorating finding. Cycles of expansion and contraction are much harder to find than cycles that repeat by the same number of years from one turn of the Wheel of Karma to the next. This is another area in which supercomputer power could be very helpful, once we can develop a means of using this method to analyze similar events in different times of history. However, this method and artificial intelligence will never experience the power of synchronicity as Jung, Einstein, and several of the top quantum physics pioneers understood it to be. Is it possible that someone could discover many more of these cycles, completely independently? Is it also possible that these discoveries might be completely independent of Helmer and Masson?

Professor Anatoly Fomenko Dramatically
Expands the Investigation

Much to my amazement, I found that a scientist had indeed independently discovered these same cycles of history, apparently in much greater detail than Helmer or Masson ever did. Back in the year 2000, after I'd already published Masson's book on my website, I found a key article in

Saturday Night, which has been Canada's leading national magazine since 1887.[592] Timothy Taylor wrote an article entitled "Time Warp," which discussed the work of a prominent Russian mathematician named Anatoly Fomenko and his colleagues. As it turns out, Fomenko was not the first Russian to discover repeating patterns in history: "The movement [to study the cycles of time] in Russia began with Nikolai Morozov (1854–1946), the rebel son of a nobleman. . . . Morozov spent his hard time poring over chronology texts and . . . drew up functions showing that the pattern of the Old Testament Judaic kings from Rehoboam to Zedekiah matched [up] almost precisely [with] the pattern of Roman Emperors from Alcinius to Justinian II—over 1,000 years later."[593]

Morozov was a prominent Russian scientist who wrote seven large volumes of investigative research on this unique subject.[594] According to Fomenko, Morozov used "the latest discoveries in mathematics, astronomy, linguistics, philology and geology" to make his case, and the first of these seven large volumes appeared in the year 1926. Fomenko and other young mathematicians at Moscow State University became captivated by Morozov's research in the 1970s. They sought to verify and further develop Morozov's model. Fomenko conducted this investigation for many years and eventually published his first academic paper on the subject in 1994.[595] Fomenko significantly enhanced the case by blending in written records for all of recorded Western history. He carried the investigation all the way back to the dawn of written history—the Sumerian clay tablets, which date back to 4000 B.C.

> Fomenko used [Morozov's] model to compare historical dynasties across a staggering range of data. He began by compiling a complete list [of dynasties] . . . from 4000 B.C. to A.D. 1800, drawing from all the nations and empires of Western and Eastern Europe, and stretching back into antiquity— through Roman, Greek, biblical and Egyptian history. Comparing one to another in every possible way, including differing accounts of the same dynasties, Fomenko found mathematically what Morozov had sketched. . . . Several dozen pairs of dynasties previously thought to be utterly

different had proximity coefficients that were very small. In other words, they were as close as your two brothers' different versions of your family tree.[596]

The wording in this excerpt is fairly technical, but the underlying concept is quite simple. Timothy Taylor is telling us that "several dozen" periods of history have repeated—far more precisely than most people could ever imagine. These patterns appear throughout all the nations and empires of Western and Eastern Europe as well as Rome, Greece, Egypt, China, and the Bible across a staggering fifty-eight-hundred-year gulf of time. Although this data set does not appear to include Australian, African, South American, or modern American history, it is still quite immense in scope and covers the vast majority of surviving historical records that are available.

This was only one method that Fomenko used to analyze history. Another method involved specific number crunching of hundreds of original written records that have survived from these various intertwining civilizations. Specifically, Fomenko analyzed how many words were used to write about these civilizations and how many pages the records were written on. This allowed him to create a mathematical function in order to see how closely the written records related to each other. He found that in some cases, when two countries had a similar pattern of historic events, their written histories were also very similar: "Fomenko claims to have found and confirmed repeating patterns between ancient and medieval Rome, and several instances where periods of the Old Testament appear statistically identical to stretches of medieval Roman-German history—from the tenth to the fourteenth centuries."[597]

Strong Cycle Connections Between Byzantine-Roman and English History

Fomenko is only one of a whole team of scientists who are now working on this research. Some of their papers can be read at New-Tradition.org. When I went back and revisited this website in March 2013, I studied a very complex paper Fomenko wrote in 2002 in which he noticed how events in Byzantine Roman history were reappearing as very similar events in the British Empire.[598] In Section 3, "Parallels Between English and Byzantine-Roman History," Fomenko finds very strong cyclical connections between three periods of Byzantine-Roman history and English history.

The first cycle shows events in Byzantine-Roman history, from A.D. 378 to 553, duplicating as events in English history from A.D. 640 to 830. Fomenko says these events are repeating by a cycle of "approximately 275 years." The second cycle reveals how events in Byzantine-Roman history from A.D. 553 to 880 are appearing in English history from A.D. 800 to 1040. Once again, these events were "approximately 275 years" apart— and this time the connections were so strong that Fomenko concluded this happened in a "rigid" form.

Let's talk about these first two cycles before we discuss the third one. One important clue is that Fomenko admitted the 275-year cycle was only "approximate." The historical records may not be perfect in all of these cases, and a certain degree of guesswork may be involved. What if the "ideal" cycle length turns out to be a mere five and a half years shorter, at 269.5 years? This is exactly half the length of our old friend the 539-year Age of the Zodiac quarter cycle. This cycle perfectly linked Joan of Arc to the student revolution in France, within days of accuracy. This same cycle also revealed that 9/11 was linked to a decisive defeat of the Germans in the Battle of Swiecino, again within days of accuracy. It also connected the Prussian-Polish alliance of the 1400s to the Democrats in modern American history, and the German Teutonic Knights to the Republican neoconservatives in several key instances. This included George H. W. Bush's loss of the election, Clinton's campaign for health care reform, 9/11, and the political defeat of the Republican neoconservative faction in the immediate aftermath of Hurricane Katrina.

The third cycle Fomenko discovered was a "rigid 120-year shift" between English historical events in the period A.D. 1040 to 1327, and Byzantine-Roman historical events from A.D. 1143 to 1453. This number immediately caught my attention. There are 360 degrees in a circle, and if you draw an equilateral triangle in the circle, each side of the triangle will be 120 degrees. Let's not forget that in Helmer's model, every cycle of history is a perfect subdivision of the Great Year of 25,920 earth years. The number 120, as a cycle length, fits perfectly into Helmer's model. There are exactly 216 cycles of 120 years in the master number of 25,920 years. Furthermore, in each Age of the Zodiac there are exactly eighteen cycles of 120 years. Once we divide the Age of the Zodiac cycle in half, we get 1,080 years. You can fit exactly nine cycles of 120 years into the Age of the Zodiac half cycle.

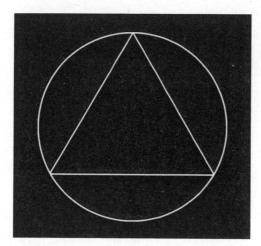

Fig. 15: A triangle naturally divides a circle into three 120-degree segments.

Therefore, Fomenko's new cycles, which he discovered through extensive scientific analysis, are a perfect fit with Helmer's original model. This may seem impossible and outrageous, but to me, the reason why both sets of researchers have discovered similar cycles is because this is how the universe really works. Fomenko hacked the source code of history and found totally new data that completely validates Helmer and Masson's findings, as well as the more recent examples featured in this book.

A Single, Large Pattern That Repeats Four Times

Fomenko's most mind-blowing accomplishment was his discovery of "a single large pattern that repeats four times" across a thirty-two-hundred-year gap, from 1600 B.C. to A.D. 1600: "[Fomenko's] most startling assertion emerges from efforts to map dozens of these 'discovered' duplications [of historical events and written texts]. . . . Specifically, there is a stretch from about 1600 B.C. to A.D. 1600 that may be mathematically deconstructed to reveal a single large pattern—that repeats four times."[599]

We will come back to this cycle in just a minute, as it ultimately makes a perfect fit with Helmer and Masson's model. First, however, we will discuss a high-profile endorsement that Fomenko's work received from one of the top thinkers in Russia.

Fomenko's Data Endorsed by the World's Strongest Chess Player

Fomenko's data is so vast in scope that it's like an incredibly complex chess game. You have to study countless numbers of different pieces and analyze the huge variety of ways their "moves" could intertwine with each other. Nothing short of a grand master chess player's mind is required in order to read and understand what they've discovered. According to Chess.com, Gary Kasparov has held the top position on the Official World Chess Federation's list twenty-three times and was rated as "the strongest player ever" after his rival chess player Fischer died in 2008.[600] Kasparov is not only aware of Fomenko's work; he is an ardent supporter of it and a featured contributor to the New Tradition website.

Although Kasparov does not agree with all of Fomenko's conclusions, he does believe these discoveries have "profound implications" for science as we now know it, creating "completely new areas of scientific research." Here is a quote directly from Kasparov.

> If indeed the dates of antiquity are incorrect, there could be profound implications for our beliefs about the past, and also for science. . . . I trust that the younger generation will have no fear of "untouchable" historical dogma, and will use contemporary knowledge to challenge questionable theories.

For sure, it is an exciting opportunity to reverse the subordinate role science plays to history—and to create completely new areas of scientific research.[601]

Fomenko's work obviously is far more complex than Helmer and Masson's cycle research. It is just about as thorough as any investigation into this subject could have been given the data that is available. However, even with such a mountain of provable evidence of neatly repeating historical events, Fomenko agreed with Morozov's original conclusion. He believed that the historians had to be faking their data and were actually reusing the same information over and over again, only making a small number of changes along the way—such as names, places, and the specific details of major events. The following quote is from one of the papers on the New Tradition website: "These parallels suggest that the traditional history of ancient times consists of multiple recounts of the same events, scattered in many locations at various times."[602] Fomenko believed these events only happened once—but were then misinterpreted as having occurred in multiple time periods.

Early Historians Caught Red-Handed?

Robert Grishin's initial essay on the New Tradition website openly accuses the people who put our historical records together of being "forgers" who have now been "caught red-handed":

> Having been armed with mathematics, the most precise of the sciences, [Fomenko and his colleagues] have shown convincingly that, for example, the whole chronology on which modern history is based is mistaken. They have been finding irrefutable proof of the fact that some of the very same events have been written under various names, and dispatched into various epochs of "ancient" history. They have caught the forgers red-handed—and exposed them before the whole world.[603]

At the time the *Saturday Night* article was written in 2000, Fomenko had concluded that we were actually only living in the year A.D. 936. He believed that large parts of our history have been "faked." Historians have disregarded Fomenko's findings and dismissed this idea as nonsense. There are many different methods they would use to argue their point, including fairly reliable carbon dating and intersecting chronologies among various, disconnected nations, though Fomenko questions both of these dating methods in his papers.[604] Nonetheless, the *Saturday Night* article reveals that these same scientists recognize that something important is going on here—and we need to find out what it is.

> Even those who don't endorse Fomenko's conclusions agree that valid mathematical questions have been raised. "It would be a massive irresponsibility not to deal with it and either prove that it's wrong or, if there's something here, find out what in the world is going on," says math professor Jack Macki. Jacques Carrière concludes, "To have a definitive answer to the thing, the problem has to be looked at by other research groups."[605]

Of course, other research groups have already investigated this subject—namely, Helmer and Masson—and have directly connected it to cycles of time that were handed down to us by ancient extraterrestrial humans that visited humanity. Many people assume these legends are purely mythological, whereas now our current level of science and technology is finally catching up. We needed to progress to a point where we could gather written records from all over the world, across vast lengths of time, in order to be able to identify these patterns. Armed with this new data, we now have the full potential to usher in an unprecedented, worldwide spiritual awakening.

CHAPTER TWENTY

Fomenko's Cycles of History—and the Book of Daniel

E ven though Fomenko believes that many historical events have been faked, he also concluded that history has a "fiber structure." This is not unlike the idea of a timeline or a repeating cycle. Fomenko compares this repeating cycle to a textbook, which breaks down into four chapters of equal lengths, as we see in this next excerpt from his own New Tradition website. This should sound very familiar by now.

> A.T. Fomenko discovered a "fiber structure" in our modern "textbook of ancient and medieval history." . . . It was proved that this "textbook" consists of four more short "textbooks" which speak about the same events—the same historical epochs. These short "textbooks" were then shifted, with respect to each other, on the time axis—and then glued together. . . . The result is our modern "textbook," which shows a history much longer than it was in reality.[606]

Unlike Helmer and Masson's work, where the intervals between wars and political events repeat themselves in shockingly precise intervals of time, even down to the day, Fomenko's longer-term cycles do not appear to fit together in such a nice, neat fashion—at first. Fomenko did notice the "rigid" cycle of "approximately 275" years and another "rigid" cycle of 120 years in the interplay between Byzantine Roman and English history, which fits our data very nicely. Nonetheless, Fomenko had no reason to see the actual lengths of time as significant. He also seems totally unaware that this same phenomenon had already been researched and written about in France. Although many of Fomenko's key papers are not yet available in English, we can find solid numbers in the graphic data available from the New Tradition website.[607]

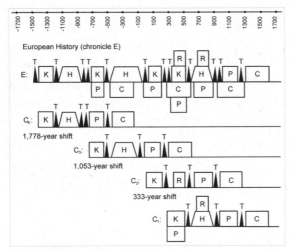

Fig. 16: Professor Fomenko's graph of the four-part "textbook" that repeats in historical events

This key graph shows four cycles that repeat between 1600 B.C. and A.D. 1600. According to the timeline at the top, each cycle is about thirteen hundred years long, though this changes slightly from one to the next. We also see that there are four subcycles, or what Fomenko called "textbooks," within each cycle. Each of these subcycles is almost exactly the same length. This remains consistent across the entire graph. This is completely in alignment with what Helmer and Masson suggested happens in history—namely, that there are smaller cycles, in even intervals of time, in which key events take place.

The 1,296-Year Cycle: The Hero's Journey, in Four Equal Sections

Now we have a single, four-part story that takes approximately thirteen hundred years to complete and could be broken up into the three-act Hero's Journey structure that all Hollywood films are based on. Let's not forget that once we include the midpoint in a screenplay, we break it up into four perfectly symmetrical pieces—pages 1 through 30, 30 through 60, 60 through 90, and 90 through 120. If Fomenko has found that the overall "story" is thirteen hundred years long, that's very interesting, because if we knock off four years and shave it down just a bit to 1,296 years, we now have another perfect subdivision of the 25,920-year precession. There are exactly twenty cycles of 1,296 years within the Great Year itself. Each of these 1,296-year cycles divides neatly into four equal parts on Fomenko's graph, giving us 324-year sections. There are exactly eighty of these 324-year cycles in the 25,920-year precession of the equinoxes.

The 720-Year Cycle: One-Third of an Age of the Zodiac

The 1,296-year cycle fits in perfectly with Helmer and Masson's model, but additional information can be found in Fomenko's graph. When, exactly, did each of Fomenko's 1,296-year "textbooks" start, and how much time occurred between them? Since Fomenko believes only the most recent cycle is the correct one, he assumes all the previous cycles must be forgeries. In the graph on his website, Fomenko gives us the exact numbers of when each of these previous cycles started. The first cycle started 1778 years before the most recent one. The second cycle started 1053 years before the most recent one. And the third cycle started 333 years before the last one.

Notice that Fomenko did not reveal how much time had elapsed between each of these cycles. Instead, he only mentioned the total

number of years that had passed between the beginning of each cycle
and the beginning of the last cycle. In order to get the actual length of
the cycle itself, we have to find out how many years elapsed between the
starting points of each cycle in the graph.

There are 725 years between 1778 and 1053 and 720 years between 1053
and 333. That means all the key historical events within the first three
cycles—which represent massive overlaps between the Roman Empire
and various aspects of later European history—take place approximately
or exactly 720 years apart from each other. The second and third cycles
are exactly 720 years apart. The first and second cycles are 725 years apart,
which is only a five-year margin of error. This might be due to a difficulty
in properly dating the records themselves. I was truly stunned when I
first did these calculations, as 720 years is exactly one-third of an Age of
the Zodiac. I immediately remembered that this same 720-year cycle was
mentioned in Masson's book and was associated with the three most
important phases of religious development.

Lastly, a gap of only 333 years separated the third and fourth cycles.
This was certainly entertaining, as I've been seeing the number 333 in
synchronistic circumstances for many years. However, in this case we
may have a nine-year margin of error. Within the "perfect" 1,296-year
cycle length Fomenko discovered, each of the four subcycles is 324 years
long. We have eighty of these 324-year cycles in the 25,920-year precession of the equinoxes. Further research may reveal that Fomenko misinterpreted certain events in the cycles and that the actual start times of
these final two cycles are precisely 324 years apart.

The first and second cycles in the graph are exactly 720 years apart.
The second and third cycles are very close to 720 years apart once again.
Masson's book gives other examples of this 720-year cycle appearing in
history. I published David Steinberg's translation of Masson's book on
my website in 1999, but I didn't read the *Saturday Night* article until
2000. At the time I first found the article, I was frustrated by the fact
that it was lacking in technical data that could have given me some
numbers to play around with. Finally, in April 2010, I dug out this old
article from my archives, which I'd been meaning to check on for many
years, while I was writing up the initial drafts of these chapters on the

cycles of history. I soon found the New Tradition website, which allowed me to locate specific numbers in Fomenko's data.

François Masson on the 720-Year Cycle in Christianity

Masson associated the 720-year cycle with the growth phases of major religions and said this cycle was originally discovered by Reverend Father Poucel. I have not been able to locate Poucel's work so far, probably because it was written in French and may have been published well before Masson wrote his book. The definition of the 720-year cycle as strictly religious in nature is too narrow to describe everything Fomenko discovered, but we can at least consider that in certain cases, major religions have followed this pattern. Masson suggested that every culture will go through stages of its spiritual and religious development that divide up into nice, neat 720-year cycles.

> 2160 / 3 = 720 years . . . pointed out by Rev. Father Poucel. The first phase of 720 years is the prophetic period of every religion. The second is the "clerical phase," and the third is that of the supremacy of the temporal [physical] power over the spiritual power. For example: [the time of] the Christ's teaching to the years 720–750 corresponds to the mystical epoch of Christianity. From A.D. 720–750 to 1440–1470, the times changed. This was the epoch of the mastery of the ecclesiastical [Church] hierarchy over peoples and governments.[608]

If this 720-year cycle apparently began with the popularly accepted time of the birth of Jesus, then the first key year we would be looking for is A.D. 720. In A.D. 726 or thereabouts, the Byzantine emperor Leo III began an open campaign of "iconoclasm."[609] This is a technical-sounding name for a culture deliberately destroying its own religious icons for political or spiritual reasons. Among other things, Emperor Leo ordered the removal of an image of Jesus's face over the entrance to the Great Palace of Constantinople.

This conflict had started accelerating as of 695, when Justinian II put images of Jesus's face on the back of his gold coins. This caused Islamic caliph Abd al-Malik, who died in 705, to stop using Jesus's face on his coins and convert them to letters only. This broke with their tradition of using Byzantine designs on their own money.[610] We also know that before Leo III ordered the idols to be smashed in 726, this rebellion had already reached epic proportions in society. In a letter estimated to be from before A.D. 726, the patriarch Germanus wrote to two iconoclast bishops, saying "now whole towns and multitudes of people are in considerable agitation over this matter" of using Jesus's face as an icon.[611]

Thus, the timing of this period of iconoclasm fits with the 720-year cycle very nicely. According to Masson, this period of iconoclasm was the "first major crisis of the Catholic Church." After this time, the church hierarchy increasingly strengthened its grip over the governments as well as the people.

Then, 720 years later we have 1440. This was within one year of when the Renaissance started, creating the dawning of modern science as we now know it. The Renaissance challenged the church's authority to proclaim the truth without question. The Renaissance also led to the Reformation, which forced the church to release control of the Bible to the people for the first time. According to Paul Robert Walker in his 2003 book, *The Feud That Sparked the Renaissance,* this social, artistic, and scientific revolution can be timed to start precisely in 1441. This was the year that Ghiberti and Brunelleschi competed over who got to design the bronze doors for the Florence Baptistery.[612]

Seven hundred and twenty years after 1440 lands us in the year 2160. This appears to be well after the time that the Great Year comes to an end and the Golden Age is predicted to have arrived in various worldwide prophecies, as I extensively discussed in *The Source Field Investigations.* However, if we are dealing with a system of cycles that is somehow guided by our own collective consciousness and was intended to reach its final resolution surrounding the end of the Great Year—which was in or around the year 2012—then perhaps other cycles took effect.

What If A.D. 720 Is the Beginning of a New Hero's Journey?

What if we take the year A.D. 720 as the beginning of a new cycle of a different length? What if A.D. 720 becomes the beginning of a new Hero's Journey story? What if the political and social climate of A.D. 720 now represents the "ordinary world," which the "heroes" of our modern era must all ultimately be inspired to join a quest to escape from, as they move from lifetime to lifetime?

The use of Jesus's face as an icon in Christianity was considered an "abomination." This was the first time that the church's authority was questioned on such a widespread level. It was the first time that the people became aware that their beloved religion had become corrupted and was being used as a tool of social and political oppression. The church militarized and became an obviously direct arm of the government for the first time in its history. What if we use A.D. 720 as our starting point for one of Fomenko's 1,296-year cycles? This would mean that the cycle will end in the year 2016. This is a very close fit with the end date for the precession and gives us another year to keep an eye on.

The 1,290-Year Cycle in the Book of Daniel

Another possible lead in our investigation is that a very similar cycle—in this case 1,290 years instead of 1,296—may have been featured in the book of Daniel in the Old Testament. Only very thinly veiled symbolism appears to have been used to describe a cycle of time in years. A variety of Bible passages reveal that a "day" can symbolize a year.[613] In 12:11, Daniel met a glowing, linen-clad man in a vision, which many readers of the Bible believe was a vision of Jehoshua. This glowing man in linen told Daniel there would be a final cycle of 1,290 "days" before the end of the age. Many Bible enthusiasts have felt this is a time-encoded prophecy, but they are not sure of the start date that we should use. Here is the

exact passage in the book of Daniel—specifically chapter 12, verse 11—
where this prophecy appears: "From the time that the regular burnt offering is taken away and the abomination that desolates is set up, there
shall be one thousand two hundred ninety days."[614]

The "regular burnt offering" is known to be incense that the church
uses as a sacred ceremonial offering. Here, the "regular burnt offering"
may be a symbol that represents the sacred, mystical aspect of Christianity's early years—the first 720-year cycle that appears throughout history, according to Reverend Father Poucel and François Masson. That
means we could potentially set the beginning of the "time of the abomination that desolates" at A.D. 720. This is the beginning of the "epoch of
the mastery of the Church hierarchy over the peoples and governments,"
according to Masson. In A.D. 720, the government and the church finally joined forces to dramatically strengthen their control over the
people. This led to many nightmares, including the Inquisition, during
which those who did not agree with the opinion of the church were tortured. Many holy wars were fought, with raping, pillaging, and mass
death, including the Crusades.

Twelve hundred and ninety years after Masson's crucial date of A.D.
720 brings us to the year 2010. I was quite surprised to see this number
emerge, as it was the year 2010 when I made this calculation. Did this
somehow indicate that the great cycles already knew when they would
be discovered? Were we on a timeline where we needed to discover them
again at a certain point in our history—and were, in fact, programmed
to discover them again? Is it possible for a prophecy to be time encoded
that far back in the past? Given the many 2,160-year overlaps between
Rome in the Age of Aries and America in the Age of Pisces, including
the exact nature of the Watergate scandal, anything is possible. "Nothing
else happened in 2010," you might say. However, at this point in Daniel's
vision, a forty-five-year transitional period begins before we receive our
"reward." We will explore this soon enough.

Let's Look at the Context: History Progressing from Age to Age
I'm sure some people will think this is a ridiculous attempt to look for
number codes in the Bible that back up the overall model. If this were

just a random Bible passage, I would definitely agree with you, so that's why we need to study the context and see what is written before we reach Daniel 12:11. In 2:20–22, we get a clear mention of history progressing from "age to age," and we see how these great cycles move us through the times and seasons, setting up and bringing down kings along the way. This definitely fits our model: "Blessed be the name of God from age to age, for wisdom and power are his. He changes times and seasons, deposes kings and sets up kings; he gives wisdom to the wise and knowledge to those who have understanding. He reveals deep and hidden things."[615]

Indeed, I would consider the knowledge of these cycles to be a "deep and hidden" aspect of "wisdom," which can be found by "those who have understanding." Now that we are in a modern technological era, we have instant, worldwide access to information and can finally understand how these cycles work.

Daniel Describes History Moving in Repeating Cycles
The plot thickens when we find out that the prophet Daniel was commissioned by King Nebuchadnezzar to interpret one of his dreams. Daniel gave the following interpretation—which shows an intimate knowledge of history moving in repeating cycles.

> You were looking, O king, and lo! there was a great statue. This statue was huge, its brilliance extraordinary; it was standing before you, and its appearance was frightening. The head of that statue was of fine gold, its chest and arms of silver, its middle and thighs of bronze, its legs of iron, its feet partly of iron and partly of clay. As you looked on, a stone was cut out, not by human hands, and it struck the statue on its feet of iron and clay and broke them in pieces. Then the iron, the clay, the bronze, the silver, and the gold were all broken in pieces and became like the chaff of the summer threshing floors; and the wind carried them away, so that not a trace of them could be found. But the stone that struck the statue became a great mountain and filled the whole earth.[616]

We clearly see an enormous statue of a man—the hero character in our story—built in layers of gold, silver, bronze and iron. Each of these layers ends up being smashed, one by one. Notice that the resulting rubble was said to look like the "chaff of the summer threshing floors." Chaff is the unusable material that falls out of a mill that is used for grinding—or threshing—grain. The grain mill is one of the most common symbolic codes embedded in dozens of different myths, worldwide, to symbolize the 25,920-year precession of the equinoxes, according to de Santillana and von Dechend. The central axis of the mill symbolizes the earth's axis as it drifts through the precession in de Santillana and von Dechend's epic model. Each section of the statue corresponds to an age. The Golden Age is represented by the head—which is the beginning of each new cycle. In the final age, everything from the previous cycles is smashed by the stone in Nebuchadnezzar's vision—and comes to a rather abrupt end.

Daniel clearly interprets each of the four main sections of the statue—gold, silver, bronze, and iron—as corresponding to a major cycle or age of human history. This begins with the Golden Age, represented here by the king. However, this vision seems to be far less relevant to Nebuchadnezzar than he may have wanted to believe at the time.

> You, O king, the king of kings—to whom the God of heaven has given the kingdom, the power, the might, and the glory, into whose hand he has given human beings, wherever they live, the wild animals of the field, and the birds of the air, and whom he has established as ruler over them all—you are the head of gold. After you shall arise another kingdom inferior to yours, and yet a third kingdom of bronze, which shall rule over the whole earth. And there shall be a fourth kingdom, strong as iron. Just as iron crushes and smashes everything, it shall crush and shatter all these.[617]

We are clearly going through the Iron Age now. Indeed, many traditional cultures have been crushed and shattered by the introduction of machines and technology. Many of these machines are made out of metal, which is signified by the iron. As we continue reading this prophecy, we find out that the people of this age are weakened by how divided they become. Nonetheless, a core of strength remains: "As you saw the feet and toes partly of potter's clay and partly of iron, it shall be a divided kingdom; but some of the strength of iron shall be in it, as you saw the iron mixed with the clay . . . the kingdom shall be partly strong and partly brittle."[618]

The degree to which this Iron Age is a prophecy of our modern world becomes clearer when we skip ahead to 7:23: "There shall be a fourth kingdom on earth that shall be different from all the other kingdoms; it shall devour the whole earth, and trample it down, and break it to pieces."[619]

Once this Iron Age comes to a close, we again return to the Golden Age. This description is given in symbolic, dreamlike terms: "And in the days of those [Iron Age] kings, the God of heaven will set up a kingdom that shall never be destroyed, nor shall this kingdom be left to another people. It shall crush all these kingdoms and bring them to an end, and it shall stand forever."[620]

Moving ahead to 12:1, we again get a clear prophecy of the difficult times we're in now, but also a revealing glimpse of what the Golden Age might be like once it finally arrives: "There shall be a time of anguish, such as has never occurred since nations first came into existence. But at that time your people shall be delivered; everyone who is found written in the book."[621]

Some may believe those in the "book" will only be "the Chosen," whomever they think those people may be. Let's consider that the "book" might actually be the story of the Hero's Journey itself. If this is the symbol that is being used, then how do we write ourselves into the book? How do we join the great story? It could be that everyone who takes up their own quest for the ancient Elixir of Immortality finds themselves in the book. Everyone who is willing to face the nemesis in the quest for a better, stronger and more loving world has dedicated themselves to the planetary healing process we now must go through. Once we defeat the nemesis on a global level, we access the treasure it has been guarding— and can now enter the Golden Age. Daniel's description of the Golden Age is very interesting: "Many of those who sleep in the dust of the earth shall awake; some to everlasting life, and some to shame and everlasting contempt. Those who are wise shall shine like the brightness of the sky—and those who lead many to righteousness, like the stars—forever and ever."[622]

This appears to be an undeniable reference to the same "fourth-density shift" that is described in the Law of One series. The next stage of human evolution, when we free ourselves from the cycles of birth and death through reincarnation, does seem to involve a movement into a "light body"—much like Jehoshua appeared after the resurrection. In chapter 21 we will discover there are more than 160,000 documented cases of Rainbow Body occurring in Tibet and China alone. This same passage also refers to "those who sleep in the dust of the earth" and then awaken. This is clearly metaphorical, not literal. It is very likely a reference to people who have remained unaware of the spiritual principles that govern the universe, rather than to dead bodies rising out of the ground, as many Christian fundamentalists believe.

The Central Passages Where the Encoded Numbers Appear
Finally, with all that context in place, we return to the central "mystery" passages where the encoded numbers appear. This begins in Daniel 12:6.

> One of them said to the man clothed in linen, who was upstream, "How long shall it be until the end of these wonders?" The man clothed in linen, who was upstream, raised his right hand and his left hand toward heaven. And I heard him swear by the one who lives forever that it would be for a time, two times, and half a time—and that when the shattering of the power of the holy people comes to an end, all these things would be accomplished.[623]

I first discovered the meaning of "a time, two times and half a time" from my friend and colleague Joe Mason in a phone call I had with him on November 9, 1996. He described a series of incredible events that led him to investigate mysteries like this. I was so fascinated that I stayed up way past my bedtime and struggled like crazy to write down everything he was saying. I soon found out that the "three and a half" symbolism appeared in a variety of different myths, worldwide, according to Joseph Campbell, the same scholar who wrote *The Hero's Journey.* In his book *The Inner Reaches of Outer Space,* Campbell suggested that the "three and a half" represented the tipping point between the third and fourth chakras, which are alleged to be energy centers within the body.

The "three and a half" symbol therefore represents the tipping point between the lower mind of the ego and the higher consciousness of the heart. Two and a half years later, in April 1999, Joe Mason wrote this up on his website, GreatDreams.com.

> In 1992, after two years of "coincidental" experiences that often related to dreams and/or crop circle formations, an incredible chain of many "coincidences" began. I read Joseph Campbell's *The Inner Reaches of Outer Space,* and was impressed with the information concerning the "midpoint of the chakras" symbolism found in diverse myths in various forms. The midpoint of the seven chakras is often expressed as three and a half. At the time, I was reading the Bible for basically the first time—although I had read a few verses over the years. Right after reading about the above mentioned concepts, I came to Revelation 11:9 and 11:11, which speak of the two olive trees/lampstands that lie dead for "three days and a half," and then stand up on their feet when a breath of life from God enters them. . . . This page details the various myths that express the "midpoint of the seven" in the various forms, and the dream-coincidences that led me to a quite convincing theory about the meaning of the Book of Revelation.[624]

Mason clearly believed this three-and-a-half point was not only the tipping point between the ego and the heart—it also represented the shift between the third and fourth dimension, or "density," in Law of One terms. This shift propels us into the coming Golden Age that had been so frequently prophesied as well. Mason explained this in another excerpt from the same article: "It seems clear that 'a time, two times, and half a time,' is yet another form of the 3 ½ symbolism. . . . In this case, there is no set period of days or years. Perhaps it means that the changes will come when the human race has reached the required level of consciousness evolution—however long that will be."[625]

This conversation with Joe Mason was of extremely high importance in my development of this investigation. I met him on a forum where I was regularly posting on the phenomenon of synchronicity and describing data I was getting from my dreams. As I listened to him talk that night, for the very first time, I was extremely tired and could barely stay awake. Yet the information he was giving me was fantastic. It was connecting hundreds of different dots for me and felt like a massive download. Even though I was half-asleep, I wrote everything he was saying down the best way I could. Joe Mason said that some of these concepts were revealing themselves to him through what he called the "Dream Voice." He said this was a quiet background murmuring that he could hear in his mind when he first woke up and could still remember a dream.

Mason told me that if you tune in to this murmuring and listen carefully, you can pick out words and sentence fragments and write them down. The very next morning, I started doing this without paying any attention to what the words were actually saying. That was a very important element of the Dream Voice protocol. As soon as you start following or understanding the words, they will quickly be distorted. After a prolonged process that generated eight pages of material, on November 10, 1996, I stopped. I then sat up, breathed normally, and began reading what I had written in my waking consciousness. I was stunned at how complex and mysterious the words were. This was my first experience with a psychic reading—and I have continued to practice and develop this ability ever since.

Daniel Requests More Information on the "Three and a Half"
Mason believed there was "no set period of days or years" in the symbolism of the three and a half. When we go back to the book of Daniel, as soon as he hears about the "three and a half" symbolism, he asks for more information: "I heard but could not understand; so I said, 'My lord,

what shall be the outcome of these things?' He said, 'Go your way, Daniel, for the words are to remain secret and sealed until the time of the end.'"[626]

This is very interesting. Could it be that "the words [that] . . . remain secret and sealed until the time of the end" are actually the "pages" of the great story itself—in other words, the knowledge of the Hero's Journey? Scholars like Joseph Campbell have only very recently discovered this common link interconnecting all the greatest mythologies in world history. Hollywood used Campbell's blueprint to write great stories and make money by reaching its audiences at the deepest possible level. The Hero's Journey story clearly seems to invoke our subconscious memory of the afterlife—and what we are really doing here on earth.

Long before the era of movies, these myths were acted out as plays—and the curtain call was arguably the most important part of the whole performance. This is where the players break the fourth wall and directly connect with the audience for the first time. In this all-important moment, we are reminded that the ordinary world as we know it is really only a stage, and there is indeed a magical world that we will once again enter. However, we do not have to die in order to access this magical world. Ultimately, we can awaken our own mystical abilities and directly access the knowledge of the universe. I began doing this on November 10, 1996, and almost immediately began getting prophecies that completely defeated my notions of linear time. The future was often being described very precisely without any seeming effort at all. The ancient story tells us that we can only reach this Elixir of Immortality—the treasure of the higher self—once we defeat the nemesis. Again, the nemesis is represented by the ego—all our doubts, fears, jealousies, suspicions, and frustrations.

This entire story appears in myths, plays, novels, television shows, and movies—but these same plot points appear, in the same sequence, throughout our history in regularly repeating cycles of time. Whoever wrote the book of Daniel seems to have understood this and was clearly not bound by linear time. The words of the book needed to remain "secret and sealed until the end," but those times may very well now be upon us. The idea that this book is the great story of the Hero's Journey, playing out in extended cycles of time, is heavily validated in the book of Daniel. As we continue, we find a clear description of a 1,290-year cycle just three sentences later. "Many shall be purified, cleansed, and refined, but the wicked shall continue to act wickedly. None of the wicked shall understand, but those who are wise shall understand. From the time that the regular burnt offering is taken away and the abomination that desolates is set up, there shall be one thousand two hundred ninety days."[627]

Now it makes more sense. Other prophecies from around the world clearly pin the Golden Age as beginning around the year 2012. The time when "the regular burnt offering is taken away and the abomination that desolates is set up" could easily be the iconoclasm in A.D. 720, when the church began strengthening its control of the people and the governments. This ended the "mystery" phase of Christianity, according to François Masson and Reverend Father Poucel. Then if we add in one of Fomenko's cycles of 1,296 years—exactly one-twentieth of the precession—we get the year 2016. The biblical mention of a figure of 1,290 years brings us even closer to the frequently prophesied date of 2012—specifically, the year 2010. Both of these numbers may be important. With the benefit of modern scientific research, we can see that the 1,296-year cycle is a perfect fit with the 25,920-year cycle—but the figure of 1,290 years calibrates this biblical passage to the end date of the entire cycle even more closely. This was also the year this prophecy was rediscovered.

The Final Forty-Five-Year Transition Period

The end date of the Mayan calendar is December 2012, or 12/12. Interestingly, in Daniel 12:12, we are told that a forty-five-year transition period will begin at or around this time. We see this appear in the difference between the 1,290 "days" and another new number—1,335: "Happy are those who persevere and attain the thousand three hundred thirty-five days. But you, go your way, and rest; you shall rise for your reward at the end of the days."[628]

In the Law of One series, we are told that the shift into fourth density begins approximately thirty years after 1981, or roughly the year 2011. The year 2011 is even closer to this apparent time-encoded prophecy in the book of Daniel. However, the Law of One series also indicates that we have to work through a transitional period of "100 to 700 years" before the shift into fourth density is complete. Before we get there, we have the opportunity to begin experiencing fourth-density abilities within our existing third-density bodies. The quotes that explain this will be revealed in the next chapter.

We've been conditioned to think that there is no magic left in the world—that science has solved all the great mysteries, and we're just here to be born, live our lives, and die, never knowing the beauty of existence again. As far as I'm concerned, these cycles make science come alive unlike anything else I have ever studied. Now I find myself taking walks and wondering if each step I take is being duplicated by some other version of me in another time cycle, either in the past or in the future. What decisions that I make will reverberate throughout these cycles? What decisions that I made have been directly influenced by what happened in other cycles? Are there certain story points built into the cycles that will steer my free will—whether I consciously realize it or not?

Life becomes a lot more interesting once you know that these cycles really exist. You can strongly question the typical atheist's idea that once we die, it's over, and there is no greater purpose to anything happening in our lives—or in world events, for that matter.

I am invigorated by the challenge of looking at weird stuff like this and seeing if there's a way we can model it. How might these cycles actually be forming? Are we moving through an energetic structure of some kind, based on the positions of the planets—and even the position of our sun around a neighboring star? I didn't solve this greatest of intellectual puzzles until August of 2012, and until I cracked the code, I did not feel comfortable trying to write this book. Once I found the answer, I realized that it had already been stated, quite plainly, in the Law of One series—I just hadn't understood what it meant at the time. This new model gave me a way to visually understand and explain the cycles of history as well as the energetic springboard that could propel us into the Golden Age.

The Hindu scriptures and others suggest that this new Golden Age will not be the first. Another Golden Age apparently occurred in our own prehistory. Did the people of this Golden Age enjoy scientific knowledge that was significantly ahead of our own in certain key areas? Were they well aware of these historical cycles that we have now redis-covered? Did our ancestors' own records of a Golden Age lead them to believe it would happen again, and even to predict when it would arrive? Did they already know that the cycles of history would converge into a single mega-event at the end of each 25,920-year cycle? Can we study the records they left behind and find the secrets to demystify the advanced science they once knew? Can we finally locate the Synchronicity Key and unlock the great treasure chest that holds the Blueprints for a Golden Age?

CHAPTER TWENTY-ONE

Explaining the Cycles and the Fourth-Density Shift

The Rainbow Body

There are more than 160,000 documented cases of people transforming into the Rainbow Body in Tibet and China alone.[629] This phenomenon has continued straight through into modern times.[630] As I revealed in *The Source Field Investigations,* this has been witnessed, scrutinized, and investigated by Father Tiso, a Catholic priest, as well as members of the Chinese military in recent times.[631] In each of these cases, a human being of flesh and blood is transformed into a "light body" and gains the ability to walk between this physical world and the afterlife. In some cases, people transform all at once, spontaneously. However, in many other instances, their bodies gradually shift into pure rainbow light over the course of seven days, while they are wrapped in a shroud.[632] These people were invariably working in highly advanced spiritual disciplines. There was nothing accidental about what happened to them. They were meditating, contemplating, and doing their best to love, forgive, and accept themselves and others and to see the universe and their own greater identity as the One Infinite Creator.[633] They had reached a point at which they mastered what this level of existence is here to teach us. That gave them the power to move into the ascended state. This is not at all what happens when most people die. Nor is this "light body" the same as what we naturally become after our physical death. It's literally a quantum leap in human evolution. Father Tiso wanted this phenomenon studied more seriously. He felt that this knowledge could help transform the lives and spiritual paths of people in the Western world.

Fig. 17: Tibetan Buddhist illustration of the "Rainbow Body"

The Harvest: Another Name for a World Transformation

The entire Law of One series is built around the idea that something very wonderful will soon be happening to us—something they called "harvest." A timeline was given for when this would begin to happen— approximately thirty years after 1981. Like many others who studied this material, I had high hopes that the Mayan Calendar end date would bring a sudden change for the positive. Although there have certainly been harbingers of positive growth at the time of this writing in April 2013, we certainly have not seen any sudden, grandiose events. We will explore exactly what the Law of One source said in much more detail later on. When you read the cumulative body of data in the Law of One series, it seems very clear that "harvest" refers to a worldwide event. After this event happens, many of us will be able to achieve the Rainbow Body state, which is often called ascension. In *The Source Field Investigations,* I presented a widespread body of data showing that many ancient prophecies are expecting this to happen as well. This includes the Sibylline mystery texts, from which "Novus Ordo Seclorum" in the Great Seal of the United States was quoted.

Fig. 18: Near-final draft of the great seal of the United States in 1782

This text was channeled by the Sybil of Cumae, an extremely accurate psychic, in or around 539 B.C. The Roman government kept it hidden in total secrecy, and considered it their greatest treasure due to its astonishing accuracy. As it says on the *Antiquities of Rome* website, "The Sibyls were gifted seers. . . . The Sybil of Cumae sold three books of prophesies to the last of the Roman kings, Tarquin the Proud. These books were highly worshipped and consulted by the Romans in their times of greatest need."[634]

These books contained a chronological timeline of events that would happen to Rome, including exact time windows and cryptic descriptions of the events. This posed a huge security threat, as anyone wanting to invade Rome could use it with devastating effectiveness, and so it was considered highly classified. It was buried deep in the Temple of Jupiter and guarded by 15 different priests[635] called the Decemvirs[636] in the ancient equivalent of Area 51. The best online resource for this text—which eventually appeared in Virgil's Fourth Eclogue—appears on MIT's page on the Internet Classics Archive. Here are some of the strongest elements of this prophecy:

> Now the last age by Cumae's Sibyl sung
> Has come and gone, and the majestic roll
> Of circling centuries begins anew:

"The majestic roll of circling centuries begins anew" was shortened to "Novus Ordo Seclorum" on the US dollar. This is a clear reference to the 25,920-year cycle. Let's see what happens immediately after the part that the Founding Fathers of America quoted from. Indeed, it gets even more interesting as we go on from there, as we seem to have a prophecy of extraterrestrials or angelic beings making themselves formally known on earth:

> Justice returns, returns old Saturn's reign,
> With a new breed of men sent down from heaven.
> Only do thou, at the boy's birth in whom
> The iron shall cease, the golden race arise,

The terms *Golden Race* and *Golden Age* are interchangeable, as I explained in *The Source Field Investigations*. This appears to be a clear reference to a worldwide light-body-type event. Let's continue from another point shortly after this and see what happens:

> This glorious age, O Pollio, shall begin,
> And the months enter on their mighty march.

> Under thy guidance, whatso tracks remain
> Of our old wickedness, once done away,
> Shall free the earth from never-ceasing fear.

He shall receive the life of gods, and see
Heroes with gods commingling, and himself
Be seen of them, and with his father's worth
Reign o'er a world at peace.

This is a prophecy of a very positive event. The earth is freed from never-ceasing fear. Extraterrestrial humans comingle with us. We then "receive the life of gods" and are "seen of them" ourselves. We are also given a time window of when this will happen—approximately at the end of the 25,920-year cycle, which we are moving through at the time of this writing. Near the end of Virgil's Fourth Eclogue, which directly quoted this greatest of all Roman treasures, we see another blatant reference to the 25,920-year cycle. Specifically, we see a reference to the tottering of "the world's orbed might." This clearly seems to refer to the slow, drifting movement of the earth's axis as we pass through this cycle.

Assume thy greatness, for the time draws nigh,
Dear child of gods, great progeny of Jove!

See how it totters—the world's orbed might,
Earth, and wide ocean, and the vault profound,
All, see, enraptured of the coming time!

The "Harvest" Discussion Is Woven Throughout the Entire Series

This same imminent event is discussed throughout the entire Law of One series—from the very first session to the last. It is clear that the main reason why these higher-level extraterrestrials are here is to try to help as many people "graduate" as possible in this magnificent event. All the different gods who visited and civilized ancient cultures and encoded this prophecy into their myths were all members of the "Confederation of Planets in Service of the One Infinite Creator," in Law of One terms. Therefore, the information that was planted into the Sybil of Cumae and eventually ended up in the Great Seal of the United States very likely started out as a positive message from the Confederation of Planets. It is interesting that despite the numerous accurate prophecies in them, the Romans were never able to use these prophecies for their own gain. I think the Confederation of Planets put enough "sizzle" in the books to attract the Romans' attention but specifically intended for this prophecy to reach us in modern times. The Law of One source announced the core beliefs of the Confederation of Planets in the very first sentence it ever spoke through Carla Rueckert, the channel:

> 1.0 The Confederation of Planets in the Service of the Infinite Creator has only one important statement. That statement, my friends, as you know, is "All things, all of life, all of the creation is part of one original thought."[637]

The exact membership of the Confederation of Planets was given in session 6:

> 6.24 I am one of the members of the Confederation of Planets in the Service of the Infinite Creator. There are approximately fifty-three civilizations, comprising approximately five hundred planetary consciousness complexes in this Confederation. This Confederation contains those from your own planet who have attained dimensions beyond your third. It contains planetary entities within your solar system, and it contains planetary entities from other galaxies. It is a true Confederation in that its members are not alike, but allied in service according to the Law of One.[638]

It took me many years to figure out what the source meant by "other galaxies." It did *not* mean anything outside the Milky Way galaxy. This was one of the more confusing things I was wrestling with when I first read all of this back in 1996. We will get back to that in a minute. Most important, the Law of One series specifically says that there will be a quantum leap changing the basic laws of physics as we now know them sometime approximately thirty years after January 1981, though the source cannot pinpoint an exact time window for various reasons. The source uses the name Ra as it once did in ancient Egypt.

> 6.16 Questioner: What is the position of this planet with respect to progression of the cycle at this time?
>
> Ra: . . . This sphere is at this time in fourth-dimension vibration. Its material is quite confused due to the society memory complexes embedded in its consciousness. It has not made an easy transition to the vibrations which beckon. Therefore, it will be fetched with some inconvenience.

> 6.17 Questioner: Is this inconvenience imminent within a few years?
>
> Ra: . . . This inconvenience, or disharmonious vibratory complex, has begun several of your years in the past. It shall continue unabated for a period of approximately three oh, thirty [30], of your years.

> 6.18 Questioner: After this thirty-year period I am assuming we will be a fourth-dimension or fourth-density planet. Is this correct?
>
> Ra: . . . This is so.

> 6.19 Questioner: [Is it] possible to estimate what percentage of [the] present population will inhabit the fourth-density planet?
>
> Ra: The harvesting is not yet, thus, estimation is meaningless.[639]

The Law of One series never got more specific than that. The Mayan calendar was never mentioned. The year 2012 was never mentioned. Hardly anyone was aware of these things back in 1981, including the members of L/L Research, who produced the material. This idea of a dimensional shift fits perfectly with the prophecies given through the Sybil of Cumae. It also explains the Golden Age prophecy that was embedded into the mythologies of more than thirty ancient cultures, as Graham Hancock popularized in 1995. Once we come into contact with this information, do we just sit back and "wait for the magic"? I certainly did not. There were enough leads given in the Law of One series to mount a comprehensive, scientific investigation. One intriguing clue I found in the early days was that the Mayan calendar, at roughly 5,125 years, is almost exactly one-fifth of this 25,920-year cycle, coming in at approximately 25,627 years.

While I was writing *The Source Field Investigations,* I discovered that each of the subcycles the Mayan calendar is tracking—260 days, 360 days + 5, 7,200 days (19.7 years), and 144,000 days (397.4 years)—was directly synchronized with the orbits in our solar system. The 260-day tzolkin is the most widely appearing of these ancient cycles in Mesoamerica. Robert Peden, an Australian college professor, found that 260 days is the smallest possible number that interlocks all the orbits of the inner planets together.[640] The Mayans built a whole system of divination around this, tracking a twenty-day cycle and a thirteen-day cycle at the same time. Each day in each of these cycles has a particular meaning, similar to astrology. The effects we experience will change as these two cycles intersect throughout the entire 260-day period. Conventional astronomers would never even believe a cycle like this could exist. The planetary orbits are not supposed to be so precisely interconnected, like the gears in a grand cosmic clock. How could something as seemingly complex as the orbits of the planets have such a simple, common denominator? Peden discovered this in 1981 but didn't publish it until releasing it freely online on May 24, 2004.[641]

Ultimately, I concluded that nothing in our solar system is random. Everything we now see is the result of a highly intricate system, perfect down to the second, which we are only just beginning to understand. So if the Mayan calendar was tracking these time cycles that correspond to planetary orbits, how did those time cycles get there in the first place?

Why are there almost exactly five Mayan calendar cycles in one 25,920-year cycle? As of the summer of 2012, I was still searching for some sort of energetic framework that could be driving these orbits and their interconnectedness. Let's say that instead of moving blindly through space, our sun is moving through an invisible matrix of some kind that is actually driving these cycles—including the 25,920-year cycle.

We Are Orbiting a Nearly Invisible Brown Dwarf Star

In the summer of 2012, right before I left for New Zealand and Australia, I realized that our sun was very likely orbiting a brown dwarf companion star, as certain scholars have argued. The natural forces given off by the brown dwarf—which we will discuss in a minute—would give us all the structure we needed to energetically drive these planetary orbits and to synchronize them.

This great orbit of our sun around another star—unknown to most people in our modern world—then becomes like the mainspring and central axis in a windup clock. Let's say the sun is orbiting another star, which is not bright enough to be easily visible. We can then use computer programs to mathematically round out that orbit into a perfect circle, in order to show it in its "idealized" form. This may be the natural form the orbit would take if it were not for the gas, dust, and pressure pushing on it as it orbits the center of the galaxy. If we regularize the orbit into a circle, the Mayan calendar cycle length then forms a perfect five-sided geometry within it. This geometry may be the hidden reason why the Mayan calendar works the way it does. This was the big missing piece that paid off so many years of research. We already see geometry appearing in a variety of different circumstances in the natural sciences. We find it in the structure of the atomic nucleus, as well as in greater groups of atoms called microclusters. We also see it in the underlying structure of continents and mountain ranges on earth known as the global grid. Additionally, it appears in the exact positioning of the planetary orbits. I had simply missed the grand finale. I had not realized what our sun was actually experiencing as it moved through space. I was thrilled to solve the mystery—suddenly, everything became explainable.

Although this is not a popular scientific notion, we can already prove that our own sun is generating geometric energy waves that structure and drive the orbits of the planets in our own solar system. The geometric spacing between the planetary orbits was proven recently by John Martineau in *A Little Book of Coincidence in the Solar System.* This is all featured in *The Source Field Investigations,* in detail. Martineau used modern computer technology to smooth out the orbits into perfect circles and then compare their relationships. Importantly, a perfect circle is also the equator of a perfect sphere if you extend it into a three-dimensional form.

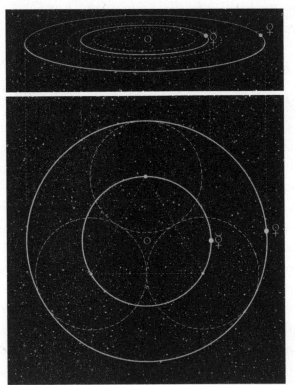

Fig. 19: John Martineau's illustration of triangular relationship between orbits of Mercury and Venus

The Platonic Solids

Each of these geometric patterns—whether in the atomic nucleus, microclusters, the global grid or the distances between the planets—is one of the five basic Platonic solids.

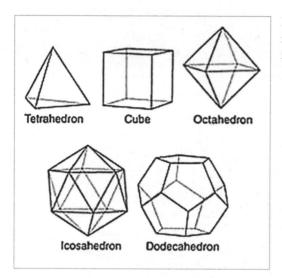

Fig. 20: The Platonic Solids: forms that naturally appear in a vibrating fluid

Why are these patterns appearing so regularly in nature? It took me years to find the answer. One early clue was that mathematicians knew these shapes had more symmetry than any other three-dimensional geometry we can generate. The Platonic solids are the most basic harmonic patterns that appear when you vibrate a fluid. This was discovered by Dr. Hans Jenny, who saw similar shapes appear when he vibrated muddy water.[642] The cloudy dirt in the water was formed by millions of tiny particles of sand. Normally, these fine particles of sand were scattered everywhere, clouding up the water. However, once Dr. Jenny vibrated the water with pure sound frequencies, the particles all mysteriously formed into very precise geometric shapes. This also left huge, empty spaces of clean, pure water in between.

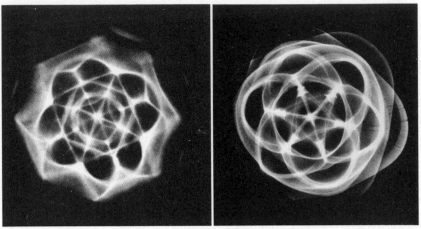

Fig. 21: Dr. Hans Jenny's illustration of geometry in a vibrating fluid. Sand particles form two different complex shapes as sound frequency changes.

These shapes stayed very solid and stable, as long as he continued to play the same sound frequency into the water. Once Dr. Jenny changed the frequency of vibration, different shapes appeared. You can see this in the change from the image on the left, which is a set of cubes in three dimensions, to the image on the right. Now we see two pyramid-like tetrahedrons, forming a six-pointed Star of David pattern when seen together.

The Big Secret of Quantum Mechanics

The big secret is that "dark matter," "dark energy," the "quantum foam," and so on—the energy most scientists now believe must be creating matter—has fluidlike properties. I call this energy the Source Field and have conclusively proven that it thinks. The Source Field is, quite literally, the energetic manifestation of a Universal Mind. The vibrations of this "universal fluid" create geometric patterns. Any vibration of the fluid—any change in its basic state—is what we could call a thought. What was the "one [and] only important statement" of the Confederation, in session 1 of the Law of One series?

1.0 The Confederation of Planets in the Service of the Infinite Creator has only one important statement. That statement, my friends, as you know, is "All things, all of life, all of the creation is part of one original thought."[643]

Fig. 22: Dr. Robert Moon's geometric model of the atomic nucleus

At the quantum level, these geometric vibrations of the Source Field—of the Universal Mind—turn into atoms and molecules. Dr. Robert Moon, who was part of a small team entrusted to develop the atomic bomb in the Manhattan Project, discovered this geometry in the nucleus of the atom in 1987.[644] Dr. Moon solved many different quantum physics problems by developing this model.[645] In Moon's model, there are no particles in the atom. Each proton in the nucleus is simply one corner of a geometric shape. Oxygen, for example, has eight protons. A cube has eight points—four on the square on top, and four on the square on the bottom.

The nucleus of the atom also has "shells" in it in Dr. Moon's new model. Once you finish building one geometry, and more energy keeps coming in, another geometry begins to form around the first one. This new model also explains how atoms can appear to be "waves" and "particles" at the same time. They can appear to be both because they are made of a fluidlike energy that is vibrating. If you measure the energy like a wave, you will see a wave. If you look for a particle, you will see one of these geometric points and find a proton. Ultimately, this means that everything we see in the universe is an energy vibration. Nothing really exists as a solid object. The mystery becomes even deeper once we see that you can create your own geometric vibrations in this fluidlike energy—which I call the Source Field—with your own thoughts. You can use this to "magnetize" certain things to you, such as in the Law of Attraction. As you become more advanced, you could use this same power to levitate objects with your mind, or even manifest physical objects out of thin air. Great masters like Jesus were able to do this because they understood the big secret: they *are* the Source Field. Thoughts are things. Or, as the young student of the Oracle said to Neo in *The Matrix:*

> ORACLE STUDENT: Do not try and bend the spoon. That's impossible. Instead . . . only try to realize the truth.
> NEO: What truth?
> STUDENT: There is no spoon.
> NEO: There is no spoon?
> STUDENT: Then you'll see that it is not the spoon that bends—it is only yourself.

Internal Vibrations in the Sun Create the Orbital Shells

In the case of our solar system, the sun has a variety of vibrations occurring inside itself, as well as on the surface. This is called "solar seismology." The surface is heaving up and down in regular cycles, as Dr. David Guenther, a professor from the Department of Astronomy and Physics at St. Mary's University in Halifax, Nova Scotia, mapped out.[646] The original observations that led to this discovery were made in 1962, by Leighton, Noyes, and Simon in their seminal work "Velocity Fields in the Solar Atmosphere," published in *Astrophysical Journal.*[647] They found that the surface of the sun appeared to be moving up and down in cycles lasting about five minutes. The sun's surface is rising and falling by only a few meters every five minutes. This is still more than enough to create waves in a fluidlike Source Field that exists throughout our solar system.

These "vibrations" within the sun create ripples that move throughout the fluidlike energy in our solar system. The waves then bounce off our solar system's outer gravitational boundary and reflect back toward the sun again. Along the way, these ripples collide with one another and form interference patterns. These interference patterns are what create the invisible geometric force fields that hold the planets in their positions. This is the force of gravity. It's not just pulling planets toward the sun; it's pushing them away as well, in a constant push-pull dance, outward and inward. The Law of One series tipped me off in 1996 that the solar system must be doing this. Here, the source describes this rhythmic action as occurring within the first star in the universe—the "central sun":

> 27.6 Intelligent infinity has a rhythm, or flow, as of a giant heart—beginning with the central sun, as you would think or conceive of this. The presence of the flow [is as] inevitable as a tide of beingness without polarity, without finity; the vast and silent all beating outward, outward, focusing outward and inward until the focuses are complete. The intelligence or consciousness of foci have reached a state where their, shall we say, spiritual nature or mass calls them inward, inward, inward until all is coalesced. This is the rhythm of reality as you spoke. . . . The basic rhythms of intelligent infinity are totally without distortion of any kind. The rhythms are clothed in mystery, for they are being itself.[648]

Gravity Is the Secret

Gravity is ultimately caused by the flow of this fluidlike energy into a planet. Gravity *is* the Source Field. This constant flow of new energy is what allows the planet to exist, moment by moment. This flow feeds each atom with new energy, as I demonstrated in *The Source Field Investigations*. My friend and colleague Dr. Nassim Haramein proved that the physics around the nucleus of an atom are effectively the same as the physics around a black hole, for example.[649] The Law of One series also heavily endorsed the work of Dewey Larson, who proposed in the 1950s that there is a parallel reality in which time is three-dimensional.[650] Larson backed up his theories with a great deal of provable evidence. In this next Law of One quote, the source endorses Larson's work. However, the source then goes on to say that a complete theory will need to include gravity and vibration in order to solve all the mysteries:

> 20.7 Questioner: Just as a sideline, a side question here: Is the physics of Dewey Larson correct?
>
> Ra: . . . The physics of sound vibrational complex Dewey is a correct system as far as it is able to go. There are those things which are not included in this system. However, those coming after this particular entity, using the basic concepts of vibration and the study of vibrational distortions, will begin to understand that which you know of as gravity and those things you consider as "n" dimensions. These things are necessary to be included in a more universal, shall we say, physical theory.[651]

Again, I read all of this in 1996. It took several more years for me to find scientific proof that the universe is made of living, conscious energy that behaves like a fluid and vibrates. These vibrations then form the geometry we have just explored, from the quantum level on up. This is all very central to the Law of One scientific model.

The Twenty-Five-Thousand-Year Cycle

The Law of One series extensively discusses the "25,000-year cycle," as the source calls it. The source says that this is a basic pattern that governs the evolution of all third-density life on any given planet in our Milky Way galaxy.

> 6.15 Questioner: What is the length, in our years, of one of these cycles currently?
>
> Ra: One major cycle is approximately twenty-five thousand [25,000] of your years. There are three cycles of this nature during which those who have progressed may be harvested at the end of three major cycles. That is, approximately between seventy-five and seventy-six thousand [75–76,000] of your

years. All are harvested regardless of their progress, for during that time the planet itself has moved through the useful part of that dimension and begins to cease being useful for the lower levels of vibration within that [third] density.[652]

In the Law of One model, there are literally millions of planets with humanlike beings on them in our Milky Way galaxy alone. Each of them is very carefully watched over and guided by beings in higher densities of existence. The humans on these planets are not expected to remain as third-density, flesh-and-blood biological life-forms forever. The universe is designed to promote our evolution into the Rainbow Body state in fixed intervals of time, spanning roughly twenty-five thousand years. Each time one of these cycles ends, it is called a "harvest" in Law of One terms, as we saw earlier. Every third-density planet in our galaxy runs through three twenty-five-thousand-year cycles before it moves out of third density entirely and fully transitions into fourth density. We will review Law of One descriptions of fourth density as we go on.

In Western astrology, the movement from the Age of Pisces into the Age of Aquarius began around the end of the year 2012. The Mayan calendar end date landed on December 21, 2012. The romantic notion was that something all-important and magnificent would happen on that very day. The reality is that nothing obvious has occurred—at least not yet. Does this mean we simply give up, say that this was all a bunch of nonsense, and go back to fear, fear, fear of the new world order, martial law, and internment camps? Or, do we simply go back into the matrix? Do we conclude that extraterrestrials do not exist, that none of this "2012 stuff" meant anything, and that life on earth is going to stay ordinary for the indefinite future? I don't think it's that simple. I'm sharing with you, in detail, some of the information I have been looking at, and meditating on, since December 21, 2012, came and went without any obvious transformative effects.

Most scientists believe this 25,920-year cycle is caused by a wobble in the earth's axis. I was taken in by this same belief and spent many years trying to understand how it worked—and *why* it worked—within the Law of One model.

25,920 YEARS

Fig. 23: The "precession of the equinoxes" is believed to be a 25,920-year
"wobble" in the earth's axis.

Why would the earth be wobbling this way? Why should such a seemingly superficial movement of our earth's axis have such massive consequences in the Law of One model? Are we moving through a geometric pattern that is tugging on the earth's axis? What geometry could cause the earth to move in a slow corkscrew fashion like this? How could this be happening on every third-density planet in our entire galaxy—as the Law of One series indicated? Even more important, how could we fit this 25,920-year wobble into the greater model of human evolution given in the Law of One series? I still hadn't solved this mystery when I wrote *The Source Field Investigations,* but I was tantalizingly close to the answer. It just took me another year to figure out what it was. As I said, the answer came thundering in on me, all at once, just days before I was about to leave on a five-city tour of New Zealand and Australia in 2012. I realized that the answer was very simple: We live in a binary solar system. We orbit our companion star over the course of 25,920 years. Our sun's companion star does not give off enough visible light to be easily observed. Stars like this are called brown dwarves. The Sumerians called this companion star Nibiru, as Dr. Zecharia Sitchin meticulously documented in several of his scholarly works, beginning with *Twelfth Planet.*[653] Various secret societies, including the Masonic Order, know all about this companion star at the highest levels and call it the Black Sun.

Almost every Masonic diagram you can find has three celestial objects at the top—the sun, the moon, and the Black Sun.

Fig. 24: This Masonic illustration shows the Sun, the Moon, and a companion star.

Fig. 25: This is another one of many Masonic illustrations showing the Sun, the Moon, and a companion star.

Sometimes the Black Sun is also depicted as the Eye of Horus. A triangle may also be drawn around the eye. A number of investigators sided with Zecharia Sitchin's conclusions and believed that Nibiru would invade our solar system, cross by earth, and cause a pole shift at any time from 2003 to the end of 2012. I never believed that was possible due to the strong geometric forces we just examined, which would repel any such large rogue object. Collisions with asteroids are one thing, but once you have objects with as much mass as a planet or star, their gravitational forces will naturally repel each other. Gravity is a push-pull force, unlike what we've been told in school. That is another basic scientific phenomenon that has apparently been hidden away by the military-industrial complex and its original founders for more than a century. This push-pull explains why the planets do not run out of angular momentum and crash into the sun. Think about it.

The sun has much more mass—and therefore much stronger gravitational attraction—than the planets. Shouldn't the planets "run out of gas" eventually, lose their speed, and crash into the sun? Why do they keep moving right along? They are being held in place—and pushed— by geometric energy fields, as Martineau documented. As our sun orbits this companion star, we are also moving through various geometric alignments.

Walter Cruttenden Gives the Proof

Walter Cruttenden sent me his book *Lost Star of Myth and Time* in 2011, and I knew that he was arguing in favor of the binary solar system model. I never had taken the time to read it, as I was too busy finishing *The Source Field Investigations*—and then I had forgotten about it. Now I realized he had to be right. I rushed over to the bookshelf and immediately started reading it, even in the last-minute rush to pack for my trip. I was delighted to see several compelling pieces of scientific proof that the Great Year of 25,920 earth years must be the direct result of our sun orbiting a companion star.

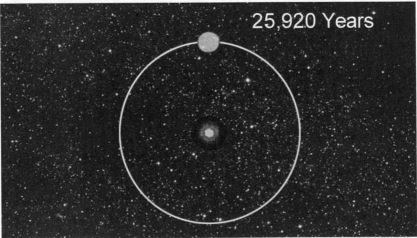

Fig. 26: Our Sun's orbit around a binary companion star, smoothed into a perfect circle—also the equator of a perfect sphere.

What if this is also one of the great Masonic secrets, and Freemasons swear on pain of death to uphold the secrets of the order? We can then begin to understand why NASA may have suppressed any evidence that would reveal this to the public. If you want to reach the higher echelons of NASA, it certainly helps to be a Freemason.

Once you survey the evidence, it becomes very obvious. In fact, the excuses that mainstream scientists have made to prop up the "earth wobble" model of the 25,920-year cycle are actually quite laughable once you see how Cruttenden lays it all out. One of the best summaries of the evidence I have found online is in the article "Is the Sun Part of a Binary Star System? Six Reasons to Consider," on the website Signs of the Times.[654] The reason why the stars move by one degree every seventy-two years through the night sky is that our entire solar system is moving like this. Every planet is affected by this cycle. This also explains why several key phenomena we see within our solar system are *not* affected by the 25,920-year cycle. If the earth's axis was wobbling on its own, then certain things like meteor showers, which repeat on the same day every year for centuries, should have started to drift—but they don't. Every year, for as long as humans have been able to write, the meteors come in, right on schedule, on the same day. Cruttenden also presents NASA evidence that fully 80 percent of the stars in our galaxy are binary stars. We can already see that they are orbiting other stars, as both of them are visible in our telescopes. There are plenty of other stars our scientists have identified that do not give off visible light. Within the Law of One system, it would therefore appear that *all* stars cluster into groups of at least two stars, if not more. By Law of One standards, any solar system that has planets with third-density life would have to be orbiting a companion star in orbits lasting 25,920 years. Stars are apparently built, by design, to travel around each other in these 25,920-year patterns—at least during the times they host third-density life.

Law of One Quotes on Star Systems as Galaxies

In the fall of 2012, while I was on my extended sabbatical in Canada, I went through the Law of One series again, extensively—and found quotes that strongly suggested that this is how it works. Our solar system was described as a galaxy. Apparently we are governed by the same laws, on a much smaller level, that the Milky Way galaxy experiences on a larger level. Could a single star be considered a galaxy? No. It has to be a "star system." This was very confusing to Dr. Don Elkins, the questioner. Take a look:

16.33 There are many Confederations. This Confederation works with the planetary spheres of seven of your galaxies, if you will, and is responsible for the callings of the densities of these galaxies.

16.34 Questioner: Would you define the word galaxy as you just used it?
Ra: We use that term in this sense as you would use star systems.

16.35 Questioner: I'm a little bit confused as to how many total planets the Confederation that you are in serves?
Ra: . . . I see the confusion. We have difficulty with your language. The galaxy term must be split. We call galaxy that vibrational complex that is local. Thus, your sun is what we would call the center of a galaxy. We see you have another meaning for this term.[655]

10.17 Questioner: Then would the nine planets and our sun we have here in our system, would you refer to that as a solar galaxy?
Ra: We would not.[656]

These Quotes Clearly Spell It Out

I didn't really examine and think about these quotes until I was aware of Cruttenden's evidence supporting a binary solar system model. Once I had that in hand, these quotes jumped right out at me in sessions 10 and 16. The source clearly says that our solar system is a galaxy. A galaxy is a star system, not an individual star. This explains why, back in session 10, the source refused to define "the nine planets and our sun" alone as a galaxy. Our sun is the center of a galaxy. It is the center of a star system. In order for us to be living in a star system, there has to be more than one star. People from the Confederation of Planets, of which Ra is also a part, clearly appear to have conveyed this knowledge to the ancients— and it appeared in the Masonic diagrams much later on. According to the Law of One series, these Masonic diagrams were hand-me-downs from ancient Confederation of Planets contacts. These contacts were originally intended to teach people how to be more loving and kind to one another in preparation for their own "graduation." Since then, much of this knowledge has been co-opted—and kept highly secret—by negative forces. The symbols and names are now hated by many.

Now I had a model that made sense. Now I could explain how both the Mayan calendar and the Ages of the Zodiac were being driven by geometric energy fields from our sun's own companion star. Once again,

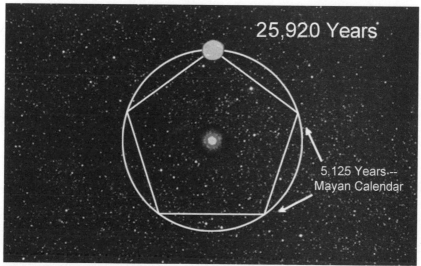

Fig. 27: The Mayan calendar divides our Sun's possible 25,920-year orbit into five equal segments, forming a pentagon or dodecahedron.

we have to take John Martineau's lead and round out our sun's natural orbit around the companion star into a perfect circle. Once we do this, the Mayan calendar cycle length, in years, cuts the circle into exactly five sections. When we play connect the dots, we get a pentagon.

In this case, what we are seeing appears to be caused by a dodecahedron that is being formed by our sun's companion. The top of the dodecahedron and the lines that extend down from it form a pentagonal structure.

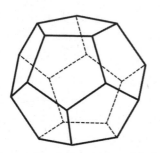

This would mean that the end of the Mayan calendar is also when we come into a geometric alignment with this massive dodecahedron created by the companion star. There is strong scientific evidence that every time we hit one of these node points on the dodecahedron, our sun has a major energetic

Fig. 28: The dodecahedron. Notice how each face is a perfect pentagon.

shift. The earth then gets a massive boost of energy. The energetic surge directly affects our climate. This cycle was discovered by Dr. Lonnie Thompson, a glaciologist. Dr. Thompson never mentioned how close the fifty-two-hundred-year cycle he discovered was to the Mayan calendar cycle of 5,125 years.

MAJOR CLIMATE CHANGE OCCURRED 5,200 YEARS AGO: EVIDENCE SUGGESTS THAT HISTORY COULD REPEAT ITSELF

Glaciologist Lonnie Thompson worries that he may have found clues that show history repeating itself, and if he is right, the result could have important implications to modern society. Thompson has spent his career trekking to the far corners of the world to find remote ice fields and then bring back cores drilled from their centers. Within those cores are the records of ancient climate from across the globe. . . .

A professor of geological sciences at Ohio State and a researcher with the Byrd Polar Research Center, Thompson points to markers in numerous records suggesting that the climate was altered suddenly some 5,200 years ago with severe impacts. . . . "Something happened back at this time and it was monumental," Thompson said. "But it didn't seem monumental to humans then because there were only approximately 250 million people occupying the planet, compared to the 6.4 billion we now have. "The evidence clearly points back to this point in history and to some event that occurred. It also points to similar changes occurring in today's climate as well," he said. . . .

Thompson believes that the 5,200-year old event may have been caused by a dramatic fluctuation in solar energy reaching the earth. . . . Evidence shows that around 5,200 years ago, solar output first dropped precipitously and then surged over a short period. It is this huge solar energy oscillation that Thompson believes may have triggered the climate change he sees in all those records.[657]

Now Things Look a Little Different

The Mayan calendar may well have been tracking our sun's movement through this giant dodecahedron. Each time we hit one of these points, all life on earth is dramatically affected.

Furthermore, the changes Dr. Lonnie Thompson observed from fifty-two hundred years ago are not going to be as strong as what we would see at the end of the entire 25,920-year cycle. This is because we are also coming into alignment with other geometries at the same time.

The Ages of the Zodiac

The Ages of the Zodiac are also the likely result of a Star of David–type geometry our sun is orbiting through—neatly dividing into twelve equal sections:

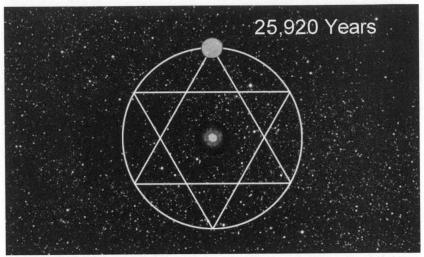

Fig. 29: The Ages of the Zodiac can be modeled by two triangles, or tetrahedrons, in a circle or sphere—forming a Star of David pattern.

Here is a breakdown of how this geometry divides the orbital circle into twelve equal sections. Each of these sections is 2,160 years long and forms an Age of the Zodiac:

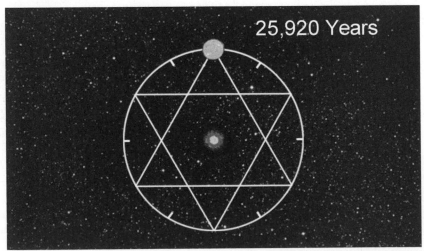

Fig. 30: The Star of David pattern cuts the circle, or sphere, into twelve equidistant segments.

This explains why the ancient Confederation of Planets extraterrestrial visitors called this 25,920-year cycle the Great Year. It is literally one "year" of the sun rotating around our companion star. Each Age of the Zodiac is one "month" within the Great Year. Once I finally saw how the pieces fit and started illustrating it, I thought it was an original discovery. I created the graphics at our Convergence conference in Phoenix, Arizona, over the weekend of November 11, 2012—11/11—less than a month after I had returned from Canada. Once I started looking through old Masonic diagrams, the same pattern I had just created in Photoshop was jumping right out at me. In Figure 31, we see in the center an S-shaped serpent with an arrow through it, surrounded by seven stars. This appears to be a representation of our companion star. Notice, again, that the sun and the moon are positioned alongside the Star of David geometry.

In Figure 32, we see an obvious connection being made between the Ages of the Zodiac—expressed here as their astrological symbols—and the geometry of the companion star. In this case, Mercury is placed at the center. This is probably the result of people copying over old diagrams and not understanding their original meanings.

Fig. 31: This Masonic/Thelemic diagram clearly indicates the Sun, the Moon, and a Star of David pattern, indicative of the companion star.

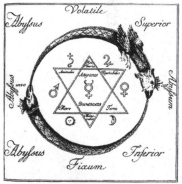

Fig. 32: This Masonic diagram again depicts the Sun, the Moon and a Star of David pattern, though by this point the original meaning may have been lost.

Part of what makes the end of the 25,920-year cycle so powerful is that we are coming into alignment with at least two different geometries at the same time:

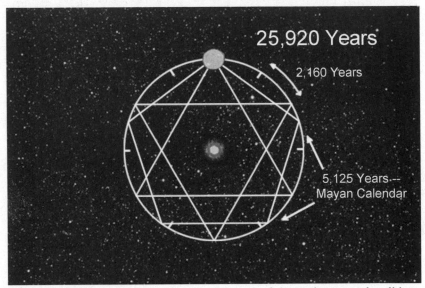

Fig. 33: The Mayan calendar pentagon and Ages of the Zodiac triangles all have points that converge at the end-date of the Great Year.

As you can see, this is the only time in the entire 25,920-year cycle where the geometries directly overlap. This will create a region of much stronger energetic charge than what we experience throughout the rest of the cycle—and since this energy is ultimately intelligent and responsible for creating biological life and DNA as we know it, this grand alignment could indeed have powerful effects on us as human beings. Once I realized that we were orbiting a companion star and moving through its geometry, I was able to decipher a Law of One quote that had puzzled me for the last sixteen years.

> 63.29 Questioner: Is there a clock-like face, shall I say, associated with the entire major galaxy—so that as it revolves, it carries all of these stars and planetary systems through transitions from density to density? Is this how it works?

Ra: I am Ra. You are perceptive. You may see a three-dimensional clock face or spiral of endlessness which is planned by the Logos [i.e., the mind of the galaxy] for this purpose.[658]

This binary system model also explained a quote I read in session 9—really for the first time. Now, based on everything we've discussed, this should make a lot more sense:

9.4 Questioner: The way I understand the process of evolution [of a] planetary population is that [a] population has a certain amount of time to progress. This is generally divided into three 25,000-year cycles. At the end of 75,000 years the planet progresses itself. What caused this situation to come about . . . [with the] preciseness of the years, 25,000 years, et cetera. What set this up to begin with?

Ra: . . . Visualize, if you will, the particular energy which, outward flowing and inward coagulating, formed the tiny realm of the creation governed by your Council of Saturn [i.e., your solar system]. Continue seeing the rhythm of this process. The living flow creates a rhythm which is as inevitable as one of your timepieces. Each of your planetary entities began the first cycle when the energy nexus was able in that environment to support such mind/body experiences. Thus, each of your planetary entities is on a different cyclical schedule, as you might call it. The timing of these cycles is a measurement equal to a portion of intelligent energy. This intelligent energy offers a type of clock. The cycles move as precisely as a clock strikes your hour. Thus, the gateway from intelligent energy to intelligent infinity opens, regardless of circumstance, on the striking of the hour.[659]

According to the Law of One series, as we move through this transitional point, we pass through "the gateway to intelligent infinity." For that moment, however brief it may appear to be in physical terms, we shift back to the primordial essence of mind that created the universe before there was physical matter. While I was on sabbatical in Canada, another quote jumped out at me—clearly suggesting that this process is not an instantaneous "cosmic light switch."

> 14.16 Questioner: There was no harvest [50,000 years ago on earth]? What about 25,000 years ago? Was there a harvest then?
>
> Ra: . . . A harvesting began taking place in the latter portion, as you measure time/space, of the second cycle, with individuals finding the gateway to intelligent infinity.[660]

Here, the source said that a "harvesting began taking place in the latter portion . . . of the second cycle." This clearly implies something that does not happen all in one moment. Notice it also said that "individuals [were] finding the gateway to intelligent infinity." This means not everyone finds the gateway at the same time. Perhaps now that we've passed December 21, 2012, if you do the work, you will be able to get results. These results are apparently the same as what happened in the 160,000 cases of Rainbow Body documented in Tibet and China.

The Transition Will Be Gradual

The Law of One series is so complex that it can take years to work through it. In September 2012, I started re-reading it for the first time in several years. I didn't work my way up to session 63 until I was finishing this book in March 2013. I then found a quote that had eluded me up until that moment—but which added significant new insights into what exactly is expected to happen, and when. This new discovery cleared up quite a bit for me, and it suggested that we will go through a transition that is significantly more gradual than I had originally envisioned.

> 63.25 Questioner: Then at some time in the future the fourth-density sphere will be fully activated. What is the difference between full activation and partial activation for this sphere?

Ra: . . . At this time the cosmic influxes are conducive to true-color green core particles being formed and material of this nature thus being formed. However, there is a mixture of the yellow-ray and green-ray environments at this time necessitating the birthing of transitional mind/body/spirit complex types of energy distortions. At full activation of the true-color green density of love the planetary sphere will be solid and inhabitable upon its own and the birthing that takes place will have been transformed through the process of time, shall we say, to the appropriate type of vehicle to appreciate in full the fourth-density planetary environment. At this nexus the green-ray environment exists to a far greater extent in time/space than in space/time.[661]

63.27 Questioner: I will make this statement and have you correct me. What we have is, as our planet is spiraled by the spiraling action of the entire major galaxy and our planetary system spirals into the new position, the fourth-density vibrations becoming more and more pronounced. These atomic core vibrations begin to create, more and more completely, the fourth-density sphere and the fourth-density bodily complexes for inhabitation of that sphere. Is this correct?

Ra: I am Ra. This is partially correct. To be corrected is the concept of the creation of green-ray density bodily complexes. This creation will be gradual and will take place beginning with your third-density type of physical vehicle and, through the means of bisexual reproduction, become by evolutionary processes, the fourth-density body complexes.[662]

63.28 Questioner: Then are these entities of whom we have spoken, the third-density harvestable who have been transferred, the ones who then will, by bisexual reproduction, create the fourth-density complexes that are necessary?

Ra: . . . The influxes of true-color green energy complexes will more and more create the conditions in which the atomic structure of cells of bodily complexes is that of the density of love. The mind/body/spirit complexes inhabiting these physical vehicles will be, and to some extent, are, those of whom you spoke and, as harvest is completed, the harvested entities of this planetary influence.

As we go back a bit further, we have a quote that clearly indicates we will live our lives, die natural deaths at whatever time is appropriate, and then reincarnate in fourth density. However, the real magic lies in the fact that if you can become "double bodied," you can start doing fourth-density magic tricks while you're still in your physical body.

63.12 Questioner: Approximately how many are here now who have come here from other planets who are third-density harvestable for fourth-density experience?

Ra: . . . This is a recent, shall we say, phenomenon and the number is not yet in excess of 35,000 entities.

63.13 Questioner: Now these entities incarnate into a third-density vibratory body. I am trying to understand how this transition takes place from third to fourth-density. I will take the example of one of these entities of which we are speaking who is now in a third-density body. He will grow older and then will it be necessary that he die from the third-density physical body and reincarnate in a fourth-density body for that transition?

Ra: . . . These entities are those incarnating with what you may call a double body in activation. It will be noted that the entities birthing these fourth-density entities experience a great feeling of, shall we say, the connection and the use of spiritual energies during pregnancy. This is due to the necessity for manifesting the double body. This transitional body is one which will be, shall we say, able to appreciate fourth-density vibratory complexes as the instreaming increases without the accompanying disruption of the third-density body. If a third-density entity were, shall we say, electrically aware of fourth-density in full, the third-density electrical fields would fail due to incompatibility. To answer your query about death, these entities will die according to third-density necessities.

63.14 Questioner: You are saying, then, that for the transition from third to fourth-density for one of the entities with doubly activated bodies, in order to make the transition the third-density body will go through the process of what we call death. Is this correct?

Ra: . . . The third and fourth, combination, density's body will die according to the necessity of third-density mind/body/spirit complex distortions. We may respond to the heart of your questioning by noting that the purpose of such combined activation of mind/body/spirit complexes is that such entities, to some extent, consciously are aware of those fourth-density understandings which third density is unable to remember due to the forgetting. Thus fourth-density experience may be begun with the added attraction, to an entity oriented towards service to others, of dwelling in a troubled third-density environment and offering its love and compassion.

63.15 Questioner: Would the purpose in transitioning to Earth prior to the complete changeover then be for the experience to be gained here before the harvesting process?

Ra: . . . This is correct. These entities are not Wanderers in the sense that this planetary sphere is their fourth-density home planet. However, the experience of this service is earned only by those harvested third-density entities which have demonstrated a great deal of orientation towards service to others. It is a privilege to be allowed this early an incarnation as there is much experiential catalyst in service to other-selves at this harvesting.[663]

Specific Quotes on the Quantum Leap

Here is the first quote that specifically mentions a quantum leap or a
quantum jump that is expected to occur. This will create enough of a
transition from third to fourth density that people may begin having the
capacity to become "double bodied" in much greater numbers after this
timeframe.

> 40.10 Questioner: I am assuming that this vibratory in-
> crease [into fourth density] began about twenty to thirty
> years ago [as of January 1981]. Is this correct?
>
> Ra: . . . The first harbingers of this were approximately
> forty-five of your years ago [1936], the energies vibrating more
> intensely through the forty-year period preceding the final
> movement of vibratory matter, shall we say, through the
> quantum leap, as you would call it.

> 40.11 Questioner: Starting then, forty-five years ago, and
> taking the entire increase of vibration that we will experience
> in this density change, approximately what percentage through
> this increase in vibrational change are we right now?
>
> Ra: . . . The vibratory nature of your environment is true
> color, green. This is at this time heavily over-woven with the
> orange ray of planetary consciousness. However, the nature
> of quanta is such that the movement over the boundary is
> that of discrete placement of vibratory level.[664]

In case you didn't catch it, the Law of One clearly predicts a "final movement of vibratory matter . . . through [a] quantum leap," in our own
present time. Its also says that "the movement over the boundary is that
of discrete placement of vibratory level." The dictionary definition of
"discrete" is "apart or detached from others; separate; distinct."[665] Therefore, this new vibratory level is a "separate and distinct" realm that is

"apart or detached from [the] others"—including third density. We do see in session 40 that the basic nature of matter, energy, and consciousness goes through a quantum shift when this "harvest" event finally happens:

> 40.5 Questioner: Thank you. Taking as an example the transition between second and third-density, when this transition takes place, does the frequency of vibration which forms the photon (the core of all the particles of the density) increase? [Does the vibration change] from a frequency corresponding to second density, or the color orange, to the frequency that we measure as the color yellow? What I am getting at is, do all the vibrations that form the density, the basic vibrations of the photon, increase in a quantum fashion over a relatively short period of time?
>
> Ra: . . . This is correct.[666]

Fourth-Density Quantum Differences

In Law of One terms, the "fourth density" state of existence has key, quantum differences from our own, in the most basic nature of our existence. This is expressed in session 16:

> 16.50 Questioner: Is it possible for you to give a small description of the conditions [in] fourth density?
>
> Ra: . . . We ask you to consider as we speak that there are no words for positively describing fourth density. We can only explain what is not and approximate what is. Beyond fourth density our ability grows more limited still—until we become without words. That which fourth density is not: it is not of words, unless chosen. It is not of heavy chemical vehicles for body complex activities. It is not of disharmony within self. It is not of disharmony within peoples. It is not within limits of possibility to cause disharmony in any way.[667]

"It is not of words, unless chosen." We will have telepathic powers that are so strong, and so fast, that speaking with our mouths is ridiculously slow. In most cases, it would also be pointless to speak this way, like going back to dial-up Internet access in the modern era of broadband. "It is not of heavy chemical vehicles for body complex activities." We now have achieved the Rainbow Body—just as we saw in over 160,000 documented cases in Tibet and China. Once we fully reincarnate into fourth density, we no longer have a flesh-and-blood body—in other words, a "heavy chemical vehicle for [the] body complex." "It is not within limits of possibility to cause disharmony in any way." Think about what this means. It is literally impossible to create anger, stress, pressure, frustration, disappointment, or humiliation—for yourself or anyone else. It is impossible to lie, cheat, steal, disrespect, badger, bully, annoy, or dishonor anyone. Everyone knows everything you are thinking—at all times.

In session 20, we get an exact estimate of how much more enjoyable it is to live in fourth density than in our current third-density level. The source specifically states that fourth density is "one hundred times more harmonious," as we see here.

> 20.24 The mind/body/spirit complex of third density has perhaps one hundred times as intensive a program of catalytic action from which to distill distortions and learn/teachings than any other of the densities.[668]

"Catalytic action" means events that cause us to grow spiritually. In Law of One terms, catalysts often appear in our lives as very difficult experiences. Many people who study spirituality would refer to this process as "burning off karma"—and it's essentially the same idea here. This means that even in fourth density—never mind fifth or sixth—life is one hundred times happier, easier, more pleasurable, and fulfilling than life in third density.

There are additional quotes in session 16 that tell us what fourth-density life is like. Now we will pick up at the exact point where we left off before:

16.50 Approximations of positive statements [for life in fourth density]: It is a plane of a type of bipedal vehicle [in other words, a two-legged body] which is much denser and more full of life; it is a plane wherein one is aware of the thoughts of other-selves; it is a plane where one is aware of the vibrations of other-selves; it is a plane of compassion and understanding of the sorrows of third density; it is a plane striving towards wisdom or light; it is a plane wherein individual differences are pronounced, although automatically harmonized by group consensus.[669]

We are still well within an acceptable window where this "quantum jump" could happen, but now there is no absolute date for us to obsess on. The closest we have to a timeline is the statement we read earlier, indicating that it would be "approximately 30 years" after 1981.

However, the source did not say "thirty-five years"—it said "approximately" thirty years. Therefore, anything much past thirty-three years from 1981 would probably have caused the source to lean toward a figure of thirty-five years instead of thirty. In some ways I am relieved that we have now passed a hurdle where there is no absolute date for us to argue over. I do believe some very significant and wonderful events are set to occur between now and whenever this shift finally happens.

It Is Difficult, If Not Impossible, to Pinpoint an Exact Time

The source also said it was very difficult to pin down exact times for certain events with precision. There are factors that influence the outcome and that are governed to a certain degree by random acts of free will. Here are some quotes where the source describes this:

89.8 Our intervening space/time has been experienced in a manner quite unlike your third-density experience of space/time.[670]

14.4 . . . We are not totally able to process your space/time continuum measurement system.[671]

65.9 The value of prophecy must be realized to be only that of expressing possibilities. Moreover, it must be, in our humble opinion, carefully taken into consideration that any time/ . space viewing, whether by one of your time/space or by one such as we, who view the time/space from a dimension, shall we say, exterior to it, will have a quite difficult time expressing time measurement values. Thus, prophecy given in specific terms is more interesting for the content or type of possibility predicted than for the space/time nexus of its supposed occurrence.[672]

17.29 Questioner: Am I to understand that the harvest will occur in the year 2011, or will it be spread?

Ra: . . . This is an approximation. We have stated we have difficulty with your time/space. This is an appropriate probable/possible time/space nexus for harvest. Those who are not in incarnation at this time will be included in the harvest.[673]

Still Well Within the Window

At the time of this writing in April 2013, we are still well within the window of "approximately 30 years." The gradual transition into the "double-bodied" state, where we have a fourth-density body available to us while still in our third-density form, does now appear to be under way. If this prophecy is true, then we can expect to see ever-increasingly powerful capabilities appearing in ordinary people. This may very well correspond with the final vanquishing of the nemesis on the global stage—and the access to the Elixir of Immortality that it has been guarding all along. This includes advanced technology that can heal our planet, as well as the absolute knowledge that we are not alone. Reconnecting with our human relatives may be a very important part of this transitional process.

The Harvest

The Law of One series specifically indicated that this marvelous event was called "harvest." Only recently did I realize that they were directly quoting from the book of Matthew. This describes a moment in time where the wicked are literally pulled into an alternate timeline—a different reality—from everyone else. Jesus used symbolism to explain this. Humans on earth, in the spiritual sense, were compared to a field of wheat that has been planted. The seeds are the spiritual teachings that are given to us by Jesus and other great masters. These spiritual teachings, if from the positive path, invariably tell us to be more loving, accepting, and forgiving of others—to realize that we are all one. Humility, patience, kindness, charity, being a good listener, and believing in and supporting the innate goodness of others—regardless of who they may be—are all key aspects of these teachings. Very few people in our modern world seem to realize that the further you go in this direction, the more likely you are to ascend and literally transform into the next level of human evolution.

However, we also have "the adversary," who plants weeds, or "tares," in the crop. These are also teachings that are made available to everyone. Our society is bursting with them. These teachings center on pursuing material things—money, power, fame, and prestige. They create, foster, and encourage narcissism, entitlement, rudeness, dominant behavior, and self-aggrandizement. Everything is built around a hierarchy. Power must not be questioned. The will of the few is imposed upon the many. We are all taught to fear "Big Brother." We know, deep inside, that seriously corrupt forces exist. We are also taught to believe they are indestructible, and our best bet is to ignore them and accept their unchanging reality in our lives. Until the rise of Internet streaming video, most people's lives were utterly dominated by corporate propaganda from watching television. We were bombarded by advertisements and taught that we had to suffer this propaganda in order to enjoy our lives. Now, all of that is changing. Each of us has the choice to focus on positive, loving material and avoid re-creating the cycles of torture and pain that have plagued us for so long.

What About the Second Coming of Christ?

Obviously, scholars of the Bible will see huge parallels with everything I'm saying here and the concept of the Second Coming of Christ. This was directly explained in the Law of One series, as follows:

> 17.22 Questioner: In our culture there is a great saying that he [Jesus] will return. Can you tell me if this is planned?
> Ra: . . . I will attempt to sort out this question. It is difficult. This entity became aware that it was not an entity of itself but operated as a messenger of the One Creator—whom this entity saw as love. This entity was aware that this cycle was in its last portion—and spoke to the effect that those of its consciousness would return at the harvest. The particular mind/body/spirit complex you call Jesus is, as what you would call an entity, not to return—except as a member of the Confederation occasionally speaking through a channel. However, there are others of the identical congruency of consciousness that will welcome those to the fourth density. This is the meaning of the returning.[674]

This clearly implies that part of our transitional process into becoming "double-bodied," with a fourth-density activation while still in a human form, does involve disclosure, when we fully realize we are not alone. Although there have been many efforts to make the public afraid of extraterrestrial life, once we realize these people are human—and that they have been helping us all along—this could be a powerful influence to enable a much greater awakening to take place. Once we find out that the world we were taught to believe in by the media was fake, it will be an unprecedented transformation. History will change so much that it is almost impossible to predict what it will look like until we actually get there. Hardly any of the pioneers in the Truth Movement have delved into the scientific knowledge that has been suppressed as I did in *The Source Field Investigations*. Until we defeat financial tyranny—or at the very least strike a truce where the Cabal allows the truth to be exposed—this information will probably never be able to reach a widespread level. The patriotic elements of the US military cannot step forward and reveal that they have had ongoing diplomatic relationships with a wide variety of extraterrestrials, as well as star gates and antigravity spacecraft.

Fourth-Density Life

Our ultimate destination in this process appears to be that we are reborn into an entirely new plane of existence. Highly advanced souls are able to spontaneously transform themselves into this state without having to undergo physical death and reincarnation. In Christian terms, this is called ascension—and I often use that same word to describe it, though I do not associate the term with any religion. There are more than 160,000 documented cases of this happening in Tibet and China alone, in which advanced masters achieved the state they called the Rainbow Body. This legend appears in many traditional cultures, as this next quote from William Henry and Mark Gray reveals:

> In Sufism it is called "the most sacred body" and the "supracelestial body." Taoists call it "the diamond body," and those who have attained it are called "the immortals" and "the cloudwalkers." Yogic schools and Tantrics call it "the divine body." In Kriya yoga it is called "the body of bliss." In Vedanta it is called "the superconductive body." The ancient Egyptians called it "the luminous body or being" *(akh)* or the *karast*. This conception evolved into Gnosticism, where it is called "the radiant body." In the Mithraic liturgy it was called "the perfect body.". . . In the Hermetic Corpus, it is called "the immortal body." In the alchemical tradition, the Emerald Tablet calls it "the golden body."[675]

De-Fanging the Vampire

Governments often rise and fall as a result of how well they can manipulate our deep-seated fears that God has abandoned us and trick us into believing we are in a grand struggle against a fearsome nemesis. They may even secretly own and control that same nemesis to ensure that they win—regardless of the outcome. The elected leaders, even at the highest levels, may at times be completely unaware that this is happening. The people may end up being terrified that their "side" is not winning, rather than realizing that there is no side. We are all children of an infinite intelligence that created the entire universe and all life within it—and loves us more than we could ever possibly imagine. My own spiritual journey led me to the direct knowing that this is true . . . and you can reach a place of stillness in yourself when it becomes obvious.

When those around us are suffering, we are suffering—and when those around us are in a state of love and peace, we feel love and peace. When the seven thousand people who meditated and made worldwide terrorist activity go down by 72 percent were creating positive energy, the energy they created didn't say, "Wait a minute. That person is a liberal. That person is a Muslim. That person is gay. That person is black. Don't go over there. Just skip that one!" Not at all. The reality is that everyone gets better. Nearly three out of four potential terrorists in the world decided not to pick up that gun, detonate that bomb, or kill that child.

The Qur'an Has Very Similar Passages

Westerners in the Judeo-Christian tradition have been barraged with media propaganda suggesting that the Qur'an, the sacred scripture of Islam, is a handbook for evil and a hotbed breeding-ground for terrorism. While I do not agree with everything in the Qur'an, just as is the case with all other religious scriptures, there are some very interesting passages in it that heavily support everything we've been talking about. These excerpts are from Lex Hixon's English translations in *The Heart of the Qur'an,* which was first published in 1988. While they are not strictly literal, word-for-word translations, Hixon does his best to convey the core of the teachings. I was quite surprised when a reader sent me this book with certain passages highlighted, as these and other passages were essentially saying many of the same things we see in the Law of One series. The Qur'an strongly suggests that some form of worldwide energetic event will occur as we go through this transitional process. This only adds to the adventure—and reminds me that we probably will never know exactly what will happen until it actually does.

> There exists only one Supreme Source, one inexhaustible Power . . . the profoundly living One, the Life beyond time that never diminishes. The One Reality never sleeps, nor even for a moment rests Its embracing Awareness. To the One alone belongs the emanation of planetary existence and the seven higher planes of Being, as spreading rays of sunlight belong to a single sun. There is no being who can turn toward the Ever-Present Source in prayer or contemplation except through the Power and love that flow from the Source Itself. Since the Ultimate Source abides beyond time, It always remains perfectly aware of what causes precede and what results follow from each event.—Meditation on Holy Qur'an 2:255[676]

> You must come to know with absolute certitude that from above your conscious being, as stars above the earth, there gaze angelic protectors. . . . Upon pages of light in the invisible book of your life, which will become visible on the Day of Truth, these heavenly beings record all your actions and reactions. Even the most secret motivations they perceive and transcribe with perfect clarity.—Meditation on Holy Qur'an 82:10–12[677]

When time suddenly disappears, in the eternal moment of illumination the brightness of the heavenly orbs will be split open and dissolved into transparent light. . . . Those who fail to live in constant expectation of the mystic Day, regarding this teaching as myth or imagination, will be severely disappointed when the Last Day actually arrives and they are not spiritually prepared.—Meditation on Holy Qur'an 77:8, 15[678]

Upon the mysterious Day when time ends, all manifest Being will tremble at the first thundering blast of Divine Resonance that will utterly stop the world. . . . This momentary terror will disappear when each soul realizes its spiritual body to be perfect, limitless and holy.—Meditation on Holy Qur'an 79:6, 13[679]

When the Day of Enlightenment dawns, the soul, expressed as a luminous body, the face of its being suffused with calm joy, awakens into the supernal garden of Divine Presence, overwhelmed to comprehend at last the full significance of its own spiritual commitment.—Meditation on Holy Qur'an 88:1–5[680]

On that timeless and transcendent Day, human beings will experience resurrection in bodies composed of light, and will be shown clearly all the thoughts and actions of their lifetimes.—Meditation on Holy Qur'an 99:4[681]

How few human beings understand the intensity and magnitude of the swiftly approaching Day of Clarification. Those who do not really comprehend the nature of the Last Day are impatient and would like to speed its arrival, whereas those who know the immense power of the Living Truth stand in trembling awe before the dawning of this infinite Day.—Meditation on Holy Qur'an 42:7[682]

This note comes from the editor of the book—and emphasizes the positive aspects of these teachings that are so often misunderstood or overlooked in the Western world.

> The Qur'an repeatedly emphasizes living a life of modesty, gratitude, honesty, justice, compassion, and love. More than any outward signs of piety, it sees these qualities as identifying . . . the person surrendered to the One Reality. . . . Ultimately, the "Lovers of Love" described by the Qur'an are those who become their own miracles of compassion and peace, whether they come to public attention in the world or not.—Editor[683]

Lastly, this message in the Qur'an is surprisingly open and honest, in showing that ultimately all of us have the choice to follow whatever spiritual teachings we prefer . . . and there are many ways back to the One.

> If each spiritual nation practices faithfully the path revealed through its own Holy Prophets, then all humanity will return together to the Source of Love.—Meditation on Holy Qur'an 5:51[684]

Looking to the Future

It is a great honor and privilege to have re-discovered this ancient science—and a huge relief to have finally put it all together into a full-length book. I knew a great deal of "homework" would be involved in creating a definitive, up-to-date work on the cycles of history, and there certainly was. It took me about three and a half years of research, meditation, lecturing and writing about these concepts to get here. This work is obviously controversial, and plenty of people have attacked and criticized my efforts in the past. I continue to do the best I can, knowing in advance that nothing is perfect, and there will always be critics out there. I can listen to a marvelous jazz ensemble performing a piece that I feel to be dazzlingly technical and beautiful, only to have others tell me they "absolutely hate jazz" and refuse to listen to it. Similarly, I have detailed exactly what I'm seeing in this book, and how I feel all these pieces fit together. I genuinely enjoyed the process, and have created something that I now feel very proud of. Undoubtedly, some people will feel that it is very inspiring and meaningful, while others will attack it with astonishing savagery and mockery.

I do feel that our investigation of the cycles of history is still in its infancy. There are many, many more avenues to explore. I could easily write another full-length book that explains all the technical details of how these cycles may actually be working, including the evidence that we live in a binary solar system. There is much more to be said about how the geometry may be helping to push the cycles along. I did have a dream in January 2013 suggesting that I think of this as a trilogy, and not to attempt to answer every technical question in this volume. *The Source Field Investigations* has many of the pieces that are needed to construct this grand model, but the real art lies in how we weave them together.

This is certainly not a book for everyone. Some people will have encountered so much psychological resistance in reading it that they probably never made it very far. Volumes of scientific evidence are only useful when we are willing to look at them. At the time of this writing, much of this information would still be considered "fringe" and "pseudoscience." Synchronicity is ultimately a personal experience—and it can be quite elusive for those who refuse to believe it is possible. Very interesting personal and global events are often dismissed by skeptics as being utterly irrelevant. The voice of the collective, as expressed in mainstream media, can be extremely compelling for many people. Shame can be a very powerful deterrent from the quest for deeper meaning and truth. There are tools available, such as hypnotic regression, that can help awaken you to the greater reality I have outlined in this book—but without that initial desire to seek the truth, these keys will probably never be used or appreciated.

Our transition into a Golden Age may continue to be a gradual process, but at some point we may very well step back and marvel at how much has happened in such a short time. Even though history may very well be repeating itself, we still have choices to make. We are not on a fixed timeline. We are not destined to experience a single outcome. We can change the story. The universe may very well be a living being—encouraging us to grow and evolve into our truest identity. Synchronicity is the key that unlocks the greatest mystery of all time.

Acknowledgments

I would like to thank the living universe, and its emissaries, for the gift of life and consciousness, and the guidance to help us remember who we really are. I would like to thank my mother, Marta Waterman; my father, Don Wilcock; and my brother, Michael Wilcock, for giving me a stable and loving family environment that helped me develop into who I am today. I also want to thank the many friends, teachers, coworkers, and colleagues I have interacted and collaborated with over the years. I owe a special debt of gratitude to the pioneering researchers and scientists who made this book possible, including Don Elkins, Carla Rueckert, and Jim McCarty, who produced the Law of One series, as well as Pete Peterson and other insiders I have had the privilege of working with. I want to thank Brian Tart, Stephanie Kelly, and the staff at Penguin for helping make this book possible, the folks at Brilliance Audio, and Tom Denney for his impressive illustration work on a strict deadline.

I want to thank Jim Hart and Amanda Welles for their consistency and support in developing the *Convergence* screenplay with me throughout this entire writing process, and my webmaster and colleague Larry Seyer for his incredible dedication to this work and his musical genius on display in *The Science of Peace* and *Wanderer Awakening,* our flagship products. I want to thank the staff at Gaiam TV for giving me an outlet to develop the philosophical teachings of the Law of One material into a fully realized television series, the staff at Prometheus Entertainment for featuring me in so many *Ancient Aliens* episodes, and the staff at REN-TV in Russia for developing six hours' worth of documentaries out of my online ebook *Financial Tyranny,* and asking me to star in them.

I also want to thank my female life partner for putting up with the incredible anxiety and stress I went through in the three and a half years it took me to develop this book. Lastly I want to thank you, the loyal reader of this book. This was easily the most difficult task I have ever taken on, and without your help, it would never have been possible. Publicity is protection—and your ongoing interest is a major part of what has kept me safe and supported on this great quest.

Notes

Chapter One

1. Don Elkins, Carla Rueckert, and Jim McCarty, *The Law of One* (West Chester, PA: Whitford Press, 1984), session 17, question 33, http://lawofone.info/results.php?s=17#33.

2. Ibid., session 19, question 18, http://lawofone.info/results.php?s=19#18.

3. François Masson, "Cyclology: The Mathematics of History," chapter 6 in *The End of Our Century,* 1979, http://divinecosmos.com/index.php/start-here/books-free-online/26-the -end-of-our-century/145-chapter-06-cyclology-the-mathematics-of-history.

4. *The Free Dictionary by Farlex,* "Morozov, Nikolai Aleksandrovich," originally published in *The Great Soviet Encyclopedia,* 3rd ed. (1970–1979) (Farmington Hills, MI: Gale Group, 2010), http://encyclopedia2.thefreedictionary.com/Nikolai+Morozov.

5. Charles Q. Choi, "DNA Molecules Display Telepathy-Like Quality," LiveScience, January 24, 2008, accessed May 2010, http://www.livescience.com/9546-dna-molecules -display-telepathyquality.html.

6. John E. Dunn, "DNA Molecules Can 'Teleport,' Nobel Prize Winner Claims," Techworld.com, January 13, 2011, accessed January 2011, http://news.techworld.com/personal -tech/3256631/dna-molecules-can-teleport-nobel-prize-winner-claims/.

7. F. Hoyle, "Is the Universe Fundamentally Biological?" in *New Ideas in Astronomy,* ed. F. Bertola et al. (New York: Cambridge University Press, 1988), pp. 5–8; Suburban Emergency Management Project, *Interstellar Dust Grains as Freeze-Dried Bacterial Cells: Hoyle and Wickramasinghe's Fantastic Journey,* Biot Report #455, August 22, 2007, accessed May 2010, http://web.archive.org/web/20091112134144/http://www.semp.us/publications /biot_reader.php?BiotID=455.

8. Ibid.

9. Brandon Keim, "Howard Hughes' Nightmare: Space May Be Filled with Germs," *Wired,* August 6, 2008, http://www.wired.com/science/space/news/2008/08/galactic_panspermia.

10. James K. Fredrickson and Tullis C. Onstott, "Microbes Deep Inside the Earth," *Scientific American,* October 1996, accessed May 2010, http://web.archive.org/web/20011216021826/ www.sciam.com/1096issue/1096onstott.html.

11. Lynne McTaggart, *The Field: The Quest for the Secret Force of the Universe* (New York: HarperCollins, 2002), p. 44.

12. P. P. Gariaev, M. J. Friedman, and E. A. Leonova-Gariaeva, "Crisis in Life Sciences: The Wave Genetics Response," EmergentMind.org, 2007, http://www.emergentmind .org/gariaev06.htm.

13. Ibid.

14. David Wilcock, "A Golden Age May Be Just Around the Corner," *Huffington Post,* August 22, 2011, http://www.huffingtonpost.com/david-wilcock/ufos-government_b_33641 .html#s336273&title=What_is_consciousness.

15. "William Braud," faculty profile, Sofia University, accessed December 2010, http://www .sofia.edu/academics/faculty/braud.php; "Curriculum Vitae, William G. Braud, Ph.D., " Sofia University, accessed April 2013, http://www.sofia.edu/academics/faculty/cv /WBraud_cv.pdf.

16. M. Schlitz and S. LaBerge, "Autonomic Detection of Remote Observation: Two Conceptual Replications," in *Proceedings of the Parapsychological Association 37th Annual Convention,* ed. D. J. Bierman (Fairhaven, MA: Parapsychological Association, 1994), pp. 465–478.

17. Malcolm Gladwell, "In the Air: Who Says Big Ideas Are Rare?" *The New Yorker,* May 12, 2008, accessed December 2010, http://www.newyorker.com/reporting/2008/05/12 /080512fa_fact_gladwell?currentPage=all.

18. Dunn, "DNA Molecules Can 'Teleport.'"

19. Hoyle, "Is the Universe Fundamentally Biological?"

20. Ibid.

21. Grazyna Fosar and Franz Bludorf, "The Living Internet (Part 2)," April 2002, accessed May 2010, http://web.archive.org/web/20030701194920/http://www.baerbelmohr.de /english/magazin/beitraege/hyper2.htm.

22. Ibid.

23. Leonardo Vintiñi, "The Strange Inventions of Pier L. Ighina," *Epoch Times,* September 25–October 1, 2008, p. B6, accessed June 2010, http://epoch-archive.com/a1/en/us/bos /2008/09-Sep/25/B6.pdf.

24. Yu V. Dzang Kangeng "Bioelectromagnetic Fields as a Material Carrier of Biogenetic Information, *Aura-Z,* 1993, no. 3, pp. 42–54.

25. Baerbel-Mohr, *DNA,* summary of the book *Vernetzte Intelligenz* by Grazyna Fosar and Franz Bludorf (Aachen, Germany: Omega-Verlag, 2001), http://web.archive.org/web /20030407171420/http://home.planet.nl/~holtj019/GB/DNA.html.

26. Gary Lynch and Richard Granger, "What Happened to the Hominids Who May Have Been Smarter Than Us?" *Discover,* December 28, 2009, http://discovermagazine.com /2009/the-brain-2/28-what-happened-to-hominids-who-were-smarter-than-us.

27. David M. Raup and J. John Sepkoski Jr., "Periodicity of Extinctions in the Geologic Past," *Proceedings of the National Academy of Sciences of the United States of America* 81 (February 1984): 801–805, http://www.pnas.org/content/81/3/801.full.pdf.

28. Robert A. Rohde and Richard A. Muller, "Cycles in Fossil Diversity," *Nature* 434, March 10, 2005, http://muller.lbl.gov/papers/Rohde-Muller-Nature.pdf.

29. Casey Kazan, "Is There a Milky Way Galaxy/Earth Biodiversity Link? Experts Say 'Yes,'" *Daily Galaxy,* May 15, 2009, accessed May 2010, http://www.dailygalaxy.com/my _weblog/2009/05/hubbles-secret.html.

30. Dava Sobel, "Man Stops Universe, Maybe," *Discover,* April 1993, http://discovermagazine .com/1993/apr/manstopsuniverse206; W. Godlowski, K. Bajan, and P. Flin, "Weak Redshift Discretization in the Local Group of Galaxies?" abstract, *Astronomische Nachrichten* 327, no. 1, January 2006, pp. 103–113, http://www3.interscience.wiley.com/journal /112234726/abstract?CRETRY=1&SRETRY=0; M. B. Bell and S. P. Comeau, "Further

Evidence for Quantized Intrinsic Redshifts in Galaxies: Is the Great Attractor a Myth?" abstract, May 7, 2003, http://arxiv.org/abs/astro-ph/0305112; W. M. Napier and B. N. G. Guthrie, "Quantized Redshifts: A Status Report," abstract, *Journal of Astrophysics and Astronomy* 18, no. 4 (December 1997), http://www.springerlink.com/content /qk27v4wx16412245/.

31. Harold Aspden, "Tutorial Note 10: Tifft's Discovery," EnergyScience.org.uk, 1997, http: //web.archive.org/web/20041126005134/http://www.energyscience.org.uk/tu/tu10.htm.

Chapter Two

32. Don Elkins, Carla Rueckert, and Jim McCarty, *The Law of One* (West Chester, PA: Whitford Press, 1984), http://lawofone.info/.

33. Richard N. Ostling, "Researcher Tabulates World's Believers," *Salt Lake Tribune,* May 19, 2001, http://www.adherents.com/misc/WCE.html.

34. Elkins, Rueckert, and McCarty, *The Law of One,* session 1, question 6, http://lawofone .info/results.php?s=1#6.

35. *Journal of Offender Rehabilitation* 36, nos. 1–4 (2003): 283–302, http://www.tandfonline .com/toc/wjor20/36/1-4#.UYbiUoKfLbs.

36. D. Orme-Johnson, "The Science of World Peace: Research Shows Meditation Is Effective," *International Journal of Healing and Caring On-Line* 3, no. 3 (September 1993): 2.

37. S. J. P. Spottiswoode, "Apparent Association Between Anomalous Cognition Experiments and Local Sidereal Time," *Journal of Scientific Exploration* 11 (2), summer (1997): 109–122.

38. Elkins, Rueckert, and McCarty, *The Law of One,* session 19, question 9, http://lawofone .info/results.php?s=19#9.

39. Ibid., session 19, question 10, http://lawofone.info/results.php?s=19#10.

40. Robert H. Van Gent, "Isaac Newton and Astrology: Witness for the Defence or for the Prosecution?" Utrecht University website, August 3, 2007, http://www.staff.science.uu .nl/~gent0113/astrology/newton.htm.

41. John D. McGervey, *Probabilities in Everyday Life* (New York: Random House, 1989).

42. Julia Parker and Derek Parker, *The Parkers' History of Astrology,* vol. 11, *Into the Twentieth Century* (1983). http://web.archive.org/web/20020804232049/http://www.astrology.com /inttwe.html.

43. Ibid.

44. Carl G. Jung, "Richard Wilhelm: In Memoriam," in *The Spirit in Man, Art, and Literature, Collected Works,* vol. 15, trans. R. F. C. Hull (London: Routledge and Kegan Paul, 1971), p. 56.

45. Arnold Lieber, "Human Aggression and the Lunar Synodic Cycle," abstract, *Journal of Clinical Psychiatry* 39, no. 5 (1978): 385–392, http://www.ncbi.nlm.nih.gov/pubmed/641019.

46. Joe Mahr, "Analysis Shines Light on Full Moon, Crime: Offenses Increase by 5 Percent in Toledo," *Toledo Blade,* August 25, 2002, http://web.archive.org/web/20110104072606 /http://www.toledoblade.com/apps/pbcs.dll/article?Date=20020825&Category =NEWS03&ArtNo=108250070&Ref=AR.

47. Ibid.

48. Fred Attewill, "Police Link Full Moon to Aggression," *Guardian* (London), June 5, 2007, http://www.guardian.co.uk/uk/2007/jun/05/ukcrime.

49. Ibid.

50. Bette Denlinger, "Michel Gauquelin: 1928–1991," Solstice Point, http://www.solstice point.com/astrologersmemorial/gauquelin.html.

51. Ken Irving, "Misunderstandings, Misrepresentations, Frequently Asked Questions & Frequently Voiced Objections About the Gauquelin Planetary Effects," *Planetos* online journal, http://www.planetos.info/mmf.html.

52. Ibid.

53. Ibid.

54. Ibid.

55. Ibid.

56. Ibid.

57. Suitbert Ertel and Kenneth Irving, *The Tenacious Mars Effect* (London: Urania Trust, 1996); Robert Currey, "Empirical Astrology: Why It Is No Longer Acceptable to Say Astrology Is Rubbish on a Scientific Basis," Astrologer.com, 2010, http://www.astrologer .com/tests/basisofastrology.htm.

58. Currey, "Empirical Astrology."

59. Carol Moore, "Sunspot Cycles and Activist Strategy," CarolMoore.net, February 2010, http://www.carolmoore.net/articles/sunspot-cycle.html.

60. Giorgio De Santillana and Hertha von Dechend, *Hamlet's Mill: An Essay Investigating the Origins of Human Knowledge and Its Transmission Through Myth*, 8th ed. (Boston: David R. Godine, 2007).

61. Graham Hancock, *Fingerprints of the Gods* (New York: Three Rivers Press, 1996).

62. Simon Jenkins, "New Evidence on the Role of Climate in Neanderthal Extinction," EurekAlert!, September 12, 2007, http://www.eurekalert.org/pub_releases/2007-09 /uol-neo091107.php.

63. LiveScience Staff, "Humans Ate Fish 40,000 Years Ago," LiveScience, July 7, 2009, http://www.livescience.com/history/090707-fish-human-diet.html.

64. Robert Roy Britt, "Oldest Human Skulls Suggest Low-Brow Culture," LiveScience, February 16, 2005, http://www.livescience.com/health/050216_oldest_humans.html; James Lewis, "On Religion, Hitchens Is Not So Great," American Thinker, July 15, 2007, http:// www.americanthinker.com/2007/07/on_religion_hitchens_is_not_so_1.html.

65. Peter Ward, "The Father of All Mass Extinctions," *Conservation* 5, no. 3 (2004), http:// www.conservationmagazine.org/articles/v5n3/the-father-of-all-mass-extinctions/.

66. Abraham Lincoln, "Emancipation Proclamation," January 1, 1863, U.S. National Park Service, http://www.nps.gov/ncro/anti/emancipation.html.

67. John F. Kennedy Presidential Library and Museum, "Report to the American People on Civil Rights, 11 June 1963," http://www.jfklibrary.org/Asset-Viewer/LH8F_oMzvoe 6RoiyEm74Ng.aspx.

68. Martin Luther King Jr., "I Have a Dream," August 28, 1963, ABC News, http://abcnews .go.com/Politics/martin-luther-kings-speech-dream-full-text/story?id=14358231.

69. RonPaul.com, "Audit the Federal Reserve," 2009/2010 version, http://www.ronpaul.com /misc/congress/legislation/111th-congress-200910/audit-the-federal-reserve-hr-1207/.

70. Ibid.

71. Melvin Sickler, "Abraham Lincoln and John F. Kennedy: Two Great Presidents of the United States, Assassinated for the Cause of Justice," Michael Journal, October–December 2003, http://www.michaeljournal.org/lincolnkennedy.htm.

72. H.R. Rep. No. 380, 50th Cong., 1st sess. (1888), in *Congressional Serial Set*, vol. 2, no. 2599 (Washington, DC: US GPO, 1888). http://books.google.com/books?id=x5wZAAAAY AAJ&printsec=frontcover&source=gbs_ge_summary_r&cad=0#v=onepage&q=E .%20D.%20Taylor&f=false.

73. Sickler, "Abraham Lincoln and John F. Kennedy."

74. Associated Press, "New Kennedy Silver Policy," *Southeast Missourian*, November 28, 1961, p. 8, http://news.google.com/newspapers?id=-q8fAAAAIBAJ&sjid=LdcEAAAAIBAJ& pg=2964,4612588; Richard E. Mooney, "Silver Sale by Treasury Ended; President Seeks Support Repeal, Kennedy Cuts Off US Silver Sales," *New York Times*, November 29, 1961,

p. 1, http://select.nytimes.com/gst/abstract.html?res=F70F1FFA3F5E147A93CBAB178AD95F458685F9.

75. "Silver Act Repeal Plan Wins House Approval," *New York Times,* April 11, 1963, http://select.nytimes.com/gst/abstract.html?res=FB0D16FE3B58137A93C3A8178FD85F478685F9; Associated Press, "House Passes Silver Bill by 251-122," *St. Petersburg Times,* April 11, 1963, p. 2A, http://news.google.com/newspapers?nid=feST4K8JoscC&dat=19630411&printsec=frontpage&hl=en.

76. "Senate Votes End to Silver Backing; Plan to Free Bullion Behind Dollar Goes to Kennedy," *New York Times,* May 24, 1963, http://select.nytimes.com/gst/abstract.html?res=F40F17F93E58137A93C6AB178ED85F478685F9; United Press International, "Senate Okays Replacement of Silver Notes," *Deseret News and Telegram,* May 23, 1963, p. 2A, http://news.google.com/newspapers?id=Z8NNAAAAIBAJ&sjid=ikkDAAAAIBAJ&pg=7119,5656491.

77. Exec. Order No. 11,110 at the American Presidency Project, http://www.presidency.ucsb.edu/ws/index.php?pid=59049.

78. Sickler, "Abraham Lincoln and John F. Kennedy."

79. Ibid.

80. Barbara Mikkelson and David P. Mikkelson, "Linkin' Kennedy," Snopes.com, http://www.snopes.com/history/american/lincoln-kennedy.asp.

81. Adam Jortner, *The Gods of Prophetstown: The Battle of Tippecanoe and the Holy War for the American Frontier* (New York: Oxford University Press, 2011).

82. John Brown Dillon, "Letters of William Henry Harrison," in *A History of Indiana* (Indianapolis: Bingham and Doughty, 1859).

83. *Ripley's Believe It or Not,* 2nd series (New York: Simon and Schuster, 1931); an updated reference is on page 140 of the Pocket Books paperback edition of 1948.

84. Randi Henderson and Tom Nugent, "The Zero Curse: More Than Just a Coincidence?" *Syracuse Herald-American,* November 2, 1980, p. C3 (reprinted from the *Baltimore Sun*).

Chapter Three

85. Richard Tarnas, *Cosmos and Psyche* (New York: Penguin, 2006), p. 50.

86. "Synchronicity," Dictionary.com, http://dictionary.reference.com/browse/synchronicity?s=t.

87. Ann Casement, "Who Owns Jung?" (London: Karnac Books, 2007), cf. p. 25, http://books.google.com/books?id=og8chpSOI3AC&printsec=frontcover.

88. Carl G. Jung, "Synchronicity: An Acausal Connecting Principle," *Collected Works of C. G. Jung, vol. 8: Structure and Dynamics of the Psyche,* (1952; repr., Princeton, NJ: Princeton University Press, 1970).

89. Wolfgang Pauli, "The Influence of Archetypal Ideas on the Scientific Theories of Kepler," in C. G. Jung and Wolfgang Pauli, *The Interpretation of Nature and the Psyche* (New York: Pantheon, 1955).

90. Carl G. Jung, "Synchronicity: An Acausal Connecting Principle," Ibid., para. 843.

91. George Gamow, *Thirty Years That Shook Physics—The Story of Quantum Theory* (New York: Doubleday, 1966), p. 64.

92. Charles P. Enz, *No Time to Be Brief: A Scientific Biography of Wolfgang Pauli* (New York: Oxford University Press, 2002), p. 152.

93. Pauli, "The Influence of Archetypal Ideas."

94. Kevin Williams, "Scientific Evidence Suggestive of Astrology," Near-Death.com, 2009, http://www.near-death.com/experiences/articles012.html.

95. Ibid.

96. Montague Ullman, Stanley Krippner, and Alan Vaughan. *Dream Telepathy: Experiments in Nocturnal Extrasensory Perception.* (1973: repr., Newburyport, MA: Hampton Roads Publishing, 2003).

97. David Wilcock, "Access Your Higher Self," Divine Cosmos, 2010, http://www.divine cosmos.com/index.php/appearances/online-convergence.

98. Don Elkins, Carla Rueckert, and Jim McCarty, *The Law of One* (West Chester, PA: Whitford Press, 1984), session 17, question 2, http://lawofone.info/results.php?s=17#2.

Chapter Four

99. Public Policy Polling. "Conspiracy Theory Poll Results." Raleigh, North Carolina, April 2, 2013, http://www.publicpolicypolling.com/main/2013/04/conspiracy-theory-poll -results-.html

100. David Wilcock and Benjamin Fulford, "Disclosure Imminent? Two Underground NWO Bases Destroyed," Divine Cosmos, September 14, 2011, http://divinecosmos.com/ start-here/davids-blog/975-undergroundbases; David Wilcock and Benjamin Fulford, "New Fulford Interview Transcript: Old World Order Nearing Defeat," Divine Cosmos, October 31, 2011, http://divinecosmos.com/start-here/davids-blog/988-fulford-owo -defeat.

101. Matt Taibbi, "Everything Is Rigged: The Biggest Price-Fixing Scandal Ever." *Rolling Stone*, April 25, 2013, http://www.rollingstone.com/politics/news/everything-is-rigged-the-biggest-financial-scandal-yet-20130425.

102. David Wilcock, "Financial Tyranny: Defeating the Greatest Cover-Up of All Time. Section Four: The Occult Economy," Divine Cosmos, January 13, 2012, http://www.divine cosmos.com/start-here/davids-blog/1023-financial-tyranny?start=3.

103. Don Elkins, Carla Rueckert, and Jim McCarty, *The Law of One* (West Chester, PA: Whitford Press, 1984), session 17, question 20, http://lawofone.info/results.php?s=17#20.

104. Ibid., session 18, question 12, http://lawofone.info/results.php?s=18#12.

105. Ibid., session 1, question 9, http://lawofone.info/results.php?s=1#9.

106. Patrick G. Bailey and Toby Grotz, "A Critical Review of the Available Information Regarding Claims of Zero-Point Energy, Free-Energy, and Over-Unity Experiments and Devices," Institute for New Energy, *Proceedings of the 28th IECEC*, April 3, 1997, accessed December 2010, http://padrak.com/ine/INE21.html.

107. Steven Aftergood, "Invention Secrecy Still Going Strong," Federation of American Scientists, October 21, 2010, accessed January 2011, http://www.fas.org/blog/secrecy/2010 /10/invention_secrecy_2010.html.

108. David Wilcock, "Confirmed: The Trillion-Dollar Lawsuit That Could End Financial Tyranny," Divine Cosmos, December 12, 2011, http://divinecosmos.com/index.php/start -here/davids-blog/995-lawsuit-end-tyranny.

109. Clive R. Boddy, "The Corporate Psychopaths Theory of the Global Financial Crisis," abstract, *Journal of Business Ethics* 102, no. 2 (August 2011): 255–259, http://link.springer.com/ article/10.1007%2Fs10551-011-0810-4; Mitchell Anderson, "Weeding Out Corporate Psychopaths," *Toronto Star,* November 23, 2011, Editorial Opinion section, http://www.the star.com/opinion/editorialopinion/2011/11/23/weeding_out_corporate_psychopaths.html.

110. Elkins, Rueckert, and McCarty, *The Law of One*, session 36, question 14, http://lawofone .info/results.php?s=36#14.

111. Ibid., session 19, question 17, http://lawofone.info/results.php?s=19#17.

112. Ibid., session 80, question 15, http://lawofone.info/results.php?s=80#15.

113. Ibid., session 36, question 15, http://lawofone.info/results.php?s=36#15.

114. Ibid., session 36, question 12, http://lawofone.info/results.php?s=36#12.

115. Ibid., session 47, question 5, http://lawofone.info/results.php?s=47#5.

116. Kevin Williams, "Scientific Evidence Suggestive of Astrology," Near-Death.com, 2009, http://www.near-death.com/experiences/articles012.html.

117. Sandra Harrison Young and Edna Rowland, *Destined for Murder: Profiles of Six Serial Killers with Astrological Commentary* (Woodbury, MN: Llewellyn Publications, 1995).

118. Dale Carnegie, *How to Win Friends and Influence People* (1937; repr., New York: Pocket Books, 1998).

119. Maxwell C. Bridges, "Sociopaths," Vatic Project, December 23, 2011, http://vaticproject .blogspot.com/2011/12/sociopaths.html.

120. Ibid.

121. Katherine Ramsland, "The Childhood Psychopath: Bad Seed or Bad Parents?" Crime Library, September 2011, http://www.trutv.com/library/crime/criminal_mind/psychol ogy/psychopath/2.html.

122. Scott O. Lilienfeld, Irwin D. Waldman, Kristin Landfield, Ashley L. Watts, Steven Rubenzer, and Thomas R. Faschingbauer, "Fearless Dominance and the U.S. Presidency: Implications of Psychopathic Personality Traits for Successful and Unsuccessful Political Leadership," *Journal of Personality and Social Psychology* 103, no. 3 (September 2012): 489–505, doi: 10.1037/a0029392.

123. Rebecca Boyle, "Fearless Dominance: Just One of Many Traits U.S. Presidents Share with Psychopaths," *Popular Science*, September 11, 2012, http://www.popsci.com/science/article /2012-09/fearless-dominance-just-one-many-traits-us-presidents-share-psychopaths.

124. Lilienfeld et al., "Fearless Dominance."

125. Barry Miles, *Paul McCartney: Many Years from Now* (New York: Henry Holt, 1997), p. 161.

126. Jen Doll, "A Treasury of Terribly Sad Stories of Lotto Winners," *Atlantic Wire,* March 30, 2012, http://www.theatlanticwire.com/national/2012/03/terribly-sad-true-stories-lotto -winners/50555/; Hannah Maundrell, "How the Lives of 10 Lottery Millionaires Went Disastrously Wrong," Money.co.uk, 2009, http://www.money.co.uk/article/1002156-how -the-lives-of-10-lottery-millionaires-went-disasterously-wrong.htm; Melissa Dahl, "$550 Million Will Buy You a Lot of . . . Misery," NBC News Vitals, November 28, 2012, http:// vitals.nbcnews.com/_news/2012/11/28/15463411-550-million-will-buy-you-a-lot-of-misery ?lite.

127. Alan Scherzagier, "Big Winners Share Lessons, Risks of Powerball Win," *USA Today,* November 28, 2012, http://www.usatoday.com/story/news/nation/2012/11/28/winner -lottery-bankrupt/1731367/.

128. Kathleen O'Toole, "The Stanford Prison Experiment: Still Powerful After All These Years," Stanford News Service, January 8, 1997, http://news.stanford.edu/pr/97 /970108prisonexp.html.

129. Ibid.

130. Ibid.

131. Ibid.

132. R. Manning, M. Levine, and A. Collins, "The Kitty Genovese Murder and the Social Psychology of Helping: The Parable of the 38 Witnesses," *American Psychologist* 62, no. 6 (2007): 555–562, http://www.grignoux.be/dossiers/288/pdf/manning_et_alii.pdf.

133. J. M. Darley and B. Latané, "Bystander Intervention in Emergencies: Diffusion of Responsibility," *Journal of Personality and Social Psychology* 8 (1968): 377–383, http://www. wadsworth.com/psychology_d/templates/student_resources/0155060678_rathus /ps/psi9.html.

134. David G. Meyers, *Social Psychology,* 10th ed. (New York: McGraw-Hill, 2010).

135. P. P. Gariaev, M. J. Friedman, and E. A. Leonova-Gariaeva, "Crisis in Life Sciences: The Wave Genetics Response," Emergent Mind, 2007, http://www.emergentmind.org/gariaev06.htm.

136. Ibid., p. 53.

137. Ibid., p. 44.
138. Glen Rein, "Effect of Conscious Intention on Human DNA," in *Proceeds of the International Forum on New Science* (Denver, 1996), accessed June 2010, http://www.item-bioenergy.com/infocenter/ConsciousIntentiononDNA.pdf.
139. Elkins, Rueckert, and McCarty, *The Law of One,* session 41, question 9, http://lawofone.info/results.php?s=41#9.
140. Ibid., session 92, question 20, http://lawofone.info/results.php?s=92#20.
141. Ibid., session 67, question 28, http://lawofone.info/results.php?s=67#28.
142. Wolfgang Lillge, "Vernadsky's Method: Biophysics and the Life Processes," *21st Century Science & Technology,* summer 2001, http://www.21stcenturysciencetech.com/articles/summ01/Biophysics/Biophysics.html.
143. Ibid.
144. Daniel Benor, "Spiritual Healing: A Unifying Influence in Complementary/Alternative Therapies," Wholistic Healing Research, January 4, 2005. http://www.wholistichealingresearch.com/spiritualhealingaunifyinginfluence.html.
145. Elkins, Rueckert, and McCarty, *The Law of One*, session 66, question 10. http://lawofone.info/results.php?s=66#10.
146. Ibid., session 4, question 14, http://lawofone.info/results.php?s=4#14.
147. Ibid., session 13, question 9, http://lawofone.info/results.php?s=13#9.
148. Ibid., session 2, question 4, http://lawofone.info/results.php?s=2#4.
149. Ibid., session 64, question 6, http://lawofone.info/results.php?s=64#6.
150. Ibid., session 28, question 5, http://lawofone.info/results.php?s=28#5.
151. Ibid., session 27, question 13, http://lawofone.info/results.php?s=27#13.
152. Ibid., session 6, question 4, http://lawofone.info/results.php?s=6#4.
153. Ibid., session 1, question 6, http://lawofone.info/results.php?s=1#6.
154. People's Republic of China, Chinese Academy of Sciences, High Energy Institute, Special Physics Research Team, "Exceptional Human Body Radiation," *PSI Research* 1, no. 2 (June 1982): 16–25; Zhao Yonjie and Xu Hongzhang, "EHBF Radiation: Special Features of the Time Response," Institute of High Energy Physics, Beijing, People's Republic of China, *PSI Research* (December 1982); G. Scott Hubbard, E. C. May, and H. E. Puthoff, "Possible Production of Photons During a Remote Viewing Task: Preliminary Results," in *Research in Parapsychology,* ed. D. H. Weiner and D. I. Radin (Metuchen, NJ: Scarecrow Press, 1985), pp. 66–70.

Chapter Five

155. Clive R. Boddy, "The Corporate Psychopaths Theory of the Global Financial Crisis," *Journal of Business Ethics* 102, no. 2 (August 2011): 255–259. http://link.springer.com/article/10.1007%2Fs10551-011-0810-4.
156. Mitchell Anderson, "Weeding Out Corporate Psychopaths, *Toronto Star,* November 23, 2011, http://www.thestar.com/opinion/editorialopinion/2011/11/23/weeding_out_corporate_psychopaths.html.
157. David Wilcock, "Financial Tyranny: Defeating the Greatest Cover-Up of All Time," Divine Cosmos, January 13, 2012, http://divinecosmos.com/start-here/davids-blog/1023-financial-tyranny.
158. Andy Coghlan and Debora MacKenzie, "Revealed—the Capitalist Network That Runs the World," *New Scientist,* October 2011, http://www.newscientist.com/article/mg21228354.500-revealed--the-capitalist-network-that-runs-the-world.html.
159. David Wilcock, "The Great Revealing: U.S. Marshals Expose the Biggest Scandal in History," Divine Cosmos, July 20, 2012, http://divinecosmos.com/start-here/davids-blog/1066-great-revealing.

160. John Hively, "Breakdown of the $26 Trillion the Federal Reserve Handed Out to Save Incompetent, but Rich Investors," December 5, 2011, http://johnhively.wordpress.com /2011/12/05/breakdown-of-the-26-trillion-the-federal-reserve-handed-out-to-save-rich -incompetent-investors-but-who-purchase-political-power/.

161. David Wilcock, "Disclosure Now: NEW 3-HR Russian Documentary Blasts Financial Tyranny!" Divine Cosmos, January 30, 2013, http://divinecosmos.com/start-here/davids -blog/1107-new-russian-doc.

162. G. Edward Griffin, *The Creature from Jekyll Island: A Second Look at the Federal Reserve,* 4th ed. (New York: American Media, 2002), http://www.wildboar.net/multilingual /easterneuropean/russian/literature/articles/whofinanced/whofinancedleninandtrotsky .html.

163. Antony C. Sutton, *Wall Street and the Bolshevik Revolution* (New Rochelle, NY: Arlington House, 1974), p. 25.

164. Cleve Backster. *Primary Perception: Biocommunication with Plants, Living Foods and Human Cells.* (Anza, CA: White Rose Millennium Press, 2003), p. 19, http://www.prima ryperception.com.

165. Ibid., pp. 78–79.

166. Ibid., chapter Six, "Tuning In to Live Bacteria," pp. 84–103.

167. Ibid., pp. 52–53.

168. Ibid., pp. 43–48.

169. Ibid., pp. 79–81.

170. Ibid., pp. 117–118.

171. Ibid., pp. 127–128.

172. M. Schlitz and S. LaBerge, "Autonomic Detection of Remote Observation: Two Conceptual Replications," in *Proceedings of the Parapsychological Association 37th Annual Convention,* ed. D. J. Bierman (Fairhaven, MA: Parapsychological Association, 1994), pp. 465–478.

173. Don Elkins, Carla Rueckert, and Jim McCarty, *The Law of One* (West Chester, PA: Whitford Press, 1984), session 93, question 3, http://lawofone.info/results.php?s=93#3.

174. Ibid., session 97, question 16, http://lawofone.info/results.php?s=97#16.

175. Ibid., session 55, question 3, http://lawofone.info/results.php?s=55#3.

176. Ibid., session 52, question 7, http://lawofone.info/results.php?s=52#7.

177. Ibid., session 97, question 16, http://lawofone.info/results.php?s=97#16.

178. Wilcock, "Disclosure Now."

179. Elkins, Rueckert, and McCarty, *The Law of One,* session 19, questions 19–21, http:// lawofone.info/results.php?s=19#19.

180. Wilcock, "Financial Tyranny."

181. Michael Chossudovsky, "Central Banking with 'Other People's Gold': A $368Bn Treasure Trove in Lower Manhattan (Op-Ed)." Russia Today, January 23, 2013, http://rt.com/ news/gold-manhattan-new-york-594/.

182. Ibid.

183. Elkins, Rueckert, and McCarty, *The Law of One,* session 11, question 18, http://lawofone .info/results.php?s=11#18.

184. Ibid., session 50, question 6, http://lawofone.info/results.php?s=50#6.

185. Adam Smith, *An Inquiry into the Nature and Causes of the Wealth of Nations* (1776), http://www2.hn.psu.edu/faculty/jmanis/adam-smith/Wealth-Nations.pdf.

186. Sterling Seagrave and Peggy Seagrave, *Gold Warriors: America's Secret Recovery of Yamashita's Gold,* rev. ed. (Brooklyn, NY: Verso Books, 2005).

187. Sean McMeekin, "Introduction to Bolshevik Gold: The Nature of a Forgotten Problem," in *History's Greatest Heist: The Looting of Russia by the Bolsheviks* (New Haven, CT: Yale

University Press, 2008), http://yalepress.yale.edu/yupbooks/excerpts/mcmeekin_histo rys.pdf; James Von Geldern, "1921: Confiscating Church Gold," Seventeen Moments in Soviet History, 2013, http://www.soviethistory.org/index.php?page=subject&SubjectID =1921church&Year=1921.

188. David Guyatt, "The Secret Gold Treaty," Deep Black Lies, http://www.deepblacklies.co .uk/secret_gold_treaty.htm.

189. Exec. Order No. 6102 at the American Presidency Project, http://www.presidency.ucsb .edu/ws/index.php?pid=14611&st=&st1.

190. Wilcock, "Financial Tyranny."

191. Edward Marshall, "Police: Fire Victims Had Been Shot," *The Journal* (West Virginia), February 7, 2012, http://www.journal-news.net/page/content.detail/id/574757/Police-- Fire-victims-had-been-shot.html?nav=5006.

192. Wilcock, "Financial Tyranny."

193. David Wilcock, "Major Event: Liens Filed Against All 12 Federal Reserve Banks," Divine Cosmos, April 13, 2012, http://divinecosmos.com/start-here/davids-blog/1047-liens.

194. David Wilcock, "The 'Green Light'—Wouldn't It Be Nice?" Divine Cosmos, June 29, 2012, http://divinecosmos.com/start-here/davids-blog/1062-green-light.

195. David Wilcock, "Will 2012 Be the Year of Freedom?" Divine Cosmos, October 7, 2012, http://divinecosmos.com/start-here/davids-blog/1085-2012freedom.

196. Victor Vernon Woolf, "V. Vernon Woolf, Ph.D.," Holodynamics, http://www.holody namics.com/vita.html.

197. Agustino Fontevecchia, "Germany Repatriating Gold from NY, Paris 'In Case of a Cur- rency Crisis,'" *Forbes,* January 16, 2013, http://www.forbes.com/sites/afontevecchia/2013 /01/16/germany-repatriating-gold-from-ny-paris-in-case-of-a-currency-crisis/.

198. Eric King, "Nigel Farage on the Queen's Tour of Britain's Gold Vault," King World News, December 14, 2012, http://kingworldnews.com/kingworldnews/KWN_Daily Web/Entries/2012/12/14_Nigel_Farage_On_The_Queens_Tour_of_Britains_Gold _Vault.html.

199. Wilcock, "Disclosure Now."

200. Violet Blue, "Anonymous Posts Over 4000 Bank Executive Credentials," Zero Day, February 4, 2013, http://www.zdnet.com/anonymous-posts-over-4000-u-s-bank -executive-credentials-7000010740/.

201. PericlesMortimer, comment 1 on Anonymous on Reddit.com, "Anonymous Releases Banker Info from Federal Reserve Computers. Banker Contact Information and Cell Phone Numbers," Reddit.com, February 4, 2013, http://www.reddit.com/r/anonymous/ comments/17uk52/anonymous_releases_banker_info_from_federal/c890its.

202. David Wilcock, "Lightning Strikes Vatican: A Geo-Synchronicity?" Divine Cosmos, February 28, 2013, http://www.divinecosmos.com/index.php/start-here/davids-blog/1111 -alliswell.

Chapter Six

203. Mary Ann Woodward, *Edgar Cayce's Story of Karma* (New York: Berkley Publishing Group, 1971), p. 15.

204. David Wilcock, "Dream: Prophecy of House Burning Down," Divine Cosmos, January 25, 2000, http://www.divinecosmos.com/index.php/start-here/readings-in-text-form /444-12500-dream-prophecy-of-house-burning-down.

205. Ibid.

206. Ibid.

207. Jose Stevens and Lena Stevens, *Secrets of Shamanism: Tapping the Spirit Power Within You*
      (New York: Avon Books, 1988), http://www.josestevens.com/.

208. W. L. Graham, "The Problem with 'God,'" Bible Reality Check, 2007, http://www.bible
      realitycheck.com/ProbwGod.htm.

209. Don Elkins, Carla Rueckert, and Jim McCarty, *The Law of One* (West Chester, PA:
      Whitford Press, 1984), session 33, question 11, http://lawofone.info/results.php?s=33#11.

210. M. Aiken, "A Case Against Hell," ed. W. L. Graham, Bible Reality Check. http://www
      .biblerealitycheck.com/caseagainsthell.htm.

211. Ibid.

212. "Gehenna," in *Collins English Dictionary*, complete and unabridged 10th ed., Dictionary
      .com, http://dictionary.reference.com/browse/Gehenna.

213. "Sin," Dictionary.com, http://dictionary.reference.com/browse/sin?s=t.

214. Ernest Scott, *The People of the Secret* (London: Octagon Press, 1991).

215. Elkins, Rueckert, and McCarty, *The Law of One*, session 17, questions 11, 19, 20, and 22,
      http://lawofone.info/results.php?s=17#11.

216. Ibid., session 11, question 8, http://lawofone.info/results.php?s=11#8.

Chapter Seven

217. Ian Stevenson, *Twenty Cases Suggestive of Reincarnation*, 2nd ed. (Charlottesville: Uni-
      versity of Virginia Press, 1980).

218. Danny Penman, "'I Died in Jerusalem in 1276,' Says Doctor Who Underwent Hypnosis to
      Reveal a Former Life," *Daily Mail*, April 25, 2008, http://www.dailymail.co.uk/pages/live/
      articles/news/news.html?in_article_id=562154&in_page_id=1770; Jim Tucker, *Life Before
      Life: Children's Memories of Previous Lives* (New York: St. Martin's Griffin, 2008).

219. Ibid.

220. Carol Bowman, *Children's Past Lives: How Past Life Memories Affect Your Child* (New
      York: Bantam, 1998).

221. Carol Bowman. *Return from Heaven: Beloved Relatives Reincarnated Within Your Family*
      (New York: HarperTorch, 2003).

222. "Reincarnation and the Bible," Near-Death.com, http://www.near-death.com/experi
      ences/origen03.html.

223. Origen, *The Writings of Origen (De Principiis)*, trans Rev. Frederick Crombie, vol.1
      (Edinburgh: T. & T. Clark, 1869), http://books.google.com/books?id=vMcIAQAAIAAJ.

224. "Chuck's List: Edgar Cayce Thursdays," Society for Spiritual and Paranormal Research,
      June 21, 2012, https://docs.google.com/document/d/1USEm_wzQTW6Rp3CduyZX
      11t8yl2LYf7hLCQCqZIzscc/edit.

225. Association for Research and Enlightenment, ed. Hugh Lynn Cayce, *The Edgar Cayce
      Reader* (New York: Warner Books, 1967), p. 7.

226. Paul K. Johnson, *Edgar Cayce in Context* (New York: State University of New York Press,
      1998), p. 2.

227. Thomas Sugrue, *There Is a River: The Story of Edgar Cayce* (New York: Henry Holt and
      Company, 1943; Virginia Beach: A.R.E. Press, 1997), http://books.google.com
      /books?id=Uo_WpADB9_gC.

228. Harmon Hartzell Bro, *A Seer Out of Season: The Life of Edgar Cayce* (New York: St.
      Martin's Paperbacks, 1996).

229. Sugrue, *There Is a River*, p. 25, http://books.google.com/books?id=Uo_WpADB9_gC
      &pg=PA25&lpg=PA25&dq=edgar+cayce+oil+of+smoke.

230. Baar Products, "Oil of Smoke," Cayce Care, http://www.baar.com/oilsmoke.htm.

231. U.S. Department of Health and Human Services, Agency for Toxic Substances and Disease Registry, "Health Effects of Creosote," *The Encyclopedia of Earth,* March 31, 2008, http://www.eoearth.org/article/Health_effects_of_creosote.

232. John Van Auken, "A Brief Story About Edgar Cayce," Association for Research and Enlightenment, 2002, http://www.edgarcayce.org/ps2/edgar_cayce_story.html.

233. Ibid.

234. Bob Leaman, *Armageddon: Doomsday in Our Lifetime?* chapter 4 (Richmond, Victoria, Australia: Greenhouse Publications, 1986), http://www.dreamscape.com/morgana /phoebe.htm.

235. Anne Hunt, "Edgar Cayce's Wart Remedy," Ezine Articles, 2006, http://ezinearticles .com/?Edgar-Cayces-Wart-Remedy&id=895289.

236. A.D.A.M. Medical Encyclopedia, "scleroderma," PubMed Health, February 2, 2012, http://www.ncbi.nlm.nih.gov/pubmedhealth/PMH0001465/.

237. Gina Cerminara, *Many Mansions: The Edgar Cayce Story on Reincarnation* (New York: Signet, 1998), p. 26.

238. Ibid.

239. Sidney Kirkpatrick, *Edgar Cayce: An American Prophet,* (New York: Riverhead Books, 2000), p. 97.

240. Cerminara, *Many Mansions.*

241. Ibid., pp. 93–94.

242. Ibid., p. 37.

243. Ibid., p. 38.

244. Ibid., p. 38.

245. Ibid., pp. 41–42.

246. Ibid., p. 112.

247. Ibid., p. 47.

248. Ibid., p. 48.

249. Ibid., pp. 48–49.

250. Ibid., p. 49.

251. Ibid., p. 50.

252. Ibid., p. 57.

253. Ibid., p. 58.

254. Ibid., pp. 58–59.

255. Ibid., p. 59.

256. Ibid., p. 107.

257. Ibid., p. 51.

258. Ibid., p. 52.

259. Ibid., p. 80.

260. Ibid., p. 87.

261. Ibid., p. 119.

262. Don Elkins, Carla Rueckert, and Jim McCarty, *The Law of One* (West Chester, PA: Whitford Press, 1984), session 21, question 9, http://lawofone.info/results.php?s =21#9.

263. Ibid., session 77, question 14, http://lawofone.info/results.php?s=77#14.

264. Ibid., session 81, question 32, http://lawofone.info/results.php?s=81#32.

265. Ibid., session 82, question 29, http://lawofone.info/results.php?s=82#29.

266. Ibid., session 83, question 18, http://lawofone.info/results.php?s=83#18.

267. Cerminara, *Many Mansions,* p. 123.

268. Mark Lehner, *The Egyptian Heritage: Based on the Edgar Cayce Readings* (Virginia Beach, VA: ARE Press, 1974).

269. W. H. Church, *The Lives of Edgar Cayce,* (Virginia Beach, VA: A.R.E. Press, 1995).

270. Ibid.

Chapter Eight

271. University of Southampton, "World's Largest-Ever Study of Near-Death Experiences," *Science Daily,* September 10, 2008, accessed December 13, 2010, http://www.sciencedaily.com/releases/2008/09/080910090829.htm.

272. Pim van Lommel, "About the Continuity of Our Consciousness," in *Brain Death and Disorders of Consciousness,* ed. C. Machado and D. A. Shewmon (New York: Kluwer Academic/Plenum Publishers, 2004); *Advances in Experimental Medicine and Biology* (2004) 550: 115–132, accessed April 2013, http://iands.org/research/important-research-articles/43-dr-pim-van-lommel-md-continuity-of-consciousness.html?start=2.

273. "Scientific Evidence for Survival of Consciousness After Death," Near-Death.com, 2010, accessed December 2010, http://www.near-death.com/evidence.html.

274. Ibid.

275. Michael Newton, *Journey of Souls: Case Studies of Life Between Lives,* 1st ed. (Woodbury, MN: Llewellyn Publications, 1994), p. 2; http://www.spiritualregression.org/.

276. Newton, *Journey of Souls,* p. 4; http://www.spiritualregression.org/.

277. Michael Newton, *Destiny of Souls: New Case Studies of Life Between Lives* (Woodbury, MN: Llewellyn Publications, 2000), pp. xi–xii; http://www.spiritualregression.org/, accessed December 2010.

278. Newton, *Journey of Souls,* p. 5; http://www.spiritualregression.org/.

279. Newton, *Journey of Souls,* p. 6; http://www.spiritualregression.org/.

280. Newton, *Journey of Souls;* http://www.spiritualregression.org/.

281. Newton, *Journey of Souls,* p. 9; http://www.spiritualregression.org/.

282. Newton, *Journey of Souls,* p. 13; http://www.spiritualregression.org/.

283. Newton, *Journey of Souls,* p. 9; http://www.spiritualregression.org/.

284. Newton, *Journey of Souls,* pp. 22–24; http://www.spiritualregression.org/.

285. Newton, *Journey of Souls,* p. 24; http://www.spiritualregression.org/.

286. Newton, *Journey of Souls,* p. 24; http://www.spiritualregression.org/.

287. Newton, *Journey of Souls,* pp. 116–120; http://www.spiritualregression.org/.

288. Newton, *Destiny of Souls,* p. 117; http://www.spiritualregression.org/.

289. Newton, *Journey of Souls,* pp. 31–32; http://www.spiritualregression.org/.

290. Newton, *Journey of Souls,* pp. 45–52; http://www.spiritualregression.org/.

291. Newton, *Journey of Souls,* p. 49; http://www.spiritualregression.org/.

292. Don Elkins, Carla Rueckert, and Jim McCarty, *The Law of One* (West Chester, PA: Whitford Press, 1984), session 69, question 6, http://lawofone.info/results.php?s=69#6.

293. Newton, *Journey of Souls,* p. 49; http://www.spiritualregression.org/.

294. Newton, *Journey of Souls,* pp. 50–51; http://www.spiritualregression.org/.

295. Newton, *Journey of Souls,* p. 78; http://www.spiritualregression.org/.

296. Newton, *Journey of Souls,* p. 75; http://www.spiritualregression.org/.

297. Newton, *Journey of Souls,* p. 88; http://www.spiritualregression.org/.

298. Newton, *Journey of Souls,* p. 123; http://www.spiritualregression.org/.

299. Newton, *Journey of Souls,* p. 170; http://www.spiritualregression.org/.

300. Elkins, Rueckert, and McCarty, *The Law of One,* session 12, questions 26–30, http://lawofone.info/results.php?s=12#26.

301. Newton, *Journey of Souls,* pp. 161–166; http://www.spiritualregression.org/.

302. Newton, *Journey of Souls,* p. 165; http://www.spiritualregression.org/.

303. Newton, *Journey of Souls,* p. 186; http://www.spiritualregression.org/.

304. Newton, *Journey of Souls*, p. 187; http://www.spiritualregression.org/.
305. Newton, *Journey of Souls*, p. 187; http://www.spiritualregression.org/.
306. Newton, *Journey of Souls*, p. 188; http://www.spiritualregression.org/.
307. Elkins, Rueckert, and McCarty, *The Law of One*, session 13, questions 16, 18, and 21, http://lawofone.info/results.php?s=13#16.
308. Ibid., session 82, question 10; http://lawofone.info/results.php?s=82#10.
309. Ibid., session 51, question 10, http://lawofone.info/results.php?s=51#10.
310. Ibid., session 75, question 25, http://lawofone.info/results.php?s=75#25.
311. Ibid., session 74, question 11, http://lawofone.info/results.php?s=74#11.
312. Ibid., session 18, question 13, http://lawofone.info/results.php?s=18#13.
313. Newton, *Journey of Souls*, p. 192; http://www.spiritualregression.org/.
314. Newton, *Journey of Souls*, p. 197; http://www.spiritualregression.org/.
315. Elkins, Rueckert, and McCarty, *The Law of One*, session 27, question 6, http://lawofone.info/results.php?s=27#6.
316. Ibid., session 27, question 13, http://lawofone.info/results.php?s=27#13.
317. Newton, *Journey of Souls*, p. 168; http://www.spiritualregression.org/.
318. Newton, *Journey of Souls*, p. 202; http://www.spiritualregression.org/.
319. Newton, *Journey of Souls*, p. 204; http://www.spiritualregression.org/.
320. Newton, *Journey of Souls*, p. 218; http://www.spiritualregression.org/.
321. Newton, *Journey of Souls*, p. 219; http://www.spiritualregression.org/.
322. Newton, *Journey of Souls*, p. 220; http://www.spiritualregression.org/.
323. Newton, *Journey of Souls*, p. 222; http://www.spiritualregression.org/.
324. Newton, *Journey of Souls*, p. 229; http://www.spiritualregression.org/.
325. Newton, *Journey of Souls*, p. 239; http://www.spiritualregression.org/.
326. Newton, *Journey of Souls*, p. 241; http://www.spiritualregression.org/.
327. Newton, *Journey of Souls*, p. 256; http://www.spiritualregression.org/.
328. Newton, *Journey of Souls*, p. 261; http://www.spiritualregression.org/.
329. Newton, *Journey of Souls*, p. 271; http://www.spiritualregression.org/.
330. Elkins, Rueckert, and McCarty, *The Law of One*, session 90, questions 14 and 16, http://lawofone.info/results.php?s=90#14.

Chapter Nine

331. Don Elkins, Carla Rueckert, and Jim McCarty, *The Law of One*. (West Chester, PA: Whitford Press, 1984), session 43, question 31, http://lawofone.info/results.php?s=43#31.
332. Christopher Vogler, *The Writers Journey: Mythic Structure for Writers,* 3rd ed. (Studio City, CA: Michael Wiese Productions, 2007).
333. Carl Jung, *The Archetypes and the Collective Unconscious,* 2nd ed., in *Collected Works of C.G. Jung,* vol. 9, part 1. (Princeton, NJ: Princeton University Press, 1981).
334. Miles@riverside, January 19, 2004, review of Jung, *The Archetypes and the Collective Unconscious,* http://www.amazon.com/Archetypes-Collective-Unconscious-Collected-Works/product-reviews/0691018332/ref=dp_top_cm_cr_acr_txt?ie=UTF8&showViewpoints=1.
335. Elkins, Rueckert, and McCarty, *The Law of One*, session 77, question 12, http://lawofone.info/results.php?s=77#12.
336. Ibid., session 91, question 18, http://lawofone.info/results.php?s=91#18.
337. George Lucas, review of Joseph Campbell, *The Hero with a Thousand Faces* (Novato, CA: New World Library, 2008), Joseph Campbell Foundation website, http://www.jcf.org/new/index.php?categoryid=83&p9999_action=details&p9999_wid=692.

338. Fredric L. Rice, *A Practical Guide to* The Hero With a Thousand Faces *by Joseph Campbell,* Skeptic Tank, 2003, http://web.archive.org/web/20090219134358/http://skepticfiles.org/atheist2/hero.htm.
339. "Arthur Clarke's 2001 Diary," extracted from Arthur C. Clarke, *Lost Worlds of 2001* (New York: New American Library, 1972), http://www.visual-memory.co.uk/amk/doc/0073.html.
340. Kristen Brennan, "Joseph Campbell," Star Wars Origins, 2006, http://www.moongadget.com/origins/myth.html.
341. Epagogix, http://www.epagogix.com.
342. Tom Whipple. "Slaves to the Algorithm." *The Economist: Intelligent Life Magazine,* May/June 2013, http://moreintelligentlife.com/content/features/anonymous/slaves-algorithm?page=full.
343. David Poland, Hot Button, October 18, 2006, http://web.archive.org/web/20120328071529/http://www.thehotbutton.com/today/hot.button/2006_thb/061018_wed.html.
344. Malcolm Gladwell, "The Formula: What If You Built a Machine to Predict Hit Movies?" *The New Yorker,* October 16, 2006, http://www.newyorker.com/archive/2006/10/16/061016fa_fact6?currentPage=all.
345. Ibid.
346. Ibid.
347. Blake Snyder, *Save the Cat! The Last Book on Screenwriting You'll Ever Need* (Studio City, CA: Michael Wiese Productions, 2005); http://www.blakesnyder.com.

Chapter Ten

348. Blake Snyder, *Save the Cat! The Last Book on Screenwriting You'll Ever Need.* (Studio City, CA: Michael Wiese Productions, 2005); http://www.blakesnyder.com.
349. Christopher Vogler, *The Writers Journey: Mythic Structure for Writers,* 3rd ed. (Studio City, CA: Michael Wiese Productions, 2007), p. 52.
350. Snyder, *Save the Cat!*; http://www.blakesnyder.com.
351. Vogler, *The Writers Journey,* pp. 207–208.
352. Dan Decker, *Anatomy of a Screenplay: Writing the American Screenplay from Character Structure to Convergence* (Chicago: Screenwriters Group, 1998).
353. Alex Epstein, *Crafty Screenwriting: Writing Movies That Get Made* (New York: Holt Paperbacks, 2002); http://www.craftyscreenwriting.com.

Chapter Eleven

354. Don Elkins, Carla Rueckert, and Jim McCarty, *The Law of One.* (West Chester, PA: Whitford Press, 1984), session 20, question 25, http://lawofone.info/results.php?s=20#25.
355. Blake Snyder, *Save the Cat! The Last Book on Screenwriting You'll Ever Need* (Studio City, CA: Michael Wiese Productions, 2005); http://www.blakesnyder.com.
356. Snyder, *Save the Cat!*; http://www.blakesnyder.com.
357. David Wilcock, "US Airways '333' Miracle Bigger Than We Think," Divine Cosmos, January 17, 2009, http://divinecosmos.com/index.php/start-here/davids-blog/424-us-airways-333-miracle-bigger-than-we-think.
358. Ibid.
359. David Gardner, "Miracle in New York: 155 escape after pilot ditches stricken Airbus in freezing Hudson River." *Daily Mail,* January 16, 2009, http://www.dailymail.co.uk/news/article-1118502/Miracle-New-York-155-escape-pilot-ditches-stricken-Airbus-freezing-Hudson-River.html.
360. Elkins, Rueckert, and McCarty, *The Law of One,* session 65, question 6, http://lawofone.info/results.php?s=65#6.

Chapter Twelve

361. Don Elkins, Carla Rueckert, and Jim McCarty, *The Law of One.* (West Chester, PA: Whitford Press, 1984), session 16, question 21, http://lawofone.info/results.php?s=16#21.

362. Ibid., session 9, question 4, http://lawofone.info/results.php?s=9#4.

363. Ibid., session 2, question 2, http://lawofone.info/results.php?s=2#2.

364. Ibid., session 1, question 1, http://lawofone.info/results.php?s=1#1.

365. Ibid., session 16, question 22, http://lawofone.info/results.php?s=16#22.

366. Joseph Campbell, *The Hero with a Thousand Faces,* 2nd ed. (Princeton, NJ: Princeton University Press, 1972).

367. Peter Lemesurier, *The Great Pyramid Decoded* (1977; repr., Rockport, MA: Element Books, 1993), p. 216.

368. Ibid., pp. 284, 287.

369. David Wilcock, "Great Pyramid—Prophecy in Stone," chapter 20 in *The Shift of the Ages,* Divine Cosmos, December 6, 2000, http://divinecosmos.com/index.php/start-here/books-free-online/18-the-shift-of-the-ages/76-the-shift-of-the-ages-chapter-20-prophetic-time-cycles; Archive.org snapshot from March 4, 2001, http://web.archive.org/web/20010304032206/http://ascension2000.com/Shift-of-the-Ages/shift20.htm.

370. François Masson, "Cyclology: The Mathematics of History," chapter 6 in *The End of Our Century,* 1979, http://divinecosmos.com/index.php/start-here/books-free-online/26-the-end-of-our-century/145-chapter-06-cyclology-the-mathematics-of-history; Archive.org snapshot from February 19, 2001, http://web.archive.org/web/20010219145152/http://ascension2000.com/fm-choo.htm.

371. François Masson, *The End of Our Era* (Virginia Beach, VA: Donning Company Publishers, 1983).

372. Library of Congress Name Authority File for François Masson, *Notre fin de siècle,* http://id.loc.gov/authorities/names/n82086698.html.

373. Masson, "Cyclology."

374. Christine Grollin, *Cahiers Astrologiques, Under the Direction of A. Volguine,* 2nd webpage, translated into English via Google Translate, http://www.aureas.org/faes/francais/cahiersastrologiques02fr.htm.

375. Christine Grollin, *Cahiers Astrologiques, Under the Direction of A. Volguine,* 3rd webpage, translated into English via Google Translate, http://www.aureas.org/faes/francais/cahiersastrologiques03fr.htm.

376. Brian P Copenhhaver. *Hermetica: The Greek Corpus Hermeticum and the Latin Asclepius in a New English Translation, with Notes and Introduction* (New York: Cambridge University Press, November 24, 1995), pp. 81–83.

377. Walter Scott. *Hermetica, Vol. 1: The Ancient Greek and Latin Writings Which Contain Religious or Philosophic Teachings Ascribed to Hermes Trismestigus* (Boston: Shambhala, May 1, 2001).

378. Prophecies of the Future. *Future Prophecies Revealed: A Remarkable Collection of Obscure Millennial Prophecies. Hermes Trismestigus (circa 1st century CE).* http://web.archive.org/web/20110203100118/http://futurerevealed.com/future/T.htm.

379. Matthew 18:21–23 (New International Version), "The Parable of the Unmercival Servant," Bible Gateway, http://www.biblegateway.com/passage/?search=Matthew+18%3A21-23&version=NIV.

380. Masson, "Cyclology."

381. Ibid.

382. "The Our World TV Show," *The Beatles Official Website*, 2009, http://www.thebeatles
.com/#/article/The_Our_World_TV_Show.

383. John Lichfield, "Egalité! Liberté! Sexualité!: Paris, May 1968," *The Independent,* February
23, 2008, http://www.independent.co.uk/news/world/europe/egalit-libert-sexualit-paris
-may-1968-784703.html.

384. Ibid.

385. Ibid.

386. Ibid.

387. Ibid.

388. Ibid.

389. Ibid.

390. Masson, "Cyclology."

Chapter Thirteen

391. François Masson, "Cyclology: The Mathematics of History," chapter 6 in *The End of Our
Century,* (1979), http://divinecosmos.com/index.php/start-here/books-free-online/26
-the-end-of-our-century/145-chapter-06-cyclology-the-mathematics-of-history.

392. Mark Lewisohn, *The Complete Beatles Recording Sessions* (New York: Harmony, 1988), p. 232.

393. George Harrison, "Within You, Without You," recorded on the Beatles, *Sgt. Pepper's
Lonely Hearts Club Band* (London: EMI Studios, 1967).

394. John Traveler, "A Look at How the Punic Wars Between Rome and Carthage Began,"
Helium: Arts and Humanities: History, http://www.helium.com/items/1530950-a-look-at
-how-the-punic-wars-between-rome-and-carthage-began.

395. "United States: Imperialism, the Progressive Era, and the Rise to World Power—1896 to
1920," *Encyclopedia Britannica,* http://www.britannica.com/EBchecked/topic/616563
/United-States/77833/Economic-recovery#toc77834.

396. "Treaty of Versailles, 1919," United States Holocaust Memorial Museum, http://www
.ushmm.org/wlc/article.php?lang=en&ModuleId=10005425.

397. John Pairman Brown, *Israel and Hellas: Sacred Institutions with Roman Counterparts*
(Boston: De Gruyter, 2000), pp. 126–128.

398. Franz L. Benz, *Personal Names in the Phoenician and Punic Inscriptions* (Rome: Pontificio
Istituto Biblico, 1982), pp. 313–314.

399. Matthew Barnes, *The Second Punic War: The Tactical Successes and Strategic Failures of
Hannibal Barca,* PICA. A Global Research Organization, 2009, http://www.thepicapro
ject.org/?page_id=517.

400. John Noble Wilford. "The Mystery of Hannibal's Elephants," *New York Times,* September 18, 1984, http://www.nytimes.com/1984/09/18/science/the-mystery-of-hannibal
-s-elephants.html.

401. Barnes, *The Second Punic War.*

402. "'Hitler Was a Great Man and the Gestapo Were Fabulous Police'": Holocaust Denier
David Irving on his Nazi Death Camp Tour," *Daily Mail,* September 27, 2010, http://
www.dailymail.co.uk/news/article-1315591/David-Irving-claims-Hitler-great-man-leads
-Nazi-death-camp-tours.html.

403. Andreas Kluth, *Hannibal and Me* (New York: Riverhead, 2013), pp. 93–94; Patrick Hunt,
"*Hannibal and Me:* A Review," *Electrum,* January 31, 2012, http://www.electrummaga
zine.com/2012/01/hannibal-and-me-a-review/.

404. Roger Manvell and Heinrich Fraenkel, *Heinrich Himmler: The SS, Gestapo, His Life and
Career* (New York: Skyhorse Publishing, 2007), http://books.google.com/books?id

=fO6Ow6jJA28C&pg=PA76&dq="Operation+Himmler"&ei=fyDOR5L2MJXGyAS
A6MmNBQ&sig=FWfI2Tk8btX7m9FZTJ8xTFz6pto.

405. Ibid.

406. Ibid.

407. Adolf Hitler, "Address by Adolf Hitler, Chancellor of the Reich, Before the Reichstag,
      September 1, 1939," Yale Law School Avalon Project, 1997, http://avalon.law.yale.edu
      /wwii/gp2.asp.

408. James J. Wirtz and Roy Godson, *Strategic Denial and Deception: The Twenty-First Cen-
      tury Challenge* (Piscataway, NJ: Transaction Publishers, 2002), http://books.google.com
      /books?id=PzfQSlTJTXkC&pg=PA100&ots=ouNc9JPz4y&dq=Gleiwitz+incident&as
      _brr=3&sig=WZF91Hk_0WybC1nqbS8Ghw7nTzw.

409. Chuck M. Sphar, "Notes: Chapter 1," *Against Rome,* http://chucksp1.tripod.com/Notes
      /Chapter%20Notes/Notes%20-%20Ch%201%20Hannibal.htm.

410. Theodore Ayrault Dodge, *Hannibal: A History of the Art of War Among the Carthaginians
      and Romans Down to the Battle of Pydna, 168 B.C.* (Boston: Da Capo Press, 1995).

411. Andreas Kossert, *Damals in Ostpreussen* (Munich: Deutsche Verlags-Anstalt, 2008), p. 160.

412. "Operation Hannibal: January–May 1945," Computrain, http://compunews.com/s13
      /hannibal.htm.

413. "Korean War," History.com, http://www.history.com/topics/korean-war.

414. Andrew Glass, "On Sept. 25, 1959 Khrushchev Capped a Visit to the U.S.," Politico.com,
      September 25, 2007, http://www.politico.com/news/stories/0907/5980.html.

415. "JFK in History: The Bay of Pigs," John F. Kennedy Presidential Library and Museum,
      http://www.jfklibrary.org/Historical+Resources/JFK+in+History/JFK+and+the+Bay
      +of+Pigs.htm.

416. Glass, "On Sept. 25, 1959 Khrushchev Capped a Visit to the U.S."

417. "Cold War I: Bay of Pigs—Timeline—1961," Oregon Public Broadcasting, 2001, http://
      web.archive.org/web/20100818012911/http://www.opb.org/education/coldwar/bayofpigs
      /timeline/1961.html.

418. Charles Tustin Kamps. "The Cuban Missile Crisis." *Air & Space Power Journal,* AU
      Press, Air University, Maxwell Air Force Base, Alabama, Fall 2007, vol. XXI, no. 3, p. 88.

419. Vista Boyland and Klyne D. Nowlin, "WWIII, A Close Call." *The Intercom,* 35 (1):
      10–11, January 2012, http://www.moaacc.org/documents/Newsletters/Jan2012.pdf.

420. "Cold War I: Bay of Pigs—Timeline—1961," Oregon Public Broadcasting, 2001, http://
      web.archive.org/web/20100818012911/http://www.opb.org/education/coldwar/bayofpigs
      /timeline/1961.html.

421. Arthur Schlesinger, *Robert Kennedy and His Times* (Boston: Houghton Mifflin Harcourt,
      2002), p. 1008.

422. "October 14, 1964: Khrushchev Ousted as Premier of Soviet Union,". History.com,
      http://www.history.com/this-day-in-history/khrushchev-ousted-as-premier-of-soviet
      -union.

Chapter Fourteen

423. "A Vietnam War Timeline," Illinois State University, http://www.english.illinois.edu
      /MAPS/vietnam/timeline.htm.

424. NPR staff, "Ike's Warning of Military Expansion, 50 Years Later," NPR, January 17, 2011,
      http://www.npr.org/2011/01/17/132942244/ikes-warning-of-military-expansion-50-years-later.

425. Eric Brown, "LBJ Tapes Show Richard Nixon May Have Committed Treason by Sabo-
      taging Vietnam Peace Talks," *International Business Times,* March 17, 2013, http://www
      .ibtimes.com/lbj-tapes-show-richard-nixon-may-have-committed-treason-sabotaging
      -vietnam-peace-talks-1131819.

426. Kathie Garcia, "Uncovering the Secrets of the Mayan Calendar," *Atlantis Rising,* no. 9, 1996, http://www.bibliotecapleyades.net/tzolkinmaya/esp_tzolkinmaya05.htm.

427. Ibid.

428. Robert Peden, "The Mayan Calendar: Why 260 Days?" Robert Peden website, 1981, updated May 24 and June 15, 2004, accessed June 2010, http://www.spiderorchid.com /mesoamerica/mesoamerica.htm.

429. John Lennon, "Imagine," Apple Records, October 11, 1971.

430. "Scipio Africanus the Elder," *Encyclopaedia Brittanica,* http://www.britannica.com /EBchecked/topic/529046/Scipio-Africanus-the-Elder/6515/Late-years.

431. Ibid.

432. Polybius Histories, book 23, chapter 14, 1–8, pp. 426–427, http://penelope.uchicago.edu /Thayer/E/Roman/Texts/Polybius/23*.html#14

433. "Scipio Africanus the Elder," *Encyclopaedia Brittanica.*

434. François Masson, "Cyclology: The Mathematics of History," chapter 6 in *The End of Our Century* (1979), http://divinecosmos.com/index.php/start-here/books-free-online/26-the -end-of-our-century/145-chapter-06-cyclology-the-mathematics-of-history.

435. Jonathan Aitken, "Nixon v Frost: The True Story of What Really Happened When a British Journalist Bullied a TV Confession out of a Disgraced Ex-President," *Daily Mail,* January 23, 2009, http://www.dailymail.co.uk/tvshowbiz/article-1127039/Nixon-v-Frost -The-true-story-really-happened-British-journalist-bullied-TV-confession -disgraced-ex-President.html.

436. "Marcus Porcius Cato," *Encyclopaedia Brittanica,* http://www.britannica.com/EB checked/topic/99975/Marcus-Porcius-Cato.

437. Ibid.

438. President Jimmy Carter, "Report to the American People on Energy," February 2, 1977, University of Virginia Miller Center, http://millercenter.org/president/speeches/detail /3396.

439. Uri Friedman, "The South Korean President's Underwear: Lee Myung-Bak Channels Jimmy Carter," *Foreign Policy,* November 28, 2011, http://blog.foreignpolicy.com/posts /2011/11/28/the_south_korean_presidents_underwear_lee_myung_bak_channels _jimmy_carter_on_energy.

440. Wayne Greene, "Saving Energy Is a Matter of Pocketbook, Patriotism," *Tulsa World,* February 22, 2009, http://www.tulsaworld.com/article.aspx/Saving_energy_is_a_mat ter_of_pocketbook_patriotism/20090222_261_g6_coalma783384.

441. President Jimmy Carter, "Report to the American People on Energy," February 2, 1977, University of Virginia Miller Center, http://millercenter.org/president/speeches/detail /3396.

442. François Masson, "Cyclology."

443. Dave Burdick, "White House Solar Panels: What Ever Happened to Carter's Solar Ther- mal Water Heater?" *Huffington Post,* January 27, 2009, http://www.huffingtonpost.com /2009/01/27/white-house-solar-panels_n_160575.html.

444. "Cato the Elder," UNRV History, http://www.unrv.com/culture/cato-the-elder.php.

445. "Jimmy Carter—39th President of the United States and Founder of the Carter Center." The Carter Center, February 1, 2013, http://www.cartercenter.org/news/experts/jimmy _carter.html.

446. Jimmy Carter, *Palestine: Peace Not Apartheid* (New York: Simon and Schuster, 2006).

447. Jimmy Carter, *The Hornet's Nest: A Novel of the Revolutionary War* (New York: Simon and Schuster, 2003).

448. "The Nobel Peace Prize 2002," Nobelprize.org, October 11, 2002, http://nobelprize.org /nobel_prizes/peace/laureates/2002/press.html.

449. Appian of Alexandria, "The First Celtiberian War," *History of Rome,* §42, http://www .livius.org/ap-ark/appian/appian_spain_09.html.

450. Titus Livius, *The History of Rome,* vol. 6, book 41, paragraph 26, http://mcadams.posc .mu.edu/txt/ah/livy/livy41.html.

451. "Soviet Invasion of Afghanistan," GuidetoRussia.com, 2004, http://www.guidetorussia .com/russia-afghanistan.asp.

452. Ibid.

453. Ibid.

454. "Soviet War in Afghanistan," Wikipedia, 2010, http://en.wikipedia.org/wiki/Soviet _war_in_Afghanistan.

455. Svetlana Savranskaya and Thomas Blanton, "The Reykjavík File: Previously Secret Documents from U.S. and Soviet Archives on the 1986 Reagan-Gorbachev Summit," National Security Archive Electronic Briefing Book No. 203, October 13, 2006, http://www.gwu .edu/~nsarchiv/NSAEBB/NSAEBB203/index.htm.

456. "White House Shake-Up: A Task Is Handed to State Dept.; Poindexter and North Have Limited Options," *New York Times,* November 26, 1986, section A, p. 12, http://www .nytimes.com/1986/11/26/world/white-house-shake-up-task-handed-state-dept -poindexter-north-have-limited.html.

457. Brown University, "John Poindexter—National Security Advisor," *Understanding the Iran-Contra Affairs,* 2010, http://www.brown.edu/Research/Understanding_the_Iran _Contra_Affair/profile-poindexter.php.

458. Savranskaya and Blanton, "The Reykjavík File."

459. Michael Wines and Norman Kempster. "U.S. Orders Expulsion of 55 Soviet Diplomats: Largest Single Ouster Affects Capital, S.F." *Los Angeles Times,* October 22, 1986, http:// articles.latimes.com/1986-10-22/news/mn-6805_1_soviet-union.

460. "Week of October 19, 1986," Mr. Pop History, http://www.mrpopculture.com/files /October%2019,%201986.pdf.

461. "Feb. 12, 1988: Russian Ships Bump U.S. Destroyer and Cruiser," History.com, http://www .history.com/this-day-in-history/russian-ships-bump-us-destroyer-and-cruiser.

462. Ibid.

463. Jason Burke, "Bin Laden Files Show Al-Qaida and Taliban Leaders in Close Contact," *The Guardian,* April 29, 2012, http://www.guardian.co.uk/world/2012/apr/29/bin -laden-al-qaida-taliban-contact.

464. "The U.S. and Soviet Proxy War in Afghanistan, 1989–1992: Prisoners of Our Preconceptions?" Working Group Report no. IV, November 15, 2005, Georgetown University Institute for the Study of Diplomacy, pp. 1–2, http://isd.georgetown.edu/files/Afghan_2 _WR_report.pdf.

465. Ria Novosti, "Tanks and Barricades on Moscow's Streets: August 19, 1991," 2013, http:// rianovosti.com/photolents/20110819/160262752_2.html.

466. "1991: Hardliners Stage Coup Against Gorbachev," BBC News, http://news.bbc.co.uk/ onthisday/hi/dates/stories/august/19/newsid_2499000/2499453.stm.

467. "Collapse of the Soviet Union—1989-1991," GlobalSecurity.org, October 1, 2012, http:// www.globalsecurity.org/military/world/russia/soviet-collapse.htm.

468. "1991: Gorbachev Resigns as Soviet Union Breaks Up," BBC News, http://news.bbc.co .uk/onthisday/hi/dates/stories/december/25/newsid_2542000/2542749.stm.

469. Masson, "Cyclology."

Chapter Fifteen

470. François Masson, *The End of Our Era* (Virginia Beach, VA: Donning Company Publishers, 1983), https://www.facebook.com/theWave1111/posts/160972590635214.

471. "Gulf War," Wikipedia, http://en.wikipedia.org/wiki/Gulf_War.

472. Jorge Hirsch, "War Against Iran, April 2006: Biological Threat and Executive Order 13292," April 1, 2006, Antiwar.com, http://www.antiwar.com/hirsch/?articleid =8788.

473. Ibid.

474. Gareth Porter, "Cheney Tried to Stifle Dissent in Iran NIE," Inter Press Service, November 8, 2007, http://ipsnews.net/news.asp?idnews=39978.

475. Ray McGovern, "A Miracle: Honest Intel on Iran Nukes," Antiwar.com, December 4, 2007, http://www.antiwar.com/mcgovern/?articleid=12001.

476. Ibid.

477. *Journal of Offender Rehabilitation* 36, nos. 1–4 (2003): 283–302, http://www.tandfonline .com/toc/wjor20/36/1-4#.UYcPUoKfLbt.

478. Harry V. Martin, "The Federal Reserve Bunk," FreeAmerica and Harry V. Martin, 1995, http://dmc.members.sonic.net/sentinel/naij2.html.

479. Ron Paul, "Abolish the Federal Reserve," Ron Paul's Speeches and Statements, House .gov, September 10, 2002, http://web.archive.org/web/20080202084948/http://www .house.gov/paul/congrec/congrec2002/cr091002b.htm.

480. "The Whitehouse Coup," BBC Radio 4: History, *Document,* July 23, 2007, http://www .bbc.co.uk/radio4/history/document/document_20070723.shtml.

481. Ben Aris and Duncan Campbell, "How Bush's Grandfather Helped Hitler Rise to Power," *The Guardian,* September 25, 2004, http://www.guardian.co.uk/world/2004/ sep/25/usa.secondworldwar.

482. Ibid.

483. David Wilcock, "Disclosure Endgame," Divine Cosmos, December 25, 2009, http:// divinecosmos.com/index.php/start-here/davids-blog/521-disclosure-endgame.

484. Peter David Beter, audio letters and audio books, http://www.peterdavidbeter.com.

485. Peter David Beter, Audio Letter No. 40, November 30, 1978, http://peterdavidbeter.com /docs/all/dbal40.html.

486. David Wilcock, "1950s Human ETs Prepare Us for Golden Age—Videos, Documents!" Divine Cosmos, July 22, 2011, http://divinecosmos.com/start-here/davids-blog/956 -1950s-ets.

487. Ibid.

488. David Wilcock, "Disclosure War at Critical Mass: Birds, Fish and Political Deaths." Divine Cosmos, January 15, 2011, http://divinecosmos.com/start-here/davids-blog/909 -disclosurecriticalmass.

489. "A New Finding in India: Extraterrestrial UFOs Have the Capabilities to Disable All Nuke Missiles in the World Including That of India's, Pakistan's and China's," *India Daily,* February 20, 2005, http://www.indiadaily.com/editorial/1656.asp.

490. Ibid.

491. Kerry Cassidy and Bill Ryan, Project Camelot, http://www.projectcamelot.org.

492. Project Camelot and David Wilcock, interview with Dr. Pete Peterson, 2009, http:// projectcamelot.org/pete_peterson.html.

493. Ibid.

494. Wilcock, "1950s Human ETs."

495. Quintus Tullius Cicero, *How to Win an Election: An Ancient Guide for Modern Politicians,* trans. Philip Freeman (Princeton, NJ: Princeton University Press, 2012).

496. Ibid., pp. xvi–xxi.

497. Ibid., pp. xvii–xxi.

498. Ibid, back cover.

499. Ibid.

500. Don Elkins, Carla Rueckert, and Jim McCarty, *The Law of One* (West Chester, PA: Whitford Press, 1984), session 57, question 7, http://lawofone.info/results.php?s =57#7.

501. "United States Elections, 2006," Wikipedia, http://en.wikipedia.org/wiki/United _States_elections,_2006.

502. "Cato the Elder (234–149 B.C.)," Roman Empire.net, http://www.roman-empire.net/re public/cato-e.html.

503. Alicia VerHage, "Cato the Elder: 234–149 B.C.," Web Chronology Project, September 19, 1999, http://www.thenagain.info/WebChron/Mediterranean/CatoElder.html.

504. David Wilcock and Benjamin Fulford, "Disclosure Imminent? Two Underground NWO Bases Destroyed," Divine Cosmos, September 14, 2011, http://divinecosmos.com/start -here/davids-blog/975-undergroundbases; David Wilcock and Benjamin Fulford, "New Fulford Interview Transcript: Old World Order Nearing Defeat," Divine Cosmos, October 31, 2011, http://divinecosmos.com/start-here/davids-blog/988-fulford-owo -defeat.

505. E. L. Skip Knox, "The Punic Wars: Third Punic War," Boise State University, http://web .archive.org/web/20110625203436/http://www.boisestate.edu/courses/westciv/punicwar /17.shtml.

506. Andrew Walker, "Project Paperclip: Dark Side of the Moon," BBC News, November 21, 2005, http://news.bbc.co.uk/2/hi/uk_news/magazine/4443934.stm.

507. Ibid.

508. Naomi Wolf, "Fascist America, in 10 Easy Steps," *The Guardian,* April 24, 2007, http:// www.guardian.co.uk/world/2007/apr/24/usa.comment.

509. Robert Parry, "The Original October Surprise, Part III," Consortium News/Truthout, October 29, 2006, http://www.truthout.org/article/robert-parry-part-iii-the-original -october-surprise.

510. Ibid.

511. Gary Sick, *October Surprise: America's Hostages in Iran and the Election of Ronald Reagan* (New York: Random House, 1991; New York: Three Rivers Press, 1992).

512. Gary Sick, "The Election Story of the Decade," *New York Times,* April 15, 1991, http:// www.fas.org/irp/congress/1992_cr/h920205-october-clips.htm.

513. Barbara Honegger, *October Surprise* (New York: Tudor, 1989).

514. "Jimmy Carter Wins Nobel Peace Prize," CNN, October 11, 2002, http://archives.cnn .com/2002/WORLD/europe/10/11/carter.nobel/index.html.

515. "Jimmy Carter's UFO Sighting," Cohen UFO, 1996, http://www.cohenufo.org/Carter/ carter_abvtopsec.htm.

516. Walker, "Project Paperclip."

517. Ewan MacAskill, "Jimmy Carter: Animosity Towards Barack Obama Is Due to Racism," *The Guardian,* September 16, 2009, http://www.guardian.co.uk/world/2009/sep/16/ jimmy-carter-racism-barack-obama.

Chapter Sixteen

518. "Rebuilding America's Defenses: Strategy, Forces and Resources for a New Century," report of the Project for the New American Century, September 2000, http://www .newamericancentury.org/RebuildingAmericasDefenses.pdf.

519. Jess Cagle, "Pearl Harbor's Top Gun," *Time,* May 27, 2001, http://www.time.com/time/ magazine/article/0,9171,128107,00.html.

520. "Rebuilding America's Defenses."

521. Anonymous, private conversation with the author, 2011.

522. "The USA PATRIOT Act: Legislation Rushed into Law in the Wake of 9/11/01," 9/11 Research, August 11, 2008, http://911research.wtc7.net/post911/legislation/usapatriot.html.

523. Ibid.

524. Jennifer Van Bergen, "The USA PATRIOT Act Was Planned Before 9/11," Truthout.org, May 20, 2002, http://www.globalissues.org/article/342/the-usa-patriot-act-was-planned-before-911.

525. Ibid.

526. "The USA PATRIOT Act: Legislation Rushed."

527. "WTC Steel Removal: The Expeditious Destruction of Evidence at Ground Zero," 9-11 Research, April 26, 2009, http://911research.wtc7.net/wtc/groundzero/cleanup.html.

528. Ibid.

529. David Wilcock, "Wilcock Readings Section 2: December 1–15, 1996," Ascension2000.com, Archive.org snapshot from January 24, 2000, http://web.archive.org/web/20000124000818/http://ascension2000.com/Readings/readings02.html.

530. "Doctors Give Mother Teresa's Heart Mild Shock," CNN World News, December 11, 1996, http://www.cnn.com/WORLD/9612/11/mother.teresa/index.html.

531. "Indian-Born Nun to Succeed Mother Teresa," CNN World News, March 13, 1997, http://www.cnn.com/WORLD/9703/13/india.teresa/index.html?_s=PM:WORLD.

532. David Wilcock, "The Advent of the Wilcock Readings," Ascension2000.com, Archive.org snapshot from April 9, 2001, http://web.archive.org/web/20010409202343/http://ascension2000.com/Readings/readings01.html.

533. David Wilcock, "Wilcock Readings Section 2," ibid.

534. Ibid.

535. Ibid.

536. David Wilcock, "Earth Very Soon to Shift Its Position," Greatdreams.com, February 23, 1999, Archive.org snapshot from October 9, 1999, http://web.archive.org/web/19991009190326/http://www.greatdreams.com/shift.htm.

537. Ibid.

538. Susan Lindauer, "Extreme Prejudice: The Terrifying Story of the Patriot Act and the Cover Ups of 9/11 and Iraq," CreateSpace Independent Publishing Platform, October 15, 2010, http://extremeprejudiceusa.wordpress.com/2010/10/10/extreme-prejudice-by-susan-lindauer/.

539. Susan Lindauer, "Public, Global Profile of SLindauer2010," Gravatar, 2010, http://en.gravatar.com/slindauer2010.

540. Bill Ryan and Elizabeth Nelson, "What Really Happened to Flight 93," Project Camelot, February 2009, http://projectcamelot.org/elizabeth_nelson_flight_93.html.

541. Elizabeth Nelson and Bill Ryan, "What Really Happened to Flight 93—Interview Transcript," Project Camelot, February 2009, http://projectcamelot.org/lang/en/elizabeth_nelson_flight_93_transcript_en.html.

542. Ibid.

543. David Wilcock, "Financial Tyranny: Defeating the Greatest Cover-Up of All Time," Divine Cosmos, January 13, 2012, http://divinecosmos.com/start-here/davids-blog/1023-financial-tyranny.

544. John Kerry, "Transcript: First Presidential Debate," *Washington Post,* September 30, 2004, http://www.washingtonpost.com/wp-srv/politics/debatereferee/debate_0930.html.

545. Kate Murphy, "Single-Payer & Interlocking Directorates: The Corporate Ties Between Insurers and Media Companies," FAIR, August 2009, http://web.archive.org/web/20120203103550/http://www.fair.org/index.php?page=3845.

546. Ben Bagdikian, *The New Media Monopoly* (Boston: Beacon Press, 2004), http://web.archive.org/web/2012101/114414/http://benbagdikian.net/; Free Press, "Who Owns the Media?" 2009–2012, http://www.freepress.net/ownership/chart/main.

547. Free Press, "Who Owns the Media?"
548. "Over Neoconservative Obstructionism and Health Care Lobbying, Health Reform Passes," Populist Daily, December 24, 2009, http://www.populistdaily.com/politics/over-neoconservative-obstruction-and-health-care-lobbying-health-reform-passes.html.
549. Imperial Teutonic Order, "The Order of the Teutonic Knights of St. Mary's Hospital in Jerusalem 1190–2010," Archive.org, March 8, 2010, http://web.archive.org/web/20100308134300/http://imperialteutonicorder.com/id25.html.

Chapter Seventeen

550. "Thirteen Years' War," Nation Master Online Encyclopedia, 2010, http://www.statemaster.com/encyclopedia/Thirteen-Years'-War.
551. Derek Bok, "The Great Health Care Debate of 1993–94," Public Talk, University of Pennsylvania Online Journal of Discourse Leadership, 1998, http://www.upenn.edu/pnc/ptbok.html.
552. Alexandra Cosgrove, "A Clinton Timeline: Highlights and Lowlights," CBS News, Washington, January 12, 2001, http://www.cbsnews.com/stories/2001/01/08/politics/main262484.shtml.
553. Richard L. Berke, "Looking for Alliance, Clinton Courts the Congress Nonstop," New York Times March 8, 1993, http://www.nytimes.com/1993/03/08/us/looking-for-alliance-clinton-courts-the-congress-nonstop.html.
554. Karen Tumulty, "Obama's Health Care Reform Bill Passed," Time Magazine/Yahoo News, March 22, 2010, http://web.archive.org/web/20100328033058/http://news.yahoo.com/s/time/20100322/us_time/08599197398900.
555. Steve Benen, "As 'Obamacare' Turns Three, the Politics Haven't Changed," Maddow Blog, MSNBC, March 21, 2013, http://maddowblog.msnbc.com/_news/2013/03/21/17401638-as-obamacare-turns-three-the-politics-havent-changed?lite.
556. David Wilcock, "6/23/99: Prophecy: Wars, Earth Changes and Ascension," Divine Cosmos, June 23, 1999, http://divinecosmos.com/index.php/start-here/readings-in-text-form/185-62399-prophecy-wars-earth-changes-and-ascension.
557. David Wilcock, "Ascension2000 Homepage," October 2, 1999, http://web.archive.org/web/19991002031519/http://www.ascension2000.com/.
558. David Wilcock, "11/24/00: Prophecy: 2000 Election Crisis Predicted in 1999," Divine Cosmos, November 24, 2000, http://divinecosmos.com/index.php/start-here/readings-in-text-form/456-112400-prophecy-2000-election-crisis-predicted-in-1999.
559. Wilcock, "6/23/99: Prophecy"; Wilcock, "11/24/00: Prophecy."
560. David Wilcock, "4/29/99: Reading: War in Kosovo," Divine Cosmos, April 29, 1999, https://divinecosmos.com/index.php/start-here/readings-in-text-form/246-42999-reading-war-in-kosovo.
561. Wilcock, "Ascension2000 Homepage."
562. Wilcock, "4/29/99: Reading."
563. David Wilcock, "ET Update on Global Politics, Immediate Future Earth Changes and Ascension Events," Ascension2000, June 23, 1999, Archive.org snapshot from March 11, 2000, http://web.archive.org/web/20000311102326/http://ascension2000.com/6.23Update.html.
564. Ibid.
565. David Wilcock, "An Ongoing Puzzle Collection from the Deepest Possible Trance State: Archangel Michael Reading #2," Ascension2000, September 30, 1999, Archive.org snapshot from April 9, 2001, http://web.archive.org/web/20010409200610/http://ascension2000.com/9.30.99.htm.

566. Ibid.

567. David Wilcock, "Archangel Michael Series #3," Ascension2000, October 1, 1999, Archive.org snapshot from March 4, 2000, http://web.archive.org/web/20000304142506/http://www.ascension2000.com/10.01.99.htm.

568. Ibid.

569. David Wilcock, "Very Powerful Reading: The Autumn Season of Humanity," Ascension2000, September 4, 1999, Archive.org snapshot from March 11, 2000, http://web.archive.org/web/20000311174059/http://ascension2000.com/9.04.99.htm.

570. Ibid.

571. "The Battle of Swiecino," Wikipedia, http://en.wikipedia.org/wiki/Battle_of_%C5%9Awiecino.

Chapter Eighteen

572. "Thirteen Years' War (1454–66)," Wikipedia, http://en.wikipedia.org/wiki/Thirteen_Years%27_War_(1454%E2%80%9366).

573. "Hurricane Katrina: The Essential Time Line," National Geographic News, September 14, 2005, http://news.nationalgeographic.com/news/2005/09/0914_050914_katrina_timeline_2.html.

574. Scott Shane, "After Failures, Government Officials Play Blame Game," *New York Times,* September 5, 2005, http://www.nytimes.com/2005/09/05/national/nationalspecial/05blame.html?_r=0.

575. Carl Hulse and Philip Shenon, "Democrats and Others Press for an Independent Inquiry," *New York Times,* September 14, 2005, http://www.nytimes.com/2005/09/14/national/nationalspecial/14cong.html?fta=y.

576. "United States Elections, 2006," Wikipedia, http://en.wikipedia.org/wiki/United_States_elections,_2006.

577. Hulse and Shenon, "Democrats and Others."

578. Michael A. Fletcher and Richard Morin, "Bush's Approval Rating Drops to New Low in Wake of Storm," *Washington Post,* September 13, 2005, http://www.washingtonpost.com/wp-dyn/content/article/2005/09/12/AR2005091200668.html.

579. Ibid.

580. "America Votes 2006," CNN, http://www.cnn.com/ELECTION/2006/.

581. Jeffrey M. Jones, "GOP Losses Span Nearly All Demographic Groups," Gallup Politics, May 18, 2009, http://www.gallup.com/poll/118528/gop-losses-span-nearly-demographic-groups.aspx.

582. Appian of Alexandria, "The Lusitanian War," *History of Rome,* §56, http://www.livius.org/ap-ark/appian/appian_spain_12.html.

583. James Grout, "The Celtiberian War," Encyclopaedia Romana, 2013, http://penelope.uchicago.edu/~grout/encyclopaedia_romana/hispania/celtiberianwar.html

Chapter Nineteen

584. Maximilien de Robespierre, *On the Principles of Political Morality* (February 1794), in *Maximilien Robespierre: On the Principles of Political Morality, February 1794,* ed. Paul Halsall, Modern History Sourcebook, August 1997, Fordham University, http://www.fordham.edu/halsall/mod/1794robespierre.asp.

585. David Andress, *The Terror* (New York: Farrar, Straus and Giroux, 2007), p. 323.

586. Simon Schama, *Citizens: A Chronicle of the French Revolution* (New York: Alfred A. Knopf, 1989), pp. 845–846.

587. Jonathan Brent and Vladimir Naumov, *Stalin's Last Crime: The Plot Against the Jewish Doctors, 1948–1953* (New York: HarperCollins, 2004).

588. M. Faria, "Stalin's Mysterious Death," Surgical Neurology International 2, no. 1 (2011): 161, http://dx.doi.org/10.4103%2F2152-7806.89876.

589. Simon Sebag Montefiore, *Stalin: The Court of the Red Tsar* (New York: Vintage, 2004), p. 571.

590. François Masson, "Cyclology: The Mathematics of History," chapter 6 in *The End of Our Century* (1979), http://divinecosmos.com/index.php/start-here/books-free-online/26-the-end-of-our-century/145-chapter-06-cyclology-the-mathematics-of-history.

591. Ibid.

592. Timothy Taylor, "Time Warp," *Saturday Night,* 2000, http://www.mail-archive.com/ctrl@listserv.aol.com/msg69058.html.

593. Ibid.

594. Nikolai A. Morozov, *Christ: The History of Human Culture from the Standpoint of the Natural Sciences,* 2nd ed. (in Russian), vols. 1–7 (Moscow, 1926–1932); vols. 1–7 (Moscow: Kraft and Lean, 1997–1998 [8 books]).

595. Anatoly T. Fomenko, *Empirico-Statistical Analysis of Narrative Material and Its Applications to Historical Dating,* vol. 1, *The Development of the Statistical Tools;* vol. 2, *The Analysis of Ancient and Medieval Records* (New York: Kluwer Academic Publishers, 1994).

596. Taylor, "Time Warp."

597. Ibid.

598. A. T. Fomenko and G. V. Nosovskij, "New Hypothetical Chronology and Concept of English History: British Empire as a Direct Successor of Byzantine-Roman Empire," New Tradition, 2002, http://www.new-tradition.org/investigation-eng-history.php.

599. Taylor, "Time Warp."

600. Bill Wall, "Who Is the Strongest Chess Player?" Chess.com, October 27, 2008, http://www.chess.com/article/view/who-is-the-strongest-chess-player.

601. Garry Kasparov, "Mathematics of the Past," New Tradition Sociological Society, http://web.archive.org/web/20100323072616/http://www.new-tradition.org/view-garry-kasparov.html.

602. Wieslaw Z. Krawciewicz, Gleb V. Nosovskij, and Petr P. Zabrieko, "Investigation of the Correctness of Historical Dating," New Tradition Sociological Society, 2002, http://web.archive.org/web/20100926092137/http://www.new-tradition.org/investigation-historical-dating.html. (At the time of this writing, the links to the full-size graphics do not work, but they do work in a mirror copy that can be found at http://www.world-mysteries.com/sci_16.htm.)

603. Robert Grishin, "Global Revision of History: Preface," New Tradition Sociological Society, 2002, http://web.archive.org/web/20101106080043/http://www.new-tradition.org/preface.html.

604. Krawciewicz, Nosovskij, and Zabrieko, "Investigation of the Correctness of Historical Dating."

605. Grishin, "Global Revision of History: Preface."

Chapter Twenty

606. A. T. Fomenko and G. V. Nosovskij, "New Hypothetical Chronology and Concept of the English History: British Empire as a Direct Successor of Byzantine-Roman Empire (Short Scheme)," New Tradition Sociological Society, 2002, http://web.archive.org/web/20101106080149/http://www.new-tradition.org/investigation-eng-history.html.

607. Wieslaw Z. Krawciewicz, Gleb V. Nosovskij, and Petr P. Zabrieko, "Investigation of the Correctness of Historical Dating," New Tradition Sociological Society, 2002, http://web.archive.org/web/20100926092137/http://www.new-tradition.org/investigation-historical-dating.html.

608. François Masson, "Cyclology: The Mathematics of History," chapter 6 in *The End of Our Century* (1979), http://divinecosmos.com/index.php/start-here/books-free-online/26-the-end-of-our-century/145-chapter-06-cyclology-the-mathematics-of-history.

609. "Iconoclasm," Wikipedia, accessed April 2010, http://en.wikipedia.org/wiki/Iconoclasm.

610. Ibid.

611. C. Mango, "Historical Introduction," in *Iconoclasm*, ed. Anthony Bryer and Judith Herrin (Birmingham: Centre for Byzantine Studies, University of Birmingham, 1977), pp. 2–3.

612. Paul Robert Walker, *The Feud That Sparked the Renaissance: How Brunelleschi and Ghiberti Changed the Art World* (New York: Harper Perennial, 2003).

613. "How a Day Can Equal a Year," Bible Prophecy Numbers, http://www.1260-1290-days-bible-prophecy.org/day-year-principle.html.

614. Daniel 12:11 (New Revised Standard Version).

615. Daniel 2:20–22 (NRSV).

616. Daniel 2:31–35 (NRSV).

617. Daniel 2:37–40 (NRSV).

618. Daniel 2:41–42 (NRSV).

619. Daniel 7:23 (NRSV).

620. Daniel 2:44–45 (NRSV).

621. Daniel 12:1 (NRSV).

622. Daniel 12:2–3 (NRSV).

623. Daniel 12:6–7 (NRSV).

624. Joe Mason, "Humanity on the Pollen Path, Part One: Symbols of the Chakras and the Midpoint," Great Dreams, April 24, 1999, http://www.greatdreams.com/plpath1.htm.

625. Ibid.

626. Daniel 12:8–9 (NRSV).

627. Daniel 12:10–11 (NRSV).

628. Daniel 12:12–13 (NRSV).

Chapter Twenty-One

629. Zhaxki Zhuoma.net. "The Rainbow Body." http://web.archive.org/web/20120301124019/http://www.zhaxizhuoma.net/SEVEN_JEWELS/HOLY%20EVENTS/RAINBOW%20BODY/RBindex.html.

630. Namkhai Norbu. Dream Yoga and the Practice of Natural Light (Ithaca, NY: Snow Lion Productions, 1992), p. 67.

631. Gail Holland. "The Rainbow Body." Institute of Noetic Sciences Review, March–May 2002. http://www.snowlionpub.com/pages/N59_9.html.

632. Ibid.

633. Ibid.

634. Giovanni Milani-Santarpia, "Mysticism and Signs in Ancient Rome: The Sibyls," *Antiquities of Rome,* http://www.mariamilani.com/ancient_rome/mysticism_signs_ancient_rome.htm.

635. Padraic Colum, "The Sibyl," *Orpheus: Myths of the World,* p. 119, http://www.livius.org/ap-ark/appian/appian_spain_12.html.

636. Milani-Santarpia, "Mysticism and Signs in Ancient Rome.

637. Don Elkins, Carla Rueckert, and Jim McCarty, *The Law of One* (West Chester, PA: Whitford Press, 1984), session 1, http://lawofone.info/results.php?s=1.

638. Ibid., session 6, question 24, http://lawofone.info/results.php?s=6#24.

639. Ibid., session 6, questions 16–19, http://lawofone.info/results.php?s=6#16.

640. Robert D. Peden, "The Mayan Calendar: Why 260 Days?" Robert Peden website, 1981, updated May 24 and June 15, 2004, accessed June 2010, http://www.spiderorchid.com/mesoamerica/mesoamerica.htm.

641. Ibid.

642. Hans Jenny. *Cymatics—A Study of Wave Phenomena.* (Newmarket, NH: MACROmedia Publishing, 2001), http://www.cymaticsource.com/.

643. Elkins, Rueckert, and McCarty, *The Law of One,* session 1, http://lawofone.info/results.php?s=1.

644. "Who Was Robert J. Moon?" 21st Century Science and Technology. http://www.21stcenturysciencetech.com/articles/drmoon.html

645. The Moon Model of the Nucleus. [List of related articles], 21st Century Science and Technology, http://www.21stcenturysciencetech.com/moonsubpg.html

646. David Guenther, "Solar and Stellar Seismology," St. Mary's University, January 2010, http://www.ap.stmarys.ca/%7Eguenther/seismology/seismology.html; "David Guenther, Professor," St. Mary's University, January 2010, http://www.ap.stmarys.ca/%7Eguenther/.

647. Robert B. Leighton, Robert W. Noyes and George W. Simon, "Velocity Fields in the Solar Atmosphere. I. Preliminary Report," *Astrophysical Journal,* vol. 135, p. 474, http://adsabs.harvard.edu/abs/1962ApJ...135..474L.

648. Elkins, Rueckert, and McCarty, *The Law of One,* session 27, question 6, http://lawofone.info/results.php?s=27#6.

649. Nassim Haramein. "Haramein Paper Wins Award!" The Resonance Project, http://www.theresonanceproject.org/best_paper_award.html

650. Dewey Larson. "The Reciprocal System: The Collected Works," http://www.reciprocalsystem.com/dbl/index.htm.

651. Elkins, Rueckert, and McCarty, *The Law of One,* session 20, question 7, http://lawofone.info/results.php?s=20#7.

652. Ibid., session 6, question 15, http://lawofone.info/results.php?s=6#15.

653. Zecharia Sitchin. *Twelfth Planet: Book I of the Earth Chronicles.* (New York: Harper, 2007), http://www.sitchin.com.

654. Ryan X, "Is the Sun Part of a Binary Star System? Six Reasons to Consider," Signs of the Times, June 24, 2011, http://www.sott.net/article/230480-Is-the-Sun-Part-of-a-Binary-Star-System-Six-Reasons-to-Consider.

655. Elkins, Rueckert, and McCarty, *The Law of One,* session 16, questions 33–35, http://lawofone.info/results.php?s=16#33.

656. Ibid., session 10, question 17, http://lawofone.info/results.php?s=10#17.

657. Earle Holland, "Major Climate Change Occurred 5,200 Years Ago: Evidence Suggests That History Could Repeat Itself," Research News, Ohio State University, December 15, 2004, http://researchnews.osu.edu/archive/5200event.htm.

658. Elkins, Rueckert, and McCarty, *The Law of One,* session 63, question 29, http://lawofone.info/results.php?s=63#29.

659. Ibid., session 9, question 4, http://lawofone.info/results.php?s=9#4.

660. Ibid., session 14, question 16, http://lawofone.info/results.php?s=14#16.

661. Ibid., session 63, question 25, http://lawofone.info/results.php?s=63#25.

662. Ibid., session 63, question 27, http://lawofone.info/results.php?s=63#27.

663. Ibid., session 63, questions 12–15, http://lawofone.info/results.php?s=63#12.

664. Ibid., session 40, questions 10–11, http://lawofone.info/results.php?s=40#10.

665. Dictionary.com, "discrete," http://dictionary.reference.com/browse/discrete?s=t.

666. Elkins, Rueckert, and McCarty, *The Law of One,* session 40, question 5, http://lawofone.info/results.php?s=40#5.

667. Ibid., session 16, question 50, http://lawofone.info/results.php?s=16#50.
668. Ibid., session 20, question 24, http://lawofone.info/results.php?s=20#24.
669. Ibid., session 16, question 50, http://lawofone.info/results.php?s=16#50.
670. Ibid., session 89, question 8, http://lawofone.info/results.php?s=89#8.
671. Ibid., session 14, question 4, http://lawofone.info/results.php?s=14#4.
672. Ibid., session 65, question 9, http://lawofone.info/results.php?s=65#9.
673. Ibid., session 17, question 29, http://lawofone.info/results.php?s=17#29.
674. Ibid., session 17, question 22, http://lawofone.info/results.php?s=17#22.
675. William Henry and Mark Gray, *Freedom's Gate: The Lost Symbols in the U.S. Capitol,* Hendersonville, TN: Scala Dei, 2009, p. 25, http://williamhenry.net/freedomsgate.html.
676. Lex Hixon and Neil Douglas-Klotz, *The Heart of the Qur'an: An Introduction to Islamic Spirituality,* 2nd ed. (Wheaton, IL: Quest Books, 2003), p. 38.
677. Ibid., pp. 65–66.
678. Ibid., p. 85.
679. Ibid., pp. 85–86.
680. Ibid., p. 86.
681. Ibid., p. 88.
682. Ibid., p. 99.
683. Ibid., p. 192–193.
684. Ibid., p. 94.

Index

About the Author

DAVID WILCOCK is an author, professional lecturer, filmmaker, and researcher of ancient civilizations, consciousness science, and new paradigms of matter and energy. His seminal thoughts and expertise have reached hundreds of thousands of people through his extensive online presence at DivineCosmos.com. David's first book, *The Source Field Investigations,* was a *New York Times* bestseller. He has appeared in multiple television programs on major networks, including eight episodes of History Channel's Ancient Aliens at the time of this writing and two prime-time documentaries investigating financial tyranny on Russian television. James V. Hart, a leading screenwriter who wrote the movie *Contact* with Carl Sagan, and has worked with directors such as Steven Spielberg and Francis Ford Coppola, has developed a feature film script with David entitled *Convergence,* and it is receiving significant interest from major production companies at the time of this writing. David also has his own weekly show on Gaiam TV entitled *Wisdom Teachings with David Wilcock*. Lastly, he cowrote and sang lead vocals on *Wanderer Awakening,* a fifty-song rock-and-roll musical, with Larry Seyer, a nine-time Grammy-winning musician and recording engineer. He lives in California.